Beyond Bollywood

Beyond Bollywood
The Cultural Politics of South Asian Diasporic Film

Jigna Desai

ROUTLEDGE
NEW YORK AND LONDON

Published in 2004 by
Routledge
29 West 35th Street
New York, NY 10001

Published in Great Britain by
Routledge
11 New Fetter Lane
London EC4P 4EE

Routledge is an imprint of the Taylor & Francis Group.

Printed in the United States of America on acid free paper.

Library of Congress Cataloging-in-Publication Data

Desai, Jigna.
    Beyond Bollywood : the cultural politics of South Asian diasporic film / Jigna Desai.
        p.   cm.
    Includes bibliographical references and index.
    ISBN 0-415-96684-1 (hard. : alk. paper)—ISBN 0-415-96685-X (pbk. : alk. paper)
    1. Motion pictures—India.   2. South Asians—Foreign countries.
I. Title
PN1993.5 .I8D48   2003
791.43′ 0954—dc21

                                                                    2003012737

Contents

Preface
Brown Skins and Silver Screens

> The "beyond" is neither a new horizon, nor a leaving behind of the past.... Beginnings and endings may be the sustaining myths of the middle years, but in the *fin de siècle*, we find ourselves in the moment of transit where space and time cross to produce complex figures of difference and identity, past and present, inside and outside, inclusion and exclusion. For there is a sense of disorientation, a disturbance of direction, in the "beyond": an exploratory, restless movement caught so well in the French rendition of the words *au-delà*—here and there, on all sides, *fort/da,* hither and thither, back and forth.
>
> —Homi Bhabha (1994, 1)

This project began in a search for the beyond. Studying observational cosmology, I then focused my desire on gleaning what I could from the light traveling over vast distance and time to arrive through telescopes onto the computer screen. Contemporaneously, I fled from the theaterless years of my childhood to the art houses of Boston to see illuminations light up other screens as they too projected the complex relations between time and space in the lives of migrant and displaced subjects. In the New England town of Newburyport, Massachusetts, at the Screening Room, I first stumbled on the play of light as brown skins crossed the silver screen in *My Beautiful Laundrette.* The large screen filled with images that I had rarely seen before outside of the snowy confines of UHF, where briefly on early Sunday mornings overexposed bodies with whitewashed faces cavorted on Technicolor backgrounds. I walked quietly out of the theater relishing the disorientation caused by this return of desire in relation to this newfound pleasure. As brown bodies trespassed the spaces of colonial anthropology and history to spaces marked as the present, I experienced a return and rupture simultaneously. Neither the savage heart eaters of *Indiana Jones* nor noble-hearted survivors of colonialism in *Gandhi,* these Laundromat owners and white boy–kissing brown boys captured some other understandings of race and culture, gender and sexuality, and identity and modernity than I had previously encountered. These moments in which brown skins flashed across the silver screen were neither Bollywood nor Hollywood and yet were both as they disoriented my presence and present.

Though it is the literature of South Asian diasporic writers such as Salman Rushdie, Michael Ondaatje, Bharati Mukherjee, and Jhumpa Lahiri that garners popular and academic attention in postcolonial and Asian-American studies, it is cinema that reaches tens, if not hundreds, of millions of viewers. Film has played a feature role in the formation of South Asian diasporic cultures, partially because of its key role in South Asia itself. Although Hollywood cinema dominates global film culture, it is Indian cinema that produces the most films per year. Vastly understudied, unlike its Western counterpart, Indian cinema, especially Bollywood, the Bombay-based, Hindi language cinema, is also a global cinema popular in the Middle East, Asia, Africa, and South Asian diasporas. Suspended between and conversant with these two giant cinemas are the films of the South Asian diaspora. This project analyzes the emergence, development, and significance of contemporary South Asian diasporic cinema.

The late 1960s and 1970s marked a time of increasing migration of South Asians from India, Sri Lanka, Bangladesh, Pakistan, Africa, and the Caribbean to the United States, Britain, Canada, Australia, and the Gulf states due to shifting geopolitical economies. Although South Asian diasporas existed in many nations prior to this time, the influx of new migrants and new technology reshaped older communities, formed new diasporas, and created new cultural processes and flows of cultural products. For example, with the growth of cable, then the VCR, and now satellite television, South Asian diasporans initiated the showing of Hindi, Tamil, and other vernacular language films on television and in movie theaters to wide audiences. South Asian language films, along with literature, music, and intellectuals, now circulate through large distribution networks that span South Asian nations and their diasporas. Able to take advantage of the extended distribution networks, films were able to reach wide audiences and they soon became central to processes of "imagining community." In recent years, the language of South Asian diasporic identity and cultural production has been the language of cinema.

Discourses of diaspora have recently emerged in the interdisciplinary fields of Asian-American, postcolonial, and feminist studies. Theories of diaspora are forwarded by those critical of the nation-state (though still claiming affiliation) as well as those who cite its demise. Reemerging in the 1980s in postcolonial Britain, diaspora is defined in discourse, on one hand as an identity in response to exclusionary and racist national narratives and on the other hand as the "third space" of postcolonial migration and hybridity. In the United States and Canada, these discourses negotiated and reinforced the expansion of multiculturalism. In the early 1990s, with the rise of discourse on the death of the nation due to globalization, diaspora was hailed as a deterritorialized geopolitical community succeeding the nation in an age of increasing globalization. This comparative project challenges the facility with which diaspora has reemerged uninterrogated in postcolonial and feminist discourse as antinational and postnational by interrogating the relationship between diaspora and the nation-state in the context of globalization. This project intervenes in and transforms significant discussions in feminist and queer studies, such as intersectionality, camp, and body theory, through the theories and methodology of diaspora and transnationalism, and, vice versa, the project genders and queers studies contemporary discussions of diaspora, postcolonial transnationalism, and globalization.

Focusing on films in English from and about the "Brown Atlantic" (South Asian diasporas in the United States, Canada, and Britain) as well as India within a transnational comparative framework, this project necessarily interrogates and reformulates the dominant emphasis on the nation and national cinema in cinema studies. *Beyond Bollywood* positions South Asian diasporic cinema as an interstitial cinema located between Hollywood and Bollywood. In this regard, this project understands this hybrid cinema as resulting from the migratory processes engendered by capitalism and postcoloniality. Consequently, *Beyond Bollywood* does not argue that diasporic cinema has transcended Bollywood through some space-clearing gesture. Instead, it understands "beyond" as posing hybrid possibilities forged out of the shifting sands of Hollywood and Bollywood. Moreover, although the project is about cinema, it is not only a project of cinema studies. The "beyond" in this context signals an investment in mobilizing an analysis of cinema to ask questions regarding significant cultural, political, social, and economic processes in globalization. In addition, this project goes beyond disciplinary rubrics and schemata by probing the analytic framework of transnational cultural studies.

> Beyond signifies spatial distance, marks progress, promises the future, but our in-timations of exceeding the barrier or boundary—the very act of going *beyond*—are unknowable, unrepresentable, without a return to the 'present' which, in the process of repetition, becomes disjunct and displaced. . . . These terms that insistently gesture to the beyond, only embody its restless and revisionary energy if they transform the present into an expanded and ex-centric site of experience and empowerment. (Bhabha 1994, 4).

This project seeks to embrace and embody that energy and spirit.

This book has been made possible by the support of numerous friends, family, and colleagues who have provided patience, encouragement, inspiration, and generosity. I am grateful to my friends who have endured endless conversations and viewings of these films: David Bael, Marie Coppola, Lara Descartes, and Nathan Yang during and since my MIT years. For providing warmth, gentle humor, and sustenance, I thank the Sullivans, Kathleen and Tom. Corinth Matera, Kathleen Sheerin-Devore, and Mary Heather Smith have read the earliest drafts of these chapters and provided much of the inspiration necessary to complete what I began so long ago. Mentorship was graciously provided by Amy Kaminsky, Helen Longino, John Mowitt, Jennifer Pierce, Naomi Scheman, and Jackie Zita.

My colleagues in the College of Liberal Arts have been generous with their comments and encouragement: Susie Bullington, Cathy Choy, Rod Ferguson, Qadri Ismail, Erika Lee, Josephine Lee, and Amanda Swarr. In particular, Ananya

Chatterjee has been instrumental in making my work not only possible but also enjoyable. To the "homegirls" of my department Richa Nagar, Gwen Pough, and Eden Torres, I owe gratitude for their unfaltering support and companionship. In addition, I want to thank the participants of the MacArthur gender workshop for their feedback. I greatly appreciate the remarkable encouragement from my distant colleagues, Sarah Casteel, Shilpa Dave, Khyati Joshi, Gita Rajan, and Pam Thoma, who have provided me with a sense of an engaged and excited community. I am highly indebted to the spirit of hospitality, collegiality and collaboration that was given by the group Sangini in Delhi, especially by Leslie, Sujata, Cath, and Betu.

I greatly appreciate the marvelous research assistance provided by Amy Brandzel and Erica Ganzell. In addition, I would like to express my deepest gratitude to Danielle Bouchard who has spent many hours poring over this manuscript, detail by detail, and provided much thought-provoking feedback. Their wonderful and sustaining conversations in addition to their careful readings indelibly mark these pages. Chapters 3 and 7 have been published in slightly different forms. Chapter 3 appears in *Diaspora* (Fall 2003) and chapter 7 in *South Asian Popular Culture* (Spring 2003, 45–61). A portion of chapter 6 also appeared in *Social Text 70* (Winter 2002, 65–89). I thank the journals for permission to publish the chapters here as well as the reviewers Rajinder Dudrah, David Eng, and Gita Rajan for comments. I also extend my gratitude to the anonymous reviewers who supported this project. My editor Matt Byrnie at Routledge deserves much of my gratitude for his patience, clarity, and generosity. Additional thanks to Alan Kaplan for his painstaking precision and attention to details in the editing process. I also wish to thank the University of Minnesota for the grants it has provided that made this book possible.

Finally, my family members have shown unqualified and limitless faith in my ability to complete this project, for which I am very grateful. I am indebted to my brother Rakesh for his humor and warmth, as well as our numerous conversations about Hollywood. From my grandparents, I have tried to learn what I can from the splinters of their stories. Even though she was unable to see the fruition of my labor in particular, I thank Ba Nirmala Gandhi for her fortitude and late-night tales that were there to remind me of what is most important. My sister Seema has proved to be a kindred spirit that sustains my everyday life. Ruskin Hunt has been a partner in every sense of the word; his patience, advice, laughter and steadfast support have sustained me through my many ebbs. This book is dedicated to my loving parents Harish and Naina Desai to whom I can finally say "yes I am done." I thank you for your unwavering encouragement of my curiosity.

South Asian Diasporas and Transnational Cultural Studies

Where the political terrain can neither resolve nor suppress inequality, it erupts in culture. Because culture is the contemporary repository of memory, of history, it is through culture, rather than government, that alternative forms of subjectivity, collectivity, and public life are imagined.

—Lisa Lowe (1998a, 22)

Only by weaving the analysis of cultural politics and political economy into a single framework can we hope to provide a nuanced delineation of the complex relations between transnational phenomena, national regimes, and cultural practices in late modernity.

—Aihwa Ong (1999, 16)

You may be an avid fan of diasporic films, eagerly awaiting the release of every new trailer and feature, or you may have casually walked by the video store and found the cover of *Monsoon Wedding* or *Fire* intriguing and brought it home. This book should be of interest and appropriate for both audiences. This book, like the films discussed below, should have a similar crossover appeal to multiple viewers—from those interested in understanding gender and sexual politics within racialized diasporic communities to those engaged with questions of agency and subjectivity in globalization and late capitalism. Therefore, this book is about film, but not only film. This project is written to be read in three simultaneous and different modalities. At one level, it is the first study of South Asian diasporic cinema and hence it asks questions generally considered of interest to those wanting to understand the emergence of this cinema, including its history, politics, and aesthetics, as well as readings of individual films. At another level, it intervenes in several theoretical debates occurring in queer, postcolonial, diasporic, cultural, feminist, and Asian-American studies, through the lens of transnationality. By focusing on significant topics such as the nation, subjectivity, agency, and embodiment in these areas, the project enriches and reshapes these conversations by suggesting new directions for analysis. Finally, this book expands transnational cultural critique, proposing a particular site of analysis, namely South Asian diasporic cultural studies. It interweaves the disparate conversations in these arenas in analyzing its object of study: South Asian diasporic cinema.

This is the first book-length analysis of South Asian diasporic cinema. The films I discuss here are located in the metropolitan centers of the United States, the United Kingdom, Canada, and India. The book outlines the emergence of South Asian diasporic cinema, paying careful attention to its narrative films and their relationships to various cinemas (e.g., Hollywood, Bollywood, national, art house, and parallel). It further poses questions regarding the production, circulation, and reception of these films. What are the various modes and contexts of production? How do we analyze the aesthetic strategies of these films in relation to their cultural politics? What happens when these films travel? Are they at home only in their place of production or elsewhere as well? What does their migration tell us about transnational communities and interculturalism? How might spectatorship and the gaze be thought within transnational frameworks? How do we understand the feminist and queer politics of these films? How do they negotiate issues of commodification? What role does South Asian and diasporic cinema play in the construction, activation, and deferment of nostalgia? The book further examines the formation and characteristics of diasporic cinema and the development of a diasporic spectatorship and subjectivity that creates a new mode of understanding transnational cultural productions, identities, and experiences. Because cinema and cultural texts are always implicated and located within changing systems and fields of power, we must reformulate and recalibrate our theoretical frameworks and methodologies, and create new conceptual models, to best account for these shifts.

Though this project focuses on a specific cinema within specific contexts, one need not be invested in South Asian diasporic cultural studies to access the analyses occurring in the book. It is the unmarked privilege of Eurocentric logic that treats discussions and analyses of white normative subjects as theoretical and universal while rendering work on ethnic or postcolonial topics as esoteric and particular. Instead, this project must be considered as of interest and import to those working on broad theoretical conversations, such as embodiment, identification, cultural production and reception, and nationalism as it seeks to expose the mutual constitution of the unmarked normative and its marked "other" in Eurocentric logic.

The book also seeks to interrogate more generally questions related to transnational cultural studies around political economy, reception, and production as well as issues of subjectivity and identity. Broad theoretical questions around issues of agency, subjectivity, and embodiment are addressed through the framework of spatiality, transnationality, and migration. In addition, discussions here of how diasporic cinema employs and transforms aesthetic and cultural strategies such as camp and disidentification are clearly linked to a variety of theoretical debates. Finally, the project expands current conversations about our understanding of diaspora, nation, and globalization in the study of transnational migration. My hope is that this study will interrupt certain types of narratives (e.g., national, heteronormative, masculine, bourgeois) as it maps the space of the "Brown Atlantic," paying particular attention to the contours of global capital, migration, colonialism, and empire in the global cities of New York, London, Toronto, and Bombay.

Studies of South Asian transnational cultures and subjectivities provide an opportunity to think through and interweave a variety of disciplinary approaches. Most important, this study attempts to disrupt and fracture the stability of disciplinary business as we know it—in other words, it does not fit neatly into the categorical disciplinary formations that drive knowledge production, rendering projects such as this at times illegible. Although in the last decade scholars in several key fields have greatly contributed to our understandings of transnational imaginings and practices, the boundaries that define the objects of study for fields such as gender, feminist, or women's studies; area studies; Asian-American studies; and cultural studies do not generally include the production of the Brown Atlantic that is outlined and performed here in this book. At the same time, paradoxically, it is these very areas of inquiry that enable and inspire this project. This project seeks to reframe disciplinary paradigms as the project places centrally disparate "subjects or objects of study": gender, sexuality, cinema, diaspora, globalization, Asian-Americans, Bollywood, and postcoloniality to name a few. In doing so, it begins to outline the necessary parameters for the formation and development of transnational cultural studies. This new creature, transnational cultural studies, integrates the fields of cultural studies, postcolonial and globalization studies, and black diasporic and Asian-American studies specifically in a way that challenges notions of culture as not being related to power relations, critiques of modernity and the nation, and political economy. In addition, this particular permutation also formulates the areas of feminist and queer studies as integral to this formation.

One contribution of this project is to locate cultural studies more strongly in relation to globalization processes. Rather than acquiescing an engagement of globalization to social scientists, I seek to understand how contemporary social, political, and economic processes can be understood through cultural production. For scholars of the Frankfurt school, such as Adorno, mass culture was a site of capitulation in contrast to the "cultural negativity" associated with modernist (high) art. In contrast, this project argues it is possible to seek complex and contradictory understandings of culture in relation to dominant institutions, ideologies, and aesthetics as well as global economics. South Asian diasporic cultural production is ideally poised to engage strategically and intellectually the macrological (i.e., capitalism and imperialism) and the micrological (i.e., discourses of everyday life) to enact analyses that examine the mutual constitution of the global and the local.[1] Migrant cultural production "does not metaphorize the experiences of 'real' immigrants but finds in the located contradictions of immigration both the critical intervention in the national paradigm at the point of its conjunction with the international and the theoretical nexus that challenges the global economic from the standpoint of the locality" (Lowe 1998a, 35). It is not necessary to seek folk or "traditional" texts as pure forms uncontaminated by capitalism and therefore to dismiss other media such as television, film, and the Internet as elitist. This project suggests that cinema provides a significant site of investigation in these negotiations not only because it is widely accessible but also because of its engagements with globalization during circulation. My suggestion here is that understanding the political economy of cultural production, circulation, and reception will illuminate the multiple and contradictory contestations and negotiations that occur with the South Asian diasporas in this moment of globalization.

Another significant contribution of this project is that it places diaspora and transnationality in the center of feminist and queer studies, pushing these areas to further consider their relationships to globalization and postcoloniality. In doing so, I produce three methods that must be deployed for South Asian diasporic and transnational cultural studies. Although lip service has been paid to asserting the significance of gender and sexuality in relation to race within diaspora studies, seldom has scholarship been able to maintain an analysis that considers all of these simultaneously.[2] Discourses of diaspora often eschew significant differences such as gender and class in favor of an emphasis on race and nation. The approach here is to explicate the ways complex and contradictory material processes and discourses construct and negotiate subjects of race, class, gender, ethnicity, religion, sexuality, and so forth simultaneously. Areas of inquiry such as Asian-American and black British cultural studies have typically paid attention to the relevance of class and gender in racial formations. This study builds on this scholarship but also emphasizes the significance of a critical understanding of sexuality, particularly heteronormativity, to these racial configurations in the context of economic globalization. The integration here of feminist and queer studies with these other areas of inquiry forces an insistence on simultaneous understandings of gender, race, and sexuality in the production of South Asian diasporic subjectivities.

This chapter is divided into four main sections. The first section on South Asian diasporic culture begins with a brief summary of the formation and politics of contemporary South Asian transnationalities and migration. It then turns to the slippery concept of culture, clarifying how it is deployed in and its relevance to this project. The second and third sections are the heart of the chapter. In the second section, I present the critical frameworks, postcolonial critique, theories of globalization, and diasporic studies that provide the modes of understanding and engaging transnationality in this project. In the third section, I elaborate on the other theoretical engagements with transnationality in this project, namely those emerging from feminist and queer theories. Finally, I end with an overview of the remaining chapters of the book, highlighting individual films and significant arguments.

South Asian Diasporas

This book seeks to explore and explicate the cultural, political, and theoretical "cartographies" of South Asian diasporas, transnationalities that are disjointed, heterogeneous, and hybrid rather than stable, unified, or coherent. South Asia refers to the nation-states of Bangladesh, Bhutan, India, the Maldives, Nepal, Pakistan, Sri Lanka, and Tibet. "South Asia" as a constructed category is often used as a strategic geopolitical or geographical term indicating political alliances, both in Asia and the diasporas, and the term is one that can configure social identities and categories without necessarily alluding to national identities. It is not to be taken as a term designating an object of study, as does area studies, but rather as designating a constructed geopolitical region with interlinked political economies and histories, a subject of study. Nevertheless, it is important to recognize the ambivalent function of the term; although South Asia provides opportunity to analyze the region because of its interconnected history, politics, and economics, it is also imagined as a homogenous community from an "external" (often Western) point of view.

Unfortunately, discussions of India dominate the study and meaning of South Asia in most (inter)disciplinary scholarship and (identity) politics.[3] The framework of "South Asian" can reflect a liberal Euro-American discourse that views the region as a homogenous monocultural area in which an Orientalized version of India represents South Asia. Thus, strategically identifying oneself or one's politics as "South Asian" can create, though does not ensure, meaningful alliances within certain contexts. Nation-states such as Sri Lanka, Bhutan, and Bangladesh, and Indian minorities including Muslims and Sikhs, as well as subaltern groups, offer multiple points to deconstruct not only the dominant national but also the Indian normative and multiple points from which to configure South Asia. Historical contexts have produced multiple oppressions and conflicts through the concept of religious difference within and between nations. In other words, the term needs to be unpacked to understand the complex relations of power that operate to consolidate a singular Hindu Indian construction of South Asia.

South Asian diasporas encompass people (and their ancestry) who have emigrated from South Asia. There are approximately 20 million people in the Indian diaspora alone (Sengupta 2003, A1). South Asian migrations are recent to the Middle East, like the guest workers, distant like the indentured servants who settled in the Caribbean during colonialism, or even multiple like the migrants who, evicted from Uganda, settled in Britain.[4] South Asian diasporas refer to migrations to Southeast Asia, the Caribbean, North America, Fiji, South America, the Middle East, England, and East and South Africa in the nineteenth century and twentieth century. Although there are disjunctural similarities between older and newer diasporas, I focus on the latter in this project. I refer specifically to migration that occurred primarily after World War II and independence (post-1965 in the United States). I am particularly interested in recent South

Asian migration to the West, specifically the United States, Britain, and Canada (Australia and New Zealand have increasing populations). The tension between similar and overlapping historical and material conditions of postcoloniality and globalization leading to migration provides the basis for this formulation of the Brown Atlantic. However, this is not to suggest a coherency or uniformity in discussing a singular diaspora but rather heterogeneous and multiple diasporas that can be discussed in relation to the specificities of their local modalities and histories.

South Asian is a useful nomenclature when referring to those who emigrated prior to the independence and partition of the Indian subcontinent. I primarily use the more specific term *Indian* when I am speaking exclusively or distinctly of India in this project to avoid masking the hegemony of India within the configuration of South Asia. In each case, I have tried to be specific as possible, referring to post-1965 U.S. immigrants as Indians but early century emigrants to Canada as Sikhs, Punjabis, or South Asians depending on the context. *South Asian* is also a strategic term for racial and ethnic identities, especially in the United States. *Desi* also has gained popularity to designate a pan–South Asian racial and ethnic migrant identity. In the Canadian and British context, *Asian*, rather than South Asian, often has been used to designate the similar identities. In these locations, South Asians tend to be the largest groups and therefore are known as Asians. (This is not the case in the United States). South Asians also identify as blacks, most frequently in Britain and Canada. South Asians in these two locations share some similar racialization processes because of a common legacy of racialized colonialism. South Asians in the United States and Canada also may share similar racialization processes because of similar immigration histories and political economies. In this transnational project, I employ *South Asian* to discuss diasporic locations. I attempt to employ the "local" moniker when possible. I have retained the nomenclatures and identities that are most significant and frequently used in specific locations, thus in the context of Britain and Africa, I employ *Asians*. Nevertheless, this study requires some fluidity and mobility in understanding shifting identification processes as it moves from South Asian to Indian or Pakistani to desi to British Asian to Asian Canadian and back again.

Public Culture

Many theories posit the homogenization of culture by the global spread of Western, namely American, cultural production, asserting that local cultures are overwritten by the hegemony of Western media. In contrast, Armand Mattelart cautions that transnational centrism is a dangerous colonizing perspective in which local subjects are reframed as "passive receptacles" of the "norms, values, and signs of transnational power" (cited in Grewal and Kaplan 1994, 13). In other words, Mattelart posits that "global" media are locally consumed and received in multiple ways that mitigate the dominance of such cultural production. Responding to such remarks, others comment that we must not be too eager to celebrate the local consumption and subversive reception of transnational products in the South without noting the profitable economic conditions of production and distribution in the North. Akhil Gupta and James Ferguson (1992, 19) argue that

> the danger here is the temptation to use scattered examples of the cultural flows dribbling from the "periphery" to the chic centers of the culture industry as a way of dismissing the "grand narrative" of capitalism (especially the totalizing narrative of late capitalism) and thus evading the powerful political issues associated with Western global hegemony.

Thus, studies examining the localized receptions of Hollywood or Bollywood films, solely at the level of reception, often ignore the economics of the production and distribution of such commodities at the level of political economy. Conversely, analyses focusing solely on production often ignore the local consumption of such works. Here, I argue that the study of the role of cultural politics of film in the production of diasporic affiliations, identities, and politics is crucial to an understanding of transnationalism and globalization.

Lisa Lowe and David Lloyd (1997) suggest that culture and cultural production, though located within the expansion of global capitalism, act as sites that may contradict and oppose capital and are not subsumed fully under the logic of transnational capitalism. They, among others, offer us an opportunity to see cultural production not as markers of the hegemony of Western imperialism and the total penetration of capital into arenas marked as separate from the economic and political but as sites in which such contestations occur. Cultural production can offer the opportunity to explore not only the relationship between culture and modes of production but also the possible ways to negotiate global processes. In this case, diasporic cinema located in the interstices of these processes promises to be a productive and unique site of inquiry that may assist in "unthinking Eurocentrism" (Shohat and Stam 1994) within the context of global capitalism.

This project analyzes transnational cultural production as described by Lowe and Lloyd (1997, 15):

> What we focus on is the intersection of commodification and labor exploitation under postmodern transnational modes of production with the historical emergence of social formations in time with but also in antagonism to modernity; these social formations are not residues of the "premodern," but are *differential* formations that mediate the processes through which capital profits through the mixing and combination of exploitative modes. What we are concerned with is the multiplicity of significant contradictions rooted in the longer histories of antagonism and adaptation.

Taking these critiques into account, the authors are considering here "the contradictions that emerge between capitalist economic formations and the social and cultural practices they presume but cannot dictate" and that these contradictions "give rise to cross-race and cross-national projects, feminist movements, anticolonial struggles, and politicized cultural practices" (p. 25). The project focuses on how transnational cultural production negotiates the nation-state and capitalism, specifically within the racialized and gendered social and political transnational spaces marked as diasporas. The cultural sphere analyzed here is one that has recently emerged. As Spivak (1999, 357) suggests, "Culture alive is always on the run, always changeful.... I am therefore a student of cultural politics. In what interests are differences defined?"

It may be useful at this point to outline some of the common characteristics that are shared by the representations and practices that are discussed here. South Asian diasporic cultural politics may differ from those in South Asia. This is in part due to the conditions of globalization and postcoloniality discussed previously, and specifically the technology that has been made accessible to these new communities. Diasporic cultural politics are mapped into this sphere of the public and popular that also negotiate nation-state policies and commercial film industries. Here the public spheres that are relevant to understanding the cultural politics of South Asian diasporas are necessarily transnational ones. This study focuses on the cultural space engendered by feature-length popular films, because of the particular ways in which they are produced, circulated, and received in the Brown Atlantic. Feature-length films popular in the West actively define and relate the central cultural debates in these transnational communities. Lesser well-known films are less likely to affect or engage South Asian transnational public cultures. Hence, although the analysis of these films is important, it is outside the theoretical framework of this project.

Unlike many conventional models, this study does not assume a split between popular and high culture. Instead, it employs the concept of public culture in its discussion of films. In their work on India, Arjun Appadurai and Carol Breckenridge (1989a and 1989b) offer the concept of public culture to create a space outside of such hierarchical approaches. They attempt to avoid these dichotomies between elite and popular, which they associate with categorical schema of Western cultures. More specifically, these dichotomies, they argue, are inappropriate for understanding culture within postcoloniality. They replace these schematic dichotomies with a framework that constructs a new cultural and theoretical space of analysis that is attentive to a variety of scales. Furthermore, Appadurai and Breckenridge propose that public culture can be employed to identify the "space between domestic life and the projects of the nation-state— where different social groups ... constitute their identities by their experience of mass-mediated forms in relation to the practices of everyday life" (cited in Pinney 2001, 7). Christopher Pinney adds, "One crucial difference between public culture and popular culture is that the former presupposes processes of globalization within which the local operates" (p. 8).

For Appadurai and Breckenridge, "the term *public culture* is more than a rubric for collectively thinking about aspects of modern life now thought about separately. It also allows us to hypothesize not a type of cultural phenomena but a *zone of* cultural debate" (1989b, p. 6). Thus, rather than classify by genre or target audience, *public culture* is concerned with complex relations between multiple groups and interests in the dominant and popular space of diaspora. Appadurai and Breckenridge, though they avoid drawing distinctions between elite and popular forms, do not suggest that all interests enter into or are equally represented in the "zone of cultural debate." Public culture, therefore, is a site of contestation of class and other interests, often articulated through the production of differences in terms of power relations. In addition, public culture identifies the space in which political, social, and economic contestations are negotiated in cultural discourses at a variety of scales and thus is not limited to the nation. This project focuses on the formation and emergence of these transnational public spheres from the local and regional to the national and global. Within the South Asian diasporic context, public spheres are the sites of contestation over social differences such as gender, race, nationality, and sexuality that are relevant to transnational subject formation. In addition, Appadurai and Breckenridge (1989b, 6–7) suggest that national culture and public cultures are sites "of an uneasy collaboration between the cultural agencies of the nation-state and the private, commercial agencies which dominate certain kinds of cultural production." It is important to note that different groups may not participate in the public cultures associated with these films. In other words, although I emphasize the space of shared cultural discourses, I recognize that not all groups and classes may access or seek participation in the dominant discourses that enter the public culture described here. For example, these transnational public cultures focused on migratory subjectivities often foreclose the politics of subalternity in their imbricated relationship with global capitalism. These films often made in the name of the agency of the transnational elite postcolonial subject may therefore claim the space of native informant in relation to the racial underclass in the North and subaltern figures in the South.[5]

South Asian diasporic migration into the West engendered by global capitalism has created complex and contradictory cultural productions and subjectivities. Therefore, differentiating this cultural production and circulation may present oppositional politics but at the same time may traffic in normativities and self-commodification to access production and circulation. Thus, the project seeks to recognize the radical and oppressive cultural politics of South Asian diasporas and explores the contradictory and complex cultural debates present in these transnational films.

Postcoloniality, Globalization, and Diaspora: Theories of the National and Transnational

This book pays attention to the uneven, contradictory, and sometimes complicit relationships between the postcolonial nation-state and global capitalism in relation to modernity through what Aihwa Ong (1999) calls the transnational practices and imaginings of migratory subjects. Transnationalism emphasizes the movement across nation-states and simultaneously implies a state of change as well; it interrogates understandings of the national and transnational through critiques offered by postcolonial, globalization, and diasporic studies. This project identifies postcoloniality and globalization as the processes and conditions that construct and constitute the Brown Atlantic and its transnationalities.

Postcolonial Critique

The arguments around the term *postcolonial* are well rehearsed.[6] Many of the contestations over "postcolonial" have sought to delineate its meaning as a social condition or a temporal period; while others define "postcolonial" as the political critique of modernity and colonialism that can be understood through analyses of the links between power and knowledge. Within this study, the former (social condition) is referred to as postcoloniality, and the latter as postcolonial critique. First, postcoloniality as a social condition (the condition resulting from a particular form of geopolitical cultural and economic domination and the subsequent struggles engaged against this domination that have been consolidated by the bourgeoisie as anticolonial nationalisms) provides a significant understanding of the histories of migration and dislocation since colonialism and independence. Furthermore, postcoloniality can be employed within varying contexts to engage shifting political struggles so that, for example, the imperialist relations of United States with decolonizing nation-states in the past six decades also can be considered within an understanding of postcoloniality.[7]

Second, postcolonial critique theoretically and politically attempts to identify and to deconstruct the universalizing Eurocentric discourses of colonialism, nationalism, and modernity through challenging universalist narratives of history, critiquing the form of the nation, and interrogating the relationship between power and knowledge. In doing so, the project of postcolonial studies seeks to disengage from the binary logic of colonial and anticolonial that characterizes elite nationalisms that do not deconstruct the Eurocentric logic of knowledge that continues to undergird anticolonial politics. Therefore, postcolonial studies, especially the project of subaltern studies, is distinguished by its focus on the nation and the project of modernity. Subaltern studies scholars, such as Ranajit Guha (1997) and Gyan Prakash (1992), have successfully employed Marxist and poststructural methodologies of "reading against the grain" of anticolonial nationalism for traces of subaltern struggles. "Reading colonial and nationalist narratives against their grain and focusing on their blind-spots, silences, and anxieties, these historians seek to uncover the subaltern's myths, cults, ideologies, and revolts that colonial and nationalist elites sought to appropriate and conventional historiography has laid to waste by their deadly weapon of cause and effect" (Prakash 1992, 9). In doing so, they have sought to dismantle the supposed hegemony of the bourgeois class in constructing the postcolonial nation. Postcolonial feminist studies scholars, such as Partha Chatterjee and Gayatri Spivak, have interrogated the nation epistemologically and politically, respectively arguing that nationalism is derivative and complicit with colonialism and consequently that anticolonial bourgeois nationalism has failed to represent subaltern subjects within the nation and that the gendered subaltern signifies the space of the conceptual failure of the nation.[8]

In contrast to the nonelite subjects of subaltern studies, postcolonial diasporic migrants often have been members of the bourgeoisie who have remained invested in employing, rather than dismantling, this Eurocentric construction of cultural difference. During British colonialism, South Asians migrated to Britain and other parts of the Commonwealth, including East Africa, Canada, and the Caribbean. More of the recent migration has been by more professional-class South Asians, people whose Indian postsecondary education and training makes them attractive to Western economies. This bourgeois class that has become transnational in the last half of the century was formed by the specific history of colonialism and could be called Macaulay's grandchildren. Lord Thomas Macaulay, a colonial administrator in India, wrote the following in his infamous 1835 "Minute on Education":

> We must at present do our best to form a class who may be interpreters between us and the millions whom we govern; a class of persons, Indian in blood and colour, but English in taste, in opinions, in morals, and in intellect. To that class we may leave it to refine the vernacular dialects of the country, to enrich those dialects with terms of science borrowed from the Western nomenclature, and to render them by degrees fit for conveying knowledge to the great mass of the population. (cited in Visweswaran 1997, 10)

Chatterjee suggests that it is this class that soon became the Indian national bourgeoisie that several generations later has transnational aspirations.[9]

With independence, this class gained access to education but not necessarily to compensatory employment and income or access to the promises of modernity. The postcolonial economy did not necessarily support the aspirations of this underemployed class that sought to migrate to fulfill its desires and capabilities. Kamala Visweswaran argues that this bourgeoisie saw themselves as forced to migrate to realize their potential. "In a sense, then, the subcontinental bourgeoisie . . . must globalize in order to realize its interests, placing the postcolonial teacher of English literature in the US academy on a continuum with the family jeweler or venture capitalist" (Visweswaran 1997, 11). The legacy of Macaulay's "Minute an Education" ensured that these English-speaking bourgeoisie, consisting of merchants, academics, doctors, and engineers, among others, had access to migration to countries such as the United States, Britain, and Canada once those nation-state's immigration policies changed. As more skilled and professional labor was needed by the economic North, immigration policies shifted to allow for the migration of certain kinds of labor, much less than certain kinds of national populations. I will return to the topic of interrelations between subjects' desires to migrate and the economic forces that propel such desires. The English-speaking class first imagined by colonialism and reformulated by anticolonial nationalism are most frequently the constituents who seek the metropolitan center that they have been taught to desire. Hence colonialism and nationalism have engendered transnationality in postcolonial migration.

In the United States, for example, an influx of South Asian migration occurred after the 1965 Immigration and Nationality Act (effective in July 1968) abolished quotas favoring northern European immigrants and assigned uniform quotas for all nation-states, granting special preference to those with capital and technical skills regardless of origin. In contrast to the "pull" for immigrant labor that recruited Asian immigrants for the exploitation of their physical labor after the end of slavery, this more recent wave arrived in the United States as part of the restructuring of global capitalism in the twentieth century. Thus, Asians, often of the middle and professional class, were able to enter the United States if they had the sufficient funds or education to do so. Many South Asians were poised for migration and did so. The postcolonial nation-states suffered economic loss with the departure of each migrant. The economic and emotional costs are an undercalculated loss for the postcolonial South Asian homelands, despite the contributions and remittances made by the diaspora.[10] The condition of postcoloniality led to a certain type of transnational migration, one that engendered South Asian diasporas marked by the legacy of colonialism. "Despite the usual assumption that Asians immigrate from stable, continuous, 'traditional' cultures, most of the post-1965 Asian immigrants come from societies already disrupted by colonialism and distorted by the upheavals of neocolonial capitalism and war" (Lowe 1998a, 16). Moreover, the colonial and Orientalist racial formations accompanied South Asian migration to Western nation-states so that although capitalism's economic imperative was satisfied by the arrival of the migrating labor, the nation-state politically disenfranchised South Asians from full citizenship.[11]

Several postcolonial scholars, such as Homi Bhabha, have sought to understand the relationship between postcoloniality and transnational migration. Postcolonial diasporas mark the return of the repressed in Bhabha's work. Having already been part of the history of the colonial nation, "it is to the city that the migrants, the minorities, the diasporic come to change the history of the nation" (Bhabha 1994, 320). The migration of Asians to Britain, for example, results directly from the aftermath of colonialism in Britain where they are excluded from and denied full citizenship because of this history. Bhabha's scholarship in its sweeping gesture does not distinguish between the subaltern nonelite, displaced diasporic, or migrant female in his postcolonial critique of modernity. Instead, his critique seeks heterogeneous sites, including postcolonial diasporas, that produce multiple cultural strategies (such as hybridity and mimicry) that critique nationalism, nativism, and modernity.[12] Postcolonial diasporic critiques of modernity pose a range of analytic possibilities that challenge many categories of modernity such as the nation and national identity but differ from postmodernist critiques in foregrounding complex histories of slavery, exile, colonialism, transnationality, and postcoloniality. Although some of Bhabha's work is aligned with the subaltern studies scholarship, it diverges in its emphasis on postcolonial diasporic migration and transnationality. The significance of the subaltern studies project then emphasizes the necessity of attending to how diasporas are characterized by elite formations and therefore often aligned with the project of nationalism.

Migration and diasporas cannot be separated from colonialism, because it is the historical condition of colonialism and postcoloniality that has led to the global displacement of South Asian peoples under various forms of migration nor can they be separated from the uneven expansion of global capitalism that also functions to provide mobility and agency to these postcolonial subjects. Bearing in mind the project of postcolonial studies, this study attempts to not only analyze the ways in which the logic of anticolonial nationalism appears in the deterritorialized nations of diasporas but also to analyze the ways in which postcolonial diasporas can provide sites for continuing to critique modernity and its universalizing narratives from a specific history and politics of transnationality.

Globalization

Most significant, globalization is understood by scholars as not only the expansion of capitalism into the "stage" of post-Fordist global capitalism and its attendant processes but also as the related intensification of compression of time and space.[13] Globalization in the works of scholars such as Lowe and Lloyd (1997, 1) describes the moment and processes of late or global capitalism, "the universal extension of a differentiated mode of production that relies on flexible accumulation and mixed production to incorporate all sectors of the global economy into its logic of commodification." The term also describes the accompanying social, political, and cultural processes. One of the political dynamics of this transformation that is of interest here is the deterritorialization of people, capital, and culture that is part of globalization.[14]

Saskia Sassen (2003, 5) comments, "Crucial to the critique of methodological nationalism is the need for trans-nationalism because the nation as container category is inadequate given the proliferation of transboundary dynamics and formation." Although scholars have debated how best to comprehend the recent processes of globalization and their subsequent impact on nation-states and transnational migrations, the models for understanding global relations often have been either totalizing or celebratory. To better understand transnational phenomena as contradictory, fragmented, and heterogeneous, scholars have made the framework of the global and the local a powerful and frequent descriptor in this scholarship on transnationality. Though they hold differing understandings of the status of the nation-state, both totalizing and celebratory positions posit the current moment of postmodernity as one in which capital, cultural products, and people cross state borders in mass migration. In terms of the former position, structuralist scholars have offered varying paradigms to describe uneven economic and political global relations under the rubric of dependency and world system theories. Positing that the integration of non-European nation-states into the world economy is accomplished through exploitation and uneven capitalist development, these Marxist theories of imperialism (in the works of Samir Amin, 1976, and Immanuel Wallerstein, 1980, for example) employ structural analyses taking the globe as a political and economic unit, with nation-states as its geographical component parts. In general, world system models conceptualize the division of the world into the core and periphery, or now more frequently, into the North and South.[15]

Other social scientists who are often more interested in framing the local as creative, resistant, and transgressive offer contrasting emphases on the impact of the local. This approach takes the global to be a uniform set of macroeconomic forces resulting from the expansion of capitalism and the local to be complex and multiple situated processes (Ong 1999, 4). In other words, although the economic and political are still associated with top-down unified global forces in these theories, transnational processes occurring on the local level are associated with cultural specificity and resistance. Here, the tendency is often to privilege the local as the site of cultural resistance and creative engagement that is best approached through the social sciences, especially ethnography.

In analyses of the impact of globalization on nation-states, scholars such as Arjun Appadurai (1990 and 1996), Ulf Hannerz, and Linda Basch, Nina Glick Schiller, and Cristina Szanton Blanc (1994) have commented on the porosity of borders, the decoupling of the nation-state, and the adaptive transnational subjects cum citizens with varying degrees of economic and political power. Arjun Appadurai writes of the postmodern condition in which culture, capital, commodities, and people are in motion in complex transnational ebbs and flows in a postnational moment. Basch et al.'s work ambitiously connects the transnational migrations of postcolonial labor groups to metropolitan nation-states, noting the complicated economic, political, and social circuits established by these groups. Their study, like others, lacks an analysis of the situated racial formation processes that occur in these places, especially in light of discourses of multiculturalism, neoliberalism, and shifting citizenship policies.[16] In response to the theories that emphasize globalization and the global as totalizing, these more celebratory discourses of cultural globalization focus on the disjunctures experienced by migratory subjects in their situated local forms of culture. As Cindi Katz (2001, 1229) comments,

> The material social practices associated with globalization work in interconnection, such as when capital, labor, or cultural products move *from* one place *to* another, but they work iteratively as well, the effects of capitalism's globalizing imperative are experienced commonly across very different locales, and understanding these connections is crucial if they are to be challenged effectively.

In contrast, Saskia Sassen (2003, 2) examines globalization as encompassing processes that though located at national or subnational levels allows involves transnational formations that connect multiple locations in networks in complex and contradictory ways.

Appadurai has been one of the strongest advocates of the celebratory approach, suggesting the collapse of the nation-state due to globalization and the possibilities of postnational and diasporic identities. "We are in the process of moving to a global order in which the nation-state has become obsolete and other formations for allegiance and identity have taken its place... and there will be a spread of national forms unconnected to territorial states" (Appadurai 1993b, "Patriotism" 421). Announcing the undoing of the hyphen between the nation and the state (also territory), the cosmopolitan possibilities of new global spatial relations and communities are seen to occur in the "local" spaces of culture that resist the "global." Furthermore, he describes these new affinities as "strong alternative forms for the organization of global traffic in resources, images, and ideas, forms that either *contest the nation-state* actively or constitute peaceful alternatives for large-scale political loyalties" (Appadurai 1993b, "Patriotism" 421, emphasis mine).

Although one could make an argument about the increase in nationalisms, Appadurai is susceptible to diagnosing the demise of the nation-state. (The case of South Asia may actually indicate the opposite as the transnational participation of migrant nationalisms plays out in religious nationalisms within the diaspora.) Creolization, diasporas, and postnationality are evoked as indications of the demise of the nation-state rather than as markers of its transformation in relation to global processes. The "post" in Appadurai's postnationality connotes "after" rather than "since." Rather than teasing out the intricate web tying together nation, state, citizenship, and globalization, this line of inquiry assumes that transnational communities have replaced nation-states. Instead of viewing the United States as "a land of immigrants," Appadurai (1993b, 423) suggests that it can be envisioned as "one mode in a postnational network of diasporas." Here, his celebratory evocations of diaspora woefully undertheorize the relevance of political economy and race to national membership and citizenship.

A wide range of scholars including Jenny Sharpe and Aihwa Ong have forwarded critiques of this cultural globalization based on the substitution of ethnicity for race and the erasure of state citizenship in privileging the transcendence of the national. Appadurai's nation of nations paradigm, writes Jenny Sharpe (1995, 189), "blurs the distinction between a racial identity formed in opposition to the idea of the United States as a nation of immigrants and an ethnic identity formed around the idea of the United States as a nation of unmeltable immigrants." His lack of attention to racial formation and racism becomes masked in the emphasis on ethnicity and the United States as perhaps the über-multicultural nation of nations. Ong pinpoints Appadurai's formulation of cosmopolitan globalism as predicated on the detachment of the nation from the state, and therefore the supposed irrelevance of the state, citizenship, and its recent reformulations due to the pressure of global capitalism. Ong's critique further presses Appadurai as she asserts the significant function and power of the nation-state in globalization, especially in regard to the regulatory and constitutive role of citizenship that occurs at multiple scales. Sassen (2003, 6) writes, "Today's re-scaling dynamics cut across institutional size and across the institutional encasements of territory produced by the formation of national states. This does not mean that the old hierarchies disappear, but rather that rescalings emerge alongside the old ones, and that the former can trump the latter."

Citizenship, as Lowe, Ong, and other Asian-American studies scholars have argued, functions as a mechanism of inclusion and exclusion. As Lowe has discussed, the immigrant has been opposed to the citizen in normative constructions of the nation. "These definitions have cast Asian immigrants both as persons and populations to be integrated into the national political sphere and as the contradictory, confusing, unintelligible elements to be marginalized and returned to their alien origins" (Lowe 1998a, 4). Lowe elucidates the ways in which the migration of Asians is situated in relation to the force of capital on one side and the desire of the nation on the other, thus creating contradictory and complex interpellations of the citizen-subject. In her account of Asian migration, Lowe (1998a, 10) suggests, "The economic contradictions of capital and labor on the national level, and the contradictions of the political national and the global economy, have given rise over and over again, for the nation to resolve *legally* capitalist contradiction around the definition of the Asian immigrant subject." In other words, capital's demand for the internationalization of labor coincides and conflicts with the nation-state's need for coherency and hegemony (Lowe 1998b, 15).[17] The resultant migration attests to the ways U.S. imperialism and capitalism converge within global economy so that Asian migration to the West is facilitated and hampered by the nation-state. "We are here because you were there" aptly summarizes the relationship between Western interests and the counternarrative offered by migrants.

This study approaches the transnational and its relationship to the postnational as advocated by the recent scholarship in American studies. Postnational American studies rather than foregoing the nation-state foregrounds the transnational and international dimensions of the United States and the Americas. In particular, it reckons with the myopic and domesticating paradigms that not only previously contained American studies to the territory of the United States but also ignored U.S. imperialism and forwarded U.S. exceptionalism. Hence, the project tries to understand transnationality in terms of multiscalar processes. In this way, it takes transnationality as "the condition of cultural interconnectedness and mobility across space—which has been intensified under late capitalism" and transnationalism as "the cultural specificities of global processes, tracing the multiplicity of the uses and conceptions of 'culture'" (Ong 1999, 4).

Furthermore, Appadurai links the expansion of capitalism and its conse-
quential migrations as liberatory actions. In this case, he fails to note that the
postnational moment of movement enabling liberatory shifts and reevaluations
of identity is also the postmodern moment of late capitalism. He does not acknowledge that liberatory mobilizations occur within specific conditions (prefer
parameters elsewhere has non-mathematical usage that is acceptable) accessible
to limited populations. Therefore, Appadurai misreads the role of the state in
the unbuckling of the nation-state; he neglects to acknowledge the shifted role
of the state in engendering global capitalism. He eulogizes the nation and its cor-
respondence to the state in his valorization of diaspora and other postnational
forms of identity and community. His example warns us that it is necessary
to locate diaspora as complicitly embedded in late capitalist formations and in
relation to the racism of nation-states. Furthermore, racialization, as I argue
later, is also linked to these economic global processes as well. In other words,
ethnicity, religion, and race continue to be mobilized and revitalized by global
geopolitics and economics. Missing in many of these accounts of globalization
is an understanding of gender and sexuality. Feminist theorists of globalization
such as Lowe, Sassen, and Cynthia Enloe (1990) have been much more attuned
to the ways in which globalization processes are specifically gendered, especially
in their analyses of labor and migration.

Scholars such as Saskia Sassen (2003, 3) argue the necessity of transforming
our theories and methods regarding studies of globalization:

> Studying the global, then, entails not only a focus on that which is explicitly
> global in scale, but also a focus on locally scaled practices and conditions artic-
> ulated with global dynamics and a focus on the multiplication of cross-border
> connections among various localities and the fact of recurrence across localities.

This project takes a multiscalar approach to studying globalization as one of the
conditions engendering South Asian diasporic transnationalities. It sees these
processes as specific flows that follow certain circuits of migration. It recognizes
that globalization processes are differentiated, reconstructing transnational circuits and regions, rather than a homogenous global structure; moreover, it
recognizes their complex relations with the local, urban, regional, national,
and international. This migration produces a certain heterogeneous and hybrid
multiscalar space—that of the Brown Atlantic.

Diaspora

Critiques of the nation have emerged not only from postcolonial and globalization studies but also from diasporic studies that have provided a complex
conceptual framework for theorizing nation, race, and transnationity in relation to cultural identities. As David Eng (1997) writes in his article "Out Here
and Over There," diaspora can be a mode of critique for studies seeking knowledge production outside of a national framework. In his work, Eng proposes

a queering not only of sexuality but also of the concept of home through the concept of diaspora. He suggests that home has been a problematic space and site that has been differently approached by Asian-American and queer studies. Bringing these methods of inquiry together through the diasporic critique allows us to query "the inevitability of these normative structures while deconstructing their mechanisms of exclusion" (Eng 2001, 206).

In the usage here, diaspora provides a critique not only of the concept of home but also of origins and the role they play in conceptualizations of nation, race, and identity. Hence, in this project, diaspora functions as a postnational critique of the nation and nationalism that is strongly associated with a critique of the concept-metaphor of home and origin. Rather than seeking to define the significance of diaspora through tracing its etymology in cultural studies, that is, seeking a linguistic origin, the project here is to understand when and why, and how it is employed in cultural politics and knowledge production. Furthermore, in posing diaspora partially as a critique of constructions of home, this project necessarily interrogates spatialized and territorialized identities not only in relation to constructions of "migrant" subjects but also in relation to the mutual constitution of "native" subjects.

Unlike Appadurai's theories on cultural globalization and diaspora, cultural studies scholarship on diaspora often has focused its constructions around a critique of the racialized formation of national identity, and has questioned the rooted, static, and sedentary logic of modernity. Challenging narratives of purity, rootedness, and timelessness, diasporic critique is positioned to dismantle nationalist constructions of belonging that link racialized and gendered bodies and space in seamless tales of bloodlines and family to the land. Reemerging in the 1980s in postcolonial Britain, diaspora is defined in discourse on one hand as an identity in response to exclusionary and racist national narratives and on the other hand as Bhabha's third space of postcolonial migration and hybridity. In the United States and Canada, these discourses negotiated and reinforced the expansion of multiculturalism. In the early 1990s, with the rise of scholarship positing the death of the nation due to globalization, diaspora was hailed as a deterritorialized geopolitical community succeeding the nation-state in an age of increasing globalization. Furthermore, although classic definitions associate the space and condition of diaspora with nostalgia for the homeland, recent articulations of diaspora decouple and disassociate this nostalgia and desire to return.[18] In current discourses on migration and transnationality, *diaspora* often is used interchangeably with terms such as *immigrant, exile,* and *refugee.* In these formulations, diaspora is forwarded as potentially undermining nationalist narratives. However, as scholars have noted, diaspora as a political category may work with and not against the nation-state.

From its Greek roots, *diaspora* means literally to scatter or sow across. The *Oxford English Dictionary* traces its usage to a reference in the Old Testament (Deuteronomy 28:25) to the dispersal of the people of Israel across the world.

Traditionally, diaspora as a translocational identity relies on the idea of a home that has been left behind or lies elsewhere. The "classic" definition of diaspora, based on the Jewish model and biblical writings, often has assumed that dispersal was due to forced exile from a "homeland" to which a "people" hopes to return eventually. Contemporary dispersed communities, known today as diasporas (including the Jewish Diaspora), differ from this classical model of exile and diaspora.

Following a schematic understanding of diaspora, William Safran (1991, 84) posits that diasporas "regard the homeland as the true, ideal home to which they or their descendants should and will eventually return when conditions are acceptable." However, he acknowledges that few dispersed communities qualify as diasporas because they fail to meet all of his defining criteria, which includes the desire to return to the homeland.[19] In defining a connection between people and the homeland, Khachig Tölölyan (1996, 14) posits, "It makes more sense to think of diasporan or diasporic existence as not necessarily involving a physical return but rather a *re-turn,* a repeated turning to the concept and/or relation of the homeland and other diasporan kin" (emphasis added). Thus, Tölölyan, rather than eliminating or evading diaspora's relationship with homeland, unfetters it from a permanent physical resettlement in favor of heterogeneous connections to both the homeland and to other diasporic locations through such forms as political commitment, imagination, memory, travel, and most important here, cultural production. For some contemporary diasporas, this reformulation of re-turn is significant as increasing transnationality makes re-turns of many kinds possible.[20] This is to suggest that not all transnational structures of feelings are nostalgia or longings for homelands.

This project attends therefore to the ways in which power manifests itself between South Asian diasporas located in the West or economic North and their nation-states of the economic South. More specifically, South Asian diasporas, unlike African diasporas, may often have more political and economic power than the nation-states of the South that are nonetheless invested often with more cultural authenticity and power. Many evocations of South Asian homelands emphasize a shared history, not of postcoloniality and globalization but of more simply some shared South Asianness. The shared South Asianness is based on an Orientalist and anticolonial nationalist formulation of Indian or South Asian difference. This project asks not only what impact does this have on diasporic politics and possibilities but, more important, how do we understand this in regard to the relationship between diaspora and postcolonial nation-states, especially ones located in the economic South. Moreover, it suggests that we understand the relationship between the construction of diasporic politics in relation to indigenous ones; I suggest that this is possible through interrogating their imbricated and problematic relationships to the concept of "native."

The relationship between diasporas and homeland requires clarification. In contrast to many constructions of diaspora that take the homeland as an a priori given or as a place of origin that exists prior to displacement, this study suggests that homelands like diasporas are produced through the material practices and cultural discourses of diasporic displacement and imaginings. For example, in my discussion of homeland and diaspora, I focus on the ways in which diasporas and homelands are produced and constructed through narratives, because diasporas, like nations, evoke a time of belonging and wholeness, the moment when the diasporic subject was neither fragmented nor disenfranchised. Narratives of exile, like classical discourses of diaspora, often privilege an originary and authentic nation as home. They are fecund in producing compensatory and fantastic imaginings that result from loss and distance. This loss is rewritten in the reinvention of a past home and nation, thus sometimes consolidating and supporting nationalism's logic of origin and authenticity. As I argue later, diasporas, rather than being derivatives of, often are mutually constituted with the homeland nation. In other words, diasporas and nations produce each other. This project examines the narratives of this mutual production, focusing on the social identities and politics articulated through these transnational cultural logics. For these reasons, it attends to the ways in which South Asian homelands imagine themselves and their diasporas as well as focuses on diasporic imaginings, consistently forwarding critiques of home and origin. Therefore, coupling an understanding of diaspora as a mode of interpreting the transnational cultural and economic politics with diaspora as the critique of the notion of an origin and homeland provides a complex framework for theorizing contemporary migrations—migrations that also require considerations of race and other social categories of difference.

In black British cultural studies, that is, as in the work of Stuart Hall (1993) and Paul Gilroy (1993a and 2000), diasporic critique primarily engages with racial formation and the exclusions of the nation-state.

> The concept of diaspora sets forth a range of analytic possibilities that offer a much-needed alternative to the Eurocentric debates based on 'post-modernism' . . . by opening up a deep historical perspective on black experiences of Western modernity which disrupts the centrality of the categories of 'nation' and nationhood that are so often taken for granted. (Mercer 1994, 246)

Hall and Gilroy overlap and differ in their theories of diaspora. Hall promotes diaspora as a cultural identity that is enacted through difference rather than through an emphasis on return to origins. Although Hall positions diaspora as antinationalist discourse, this is not the primary function of the term. He understands diaspora, not in schematic terms, as a frame for understanding antiessentialist identities articulating difference. In expanding Hall's strategic use of diaspora primarily in relation to race and cultural identity, my deployment here situates difference through multiple axes of social differentiation, including religion, gender, class, and sexuality. Diaspora is an attempt to reconstruct, reposition, and rearticulate these differences in global capitalist modes of production.

Citing the cosmopolitan transnational politics of the African (and Jewish) diaspora as exemplary, Gilroy emphasizes forced dispersal as leading not to common essential experiences but to shared racial politics. In this formulation, diasporic identity is focused "less on the equalizing, pre-democratic force of sovereign territory and more on the social dynamics of remembrance and commemoration defined by a strong sense of the dangers involved in forgetting the location of origin and the tearful process of dispersal" (Gilroy 2000, 123–24). Thus for Gilroy, diaspora primarily functions as a mode of identification and disidentification in relation to the nation and against nonsituated postmodern celebrations of mobility.

Gilroy (1993a, 7) calls for challenging frameworks that privilege the national for two reasons: (1) the necessity of interrogating the nation-state as a cultural, political, and socioeconomic unit, and (2) the necessity of challenging the essentialist politics of purity that haunt modernity's construction of culture. *There Ain't No Black in the Union Jack* (1987), *The Black Atlantic* (1993a), and *Against Race* (2000) assert the significance of transnational circulation to understanding racial formations and the cultural processes.[21] Moving from diaspora as an abstraction, Gilroy posits the Black Atlantic as a specific transnational and intercultural site that encourages us to see mobility and movement in a hemispheric circuit. His proposition is that intellectuals, artists, writers, and activists crisscrossed the Atlantic as part of a transnational political and cultural movement linking the United States, Canada, Britain, and the Caribbean in a counterculture of modernity (Gilroy 1993a, 16). The tension between speaking of black diasporas and forwarding an autonomous circuit is imbalanced in Gilroy favoring the oceanic framework of the Atlantic. Although Gilroy's formulation evokes a specific geographic site framed through the hemispheric understanding of the Atlantic as a circuit of travel, Michael Hanchard (1990, 40), like Hall and other scholars, speaks of a black diaspora without a geographic specificity, but nevertheless critical of territorialized national cultures and cultural nationalisms:

> Embedded in the tale of diaspora is a symbolic revolt against the nation-state, and for this reason the diaspora holds a dual significance. It suggests a transnational dimension to black identity, for if the notion of an African diaspora is anything it is a human necklace strung together by a thread known as the slave trade, a thread which made its way across a path of America with little regard for national boundaries.

Theories of the black diaspora, like Gilroy's or Hanchard's, historically locate diasporic displacement directly in relation to the history of slavery, suggesting that these diasporic discourses cannot be reapplied easily to other diasporas without regard to their modes of displacement or historical formations.[22] Resisting an appropriation and misapplication of scholarship on black diasporas raises the question of the suitability of these theories of diaspora in regard to other transnational formations, particularly South Asian ones. South Asian diasporas, resulting not from slavery but from various modes of displacement including indentured servitude, colonialism, and uneven capital development do not produce the same political possibilities in their subsequent conceptualization of diaspora and diasporic politics. In other words, with different but overlapping histories and political economies, not only do these transnational formations vary but so do the frameworks necessary for analyzing them.[23] We must theorize differently contemporary South Asian migrant subjects who indicate different geopolitical positioning in their negotiations of the nation-state, capital, and modernity.

Building from these disjunctive understandings of diaspora, I am less interested in offering a definitive understanding of diaspora that is applicable universally than I am in forging a fractured and flawed methodology of theorizing transnational cultural politics through differences. Stretched over corners and mistranslating phrases, these theories of diaspora pose possibilities and limitations in their understandings of South Asian transnationalities. One productive point of engagement may be the ways in which diaspora is inadequate to the task in considering the disjunctures and gaps provoked by the productive and failed moments of engagement. For example, in the case of South Asians, one could argue that transnational migration creates a compatible and contradictory relationship between postcoloniality and capitalism that is negotiated in the creation of new cultural logics that employ tropes of cultural difference and at the same time make these differences compatible with capitalism. This project explores these new cultural practices and strategies that are employed by transnational subjects in cultural production.

Although I have argued for a theoretical understanding of diaspora that serves to challenge reified searches for origins, essential identities, and predominantly nation-based analyses, I am also forwarding a specific analysis within this book that accounts for the differences not only between diasporas but also within them. Rather than suggest that the discourses of diaspora as articulated here are representative of all South Asian diasporas, my analysis of the Brown Atlantic is offered in the spirit of opening up transnational theoretical space for analysis that challenges the idea of a single or national framework. It attends to multiscalar differences in its contrast and comparison of the nation-states, global cities, regions, and networks that frame the Brown Atlantic in complex, contradictory, and enmeshed power relations.

Paradigm Lost and Regained—Transnationality, Diaspora, and Asian-American Studies

In the United States, some critics argue that the emphasis on diasporic and transnational connections marginalizes antiracism, which is seen as a driving and defining force of Asian-American studies. The framing of "transnational" as a new paradigm presents a monolithic history of Asian-American studies and the Asian-American movement, erasing and rewriting earlier frameworks and politics.[24] This is not to cite some pure origin from which we have fallen but rather to assert that different formulations of Asian-American studies become marginalized as a dominant definition becomes institutionalized and to suggest the contested nature and terrain of Asian-American studies.[25] The debate of the hyphen is an enduring contention in Asian(-)American studies. Many of the arguments for and against the hyphen revolve around the politics and possibilities of cultural nationalism that depend on the claim to the nation that is forwarded by the unsplit and unambiguous unhyphenated term.[26] In nonhyphenated terms, *American* stands for the nation with *Asian* as an adjective indicating a particular formation of the nation. The hyphen does not indicate an equation in which one side (Asia) is balanced by the presence of the other (America), rendering both sides transparent. Therefore, in neither formulation should "Asian"(-)American be read as identical to Asian. The hyphen in coupling Asian with American indicates an uneven history and set of power relations in which the mutual constructedness of Asia and America is foregrounded. Questioning the construction of both terms also complicates an idea of what it means to claim membership and citizenship in either. Finally, functioning as a hinge, the hyphen in Asian-American studies allows us to forge political alliances and links with other locales that are too mutually involved in similar contestations.

Sau-ling Wong's (1995) essay "Denationalization Reconsidered" asserts that a diasporic project lacks local commitment. She outlines the dangers of defining a shift to a diasporic perspective as the most advanced phase in the development of Asian-American studies based on the completion of the cultural nationalist project. She objects to projecting diaspora as a teleological consequence of the cultural nationalist project by signaling the end of racism and the celebration of boundary crossing. In the article, Wong also positions diaspora as an unlikely and impossible place from which to organize and act politically, writing that diaspora has a "potential to glamorize a noncommittal political stance in one's land of principal residence" (p. 17). Thus, the dangers of diasporic studies can be summarized as a valorization of migration without attention to citizenship and the nation-state, an emphasis on the global at the price of the local, and consequently, a subsumption of race to political economy.[27]

In light of different processes of globalization, it is important to recognize that strategizing across national borders is as important as strategizing within them. Within globalization, diaspora strategically positions a bifocal commitment rather than absolving diasporans from a political stance in local struggles. Wong's transnational framework not only maintains a binary between local and global (a common oversimplification) but also privileges the national above all else. In many conceptualizations of the local and the global, the global is framed as monolithic and universal and the local as historical, fluid, and particular, thus erasing their multiplicities, similarities, and overlaps; frequently, "the national and the global scales are viewed as being mutually exclusive rather than relational and co-constitutive" (Brenner 1997, 138). Global and local are not mutually exclusive predetermined units, but shifting lenses that recognize multiple and enmeshed scales of analysis. "From this perspective, globalization is a multiscalar transformation of global social space, and one of its major organizational-institutional dimensions is constituted through the territorial state itself" (Brenner 1997, 139). One consequence of this argument is that claiming America cannot be understood or accomplished outside of a transnational project as we seek to explore the ways in which a hyphenated Asian-American critique transforms and revamps the more insular approaches to interrogating America. Moreover, understandings of Asian-America need to be understand in relation to U.S. Orientalism and imperialism. Therefore, I suggest that Asian-American critique, like postcolonial critique, is a mode of critique that addresses these particular formations of power and knowledge.

Similarly, this is not to suggest that we are beyond race but that we must further develop transnational-understandings of racialized subjects. Scholars have continually noted the ways in which the expansion of colonialism and capitalism has relied on racializing processes. These scholars suggest that the international components of racialization are hardly new and are linked to national and global class formations as well. In analyzing the Brown Atlantic, this study examines how racializations shift and change and how minor(ity) discourses adapt, negotiate, and sometimes challenge these racial processes at multiple scales.

Recent geopolitical events (e.g., the subsequent anti-immigration backlash and suspension of civil right since 9/11, the wars in Afghanistan and Iraq, the possibility of Indo-Pakistan nuclear deployment) have proliferated and consolidated racialization of South Asians as well as intensified the racialization of Muslims and Arabs (i.e., the racialization of religion). "Brown" peoples, including South Asians, are increasingly associated with terror and foreignness. Many of these discourses revitalize and forward the differentiation between those who are citizen and foreign on racial terms (see Lowe 1998a and Okihiro 1991). Moreover, these racialization processes are shared not only in the United States but throughout the Brown Atlantic. The increased surveillance and state policing of Arab, Muslim, and South Asian migrant subjects by the West has been fostered by the passing of laws such as the USA PATRIOT Act. Scholars argue that racial formations are produced by the constant renegotiated relations between social formations, capitalism, and the nation-state. These recent events have expanded the differentiation and racialization of South and Southwest Asians, Arabs, and others with "brown" skin as "aliens." Prior to the incidents of 9/11, South Asians in Canada, the United States, and Britain shared fewer racial processes. In this case, state responses have been similar in the Brown Atlantic, resulting in racial formations that are increasingly congruent and comparable. (Of course differences between nation-state policies nevertheless exist as Pakistani-Americans seek asylum in Canada from the latest surveillance laws passed by the U.S. INS.)

The U.S.-initiated wars (waged on two fronts—"against terrorism" and members of the "axis of exil") have created a sociopolitical environment that not only infringes on rights and citizenship through proliferating racialized discourses in the national culture but also initiates a new regime of imperialist domination by the United States and its allies on non-Western nation-states and peoples. Despite the questioned legality of the state surveillance and harassment, the imprisonment of South Asian, Southwest Asian, African, and Arab migrants has increased in Britain and United States. With covert and overt neocolonialist "counter-insurgency" tactics, U.S.-led state forces have created decentralized and proliferating sites of military intervention both internationally and domestically. Identified as the new way of waging war in the twenty-first century, discourses justify this growing militarism in the public and private spheres in racialized terms. Thus, under the guise of peacekeeping, safety, and civilizing missions, the nation-state fosters transnational racial processes. These racial processes twist and turn to accommodate and negotiate the conflicting needs of U.S. imperialism (having allies in the Middle East, North Africa, and South Asia) and of global economy (furthering trade and maintaining supplies of immigrant labor) in relation to competing national discourses (those of multiculturalism and racialization). For example, ideologies of multiculturalism that are now accepted in the public sphere necessitate the differentiation of "good" and "bad" immigrants (whether South Asian, Arab, or Muslim). The heightened visibility of brown subjects, in some ways, forces these competing interests to appear in competing representations that celebrate the model minority assimilated and Westernized Asian migrant who is worthy of citizenship as different from the alien and foreign noncitizen. Increasingly, it is citizenship that is used to differentiate these racialized subjects in Western nation-states. This study of the Brown Atlantic poses that a hyphenated project that interrogates the meanings of racialization and transnationality in relation to each other is necessary for Asian-American scholarship that seeks to go beyond simple claims of nationalism or generalized disavowals of the nation-state that recognizes their mutual implications and dependencies.

Transnational Feminist Politics

In forging transnational feminist politics, scholars have begun to think through the necessities of frameworks that jump scale and cross geographies to create social change. Feminist theories and methods, especially intersectionality and the politics of location, have been central to discussions of globalization, transnationality, and nation in this project. Many women of color and postcolonial feminists have argued for feminist methods that analyze the experience of multiple differences such as race, class, gender, sexuality, nationality, and so forth as being simultaneous. Forging transnational feminist politics, scholars have created a significant space for critiquing the nation-state, capitalism, and globalization with attention to gender, race, and sexuality.

Feminists such as Gloria Hull (1982), Combahee River Collective (1983), Pratibha Parmar (1997), Avtar Brah (1996), Audre Lorde (1984), Angela Davis (1981), June Jordan (1998), Toni Morrison (1992), Lisa Lowe (1998), bell hooks (1990 and 1992), and Gloria Anzaldúa (1987) have offered theories to understand how multiple differences operate in relation to subjectivity and power. These women of color, antiglobalization, postcolonial, and critical race feminists have provided the theoretical frameworks and methodologies for analysis here. *Intersectionality,* a term introduced by Kimberlé Crenshaw (2000), has been a method for understanding the simultaneity of multiple differences in the experiences of women of color. Since then the term has been expanded to employ analyses of many multiple and contradictory differences in understanding experiences immersed in uneven power relations, hence focusing not only on understanding oppression but also privilege.

Clearly, "race, class, and gender" has become a theoretical and methodological cliché in U.S.-based feminist studies. The mantra associated with a "been there, done that" exasperation by many feminists does not address the ways in which contemporary feminist scholarship has barely begun to understand how an analytic based on multiple and simultaneous contextual differences might affect feminist theories. In other words, the assumption that all feminists consider intersectionality or account adequately for these differences in their scholarship is premature and problematic. Furthermore, the triumvirate of race, class, and gender, which is sometimes expanded to include ethnicity and sexuality, often is thought of as a laundry list of categories rather than understood as a contextual and historical explication of the relevant differences that are in play within a specific field of power. Hence, my understanding of intersectionality is deconstructive in that difference is not thought of as being a priori to power relations and instead seeks to identify which differences are relevant and how they operate. Finally, in asserting an attention to difference, most feminist scholarship has focused on associating difference only with the subordinate categories and not with the dominant categories (such as whiteness and heterosexuality), leaving the superordinate as normative, unmarked, and privileged. Amy Brandzel expands the possibilities of employing intersectionality in her work by strongly emphasizing its basis in critical race and feminist theories. She suggests that as a method it can be deployed to emphasize

> the material impact of subordination, a critique of neutrality based claims and awareness of how privileges and subordinations are furthered by them, an awareness and attention towards discursive productions of categories from seemingly neutral discourses, and an ability to see experience not as the only source of knowledge, but as a critical source of particular types of knowledge that can serve as sources of critique. (Brandzel 2002, 21–22)

Thus intersectionality can be a powerful tool in exploring the production and expression of multiple and shifting differences in relations of privilege and power.

Postcolonial feminism also gives us a method to critique the politics of representation and knowledge production, especially in regard to Eurocentric theories of "Third World women." In the past fifteen years, scholars such as Gayatri Spivak (1991 and 1999), Chandra Mohanty (1991), Radhika Mohanram (1999), Inderpal Grewal and Caren Kaplan (1994), M. Jacqui Alexander (1994), Sara Suleri (1992), Ella Shohat (2001), and Trinh T. Minh-ha (1989) have argued against dominant constructions of the "Third World woman" as a victim who requires saving by First World feminists. A significant strand of this critique has posited that these constructions of the Third World woman foster formulations of First World subjects as liberated agents. Mohanty's (1991) work describes the homogenizing moves of Western discourse that consolidates Third World women as victims par excellence of colonialism and native patriarchy, situating them as a transparent and coherent object of inquiry that is knowable and unknowing. These constructions bolster the imperialist logics of superiority that underlie white liberal feminism and ideologies of Western subjectivities.

Postcolonial feminist critiques have further warned against homogenizing all non-Western and nonwhite women as the same despite discourses of alliance building based on the category "Third World women." For example, place is significant in considering the difference between a South Asian woman in Britain and in Pakistan particularly because Third World women in Western academic institutions are positioned as native informants of the other. Spivak, in particular, forwards the incommensurability of the subaltern, making her the bearer of meanings that are in excess of Western knowledge production and strategically investing in the figure of the subaltern anticolonial resistance that must be attempted to be read by the transnationally literate academic feminist. She writes,

> The disenfranchised woman of the diaspora—new and old—cannot, then, engage in the *critical* agency of civil society—citizenship in the most robust sense—to fight the depredations of "global economic citizenship." This is not to silence her, but rather to desist from guilt-tripping her. For her struggle is for access to the subjectship of the civil society of her new state: basic civil rights. Escaping the failure of decolonization at home and abroad, she is not yet so secure in the state of desperate choice or chance as to even conceive of ridding her mind of the burden of transnationality. But perhaps her daughters or granddaughters—whichever generation arrives on the threshold of tertiary education—can. (Spivak 1997, 252)

The diasporic woman is often called forth by the West to occupy the position of the postcolonial subaltern or the disenfranchised transnational migrant of labor. According to Spivak, the diasporic woman is positioned by multiple nationalisms, contested citizenships, strained patriarchies, and the expansion of capital in the new nation-state. Her agency in global and local cultural politics is circumscribed by her transnational positioning, a point to which I will return later.

It is against these flights into ethnocentric universalization and homogenization that feminists have proposed situated analyses of knowledge production and power. In particular, some postcolonial feminists have advocated a "politics of location" to build solidarities across space and place based on commonalities or similarities through better understandings of knowledge production as located in power. Adrienne Rich's (1986) theory of "the politics of location" has been retooled and developed to argue against these sweeping constructions of a singular global feminism to produce multiple and transnational feminisms. As a transformative method of feminist scholarship, the politics of location has been employed to produce accountability and specificity of knowledge. This politics of location attempts not only to recognize that knowledge is situated, that is, produced from and for specific material, geographic, epistemological contexts that are enabled by specific power structures and alliances, but also to mark and make visible these locations of feminist scholarship to build alliances and solidarities. Similarly, feminist geographer Cindi Katz (2001, 1230) comments,

> If situated knowledges suggest local particularities of the relations of production and reproduction, their conscious apprehension in a globalized and multiply differentiated world offers fertile political connections across space and scale that have the fluidity to match and confront the deft and global mobility of capitalist investment and disinvestment successfully.

Feminist geographers have additionally posited that not only is a metaphoric politics of location necessary but also a formulation of knowledge production as embedded in material place and space is necessary. Therefore, the politics of location as a method should recognize how and where knowledge is produced as well as what possible politics it produces through the metaphoric and material.[28] Therefore, politics of location could be used to point out accountability in terms of interests and investments, which would enable the possibility of building solidarities. Like other forms of identity and place-based formulations, such as multicultural coalitions, a feminist politics of location attempts to work through "grounded" and specific localities, commonalities, and similarities that provide the possibility of solidarity based on concrete and abstract knowledges.

Cindi Katz (2001) argues that creating new political engagements with globalization requires retooling comparative feminist methods. Thus, feminist geographers in particular have encouraged feminists also to think through a politics of scale to illuminate spaces and processes necessary to imagine and create cooperation by linking physically discontinuous spaces and negotiate multiple frameworks. Katz constructs a methodology of critical topography that draws contour lines marking similar and linked global processes. She therefore mobilizes topography to examine "some part of the material world, defined at any scale from the body to the global, in order to understand its salient features and their mutual and broader relationships" (p. 1228). This project also draws contour lines between those places with similar and linked relations to transnational processes within the circuit of the Brown Atlantic. Employing the metaphor of topography, this project assumes that space bears and reinforces social relations as well as elucidates the intersections of economic, political, social, and cultural processes. This feminist topography will hopefully make visible specific power structures and global processes in various locations, enabling the possibility of creating social change based on clearer understandings of the similar processes and conditions of gendering, racialization, globalization, and postcoloniality in South Asian diasporas.

Queer-ing

Few studies of postcoloniality and globalization have focused on the ways in which sexual and gender norms are affected by postcolonial nationalisms and global capitalism.[29] South Asian postcolonial discussions of sexuality, in such collections such as Kumari Jayawardena and Malathi De Alwis' *Embodied Violence* (1996), have focused on the impact of male power on women, which is exerted through heterosexuality. More recently, more attention has turned toward nonheterosexual female sexuality in Mary E. John and Janaki Nair's discussion of sexual economy in *Question of Silence* (1998) and in the lesbian anthology *Facing the Mirror* (Sukthankar 1999). With the exception of some queer studies scholars who have engaged with some of the implications of postcolonial critiques in sexuality studies (in texts such *Nationalisms and Sexualities* (Parker 1992), *Queer Diasporas* (Patton and Eppler 2000), and the special issue of *The Gay and Lesbian Quarterly* titled "Thinking Sexuality Transnationally"), (Povinelli and Chauncey 1999) most of the dominant literature argues for the emergence and development of global gay identities and movements. These dominant strands of feminist and gay/lesbian/bisexual/transgender/queer studies based on a teleological logic of modernity deny coevalness to postcolonial subjects, posing Third World sexualities as backward, undeveloped, and unliberated.

In contrast, M. Jacqui Alexander (1994) interrogates the ways in which postcolonial laws mediate membership to and citizenship in the nation-state through identifying and sanctioning normative and deviant sexualities. She argues that postcolonial nation-states employ the criminalization of deviant (i.e., nonheteronormative) sexualities as a technology of control. Alexander further posits that the postcolonial nation-state opposed to colonialism and neocolonialism but, nevertheless, compromised by global capitalism, blames shifts and transformations on sexual and gender deviants (prostitutes, unwed mothers, gays, and lesbians). Her attention to the production of deviant and normative national sexualities exposes how gender and sexual norms coincide in bourgeois constructions of women's and the nation's honor.

Similarly, I too seek here to locate sexuality and gender in relation to postcolonial political economy, examining the links between nation-state, capitalism, (neo)colonialism, sexuality, and gender. Therefore, in addition to feminist methods, this project employs a queer framework. It follows the work of queer studies scholars such as Alexander (1994), Lauren Berlant (1997), and David Eng (1997 and 2001) who have begun to queer the nation-state and capitalism, critiquing the heteronormativity of national narratives of belonging and citizenship. This book takes these inquiries one step further, queering not only the nation-state but also transnationality in regard to postcoloniality and globalization. More specifically, it sketches out the ways in which sexuality is normalized and embodied in citizenship and nationalism, circulated through capitalism, and mobilized in the terrain of postcoloniality. Furthermore, it argues that sexuality and sexual norms are central to the gendered construction of tradition and modernity through which cultural citizenship and identities are negotiated in South Asia and the South Asian diaspora.

Queer methodology does not suggest attention to homosexualities or homosexual identities only. Instead, to "queer" here is to provide a critique of the normative, particularly the heteronormative, as suggested by queer studies scholars Berlant (1997), Michael Warner (1993), and Lisa Duggan (1994). As Warner (1993, xxvi–xxvii) suggests, the queer paradigm defines "itself against the normal rather than the heterosexual" and against "not just the normal behavior of the social, but the *idea* of normal behavior," that is, "regimes of the normal." Queer theory stresses the analysis of the powers and structures that construct norms and deviances. Thus, queer method here is less about excavating lesbian and gay identities and subjects than it is about interrogating the ways in which heterosexuality and other modalities of power (such as whiteness and maleness) are normative and are identifying the multiple spaces of nonnormativity.

I argue that diasporas maintain and consolidate connections and imaginings of the homeland by performing national identities through gender and sexual normativities. This study takes the investigation of dominant white Western heteronormativity and South Asian diasporic heteronormativity—properly married, intraracial, intrareligious, bourgeois, and intranational heterosexuality—as central to its project. Heteronormativity, I argue in later chapters, operates as a crucial sign of belonging in diasporas. With gender, heteronormativity functions as a site of cultural authenticity articulated through the discourses of morality, cultural values, and ethnic identity. Thus, heteronormativity functions as a key component of South Asian diasporic cultural nationalisms.

This analysis integrates feminist and queer methods to understand the ways in which gender, racial, and national norms also function in relation to sexuality and subjectivity. Eng (2001, 217) poses a critical queer methodology "that exceeds the question of sexuality as a narrowly defined or singular category by considering the ways in which other critical and intersecting axes of difference give legibility to our social identities" that can function "as a wide method of racial critique, considering at once a network of social difference and political concerns as it dynamically underpins the formation of Asian-American subjectivity." His deployment of queerness is clearly intersectional in its approach to race and gender and may also enable feminist politics of location as well. Moreover, his interrogation of subjectivity in relation to ethnic cultural nationalism from a queer perspective offers a productive model for this study.

Like singular global feminism, dominant gay and lesbian (as well as queer) studies needs to be wary of producing an ethnocentric narrative of its own imperialist superiority. Queer theories must engage with their own sense of a politics of location that focuses on how queer theory functions in relation to globalization and postcoloniality. It must account for its privilege and struggle to clarify and work against its own imbricated inextricable location in relation to capitalism, empire, and neocolonialism. Queer methods prove useful in understanding not only sexual norms but other norms, such as gender, as well. Therefore, this study proposes that queer politics pose possibilities for cultural politics across many differences.[30]

Taking seriously the charge made by Ong (1999, 3) to attend "to the transnational practices and imaginings of nomadic subjects and the social conditions that enable his [sic] flexibility," my approach is a comparative transnational framework in which I examine South Asian diasporic cinema of the United States, Canada, Britain, and India. This oxymoron of transnational (hence linked) comparative (hence discrete) conveys the complex analytics of this project, as I have discussed earlier. *Beyond Bollywood* attempts to recognize and negotiate these contradictions in diasporic cultural politics. The status of South Asian diasporic public cultures expressed through film is historically linked with postcoloniality and globalization, and I read these public cultures to understand the transnational practices and imaginings of South Asian diasporic subjects. I employ the transnational to emphasize negotiations with governmentalities of the nation-state and the material processes of capitalism in relation to social, cultural, and psychic imaginings of migrant subjects. Furthermore, by emphasizing the link between political economy and cultural production, I seek to recognize the contradictory and limited but nonetheless viable contribution of diasporic cultural studies as a site of resisting subjectivities and struggles in globalization. In the past four decades, there has been increased migration to the global cities of the West and these sites offer a unique opportunity for engaging with dominant discourses on modernity, capitalism, and the nation. The Brown Atlantic, located in the heart of the beast, provides a foray into understanding negotiations of South Asian transnationalities with U.S. imperialism, British colonialism, and global capitalism.

Summary of Chapters

In the next chapter, "Between Hollywood and Bollywood," on the political economy of South Asian diasporic cinema, I outline the sociohistorical and economic context for the formation and development of South Asian diasporic cinema in the Brown Atlantic and provide a detailed overview of the emergence of particular films and filmmakers. Recognizing this interstitial location between larger, more established cinemas such as Hollywood, Bollywood, Third World, and specific national "art" cinemas, I explore in this chapter the political, economic, and social contexts that enable and disable the emergence and development of South Asian diasporic films. I conclude the chapter by focusing on the black British cultural studies, discussions regarding the politics of representation in cultural production, circulation, and reception.

In the following chapters (3 through 5), I focus on the United States, Canada, and Britain, respectively, in an analysis of popular feature films, while addressing significant issues in queer, feminist, and diasporic cultural studies. In chapter 3, "When Indians Play Cowboys," I focus on U.S. discourses of mobility and migration in Mira Nair's (1991) Hollywood film *Mississippi Masala*. I argue that tropes of westward migration in South Asian–American films can become postmodern narratives of uprooted mobility and surplus service labor. In contrast to these narratives, the British film *Wild West* exposes the myth of the frontier and its promise of continual self-reinvention and available unclaimed territory. I further examine how postcolonial diasporic studies must engage with the politics of indigeneity as the idea of the "native" informs them both.

In chapter 4, "Reel a State," I discuss Srinivas Krishna's Canadian film *Masala*, which interrogates the shifting relationship between ethnic and racial identities and the politics of the pluralist multicultural nation-state and suggest that planes function as chronotopes for the experiences of diasporic displacement. More significant, I explore how *Masala* parodies the nostalgia that is associated with diasporic spectatorship of Bollywood cinema and South Asian cultural production and advocate foregrounding a diasporic spectatorship that is based on the queer cultural politics of camp. Foregrounding the conflicted heterogeneity of South Asian diasporas, I compare and contrast Hindu-normative and Sikh understandings of diasporic affiliation.

In chapter 5, "Homesickness and Motion Sickness," I probe the idea of nostalgia further and discuss how it is gendered and embodied in Gurinder Chadha's (1994) *Bhaji on the Beach*. I examine how *nostos*, meaning return to home, and *algos*, meaning pain, suggest a physical embodiment of the postcolonial diasporic condition of homesickness. I explore how women's bodies reflect homesicknesses—the gendered social and physical illnesses that result from the production of home.

In the sixth and seventh chapters, I return to the "homeland" to interrogate the reception of diasporic cinema and the development of a diasporic-influenced transnational and cosmopolitan cinema in India. In chapter 6, "Homo on the Range," I turn to the relationship between diaspora and homeland to explore the transnational gender and sexual politics of Deepa Mehta's (1997) film *Fire*. I argue that the responses to *Fire* raise questions regarding the transnational production, circulation, and reception of the cultural politics of diasporic films within a global market. I analyze the controversial film and its infamous reception within the framework of a political economy of queerness. In chapter 7,

"Sex in the Global City," I continue the discussion begun in relation to *Fire* and interrogate the cosmopolitan cinema in English emerging in India in response to diasporic films. This new cinema, characterized by such films as *Bombay Boys* and *Hyderabad Blues*, emerges from the subcontinent to register and dissect critically the increasing presence of diaspora within the postcolonial nation-state in the moment of increasing globalization processes. I also examine the gendered and sexualized logics of transnationality at work within these films.

In the conclusion, I probe the recent developments in South Asian diasporic cinema and comment on the divergent directions emerging in the various parts of the Brown Atlantic and the homelands. In the main portion of the chapter, I focus on Nair's (2002) *Monsoon Wedding* to understand better the economic, cultural, and political implications of its international popularity. I also tie the increasing popularity of cross-cultural wedding films to particular deployments of feminist sexual agency. I suggest that heteronormativity is significant to the success of recent films by Nair, Mehta, and Chadha and indicate further questions for exploration in feminist and queer understandings of transnational cultural studies. I conclude the chapter by locating these films about heteronormative feminist South Asian migrants within the context of transnational feminist theories of migration and globalization to argue that the migrant woman becomes the site of transnational desire for Western eyes who seek in her the formulation of the authentic native informant.

2
Between Hollywood and Bollywood

We have been trying to theorize identity as constituted, not outside but within representation; and hence of cinema, not as a second-order mirror held up to reflect what already exists, but as that form of representation which is able to constitute us as new kinds of subjects, and thereby enable us to discover places from which to speak.

—Stuart Hall (1993, 402)

Writing on work that could comprise an Asian diaspora or a South Asian film category, is sparse and critical engagement with these films is important. It may be that the links between the films and filmmakers within these categories are fragile; links which may or may not exist but which, however, deserve exploration and explanation.

—June Givanni (1994, 2)

The aridity of those three cultural terms—production, circulation, and consumption—does scant justice to the convoluted outernational processes to which they now refer. Each of them in contrasting ways, hosts a politics of race and power which is hard to grasp, let alone fully appreciate, through the sometimes crude categories that political economy and European cultural criticism deploy in their tentative analyses of ethnicity and culture.

—Paul Gilroy (1993a, 103)

Film is the most popular and significant cultural form and commodity in the transnational South Asian cultural and political economy. More important, South Asian diasporic identificatory processes are centrally configured and contested through the cinematic apparatus. This project examines cinema primarily in relation to the contestations over meaning in relation to the political struggles of (dis)identification within transnational South Asian public spheres. In this case, I pay specific attention to the contestations over national claims (American, British, Canadian, and South Asian) and to the varying and shifting social differences (e.g., gender, religion, class) that inflect these claims. South Asian diasporic cinema is a developing cinema that negotiates the dominant discourses, politics, and economies of multiple locations. This political and cultural economy affects the form, production, and circulation of the films. South Asian diasporic cinema negotiates and traffics among the two largest global cinemas—those of Hollywood and Bollywood—as well as individual national cinemas including British, Canadian, alternative U.S., and alternative Indian. Thus, South Asian diasporic films function significantly as part of the shifting economic, political, and cultural relations between global capitalism and the postcolonial nation-state, raising questions regarding the negotiation of cultural politics of diasporas located within local, national, and transnational processes.

Most frequently, films are institutionalized within the canons of national cinemas that are nation-building projects. Hence, cinema functions significantly in narrating nations and producing national identities. South Asian diasporic films are usually incorporated into these national paradigms through the logic of multiculturalism and cultural nationalism or through nationalist forms of nostalgia. When films such as *Fire* or *The Warrior* do not conform to these expectations, they are rendered illegible or primitive in dominant national and international discourses. This project takes into consideration how South Asian diasporic filmmakers negotiate this institutionalization and identification and it attends to these negotiations which occur at multiple levels, from the content and aesthetics to the technology and economics, in relation to complex political and social formations.

It is the interstitiality of these films that prevents full co-optation and incorporation into institutionally privileged canons. These films often (but not always) "disidentify" with dominant ideologies.[1] Hence, the project seeks to elucidate how these films negotiate the hegemony of multiculturalism that serves as the logic of incorporation into national cinemas. More important, minority-made films are often assimilated into larger national canons and cinemas by interpreting the texts as conforming to dominant aesthetics and forms. Although many of these films are read as Hollywood, British, or even Bollywood films, their disjunctures, heterogeneity, and hybridity belie this attempt to define texts by their relation to these dominant cinemas. In particular, these heterogeneities and multiplicities indicate the different material and historical conditions of production that create specific and local cultural politics in relation to dominant forms. The aesthetics and content of the films reflect these material conditions and the resultant contestations. Furthermore, South Asian diasporic films are intertextually related to each other and to other minor cinemas with which they align themselves; they also may respond to, mimic, and otherwise engage dominant cinemas. In this manner, many films are characterized by polyvocality or in Bakhtinian terms *heteroglossia* in that they contain multiple speech and language types.[2]

It is a difficult task to outline the characteristics of South Asian diasporic cinema outside of the logic of cultural nationalism or essentialism. For example, defining any such body of works based entirely on the racial identities of the filmmakers can be an essentialist project. Suggesting that South Asian diasporic cinema is constituted by films made by South Asian diasporic filmmakers insufficiently characterizes what is at stake in discussing South Asian diasporic films as a cinema.[3] This is not to say that the identities of participants in control of the filmic production are irrelevant; access to the means of production has been systematically unavailable to people of color, including South Asian migrants. Clearly, the dilemma is more complicated than a game of simple identity politics, and attempts have certainly been made to categorize or distinguish certain kinds of films from others based on the identities of those involved in production. For example, in the British publication *A Fuller Picture*, Onyekachi Wambu and Kevin Arnold (1999, 9) ask, "Are black films only films made by black directors with black themes? Supposing a film is made by a black director, with a black crew and a white theme, does this count as a black film?" In their answer to this question and analysis of the black British context, Wambu and Arnold assign point values to films based on content and on the identities of the producers, writers, directors, and so on to identify films as black films. Critiques of the oversimplified identity politics and cultural authenticity that implicitly underlie these discussions are complex and well rehearsed. As Isaac Julien (1995) remarks, "Being black isn't enough for me. I want to know what your cultural politics are."

In this project, I am less interested in drawing such distinctions than I am in understanding how South Asian diasporic films constitute and contribute to the formation of the public culture of the Brown Atlantic. In this study, I concentrate thematically on films that are primarily about South Asian diasporas, especially those with South Asian diasporic writers or directors, rather than attempt to discriminate boundaries based on the identities of those involved in the filmic production. Therefore, certain films (such as *The Sixth Sense, What's Cooking*, or *Elizabeth*) made by South Asian diasporic directors are not discussed, whereas others (such as *Seducing Maarya* made by Singaporean Canadian Hunt Hoe) could be included in this discussion. In this chapter, I narrate a brief history of the emergence of South Asian diasporic films in the United States, Canada, and Britain, including a discussion of the cultural producers and the material and social conditions enabling filmic production, distribution, and reception. Hence, the book focuses on films and filmmakers that have been significant to constituting and contributing to South Asian transnational public cultures.

This chapter is divided into three sections. In the first section, I provide a context for understanding the aesthetics, mode of production, and cultural politics of South Asian diasporic cinema by positioning it in relation to Hollywood, Bollywood, and nondominant cinemas.[4] In the second section, I present a genealogical overview of the emergence of South Asian diasporic public cultures and cinema in Britain, the United States, and Canada, with attention to the context of production and thematic subjects of individual films; this particular section is important in that it provides a historical narrative that can be referenced for future studies at the same time that it maps out specifically and in detail the contours of South Asian diasporic cinema. The theoretical discussion is located primarily in the final section, in which I look specifically at black British cultural studies as the site of emergence for Asian British diasporic cinema. In this section, I examine the links between the production of the films and the national and transnational politics of representation, subjectivity, and reception. Thus, my purpose in the chapter is to relay not only the material and historical conditions facilitating the means and mode of production but also the relationship between these conditions and the textual content and form of the films themselves especially in relation to politics of representation.

In the Shadow of Hollywood

The question here is how to understand the situated place of these diasporic and transnational filmic productions in relation to dominant global and national cinemas. In relation to the global hegemony of Hollywood, diasporic filmmakers wrestle not only to justify the validity of South Asian–based content but also to harness the means of production and gain entrance into vertically and horizontally integrated film industries. South Asian diasporic filmmakers have gained access to resources in many different ways, including Hollywood financing, state funding, and multinational sponsorship. Hollywood (and its postindustrial mode of production) overly determines not only U.S. filmic production but also the circulation and consumption of diasporic films.

Marxist cultural and postcolonial studies scholarship has noted the function of cultural production in colonialism and late capitalist political economy. Scholars have commented on the role of the cinematic apparatus in colonialism through its production of difference particularly in relation to disciplinary formations such as ethnography, anthropology, and sciences. In addition, the global domination of media by U.S.-based transnational corporations as well as the role of Hollywood in U.S. imperialism also has been discussed by many scholars (e.g., Fredric Jameson (1991) and Armand Mattelart, 1994). Similarly, Asian-American scholarship on media has identified the ways in which cinematic texts produce Orientalist racial formations; for example, the roles of film and television in constructing Asian-Americans as perpetually foreign noncitizens is discussed by scholars such as Gina Marchetti (1993) and Darrell Hamamoto (1994 and 2000).[5] These scholars contend that Hollywood dominates globalized cultural production not only through its control of transnational networks of production and distribution but, more important, as the hegemonic producer of imperialist texts and ideologies.

Hollywood (and less so Bollywood) operates within a postindustrial mode so that it seeks to acquire and distribute "independent" alternative films without involvement in production. Hence, the films can be funded by cobbling together various sources; however, commercial success ultimately lies with entry into the vertically and horizontally integrated systems of distribution and circulation. Linked to other globalization processes, the postindustrial mode is flexible and far reaching as it expands to accommodate alternative modes and materials (Naficy 2001, 42). National film industries, especially those in Europe, attempting to protect themselves through regulation and quotas have not been very successful in challenging the hegemony of Hollywood. In the case of Britain, the logic seems to be "if you can't beat them, join them" because the national film industry has sought not only to sponsor and support forcefully British film-makers but also to encourage collaborative and cosponsored projects as well as mimicking the Hollywood formats of big-budgeted blockbusters. Unable to compete, British cinema has found itself ambivalently recognizing the role that black British filmmaking has played in fostering its international markets and image. Nevertheless, as Naficy (2001) writes, "The dominant mode of cultural production exists side by side with the alternative and emergent modes, which serve other functions and can mobilize other values" (p. 43). South Asian diasporic and transnational films are therefore imbricated very clearly in a complex system of capital and culture.

In terms of mode of production, these transnational films are located in the interstices of Hollywood and Bollywood. Non-Anglophone films (and frequently non-Hollywood Anglophone films as well) have been located within national cinemas through the construction of the development of the art-house film. The primary audience for international films are identified through the specific class-identified spectatorship of art-house films. The phenomenon of the art house is based on positioning "foreign" films as ethnographic documents of "other" (national) cultures and therefore as representatives of national cinemas. In particular, foreign Third World films that can be read as portraying the other through cultural difference (i.e., gender and sexual experiences or nativist renderings of rural village life) are deemed most authentic. Mapping to and from racialized transnational postcolonial bodies, diasporic filmmakers frequently occupy the position of native informant, as was the case of Mira Nair and her first film *Salaam Bombay!* Similarly, Asian films have been included into "global cinema" on an individual basis so that filmmakers Satyajit Ray, Wayne Wang, and Akira Kurosawa may be a familiar name to art-house cinema fans, whereas the popular Amitabh Bachchan may not.[6] Thus, these auteur directors are deemed significant enough to be associated with the art cinema of European filmmakers (e.g., Francois Truffaut or Jean Luc Godard).

Bollywood Abroad

That the first annual International Indian Film Awards were recently convened in London in 2000 suggests that Indian cinema, although a national cinema, has deterritorialized so that its boundaries are no longer identical to those of the nation-state. Celebrating the achievements of Indian film industries, the occasion was marked by the presence of Indian and Asian British filmmakers and stars. Set in London, the award ceremony strategically sought to capitalize on its overseas markets, particularly on its British viewers. The location can be explained by the significance of the South Asian diaspora in Britain and its centrality to the production and consumption of Indian cinema. One of the event's goals was identified by the keynote speaker of the evening—Amitabh Bachchan (entertainer of the millennium according to a British survey), who defined and promoted Indian cinema as a global cinema, a cinema to be reckoned with. Suggesting that Indian cinemas, and especially Bollywood, are poised on the brink of deterritorialization at a grand scale, Bachchan was discussing Bollywood as a global, not just local, alternative to Hollywood.

South Asian diasporic films also are located in relation to the expanding (dominant but not hegemonic) power of the Bollywood, which has sought to challenge the global domination of Hollywood cinema by positioning itself as a global cinema. Though unknown to many Westerners, Indian cinema has a long past and has been an international cinema familiar to viewers from Russia and the Middle East to parts of Asia and Africa for many decades.[7] In addition to the Middle East and other parts of South Asia, the earlier South Asian diasporas (prior to the sixties) in Fiji, Trinidad, and Africa imported Indian cinema for more than forty years. Increasingly, many non-Western audiences cite Indian cinema as appealing because it is seen as an alternative to the Americanness of Hollywood in its Third World or postcolonial sensibilities and structures of feeling.[8] Bollywood is seen to provide an alternative model of modernity. These and other factors contribute to the growing familiarity and popularity of South Asian cinemas abroad.

Due to increasing transnational migration and circulation of cultural commodities, Indian media, especially Bollywood, has had an increasing presence in South Asian diasporas in the past decade. The development of communication and media technology within globalization has greatly affected the transnational distribution of cultural products, including both those of the economic North and the South, though of course not evenly. The late sixties and seventies marked a time of increasing migration of South Asians from India, Sri Lanka, Bangladesh, Pakistan, Africa, and the Caribbean to the United States, Britain, Canada, Australia, and the Gulf states due to shifting geopolitical economies. Although South Asian diasporas existed in many nations prior to this time, the influx of new migrants reshaped older communities, formed new diasporas, and created new cultural processes and flows of cultural products. For example, with the growth of cable, VCR, DVD, and now satellite television, South Asian diasporas initiated the showing of Hindi, Tamil, and other vernacular-language films on television and in movie theaters to wide audiences. Although television (satellite and cable) and music are popular media in South Asia and the diasporas, cinema remains the paradigmatic and dominant cultural medium. In general, the past two to three decades have witnessed the increased global consumption of specifically Indian media in and out of the diaspora. South Asian diasporas are one of the largest sites of consumption of Bollywood films and are considered a distribution territory by the Indian film industry.

But during this time, diasporas hardly registered in the national filmic imaginary; in other words, diasporic lives and experiences rarely were the subject of films. This is clearly not the case anymore, because Indian film industries have "discovered" the diasporas (as lucrative markets). More recent export of films has occurred between India and its newer diasporas in Britain, North America, Australia, the Gulf states, and New Zealand. British Asians with greater disposable income have been significant in asserting the primacy of diasporic markets and spectators according to Vijay Mishra (2002) in *Bollywood Cinema*. This interest accompanied by the shifting of the political economy of India has generated an investment in representing diasporas in different ways. As Purnima Mankekar (1999a) argues in "Brides Who Travel," the deterritorialized nonresident Indians became imagined as crucial to the Indian economy and nation-state in filmic national narratives such as *Dilwale Dulhaniya Le Jayenge*. Since then, the deterritorialized Indian has been imagined as internal and integral to the Indian nation-state. Consequently, filmic representations as well as state policies have shifted to reflect this discourse. In relation to this study, the globalization of Bollywood has seriously affected the production and circulation of diasporic films with the result, most recently, of blurring these categories with such films as *Bollywood/Hollywood* and *Monsoon Wedding*.

Many hopes have been pinned on the success of Bollywood as a global cinema. From the recent showcasing of *Devdas* at the Cannes film festival and nomination of *Lagaan* for an Academy Award to the opening of Andrew Lloyd Webber's *Bombay Dreams* in London, expectations are high for the crossover appeal of Bollywood cinema into Western theaters and for white Western audiences. These hopes result partially from the increasing commercial success of Indian films recently in Britain. British Asians have propelled Bollywood films into dominant culture in complicated ways where they have entered multiplexes, luring not only British Asians but also white British to the theaters. Films like *Kuch Kuch Hota Hai*, *Hum Aapke Hai Koun*, *Dilwale Dulhaniya Le Jayenge*, and *Taal* have consistently appeared in the annual list of top twenty most popular foreign-language films in Britain for the past five years. For example, *Kuch Kuch Hota Hai* was the top-grossing foreign-language film in 1998, earning almost 1.5 million pounds. In 2002, the British Film Institute launched its focus program titled *ImagineAsia* on South Asian and South Asian diasporic films. This program was designed to boost the visibility and presence of non-Hollywood films in Britain as well as recognize the significance of South Asian cinemas. In the United States, the popularity of Mira Nair's hybrid *Monsoon Wedding*, references to Bollywood in *Moulin Rouge* and *Ghost World*, and the commercial success of Ang Lee's *Crouching Tiger, Hidden Dragon* have prompted an increasing awareness and interest in Asian cinema and popular Indian films in particular.

Most commercial Indian films are often characterized as unappealing to Western viewers (even to those art-house audiences interested in foreign films) because of their content and aesthetic forms that derive from diverse Indian sources including Parsi theater and Hindu performances. These three-hour films are often identifiable by their all-encompassing forms that include elements of comedy, (melo)drama, action, romance, and music that do not fit Western aesthetic expectations; in particular, the elaborate and often extradiegetic song and dance numbers, usually six to eight per film, often pose difficulties for Western viewers. These films nevertheless are highly influential on South Asian diasporic filmmaking.

As I discuss throughout the book, the impact of Bollywood on South Asian diasporic filmmaking is multifold. One primary example is the frequency with which Bollywood is referred to thematically within the films themselves. For example, *Bollywood Calling* by Nagesh Kukunoor is about the film industry. *Bombay Dreams* (the Andrew Lloyd Webber musical) centers on the Bollywood film industry and fantasies it produces. *East Is East* features a scene in which the family goes to see a Bollywood film, and *American Desi* posits that a familiarity and appreciation of Bollywood is essential to a nonassimilated ethnic identity. In addition, Bollywood conventions are reflected in the aesthetic forms and narrative structures in a variety of films. *Masala* and *Bhaji on the Beach* employ musical sequences, whereas *Mississippi Masala* and *Fire* feature Bollywood music both as background music as well as part of the narrative structure. Also, there is crossover in terms of performers: Shashi Kapoor, Zohra Seghal, Om Puri, and Shabana Azmi are all actors who have appeared in Indian and diasporic productions. Finally, diasporic filmmakers have employed the networks of distribution that circulate Indian films. *American Desi,* for example, has had little access to mainstream theaters and has instead played at venues in major metropolitan locations with South Asian communities that regularly feature Bollywood films. On video, *American Desi* was primarily rented and sold (both legal and bootleg versions) through the many South Asian video stores distributed throughout the United States. Conversely, Nair and Mehta, whose films appeal simultaneously to multiple audiences, pursue the possibility of maximum exposure within India for their films, attempting to simultaneously locate them within North American national cinemas as well as in relation to Indian cinemas. Nair, for example, forwarded *Monsoon Wedding* as India's nominee for Best Foreign Film for the U.S. Academy Awards; the film, however, lost the nomination to *Lagaan,* which had its own aspirations to national representation and transnational access following the international and Western success of *Crouching Tiger, Hidden Dragon.* In the previous examples, at times, Bollywood and Indian cinemas can be seen as providing an oppositional aesthetic to that of Hollywood to diasporic filmmakers; consequently, references to Bollywood and Indian cinematic forms and aesthetics signify not only alternatives to dominant Western cinematic practices but also a self-reflective claim to the cinematic apparatus itself in the name of the non-Western. However, as I discuss later, diasporic films may share a contested relationship with Bollywood as well as with Hollywood.

Nonnational Cinemas

In addition to Bollywood and Hollywood, diasporic cinemas also have contested relationships with national cinemas. Although much of diasporic cinematic

production has been located in relation to its contestations with national cinemas such as (Asian-)North American or (black) British cinema, other frameworks besides those centered on the nation have been proffered by various
scholars. In other words, non-Western cinema is characterized by various
nomenclatures and embraces a variety of cultural practices. Cinema studies
scholars have theorized the category of independent and alternative films that
challenge and "unthink" the Eurocentrism (Shohat and Stam, 1994) of dominant cinemas based on mode of production or ideology. Developed as an alternative to the binary of hegemonic Hollywood and auteur and avant-garde
cinemas, third cinema has been theorized as a political and antihegemonic
cinema emerging primarily in the Third World since the sixties. As an antico-
lonialist category, third cinema was thought to have a different aesthetics and
constituency. The third cinema was associated with a number of Third World
cinemas including those of Latin American, Africa, and the Middle East. In addition to concepts such as Third World cinema and third cinema, scholars have
proffered various paradigms for smaller migrant or racialized cinemas such as
minor cinema (Deleuze and Guattari 1990), intercultural cinema (Marks 2000),
and accented cinema (Naficy 1999 and 2001).[9] These cinemas are defined in
opposition to the hegemony of dominant cinemas.

More specific than the third cinema, it is inextricably imbricated within its
particular nexus of the local, national, and transnational. Like Naficy's accented
cinema, diasporic cinema addresses the social processes of exile and migration. The films discussed here thematically emphasize issues of mobility and
location, including displacement from homelands as well as exclusion in Western nation-states. Diasporic films are not always oppositional, however, they
employ repetition with a difference and are focused on the politics of displacement, alienation, or loss. For example, although they employ social realism
(from dominant Western cinema) or melodrama (from Indian cinemas), their
treatment redefines and reproduces these styles in their deployment of the cinematic apparatus. However, these strategies are not necessarily specific to any one
nation or filmmaker as many directors produce films that engage with issues in
different ways. In that sense, diasporic cinema and its categories of inquiry are
fluid and heterogeneous rather than fixed and unitary.

Diasporic cinema is characterized by all modes of production—dominant,
interstitial, and collective. Films made with the interstitial mode of production according to Naficy (1999, 134) "operate within and astride the cracks and
fissures of the system, benefiting from its contradictions, anomalies, and heterogeneities." The collective mode of filmic production has been less present
than the interstitial mode in South Asian filmmaking in the diaspora. However,
many of the filmmakers, especially those from the British context, participated
in the workshops and collectives that arose in London in the eighties. The films
discussed in this book, as well as most South Asian diasporic films, are situated
within and work inside mainstream film industry and society. Furthermore,

many of them engage thematically and explicitly with modes of production and the related issues of form and aesthetics. Although not all of these films have had access to dominant modes of distribution, the films discussed in this book are feature-length narrative (fictional) films that did have access or may potentially acquire access to wide distribution. This is to say that I am not comparing apples and oranges in looking at documentaries, experimental, or avant-garde films that have less access to commercial distribution and thus are available through different media venues.[10]

With the strong commercial presence of cinema in India since before independence, South Asian diasporic cinema has been located more in relation to the dominant Indian commercial cinemas (as well as their parallel or art cinemas) than third cinemas. Many of the films that are discussed here, especially those from Canada and Britain, were financially supported by state-funded grants, especially those designated for multicultural productions, whereas others were funded transnationally through large production companies. As I discuss in the next section, state funding of multicultural film and television productions became available in the eighties as civil rights social movements demanded the means to the modes of reproduction and representation. Television funding is of import, because national film industries rarely see themselves as being able to compete with the domination of Hollywood and frequently develop low budget films directly for television programming. In the case of films that achieved some commercial profit, the filmmakers were sometimes able to access either funding by major studios or by international funding. In the case of the latter, however, filmmakers were often required to pursue multiple production companies to acquire the full funding for their films. For South Asian diasporic cinema, funding remains a significant concern. The impact of this is different in each case and something I specifically discuss in relation to the films themselves later.

Emerging South Asian Diasporic Public Cultures

In these transnational migrant communities, heterogeneous South Asian diasporic artists and intellectuals have wrestled with cultural production elucidating the histories and politics of racism, colonialism, and modernity. In the latter half of the century, postcolonial migration to Britain has created one of the most diverse diasporic locations. Although migration occurred throughout the century, British citizenship laws changed in 1962 to decree that only those born in Britain could gain British citizenship; this law, rather than stemming migration, created an increase in migration. In these early years, the first feature films produced were *Towers of Silence* (1975) by Jamil Dehlavi, *Private Enterprise* (1975) by Dilip Hiro, is listed by director Peter Smith, and *Majdhar* (1984) by Ahmed Jamal of the Retake Collective.[11] These early films were characterized by their emphasis on the difficulties of displacement (e.g., the isolation and lack of support due to migration and social alienation) and the institutional impacts of racism (e.g., lack of financial opportunities and access to education) on the lives of migrants. Several of the black British films of this period also anticipated and instigated much of the discussion between access to the nation through cit izenship and the politics of representation that characterize the later films.

The emergence of these films and others in the eighties and nineties marks a moment in which South Asian diasporic filmmakers in Britain gained access to the means of greater circulation and production. Although films emerged in the seventies, the political economy of minority cultural production did not enable the entrance of minority discourses into national public spheres as it did in the eighties and nineties. Discourses of multiculturalism in the United States, Canada, and Britain were significant to these filmmakers who employed them to gain wider access to production and distribution, which meant negotiating the preestablished media networks of dominant white society. Able to take advantage of the extended distribution networks, some films were able to reach wide audiences and soon became significant to the process of imagining diasporic communities and identities.

Kobena Mercer (1994, 74) writes that as black filmmaking moves away from being a minor cinema as well as

> expands and gets taken up by different audiences in the public sphere, it becomes progressively demarginalized, and in the process its oppositional perspectives reveal that traditional structures of cultural value and national identity are themselves becoming increasingly fractured, fragmented and in this sense decentered from their previous authority and dominance.

Mercer comments on the institutionalization of black and Asian British film-making and cultural politics that result from this institutionalization. This institutionalization constituted not only new national public spheres but also emerging transnational ones. The viability of financial success of diasporic films depends on several factors that help facilitate its inclusion in global cultural circuits. The South Asian diasporic cinema in English is most likely to achieve commercial success due to the global hegemony of English and specifically Hollywood. Filmmakers in Britain, Canada, and the United States (the English-speaking locations in the diaspora) are much more likely to gain access to resources and be marketed commercially.[12] (In South Asia, English marks an upper and middle class, specifically an expanding transnational cosmopolitan middle class that is relatedly developing its own English-language postcolonial cinema.) As I discuss later, those films most likely to circulate transnationally are those that are more "Western friendly," adopting familiar genres, narratives, or themes in their hybrid productions. This does not mean though that these films are not indebted to other non-Western cultural forms and practices; to the contrary, the crossover appeal of the exotic that is associated with Bollywood cinema, for example, also increases the popularity of some South Asian diasporic films.

The first wave of diasporic cinema emerged amidst the development of black British cultural critique in Britain. Coming out of the Thatcher regime, Hanif Kureishi's *My Beautiful Laundrette* (1986) and *Sammy and Rosie Get Laid* (1988) were two of the first diasporic films to gain access to distribution and reach international audiences. Asian-Trinidadian British Horace Ové's film *Playing Away* (1986) also emerged during this time. There were other films, such as *Towers of Silence* and *Private Enterprise* that were made by collectives and in workshops that did not circulate as broadly. The response to Margaret Thatcher and Enoch Powell's racist nationalisms in the works of Kureishi, Ové, and Pratibha Parmar, strikes at the oppressions of the nation-state, similar to the works of Hall and Gilroy. Kureishi's films emerged out of the state-funded workshops designed to further black British cultural producers and were, therefore, able to garner access to distribution. *My Beautiful Laundrette* unabashedly explores the unlikely interracial romance between a Pakistani-British man and his white skinhead employee as they vibrantly renovate a laundrette in Thatcher's London. Placing London and its historical and cultural politics under a microscope, *Sammy and Rosie Get Laid* follows the complicated lives of a white feminist social worker and her hedonistic Pakistani British husband as they negotiate the return of his father, a known torturer in Pakistan.

Wild West (1993), written by Harwant Bains and directed by David Attwood, is a parodic comedy about a trio of Pakistani British brothers who sing in their own country and western band; the quirky film's dark and satirical humor did not make it amenable to crossover audiences. It was almost eight years after Kureishi's *My Beautiful Laundrette* that another British Asian film—Gurinder Chadha's *Bhaji on the Beach* (1993)—gained access to mass distribution and popularity. The director Chadha and the writer Meera Syal also were aided by the workshops and worked in television before entering into filmmaking. About a group of South Asian British women on a day trip to the sea resort of Blackpool, the film, despite its modest release, circulated in Britain as well as internationally.

Canada's national film industry and cinema, like those of Britain, are structured in relation to the hegemony of Hollywood. Writer and director Srinivas Krishna was supported by state-funding programs, which like their British counterparts, were designed to encourage the development of multicultural artists in the national cinema and film industry. Krishna's film *Masala* (1991) emerged as a challenge to multiculturalism at the same time as the national cinema tried to reimagine itself within a multicultural framework. That same year, Deepa Mehta also released her first South Asian–Canadian film *Sam & Me* (1991), interrogating the different conditions and constructions of diaspora in the context of racial formations and political economy for a bourgeois Jewish family and recent disenfranchised South Asian male migrants in Toronto.[13] The film was partially financed by a privately owned British-based television programming company. As migrant filmmakers, Krishna and Mehta, like the Armenian migrant Atom Egoyan, contributed to the transformation of Canadian cinema that was occurring due to the activism of migrant and indigenous groups. However, the Canadian nation-state's support was not always necessarily sufficient in and of itself to facilitate access to developing artists. For example, in the case of Mehta, the director also relies on the networks she had established through her collaborative work with her former white Canadian husband.

In the United States, the civil rights movement in the sixties and seventies influenced the development of Asian-American independent filmmaking with the formation of federally funded art programs as well. During this time period, activist-artists formed community and collective organizations such as Visual Communications (Los Angeles) and Asian CineVision (New York) to aid in the production and distribution of film and video. (Unlike in Britain, access to filmmaking was focused in film schools rather than in community organizing and collective workshops.) More recently, the National Asian-American Telecommunications Association (NAATA, San Francisco) also became a major distributor for Asian-American media, especially for television programming. Funded by state agencies, Asian-American filmmakers have slowly gained limited access to production. Many of these organizations have showcased the work of transnational filmmakers (including Wayne Wang and Ang Lee) at film festivals providing visibility and exposure (Hamamoto 1994, 3). These collectives and organizations have worked to forward an Asian-American identity, that is, the formation of a pan-ethnic coalition, and to support media production in the name of community empowerment and self-representation. In producing films for particular audiences, these organizations actively constitute and shape identities, communities, and culture. Because South Asian–Americans have had an ambivalent and ambiguous relationship with Asian-American identity, they did not participate in many of the earlier Asian-American media production initiatives.

Hence, in the North American case, it was primarily those filmmakers who had experience prior to migration or through venues other than state funding who first produced films in the diaspora. In the United States near the end of the Reagan-Bush years, Mira Nair was the first South Asian–American (woman) director to gain access to Hollywood and was not followed by another until the emergence of M. Night Shyamalan almost ten years later. Nair's entrance into the film industry was greatly facilitated by her location as a filmmaker in India. Nair migrated from India to the United States, where she studied filmmaking at Harvard. Her earliest foray into U.S. theaters with *Salaam Bombay!* (1988), a fictionalized depiction of Bombay life told from the perspective of those who are disenfranchised most—children and women—played in film festivals and art houses in the late eighties. The film was controversial and received heavy criticism from those who felt she pandered to the West with images of a destitute and victimized India in her role as native informant or cultural insider. Her second major release, *Mississippi Masala* (1991), like Kureishi's and Chadha's films, addresses issues of immigration and racism and inaugurates the visibility of South Asian diasporic cultures into dominant cinema in the United States. Nair sought out support from not only U.S. sources but also transnational ones. One can see the transnational networks of the Brown Atlantic in the production of the film, because it was jointly financed by British and U.S. producers (including Channel Four Films); in addition, Farrukh Dhondy (a heavily influential British television and film producer) is thanked in the credits of the film. The film, like *The Joy Luck Club* (1993), inspired heated debates in South Asian–American communities for its depiction of a relationship between a South Asian–American woman and an African-American man. *Mississippi Masala* has been held up by some Asian-American studies scholars as an excellent example of understanding and critiquing identity politics or as an example of multiracial political alliances.

The situation in Britain is strikingly different, as British Asian filmmakers have been less interested in representing India in the form of transnational cinema. This difference may be related to the material issues of production and funding conditions. For example, in Britain, state support and funding more readily recognized the necessity of addressing the nation. In Canada, similarly, films focused on Canadian settings and topics were more likely to get funded. Thus, these filmmakers have faced somewhat greater difficulties because of their complex relationship to British and Hollywood cinema. Consequently, it appears that British Asians are more reliant currently on state support of cultural production than their U.S. counterparts. Although the British nation-state initiated programs to promote the development of black British films, it did little to ensure the commercial success of these films.

These films in the United States, Canada, and Britain are the first cluster of South Asian diasporic films in English that were commercially successful and circulated internationally. How are we to understand the complex locations of diasporic cinema as being situated not only as minority cultural production within a national framework but also within a transnational one? Thematically, these films tackled many similar topics in their content, including an emphasis on racism, multiculturalism, and constructions of home, as well as gender and sexual politics. Many of the films, negotiating their location in the West, carefully identified the political, economic, and social ramifications of racial exclusions and Eurocentrism on South Asian communities. Positioning themselves in relation to their situated national identities (whether it be black British, Asian-Canadian, Asian-American, or people of color), many of the films also manipulate and employ discourses on race and the nation to create disidentifications and heterogeneous representations. In addition, they expose the ways in which nationalist and diasporic discourses are gendered and sexualized, asserting these as central sites of social, economic, and political contestation. In these early articulations of diaspora, the films' protagonists often imagine and seek home in mobilized "routes" in the diaspora rather than national and cultural "roots" in the homeland; thus, they refuse to evoke "natural" and "organic" roots in the homeland through nostalgia and memory.

By the mid-nineties, many of these directors, having exhibited commercial viability to Western distributors, were making additional films, not all centered on South Asian diasporic themes and unfortunately not all doing well at the box office. Nair's major next release, *The Perez Family* (starring Marisa Tomei, Alfred Molina, and Anjelica Huston, 1995) is a portrayal of the complicated politics and lives of a group of Cubans who pose as a family because the Immigration and Naturalization Service gives priority to family over individuals. Working within Hollywood, Nair struggled with studios over the control of the film, claiming dissatisfaction with the final product. Kureishi's self-directed third film *London Kills Me* (1991) is a comedy focusing on a homeless young man who takes a restaurant job in the attempt to break out of the drug business. Gurinder Chadha also made a Hollywood multicultural film *What's Cooking?* (2000) about four neighboring families in Los Angeles on Thanksgiving day, starring Kyra Sedgwick and Juliana Margulies. Krishna's sophomore film *Lulu* (1996) investigates the global economy of race, gender, and sexuality by portraying the complicated life of a Vietnamese mail-order bride in Canada. Mehta, becoming more involved in Hollywood, worked on television programming including the *Young Indiana Jones Chronicles* (1992), as well as the moderate-budget *Camilla* (1994), starring Jessica Tandy.

Simultaneously during the mid-nineties, access to South Asian cultural production increased significantly in the diasporas, so that Bollywood and other texts in South Asian languages other than English slowly gained everyday status in South Asian households and communities. With this circulation and the liberalization of the Indian economy, some migrant filmmakers such as Mehta and Nair re-turned their cameras to the homeland of India to explore the changes in cultural processes in urban middle-class culture in South Asia. Set during the sixteenth century, *Kama Sutra* (1996) is an exotic and erotic historical romance exploring the sexual politics of the lives of a courtesan and a queen. Nair had difficulty with the censor board when she attempted to release *Kama Sutra* in India, and was forced into extensive court battles over the mandated cuts. Nair also was criticized for pandering to Western audiences with the Orientalist narrative. Despite these difficulties, Nair later adapted for Showtime Dr. Abraham Verghese's memoir *My Own Country* (1998) about working with patients with AIDS as a migrant doctor living in the South. After *Camilla*, Mehta began work on a trilogy (*Fire, Earth,* and *Water*) based on the changing lives of women in South Asia. The first of these films, *Fire* (1997), was an international success at festivals and at the box office. *Fire* (starring Shabana Azmi and Nandita Das) was protested by Hindu nationalists in India who objected to its narrative about two women who fall in love. Made in Bollywood, the second of the trilogy, the Hindi film *Earth* (1998) is based on Bapsi Sidhwa's (1991) novel about Partition *Cracking India* (starring Nandita Das and Aamir Khan). Mehta has been unable to finish her trilogy, because the shooting of *Water* (with Shabana Azmi and Nandita Das playing widows in Varnassi of the 1920s) was thwarted by the same Hindu nationalists who protested *Fire,* arguing that the film was offensive to Hindus. On one hand, Mehta and Nair have gained greater acclaim from the West for their films that focus on South Asia. On the other hand, though *Fire* was popular in India, Nair and Mehta have faced difficulty with their films. Their films sit in precariously balanced positions in regard to Bollywood and other Indian cinemas. Diasporic films are involved in complicated struggles over representation not only with Bollywood but also with other cinemas in India, for example, the growing transnational cosmopolitan English-language cinema. As I discuss later, films such as Kaizad Gustad's *Bombay Boys* (1998), Nagesh Kukunoor's *Hyderabad Blues* (1998), and Dev Benegal's *Split Wide Open* (2000) are being made by young transnational Indian male filmmakers who openly contest dominant Bollywood and diasporic constructions of India in their films.

After a long silence in Britain, Ayub Khan Din (the actor who played Sammy in Kureishi's *Sammy and Rosie Get Laid*) released his film *East Is East* (1999), which was soon followed by an adaptation of a Kureishi short story titled *My Son the Fanatic* (1997), directed by Udayan Prasad. *East Is East* (starring Bollywood actor Om Puri), based on a play of the same name, portrays the lives of a British family headed by a Pakistani father and an English mother. The film was one of the overall top-grossing films in Britain during 1999, earning more than 7 million pounds at the box office. The film surprised many with its popularity and box office success as it simultaneously created controversy. On one hand, it was celebrated for its achievement in the extent of its box office success; on the other, it was criticized severely for perpetuating stereotypes of British Asians, especially in the character of the patriarchal and abusive father. In contrast, *My Son the Fanatic* (also starring Om Puri) portrays a liberal and secular father losing touch with his son who becomes increasingly immersed in Muslim fundamentalism, partly in response to racial formations and racism. Most recently, Chadha's *Bend It Like Beckham* (2002) features a young Punjabi British woman in her quest to play soccer as well as her idol does. The film has surpassed all box office expectations, earning approximately 26 million dollars at the U.S. box offices alone, and has been selected as best comedy film of the year in Britain. Arguably, it is both the visibility of Chadha as a filmmaker (and the popularity of soccer and player David Beckham) that facilitated this access and success. Other Asian-British films have been recently released such as the adaptation of V. S. Naipaul novel *The Mystic Masseur* (2002) and *The Guru* (2002). The winner of the London Film Festival's top prize, Asif Kapadia's *The Warrior* (2001) contains less than ten minutes of dialogue (all in Hindi) as it narrates the journey of a man traveling from Rajasthan to the Himalayas. Interestingly, although the British national cinema defined this film as British and nominated it as Britain's entry to the Oscars, it was recently rejected by the Academy of Motion Picture Arts and Sciences because the film is in Hindi. As a testimony to U.S. domination and colonial logic, the judges decreed that it was not eligible because Hindi is not an indigenous language of Britain (though it is spoken by more than a million people in Britain). They further justified that if the film had been about Hindi speakers in Britain, then the film would have been acceptable.[14]

In Canada, Mehta, unable to complete the film *Water,* recently released her Toronto-based film *Bollywood/Hollywood* (2002). Her latest project revitalizes the "hooker with a heart of gold" narrative by cheekily satirizing the primacy of marriage within South Asian families; in this case, the Asian Canadian son who feeling family pressure to marry hires a woman to pose as his fiancée. The film attempts to capitalize on the significance of Bollywood cinema in the diaspora, amply employing song and dance sequences (featuring a drag queen), campy portrayals of melodramatic mothers, and tongue-in-cheek cross-class romance. In the past five years in the United States, Shyamalan has broken into the Hollywood industry as the director of blockbuster films such as *The Sixth Sense* (starring Bruce Willis, 1999) and *Signs* (starring Mel Gibson, 2002); the former film is one of the top-grossing films in the history of Hollywood. His films have grossed more than 1 billion dollars. Although Shyamalan's blockbusters do not engage with South Asian–American or diasporic cultural subjects, his earlier work, including his first film *Praying with Anger* (1992) about a young South Asian–American discovering his roots in Chennai, does. The film, Shyamalan's first project after attending art school in New York, played in a few film festivals and was restrictively distributed for a week in select urban theaters. His next film *Wide Awake* (1998) despite its low-grossing return did not prevent Shyamalan from garnering attention for the script of *The Sixth Sense.*

In contrast, smaller U.S. "independent" productions such as *American Desi* (2001), *ABCD* (1999), *Mitr (My Friend)* (2001), *American Chai* (2001), *Namaste* (2002), and *Chutney Popcorn* (2000) have emerged onto the scene. Of these films, *Chutney Popcorn* and *American Desi* have gained the most access to distribution and been popular with different audiences. *Chutney Popcorn* features the writer and director Nisha Ganatra as a lesbian daughter (in a relationship with a women portrayed by Jill Hennessy) who is trying to get pregnant for her infertile sister. Because of its limited distribution, the film has done better in video rental and sales than in theaters. The film criticizes how heterosexuality, marriage, and reproduction are at the center of respectability and acceptance in South Asian–American communities; within the film, the lesbian daughter seeks to prove herself by succeeding where her sister has failed. The film emphasizes how those who are nonheteronormative are marked as outside of South Asian–American communities as inauthentic and Western.[15]

Several recent films by South Asian–American filmmakers reify heteronormativity in their interrogation of South Asian–American or desi identities. These films made by one and a half- and second-generation Indian Americans frequently depict South Asian–American identities as confusing and confused. These culturally nationalist films that characterize desi identity as being caught between two cultures inadvertently forward a homogenous, normative, and transparent understanding of desi subjectivity. Very few films render the possibility of culture as open and dynamic, instead seeking to define South Asian–America as a space suspended between the Manichean binary of East and West, in lieu of a space that is heterogeneous and hybrid. For example, *American Desi, Namaste,* and *ABCD,* although explicitly focused on issues of belonging and authenticity in desi culture, rely on asserting normative gender roles and sexual practices to consolidate these identities. Furthermore, these second-generation filmmakers have had difficulty accessing the means of production and distribution. Their access has been developed not through the channels of alternative or Hollywood filmmaking or even Asian-American filmic production but rather through the networks established for the transnational circulation of Bollywood and other South Asian media. It is ironic that these South Asian–American productions are more likely to enter markets through these circuits than through those of independent cinema in the United States, thereby limiting their potential earnings. Overall, the presence of so many South Asian diasporic films indicates the growth and establishment of a desi public sphere in North America, especially for those South Asian–Americans who are able to acquire the material resources to produce a low budget film that can be distributed in DVD and video through retail stores featuring South Asian media.

Re-turning the director to India, Nair's *Monsoon Wedding* (2002) presents a wealthy Punjabi family in New Delhi as they prepare a lavish wedding for the daughter's marriage to a diasporic man from Houston, Texas. Combining elements of Hollywood and Bollywood, the film is the seventh top-grossing foreign film in the United States and cost just over a million dollars to make. Quickly following up on her success with *Monsoon Wedding,* Nair made *Hysterical Blindness* (2002) for HBO, about two working-class women seeking love and happiness in New Jersey. She has also completed a short film that is part of an anthology titled *11'09"01* (2002) based on the true story of Salman Hamdani, a Muslim-American man who disappeared in New York during 9/11. The film depicts his family's anxiety and pain as they are repeatedly harassed with accusations that he was the "missing hijacker" until his remains are discovered among the rubble of the World Trade Center, where he had apparently rushed to aid distressed survivors, and he is named a hero. The film has been branded anti-American by some critics. Nair has garnered incredible attention for her film and has accepted several major projects for the next few years, including the offer to adapt and direct *Monsoon Wedding* as a Broadway musical due out in 2004; this project strikingly parallels the Meera Syal–Shekar Kapur–A. R. Rahman collaboration of *Bollywood Dreams* sponsored by Andrew Lloyd Webber. In addition, she also has agreed to direct the upcoming adaptation of William Thackeray's *Vanity Fair* starring Reese Witherspoon with a multimillion dollar budget. Nair also has signed a contract to develop a comedy series based on the lives of a motel-owning Indian-American family for television. Overall, film-makers in North America, like Nair and Mehta, seem better poised to legitimate their films and gain access to the production of films at a larger scale. I return to this discussion of the popularity of various filmmakers and films in the conclusion.

Thus, although the United States has enabled different access to filmmaking, Coco Fusco comments that U.S. minority communities are "still faced with a dearth of critical language on black independent cinema....In general, film culture in the U.S. is far less integrated with academic research" (Fusco 1988, 37–38). In fact, I argue, it is black British cultural studies that provides a great deal of the theoretical framework for understanding the production of South Asian diasporic (including British Asian) cinema.[16] For this reason, in the next section, I explore how British cultural studies, (especially in the work of Hall, Gilroy, and Mercer) theorizing of the politics of representation, production, and reception informs South Asian diasporic cultural studies. Conversely, I also hope to demonstrate that Asian British films have been central to cultural debates in Britain and therefore to the formation of British cultural studies, a point that is lost in the way that African-American studies takes up black British cultural studies.

Black and Asian-British Cinema or Cool Brittania

South Asian diasporic films emerged primarily in Britain because of favorable conditions during the eighties. The political economy of Britain created opportunities for access that were previously severely limited. Thus, this period saw the increased production and integration of black British academic and artistic production. This period, which seems quite distant from the current moment in which so many of these cultural forms have been co-opted in the name of multiculturalism and globalization, nevertheless was identified by many scholars such as Hall and Mercer as salient in shifting discourses and practices of the nation-state and race. Hall, writing in the eighties, commented, "Young black people in London today are marginalized, fragmented, unenfranchised, disadvantaged and dispersed. And yet, they look as if they own the territory. Somehow, they too, in spite of everything, are centered, in place: without much material support, it's true, but nevertheless they occupy a new kind of space at the center" (cited in Mercer 1994, 19). The protests and movements during this time period resulted in the formation of state-sponsored organizations structured to facilitate the emergence of black British cultural producers. Furthermore, these discourses were coupled with charges to the nation-state to provide the material and ideological support for transformation. Hence, coalitions of African and Asian diasporic peoples organized as "black" in challenging dominant discourses on the nation. Based on memories and personal and collective narratives, films like *Handsworth Songs* (Akomfrah 1986) and *The Passion of*

Remembrance (Julien and Blackwood 1986) challenged and rewrote histories of colonialism and migration.

South Asian British and black British films of the eighties neither were easily incorporated into British national cinemas as the films openly contested national narratives and identification processes nor were able to enter the national film industries without intervention from social movements on the state. British scholar John Hill suggests we may want to clarify what we mean when we say that we are discussing British films (Hill 1992, 10). Hill speaks specifically about the distinction between a national film industry versus a national cinema. Most generally, the latter is thought to represent the nation, which increasingly is seen as threatened from the inside (minorities) and from the outside by the hegemony of Hollywood, while the former may be considered a commercial profit-seeking enterprise that often is protected as a national industry against other international producers of similar commodities. Discussions of national film industries are therefore concerned with what are often the economics and politics of production ranging from issues such as the employment of nationals to tariff and trade agreements regarding the import and export of films. Of course, as other scholars have noted, the division is hardly a simple one. National cinemas and film industries often are inextricably linked, because perceptions of what is the nation and national culture inevitably inform the material processes, which are the concern of film industries.

Clearly, the work of scholars such as Pierre Bourdieu (1984) has furthered understandings of the relationship between socioeconomic class and culture, especially in considering how concepts of art and high culture operate in relation to bourgeoisie social formations.[17] When we speak of British cinema, the implicit understanding is that British cinema is a coherent body of films that represents the nation and national culture. British cinema, because it is viewed as representing the nation, is a site where national identities are contested. Within the national imaginary, British cinema is generally associated with certain types of "highbrow" literary films. Correspondingly, viewers who consume these films also are imagined and are constructed as constituting national audiences. National cinema assumes a "tight, symbiotic relation between films and audiences and a clear, unified version of national identity and national preoccupations" (Hill 1992, 16). These films are assumed, therefore, to be popular with these national audiences, as well as international audiences who are seen as expecting and desiring a similar image of British culture in the films. Hence, international (i.e., American) perceptions of British culture and cinema are highly influential as well. British scholars concurred until the eighties that appealing to international audiences requires presenting nostalgic images of a romantic and pastoral England. Within the national and international imaginary, British films most often are perceived to be heritage films (e.g., Merchant-Ivory productions such as *Room with a View* and *Howards End*) and nostalgic Raj (colonial) films (e.g., *Passage to India* and even *Gandhi*). Debate among British scholars has focused on the function of these heritage films in local and global perceptions of British culture, with some arguing that global interests force the production of such films and others arguing for the increased production of such films. It was not until British films such as *My Beautiful Laundrette, Bhaji on the Beach, The Crying Game, Trainspotting,* and *East Is East* that these assumptions began to be questioned and challenged.

Andrew Higson (1989, 36) posits that the "parameters of a national cinema should always be drawn at the site of consumption as much as the site of production of films," including "the activity of national audiences and the conditions under which they make sense of and use the films they watch." Hill disagrees with this assessment, positing instead that consumption is not a fine enough marker because the consumption of Hollywood films by British viewers would be therefore included in an understanding of British cinema. Hill does not note that many discussions of British cinema also focus on the consumption of these films internationally. Hence, an aspect of Higson's argument is already integrated into discussions of national cinema, and Higson's main contention that consumption must be considered cannot be easily brushed aside. Moreover, the relationship between production and consumption is especially significant to minority filmmakers whose access to resources is generally limited. As in discussions of British films overseas, the significance of consumption also is implicit in this discussion because of the ways these texts circulate within the transnational network of the Brown Atlantic.

Black Critique of the Nation

Studies of British cinema in the eighties and nineties reflect the contestations over national identity that were occurring in national discourses as well. In particular, Britain was confronting the legacy of its colonialism that was manifested in the postcolonial immigration that reshaped the nation-state. Many scholars who are now associated with cultural and postcolonial studies including Bhabha, Gilroy, and Hall focused on the impact of the postcolonial "return" to the metropolitan center and the necessity of consequently transforming discourses on race, nation, and culture. Oppositional discourses on British cinema also questioned the history of colonialism that was being written large into the national imaginary by nostalgic films of the Raj Quarter and *Gandhi.* Many black artists and scholars were critical of the colonial nostalgia exhibited in the heritage films and sought to make films that depicted postcolonial subjects in the metropole, rather than hot, dusty, and exotic colonies. In general, black scholars and activists challenged the racist practices and policies of the nation-state during Thatcher's reign as prime minister.

Black identity and politics emerged in the sixties and seventies and functioned as a fragile political strategic identity for Asian and African diasporic peoples in Britain. Sallie Westwood (1995, 197–221) suggests that black was imported from U.S.-based black politics and then became an oppositional but hegemonic and unified political identity. Since this initial employment, there has been an increasing movement toward a politics of differentiation in which British Asian has gained currency, thus emphasizing a diasporic South Asian identity, whereas African Caribbean identity similarly stresses affiliations to African diasporas. Hence, both differentiated identities forward diasporic and transnational associations over the national ones implied by the use of *black*. In other words, the term is contested as a site of alliance by critics who contend that *black* homogenizes disparate experiences under one category.[18] Moreover, it is the specificity of Asian experiences that are supposedly erased with the use of the strategic term. The former criticism presumes that there is more cohesion and similarity within Asian communities, despite their differences, than there is between black and Asian communities. In other words, this criticism assumes homogeneity within communities and difference between communities. Alternatively, one could argue that the term need not mask differences between or within communities. Gilroy argues that we need a polyphonic and multiaccentual understanding of blackness, in other words, that we see it in heterogeneous terms. Consequently, he argues that blackness needs to account for heterogeneity and difference. Black British films marked a shift from earlier race relation approaches (which framed minorities as the objects of study and regarded race as a "problem" to be solved) to reformulations of the nation and national identities that rendered racialized subjects as plural and complex. Eschewing much of the cultural nationalism that characterizes dominant discourses of racial minority communities, many of the black British discourses in the eighties incorporated intersectionality and poststructuralism into their critiques, suggesting plurality, hybridity, and multiplicity in the place of unity, purity, and homogeneity.

Black Filmmaking

Black filmmaking involved different modes of production in the eighties. In the wake of uprisings against institutional and systemic racism in the eighties, the demands for black representation in national and state institutions motivated state support, and the nation-state became active in supporting and facilitating the production of cinema by establishing workshops. British Asian artists were active in the government-supported workshops and also were encouraged by organizations such as the British Film Institute and the developing Channel Four.[19] Television coupled with the state grant-supported workshops and collectives led to the production of numerous independent films during this period.

At the same time, the participation of the state and its tokenist politics of multiculturalism had implications. The funding allowed the state to shape and structure the relationship between filmmakers and audiences. Black filmmakers confronted the racial politics of representation that accompanied state and institutional funding. The institutional structures, especially funding, confronted the issues of tokenism, competition, and nepotism (Gilroy 1988, 46). These situations occur when the state seeks to select and designate certain minority artists as spokesmen or representatives of ethnic communities. Hall (1995, 14) posits that this relationship was "powerfully mediated and transformed by the apparatuses, the discursive strategies, organizational practices, professional knowledge and technologies"—all of which he identifies as the governmentality of media.

The workshops emphasized a different form of production and distribution than did the television-supported programming. These workshops were set up to facilitate collective filmmaking by minority communities to express their politics and desires in both content and form. The films produced by Sankofa, for example, were nonmainstream films that interrogated not only the sociological approach to race relations but also its standard aesthetic form of realist documentary. They questioned narrative and representative strategies of cinematic form in their films. The collectives argued that their form of production created integrated practices that developed new narratives and aesthetics not possible within commercial media industries. In contrast, proponents of larger production companies maintained that more conventional programs and cultural products would gain access to wider distribution and hence larger audiences (Mercer 1994, 80). As I discuss later, this particular debate returns repeatedly in British discourses on black and Asian filmmaking. James Snead (1988, 47) proposes that the category black independent film "seems custom-made to cover-up the 'questions of political power and ideological control.' . . . It invents some people who just happen to have declared some putative artistic and/or financial independence." Discussions of these films in the eighties are less marked by an emphasis on their commercial viability than are films produced in the mid-and late nineties in Britain. These debates impose and produce a false binary suggesting that only commercially viable films or collectively produced aesthetically radical films are significant. Both sets of films challenge dominant discourses of the nation but from different public spheres. In the early eighties, mode of production was less a factor limiting than it became later. Furthermore, the different modes of production enabled access to resources for filmmakers and also diversified the aesthetics and topics associated with minority filmmaking (Mercer 1994, 81). Both modes of production contributed to the formation of black public cultures and enabled transnational public cultures.

Though they did not acquire mass distribution, these texts had great impact and saliency in the African diaspora, especially in the United States. Fusco remarks that the films were popular among certain groups in the United States precisely because they allowed liberal audiences to view a racial narrative from a distanced gaze. She argues that British racism did not translate into American terms as directly, and viewers were able to disassociate these issues from the U.S. context (Fusco 1988, 38). Snead suggests that this distancing is made possible by the ways the U.S. audiences associate British accents and culture with a certain sense of superiority and so that even though characters may be speaking about racism, oppression, or marginalization, they are perceived as being elevated and privileged (Snead 1988, 48).

A difference between black and Asian filmmaking might be tentatively identified here as well. Kureishi's films, directed by white director Stephen Frears, were not made in the workshop mode and can be differentiated from the films made by Sankofa, Black Audio, Retake, and so on. In fact, although Asian filmmakers have used alternative and avant-garde forms, they have tended toward more conventional narratives and accessed larger commercial distribution. In the case of Chadha and Kureishi, their works are more conventional in their narrative form, which makes them more easily distributable and consumable by audiences. Circulation can expand what is seen as standard format and build audiences through exposure, in that viewing films is a mutually constitutive practice and form is not simply there waiting to be discovered but is produced as viewers see films and learn to read films differently.

Burden of Representation

The films eschewed the representative politics that were expected of them. Mercer (1994) calls this expectation "the burden of representation," while Kureishi labels it the "brown man's burden" (Kureishi 1995, 6). Both refer to the expectation and perception that cultural production by nondominant producers represents (in the sense of renders fully transparent and representable) the subjectivities, identities, and experiences of minority communities. In the case of Britain, institutional support created expectations that the films would "speak for" minority communities. Mercer (1994, 92) argues that "this legitimates institutional expediency (it 'demonstrates' multiculturalism) *and* the rationing of access to meager resources (it polices a group's social rights to representation)." Minority communities also apply pressure to artists to represent them, often in "positive" terms. Minority communities are aware of and experience the lack of access to creating their own cultural representations within national culture and seek to counter dominant constructions of minorities as "negative" with images that are "positive." Thus, the binary logic of dominant discourses continues to determine the terrain of contestation. In other words, the pressure is on minority filmmakers to present and represent communities in ways that are already predetermined by dominant discourses; in this case, minority communities often expect cultural producers to work to "correct" these misconceptions by substituting images that conform to dominant normativities in place of stereotypes. Furthermore, these expectations perpetuate the idea that someone can speak for or represent a community, thus ultimately reinforcing the marginality of the community.

Kureishi's (as well as Gurinder Chadha's) filmmaking provides an excellent example of how different modes of production intertwine as Kureishi was introduced to scriptwriting and filmmaking through workshop production and television programming but then accessed theater distribution.[20] *My Beautiful*

Laundrette was also the first and most successful film of the independent production company Working Title, which worked with many Asian British productions. It transformed the playing field. Kureishi's films irreverently approach the experience of Asians in Britain, challenging dominant conceptions with their plurality of identities and rejection of essentialism. *My Beautiful Laundrette* and *Sammy and Rosie Get Laid* were written by Kureishi and directed by Frears. These were followed by Kureishi's self-directed *London Kills Me* as well as several adaptations of Kureishi's writings including *My Son the Fanatic* and the television miniseries *The Buddha of Suburbia*. Kureishi writes in *My Beautiful Laundrette and the Rainbow Sign* that he was "tired of seeing lavish films set in exotic locations" that were basically the product of "aiming a camera at an attractive landscape in the hot country in front of which stood a star in a perfectly clean costume delivering lines from an old book" (1986, 43). *My Beautiful Laundrette*, nominated as best foreign film in the Academy Awards, was the first Asian British film to reach international audiences. *My Beautiful Laundrette* and *Sammy and Rosie Get Laid* interrogated and redefined the meaning of British from a variety of positions; the films foregrounded not only racial but also class, sexuality, and gender politics. Furthermore, they challenged the construction of national cinema as consisting of heritage films or associated primarily with a nostalgic modern English upper class. As the first highly visible Asian British filmmaker, Kureishi was particularly burdened with the weight of representation resulting from material inequalities and lack of access to the means of filmic production. Nevertheless, *My Beautiful Laundrette* was also one of the first films in the public culture of the Brown Atlantic.

My Beautiful Laundrette revolves loosely around Omar, a young Pakistani British man who manages his uncle's laundrette, transforming it from dilapidated wreck to a clean, sparkling, and soon-to-be successful business with the help of his lover Johnny, a former skinhead. It is the laundrette that enables Omar to employ Johnny and mitigate the racialized power relations between them. The significance of class and capital in relation to racial formations is commented on by several characters: Omar's cousin Salim the drug dealer reasons, "We're nothing in England without money." Similarly, Omar's Uncle Nasser advises him to invest in ways that make him "indispensable" to the British society and economy: "What is it that the gora [white] Englishman always needs? Clean clothes." The laundrette stands at the center of this interrogation of race, class, gender, and sexuality in Thatcher's England, where Asian British men negotiate a place in society only through acquiring capital. Capital is the most powerful instrument of negotiation suggests the film. Within the film, Asian British businessmen squeeze and exploit who they can, in this case, the white underclass, though not without repercussions. Nevertheless, capitalist enterprise provides the opportunity to mitigate some of the relations of power. Asian British women, on the other hand, cannot access these same spaces. Omar's female cousin Tania, for example, is left only with the option to leave home and family. The film ends

with Omar and Johnny intimately having sex in the back of the beautiful laundrette, a temporary and interstitial space that has been negotiated between the
two of them.

In *Sammy and Rosie Get Laid,* the city of London still remains that site
of oppressions and possibilities. It is in the interstitial spaces of the city that
Kureishi locates the successful and failed resistances to exploitation, racism,
marginalization, and state violence (both of the postcolonial nation-state and
the metropolitan nation-state). The film interweaves the lives of Sammy (a
hedonistic Asian Brit whose father has returned to London from Pakistan) and
Rosie (Sammy's wife and a liberal white social worker) into the network of lives
in the communities around them.[21] Its dystopic view of Thatcher's England
is similar to that of *My Beautiful Laundrette* but is painted in darker hues.
With both films, transgressive sexual practices become one possible strategy of
resistance that challenges dominant social mores and power structures. In other
words, the films frame sexual encounters as spaces of social and political contact
that negotiate gender, class, and race.

Kureishi's films (and writings) made a significant impact on British and
Asian British culture of the eighties and nineties. *My Beautiful Laundrette* and
Sammy and Rosie Get Laid unabashedly portrayed life in a black Britain that was
not suspended between two cultures thus trapped in some Manichean binary of
East and West but that rather complexly rendered the heterogeneous and hybrid
subjects of postcolonial Britain and specifically a global London. These films
produced a space for the emerging identities of British and diasporic subjects
to be articulated. They presented complex, nonessentialist, and nontransparent
subjectivities that did not attempt to represent British Asian identity as singular
and static.

Commenting on the impact of Kureishi's and other black and Asian films,
Andrew Higson (2000, 35) suggests a postnational model for British cinema, one
that focuses on "multiculturalism, transnationalism, and devolution." However,
Kureishi's films were controversial and not lauded by all critics. *My Beautiful
Laundrette* was attacked by neoconservative British critics who disapproved of its
"disgusting" and "sick" view of Britain (Mercer 1994, 73). These disagreements
signal the contestation over British identity and culture occurring through a
discussion of these films as part of national cinema, on one side by dominant
voices who are threatened by its dissection of the nation and on the other side
by British Asians who seek positive images to challenge racist stereotypes.[22]
Kureishi received criticism from many Asian British who saw his films, especially *My Beautiful Laundrette,* as airing dirty linen in public and furthering
stereotypes. Some of the critics saw the films as presenting Asians as sex and
money crazed. Independent producer Mahmood Jamal considered such films a
form of neo-Orientalism reinforcing "stereotypes of their own people for a few
cheap laughs" (Jamal, cited in Mercer 1994, 73). The audiences were not the same
for these films internationally. In the United States, James Snead suggests that

Kureshi's films were ignored by African-American communities as the films were not seen as black films (Snead 1988, 48). As Colin MacCabe (1988, 32) suggests,

> The realization that there are no essential identities needs to be paralleled by the realization that there is no single audience, that the national culture cannot be understood as a totality which provides a unified audience but as a series of differences, a multitude of audiences. To take such a position is immediately to allow a much more plural set of aesthetic values than has been permissible within the western tradition or, at a more local level, than was evident in the debate about the films discussed.

Furthermore, such formulations assume that black filmmakers belong to only one community and have only a singular identity. As Fusco (1988, 38–39) comments,

> The only way I propose to break down all these problematic assumptions is to work on several fronts through different forms of cultural production, including (but not exclusively) criticism. We must be able to demonstrate that limited visions of black cinema and black identity won't hold. . . . (F)ilm is a cultural form that relies on building many different audiences to sustain it.

Kureishi's films are not concerned so much with presenting a "positive" representation of Asian or black British people. In one scene of *Sammy and Rosie Get Laid*, Sammy is the perfect example of the excesses of capitalist consumption as he masturbates to porn while listening to music and consuming fast food burgers and cocaine. The films depict complex and layered categories that reflect subjects in relation to multiple rather than singular differences. Thus, Rita in *Sammy and Rosie Get Laid* appears as British Asian, feminist, and lesbian, which positions her differently even from Omar in *My Beautiful Laundrette*. Kureishi is attentive to intersectionality and the complex positions occupied by individuals in relation to both white and Asian British communities. Scholars, such as Mercer, contend that such heterogeneous and hybrid depictions actually challenge stereotypes and misconceptions as they depict differences within communities assumed to be monolithic, unified, and transparent; furthermore, they posit that the myth of transparent and homogenous black identities and experiences is a foundational belief in many ideologies of racism.

This hybridity is made visible in the formal aspects of Kureishi's films, albeit differently from those that incorporate elements of Bollywood cinema into their formal structures. Kureishi's films nevertheless are hybrid, blending styles and forms. *My Beautiful Laundrette* combines comedy and surrealism in its realist and allegorical presentation. *Sammy and Rosie Get Laid* similarly uses slapstick and melodrama (and even the western). One of the most striking examples of its innovation is its use of triple split screen in what Kureishi (1988, 25) calls the "fuck sandwich" to render multiplicity and heterogeneity.

The mid- and late nineties brought a shift from the hopeful period of the eighties in Britain. The eighties were marked by a struggle to acquire visibility and access such that cultural producers had to struggle with and negotiate the state and its apparatuses to gain the means of production and distribution. First, in the nineties, invisibility was less the issue. Although discourses of voice and visibility still had cultural capital, they no longer functioned in the same way. Once institutions and public discourses could point to a few highly visible black and Asian cultural producers and argue that minorities now had access and were successful employing a tokenist logic, then black and Asian cultural producers could less powerfully wield "visibility" as strategic rhetoric. What remains an issue, however, is the way in which filmmaking is restrictive due to its requirement of great economic investment. In other words, as scholars and cultural producers have argued strongly, political economy and material conditions are central to discussions of filmic and media production. In addition, Mercer (1999–2000, 62) suggests that within postmodernity, the gaining of voice and visibility no longer equal a change in the structure of power. Cultural difference in multiculturalism became an additive strategy in which a few black cultural producers are included in cultural institutions without dismantling, altering, or neutralizing the systemic economic and political discrimination of social structures. Without an emphasis on the conflicts and tensions produced by a pluralist society and the necessity of transforming material conditions, visibility can become a way to spice up culture without a compensatory interrogation or shift of values and epistemologies.

Second, "It was the institutional response to the agenda, during the late Eighties moment, that brought about a sea-change in the 'relations of representation,' that created the scenario in which Nineties black artists sought distance from the hyper-politicization of difference" (Mercer 1999–2000, 56). Black politics became more fragmented rather than polyphonic. Internal differentiation and particularity, rather than similarity, were emphasized. In some senses, this change can be read as a response to critiques of the burden of representation, as the focus shifted from producing a singular and transparent representation of ethnic communities in the form of cultural nationalism to representations that were based on specific intersectional analyses of social and historical conditions. Hall (1995, 16) suggests that black cultural production became "far less 'collectivist' in spirit" and consequently less focused on an antiracist agenda. Mercer identifies this period differently than Hall, suggesting that after the eighties, racial politics had become commodified and institutionalized in a form of multiculturalism that too needed to be challenged. Mercer asserts that blackness (race and ethnicity in general) became hypervisible so that cultural and racial difference became normalized and commodified in dominant discourses. The emphasis on the commodification of cultural difference and its incorporation into mainstream commercial consumption overshadowed discussions linking cultural production to social, political, and economic transformation.

Director David Attwood and writer Harwant Bains's film *Wild West* is hyperaware of this commodification, commercialization, and tokenist visibility and incorporates this awareness into the narrative. *Wild West* depicts the trade in multicultural media production in suggesting that Asian (female) artists can be deployed to satisfy the latest demands for the exotic and erotic in dominant culture. The film parodies and exposes this "interest" in Asian cultural production suggesting that "Asianness" serves as a clever gimmick for commercial industries that are ever ready to incorporate difference in the name of profit. Asian British filmmakers and films, such as *Wild West*, frequently attempt to thematize and narrate the economic power relations and social conditions of production. I will return to this issue of hypervisibility and commodification.

Much of the British cultural studies scholarship in the nineties is characterized by an emphasis on audiences. Scholars emphasize audiences as ways to negotiate the issue of the burden of representation. Hall and Gilroy both theorize the ways that black cultural production negotiates the burden of representation with similar strategies. Hall (1995, 13) writes, "We do have to speak responsibly about black subjects and black cultures, which are indeed the subjects of our representational practices, and we have to learn to speak responsibly to black and other audiences." Hall attempts to reconcile the burden of representation with the responsibility placed on cultural producers in relation to their audiences because of material conditions. Gilroy (1988, 46) similarly forwards a "populist modernism" that is enacted through the cultural producer's responsibility to "articulate a core of aesthetic modernism in resolutely vernacular formats." How do we interpret this responsibility and our understandings of what it means to speak to black audiences? Hall and Gilroy recognize that the political economy of minority cultural production within the dominant national public sphere forces cultural producers to articulate oversimplified or problematic identities (and therefore relationships to communities). Their strategy is to turn to the question of audience. The issue of audiences is primary in many of the discussions of black cultural production in the nineties by scholars such as Gilroy and Hall and also by the media industries themselves.

Mercer critiques populist modernism and the emphasis on "black audiences":

> The notion of a given, and hence naturalized, set of ethic "obligations" immediately sets up a moral problematic in which questions of structure are displaced by a voluntaristic emphasis on individual agency. This implies a contractual model of subjectivity in which black artists are assumed to have a fundamental "freedom of choice" that has to be reconciled with their "accountability" to the community. (Mercer 1994, 240).

Trinh T. Minh-ha (1990) suggests that splitting the "masses" from the elite implies not only a passive audience that consumes but also one that is separate from the artist. Hall's and Gilroy's formulations shift the emphasis from the text to the artists who make them and their intentions toward their perceived audiences. Mercer argues such formulations are based on certain understandings of "audience" that essentialize black audiences in the name of the vernacular and authenticity. Therefore, not only do they presume distinctions between black and other (mainly whites) audiences but they also implicitly prioritize certain formations of minority audiences over others. "Moreover, in assuming that authorial intentions determine the socioeconomic composition of audiences, the argument risks the return of a certain class reductionism, whereby the value of an artwork is judged by the race/class composition of the audience for which it was intended" (Mercer 1994, 242). This caution suggests that cultural nationalism is produced whenever an association between class and "authentic" aesthetics is forged. Mercer argues instead for the necessity of maintaining the heterogeneity and multiplicity of blackness.

Though the film did not garner box office monies to cover its costs, *Bhaji on the Beach* was one of the most successful films characterizing the early and mid nineties and eventually recovered its production costs through video sales. Gurinder Chadha received awards for her debut feature film released in 1994. It was the first commercial film released by a black woman in Britain. Although the film was less focused on black and white relations even within an antiracist agenda, it was unequivocally concerned with black cultural politics. Chadha posits that her entrance into filmmaking was in a time in which there was much more awareness about black cultural production in the dominant media. "The era of workshops and the dependent relations they institutionalized may be passing. But the space they provided nurtured some of the most seriously creative and innovative black work to appear in film and TV" suggested Stuart Hall (1995, 25). Chadha is one filmmaker who achieved access to "mainstream" media production through the state-supported funding. Although fluent in the debates outlined previously, Chadha's *Bhaji on the Beach* pursues the more commercial venue that becomes the primary focus of Asian filmmaking discourses in the last half of the decade. In addition, the film relies on more conventional narrative structure and frameworks, thus marking its potential for crossover appeal.

However, Hindu cultural nationalists found the film questionable. As Gargi Bhattacharyya and John Gabriel (1994, 57) comment, *Bhaji on the Beach* too was attacked by a militant Hindu organization identifying itself as Arya Samaj; the group charged that *Bhaji on the Beach* degraded Indian culture. Bhattacharyya and Gabriel report that one of the scenes that the group found morally offensive was one in which Chadha parodies an Indian film *Paurab Aur Paschim* (*East or West*) in depicting the Westernization of a diasporic woman by portraying her as a miniskirted and blonde wig–wearing cigarette smoker prancing around in front of an idol of Rama in a Hindu temple. Chadha pursues a homogenous understanding of audience in her response to these events as she reports being hurt by these critiques as she makes her films for "all Asians" (cited in Bhattacharyya and Gabriel 1994, 57).

In contrast to the discourse of black cultural studies scholars, contemporary dominant discourse concentrates primarily on the hegemony of Hollywood, focusing especially on developing the national film industry to compete with Hollywood films in Britain. For many national cinemas, the hegemony of Hollywood often provides the standard for success, especially as the United States has a self-sustaining audience that can produce box office profits that offset production costs. In the case of Britain, consumption can match production for low to moderate budget films. Big-budget films must be like American blockbusters and must reach international (i.e., U.S.) audiences to recoup costs. This, of course, conflicts with the idea that British films and cinema are produced for the British audience. More specifically, that heritage-based national narratives were deprioritized as globalization processes further commercialized the state and its cultural and filmic production.

The general perception became that there were only two viable options—either to continue to produce the British niche market of heritage films (or the equivalent of *Four Weddings and a Funeral*) that marketed a certain vision of Britain to a sizable art-house audience or to emulate Hollywood. Emulating Hollywood meant, at some level, producing action spectacles with high budgets and mainstream international audiences. The report *The Bigger Picture* suggested exactly this—that the British film industry needed to invest in higher production cost action films. The success of certain films that did not fit into the heritage mode, such as *The Full Monty, The Crying Game, Trainspotting*, and *Lock, Stock, and Two Smoking Barrels* challenged both of these perceptions (and revitalized British cinema and the role of British films in U.S. art-house cinema).[23] Although the nation-state is still heavily involved in financing the British film industry, the shift from the eighties to the contemporary moment is the move away from an emphasis on multiculturalism to one primarily on profit. However, the vision of a homogenous white national cinema hardly remains intact considering the popularity of these films. Higson (2000) characterizes contemporary British cinema as postnational in its transnationality and multiculturalism.[24] Chadha comments that *Bhaji on the Beach* is seen as an English film in the United States regardless of how contested it might be in England: "Yes, it's important that it's set in England, and an England they don't often see, but *Bhaji on the Beach* is so English that they relate to it even if it means that they come to it via *Howard's End, My Beautiful Launderette, Enchanted April*, and now *Four Weddings and a Funeral*" (Chadha cited in Bhattacharyya and Gabriel 1994, 63). Increasingly in these discussions, the focus switched from an emphasis on national production to consumption that was measured in the commercial popularity of the film in Britain and in the United States. Consequently, the emphasis has shifted from viewers and audiences to markets.

The trend in British analyses is to adopt increasingly the U.S. model of markets, commodities, and targets. Cultural production also shifted in relation to the nation-state as the culture industry sought to pursue a market-driven strategy that still marks cultural production and state policy in Britain. The funding strategies have shifted to a lottery system that too is severely criticized when films fail to become commercial successes. This capitalist discourse occurs even within minority production and programming. Discussions of Asian and black films increasingly focused on the consumption by white British and international, namely U.S., audiences, rather than Asian and black ones. Onyekachi

Wambu and Kevin Arnold (1999, vi), in *A Fuller Picture,* argue that since this is the commercial context in which black films must exist, they suggest "targeting and expanding the audience base for black films." One suggestion that they forward is to develop target theaters directed toward black audiences, similar to the development of the art-house cinema (p. 24).

Moreover, cultural producers, seeking to avoid the stigmatization associated with tokenism and the burden of representation also began to speak in terms of "markets" and crossover demographics. Discussing television, Hall (1995, 19–20) comments,

> It seems appropriate, therefore, to ask the newly converted "free marketeers" and self-helpers why they are so convinced that their programmes and ideas will survive in an absolutely unregulated "open market." Without some dedicated funding, some dedicated space in the schedules, some policy directives linked with funded initiatives, won't the old habits, the old conceptions of the audience, the old address books and contact phone-numbers, simply reassert themselves?

"Crossover" in relation to discussions of black British cultural productions usually signifies the success of texts with white audiences. If profits are the primary measure of success and significance, then the importance of appealing to black audiences becomes secondary. The nineties marked a period in which black cultural production as an alternative culture became recognized by the British film industry as a potential site of profit as the industry attempted to incorporate black cultural production into the categories of mainstream and alternative.

Crossover also assumes that there are certain audiences that are commensurate with communities and demographic populations. Consequently, the emphasis on crossover success shifts discussion away from the issues associated with the burden of representation and the relations between cultural producers and black British communities to appealing to white demographic markets. Hence, the discourse implies the differentiation of national viewers into target demographic groups but focuses on those white and other audiences interested in "multicultural fare." Consequently, unified national cinema and culture are no longer seen as serving a unified nation, instead, late capitalist diversification has brought a decentralized approach that favors plurality in constructing and penetrating its differentiated target markets. These shifts do not mean that black visibility is no longer regulated by dominant interests. To the contrary, the visibility of black representation in the public sphere is still dependent on the political economy of the culture industry and has been integrated into capitalist expansion through the logic and rhetoric of multiculturalism.

Conclusion

Some scholars have been critical of these recent trends. For example, Karen Alexander (2000) critiques the British Film Institute/Black Film Bulletin report

A Fuller Picture for focusing solely on market forces and neglecting questions of culture and aesthetics in relationship to the issue of the marketing of black films to specific audiences. Posing the question of "what will it mean for our collective imaginations if the primary audience for our national cinema continues to be positioned as white?" (p. 109), Alexander also questions the concept that black films are of interest only to (and thus should be marketed only to) black audiences.

Crossover appeal has been a characteristic of several Asian British filmmakers like Din and Chadha who have pursued comedy over drama. In their films, feminist challenges to gender normativities and patriarchal power within the family have had a particular appeal to multiple audiences. In *East Is East,* the Muslim father is depicted as an abusive and controlling patriarch who attempts to enforce conservative law in the family, punishing defiance and deviance. Deviance, such as homosexuality, is seen as familiar to white liberal audiences who can feel empathetic with British Asians and feel that homosexuality is a sign of assimilation into Britishness. *East Is East* emphasizes these conflicts as being determined by generational differences that result from acculturation. Thus, the "traditional" Muslim father is framed as restrictive and abusive in regard to his liberal and progressive children and wife.[25] The father's physical and psychological abuse is, however, often naturalized as it is associated most frequently with traditional discourses on gender and sexuality rather than located more clearly in relation to the geopolitical, historical, and socioeconomic contexts.

In contrast, *My Son the Fanatic* does not portray the father as the source of derision or loathing but rather as a complex, sympathetic, and sexually deviant (he befriends a sex worker) figure who is not easily placed into simple categories. The father drives a taxi away from the metropolitan London, eking out a living from business travelers and sex workers. Distant and alienated from his family, he is unable to wield any power when his son decides to break off his engagement with a white woman and becomes a militant Muslim fundamentalist in response to his own alienation and in opposition to British dominance. *My Son the Fanatic* probes and exposes the constructed nature of tradition as it switches the expectations of audiences. In the film (like the short story on which it is based), it is the son rather than the father who seeks resistance in discourses of tradition, specifically, in religious discourses of Islam. In this narrative, Muslim fundamentalism is not a continuous and inexplicable tradition as framed by the Orientalist imagination but rather is a contemporary phenomenon engendered by the location of the minority Muslim in modernity. Hence, the film explores the function and problems of religious identity as a form of resistance to Western imperialism. In fact, what *My Son the Fanatic* does is suggest that this idea of speaking to and for audiences is difficult and fraught. The film does not forward a black identity per se. Instead, in the nexus of discourses on the nation, capital, and modernity, it locates contradictory positions. Furthermore, it does not suggest that black conceived as being a multiple signifier of African and Asian identities is meaningful, coherent, sound, or even politically strategic. Instead, it probes the sites of dissonance and discord within Asian communities. Although the film is unable to create a productive dialogue between the conflicting voices, it certainly suggests the necessity of doing so. The response of different groups to the Salman Rushdie affair as it is popularly called reveals the differing and conflicting positions even within black Britain. Muslims in diaspora are increasingly formulated as the most dangerous and least assimilable of minorities, Europe's most terrifying and volatile other. Kureishi and Prasad emphasize lack of coherency and unity to the idea of a black community. They do so, not simply by suggesting that black is insufficient to recognize the diversity of African and Asian experiences but by forwarding the serious contradictions and disagreements that exist within these communities. The conflict between father and son in *My Son the Fanatic* is quite different from the one portrayed in *East Is East*. I suggest that this difference also accounts for the difference in their appeal to audiences, wherein *East Is East* can garner dominant and nondominant audiences (in light of its tropes of oppressive Asian patriarchal traditions) and *My Son the Fanatic* is marginal to both.

For the moment, South Asian and Asian British media productions are highly visible in Britain, which seems to have embraced at least a few female artists including Gurinder Chadha and Meera Syal. More recently, Chadha's new film about soccer and "Asian life" made a significant impact in 2002. *Bend It Like Beckham* opened in more than 400 cinemas its first weekend, in contrast to the five that featured *Bhaji on the Beach*. The film grossed more than 2 million pounds (almost 4 million U.S. dollars) that weekend, making it the seventh highest opening for a British film and earning Chadha the title "queen of the multi" (which can ambiguously mean both multiplex and multiculturalism). Featuring an interracial romance between the protagonist Jess and her Irish soccer coach Joe, the film's narrative follows the conventions of the genre with a political critique of the way sports participates in gendered and racialized national discourses. Sports and particularly soccer/football is a site in which the British Asian woman is interpellated into British heteronormativity. I return briefly to this film in the conclusion.

In addition, an adaptation of Syal's first novel *Anita and Me* (1996) is also forthcoming (2003–4). Syal's second novel *Life Isn't All Ha Ha Hee Hee* (2000) is also an immensely popular best-seller. Similarly, television continues to be a site featuring the productions of Asian artists such as Syal's *Goodness Gracious Me* and *The Kumars at Number 42,* which have garnered critical and popular accolades. Hypervisibility has become an issue, because British Asians as representations of Asianness are everywhere (most recently featured in the center display of the department store Selfridges). This visibility is occurring simultaneously with the heightened racialization processes following the globalization of the events of 9/11. Hence, this visibility is accompanied by a bifurcation in which Asianness is hip, cool, and British, and Asians themselves are dangerous and foreign.

Many Asian British films of the past fifteen years have sought to destabilize essentialist notions of identity, including those identities associated with dominant and cultural nationalism. The shifting historical and social conditions in Britain during this time have affected not only the means of production but also the modes of production. As the social and political contexts of racial formation and nationalism have continually changed due to local, national, and transnational forces, different forms of production and consumption have characterized Asian British filmmaking. Consequently, changing discourses on race, multiculturalism, and identity also have led films to adapt their politics and aesthetics. The hypervisibility mentioned previously may be seen as the flip side of the invisibility that characterized racial and cultural politics earlier in Britain; the burden of representation has now become the spectacle of representation. Mercer (1999–2000, 55) critiques what he calls "excess visibility" in relationship to this link between "corporate internationalism and repressive localism"—the increasing representation of "cultural difference" in a depoliticized, commodified, and narrowly nationalist form. South Asian British and diasporic films are called on to negotiate the growing xenophobia of contemporary racialization processes as they simultaneously contend with a blasé and consuming cosmopolitanism in a post-Empire Britain. Seeking to precariously balance the growing U.S. commercialism with their attention to audiences, diasporic filmmakers are contradictorily and complexly positioned at the nexus of local, national, and transnational forces.

This project interrogates such constructions and shifts in South Asian diasporic cinema. It explores how the multidirectional circulation of cultural products affects the ways in which diasporic cinema and spectatorship are constructed. It pays close attention to which films circulate and why, asking how do the influences of Bollywood and Hollywood cinemas resonate in diasporic cinema? What is the relationship between South Asian diasporic film and Indian cinema? The book seeks to understand how this infrastructure facilitates further filmmaking in the diaspora. With the increase in transnational projects and transactions, filmmakers have greater access to the means of production. Consequently, it is significant to attend to how exactly those means shape and produce certain narratives and representations. It remains to be seen what kinds of expanded networks and formations will develop as diasporic filmmakers operate within global cities and other nodes of diasporas that are supplementary to a national framework. Globalization has already and will increasingly create hypervisibility of certain films; we must ask which films and why. How are they located in certain circuits of circulation and reception? What kinds of transnational imaginary will they produce that coincides, rewrites, and contradicts previous colonial, national, gendered, sexual, and racialized narratives? In this chapter, I have provided a historical overview of the discussions of some of these issues that I will now pursue in the following chapters in more a complex manner.

3

When Indians Play Cowboys: Diaspora and Postcoloniality in Mira Nair's *Mississippi Masala*

> What was initially felt to be a curse—the curse of homelessness or the curse of enforced exile—gets repossessed. It becomes affirmed and is reconstructed as the basis of a privileged standpoint from which certain useful and critical perceptions about the modern world become more likely.
>
> —Paul Gilroy (1993a, 111)

In W. E. B. DuBois's *Dark Princess: A Romance* ([1928] 1995), the radical African-American protagonist Matthew Townes successfully proves himself and the pan-African peoples qualified to join an international movement of the "darker" peoples planning to overthrow white imperialism. Though Orientalist, especially in its gendering of discourses, the novel professes DuBois's complex internationalist, anti-imperialist, antiracist, Marxist politics through the romance between the protagonist and an Indian princess. Only the leader and global voice of this anti-imperialist movement, the princess Kautilya, recognizes the centrality of the African diaspora to the anti-imperial struggle for liberation as she falls in love with Townes. In contrast, the princess' pan-Asian entourage, spouting an antiblack racist rhetoric, promotes an Asian exceptionalism and a wholesale dismissal of blacks. The text focuses not only on the infamous color line between "darker peoples" and whites in the United States and transnationally but also on the racial hierarchies among people of color that impede political anti-imperialist solidarity. Through the romance in the novel, DuBois launches a critique of the "shadow of a color line within a color line" maintained by Indians and other Asians who dismiss the possibility of African and African diasporic contribution and participation in the formation of an internationalist solidarity movement. Townes proves himself capable and resourceful not only as a political comrade but also as a worthy spouse for the princess. His unique contributions are based on his racialized double consciousness and, more important, on his location in the African diaspora as a black proletariat.[1]

In *Dark Princess,* DuBois employs the convention of the global and multiracial heterosexual romance to resolve the racial hierarchies preventing the formation of international alliances necessary for an anti-imperialist internationalist movement. The novel literally couples anti-imperialist movements in

Asia with African-American struggles producing as their offspring the son of Townes and Princess Kautilya—the "Messenger and Messiah to all the Darker Worlds" (p. 311). DuBois is writing against Western white supremacist and colonial discourses that characterize the black and Asian women in deviant or denigrating terms (such as Katherine Mayo's indictment of Indian women in *Mother India*) (Mullen 2003, 223). For DuBois, radical politics are expressed through gendered and sexualized tropes of heterosexual romance and family.

DuBois furthers his query of the role of the African-American proletariat in the internationalist movement against capitalism in a vision that is not Afrocentric but is simultaneously international and nation based. *Dark Princess* presents the African diaspora in the United States as a privileged site of political engagement while suggesting that race needs to be considered in its transnational dimensions and linking the struggles of the black diaspora to those of anti-imperialist Asia.[2] Bill Mullen (2003, 219) writes,

> *Dark Princess* thus stands as a central text of African American discursive engagement with the American, Asian, and international left in this century, and it constitutes a key text for understanding how resistance, particularly to Eurocentric discourses of race, led to the radical recasting of Afro-Asian relationships as central to twentieth-century world revolutionary struggle.

At the end of the century, after the successes and failures of postcolonial independence and civil rights, a South Asian diasporic and Hollywood film also imagines the union of an African-American man and a South Asian woman in relation to the continuing struggles of people of color. About a family exiled from Uganda living in the U.S. South, Mira Nair's *Mississippi Masala* focuses on the daughter Mina who, despite her disapproving community's sense of superiority and racism, falls in love with an African-American man, Demetrius. Exploring the implications of the "shadow of the color line," the film analyzes contemporary South Asian (American) racial identity formations. It makes visible the antiblack racism of South Asians and the overshadowed and invisible racial formation processes of South Asian–Americans themselves. The film explores the ways in which the racialization of (South) Asian-Americans is hidden by U.S. binary discourses of race as black and white, simultaneously producing racial discourses framing South Asians as always foreign and as near-white model minorities. More important, the film, like DuBois's novel, finds resolutions through the interracial heterosexual romance configuring a global racial politics of alliance with the erasure of the black woman. DuBois's novel *Dark Princess* explicitly ends in the South in an attempt to connect to the Africa and Asia it faces, searching continually for connection and inspiration between African diasporic and Asian liberation struggles. In contrast, *Mississippi Masala* detaches itself from Africa and moves away from Mississippi (and the South) to separate the couple from their disapproving communities, offering little connection through liberation struggles in the postcolonial new order. The film closes not in the South facing and reaching toward Africa and Asia but in an empty field, moving into an unmarked America. This uninscribed land (the American range) leads us to question the mobility, trajectory, and destination of the film, especially in contrast to the novel. Although the novel suggests African-American politics in relation to Asian and internationalist movements, the film domesticates the South Asian diasporic into the new multicultural American.

Although *Mississippi Masala* has been discussed extensively by South Asian, Asian-American, and American studies scholars, here, I reframe and probe the issues raised by the film, particularly in the context of South Asian diasporic cultural production and politics. Most readings of *Mississippi Masala* celebrate the romance between Demetrius and Mina as a vehicle to overcome the South Asian antiblack racism that impedes the formation of multicultural alliances. Furthermore, many of the previous discussions of the film frame it as a paragon of a refusal of nationalism and nostalgia. In regard to multicultural alliances, I reexamine the ways in which diasporic politics in the film are sutured through the South Asian migrant woman and the African-American man, specifically regarding the ways romance functions in the film in relation to gender, sexual, and racial normativities. I seek to do more than celebrate that nostalgia and nationalism are refused but also to deconstruct and evaluate the specific modes and strategies of refusal.

The film turns to mobility and the heterosexual mixed-race romance as a resolution to displacement and exclusion. It shifts discourses of diaspora from an emphasis on a return to homeland to a refusal and replacement of the homeland with a desire for westward movement and travel; thus, diaspora as exile is rejected in favor of diaspora as the frontier. I suggest that the specifically American articulation of diaspora as a "home on the range" captures several of the nuances and dangers of this frontier myth or U.S.-domesticated nomadism. Although *Mississippi Masala* challenges the idea of a naturalized habitat in relation to identity and subjectivity, it succumbs to the myth of a "home on the range"—both a western frontier home and a home within constant movement. This narrative of home on the range is grounded therefore in narratives of American exceptionalism, expansion, and imperialism.

Different meanings stem from the use of the term *range* in its various forms: "an extensive area of open land on which livestock (and their cowboys) wander and graze"; "to pass over or through an area or a region"; "to wander freely; roam"; "the geographic region in which a given plant or animal normally lives or grows"; and "the maximum extent or distance limiting operation, action, or effectiveness" (American Heritage Dictionary 1982). Looking at the contradictory meanings, one can see how a home on the range can mean both a nomadic movement and the temporary rootedness of a homeland. The tendency to perceive only the United States as containing the range of possible cultures, peoples, and groups is part of a myopic nationalism that domesticates transnationalism into multiculturalism, formulating America as a microcosm of the global. I foreground these particular issues in seeking to locate this discussion of the film in relation to ongoing conversations in Asian-American, postcolonial, postnational American, and cultural studies.

Discourses of Diaspora and *Mississippi Masala*

> It may be that writers in my position, exiles or emigrants or expatriates, are haunted by some sense of loss, some urge to reclaim, to look back, even at risk of being mutated into pillars of salt. But if we do look back, we must also do so in the knowledge—which gives rise to profound uncertainties—that our physical alienation from India almost inevitably means that we will not be capable of reclaiming precisely the thing that was lost; that we will, in short, create fictions, not actual cities or villages, but invisible ones, imaginary homelands, Indias of the mind.
>
> —Salman Rushdie (1991, 1)

Rushdie muses that the homelands of many first-generation South Asian diasporic writers are often the production of the nostalgic imagination. Many South Asian diasporic films redefine diaspora in relation to and as a challenge to exclusionary Western nationalisms. Echoing the sentiment, "it ain't where you're from, it's where you're at," their works focus primarily on the nation-state of residence and its racial politics. In doing so, they have produced narratives that decouple diaspora from homeland in hope of avoiding essentialist or imaginary narratives of belonging and origins. Therefore, while many South Asian diasporic films depict yearnings for the homeland, it is rarely the protagonist that is depicted as longing nostalgically. These narratives encode diasporic affiliations primarily through the difference of generation, associating nostalgia with middle-age first-generation migrants.[3] Many of Nair's features portray the failure of the postcolonial nation-state, and among these, many focus on the exilic or diasporic displacement.[4]

Nair's contribution to the formation and emergence of South Asian diasporic cinema, especially *Mississippi Masala* and *Monsoon Wedding*, cannot be overstated. With the exception of her first full-length feature *Salaam Bombay!*, her films have been made in the mode of Hollywood cinematic production. Nair reports that it was a struggle to be able to portray the themes of *Mississippi Masala*, diasporic displacement, national identification, interethnic racism, and interracial desire, on Hollywood celluloid and without white leads. Produced with a sizable budget and distributed by the major studio Samuel Goldwyn, the film features Denzel Washington, an African-American male actor with white crossover appeal, in one of its starring roles. Washington was cast opposite first-time actress Sarita Choudhury in this revised multicultural Romeo and Juliet romance to capitalize on his popularity following several Hollywood blockbusters. The film, funded by U.S. and U.K. sources, grossed a modest $7.3 million.

Mississippi Masala opens with Idi Amin's expulsion of Asians, including Mina (Sarita Choudhury) and her parents Jay (Roshan Seth) and Kinnu (Sharmila Tagore), from Uganda in 1972. The prologue introduces Jay being imprisoned for his statements criticizing Amin on the British Broadcasting Corporation (BBC) and subsequently being released because of his African friend Okelo's offerings of bribes. The family's trajectory of exile from Uganda to Britain and then to the U.S. South is cartographically traced on a map during the opening credits. This westward migration locates the family in a small city in Mississippi in the early nineties. Upon exile, Jay, unlike other members of his family, longs for his homeland nation-state of Uganda, pursuing litigation against the Ugandan government to recover his lost home. The homeland metonymically becomes the family house as Jay obsesses about reclaiming his property after his expulsion. Jay, unlike his wife Kinnu and daughter Mina, seems also to carry a sense of bitterness and betrayal in regard to his friend Okelo who saved his life and urged him to leave Uganda. The family suffers downward class mobility because of their expulsion, and in Mississippi they are financially dependent on relatives, living and working in a friend's motel business.

The main portion of the film begins in Mississippi, interweaving Mina's romance with the African-American carpet-cleaning Demetrius (Denzel Washington) with the story of the family's exile through a series of flashbacks. Mina first encounters Demetrius when she inadvertently rear-ends his van at a red light. They meet again later when she is on a date with Harry Patel, a self-satisfied, uptight, and financially successful South Asian–American man whom Mina should apparently be grateful to date because of her lower status in the community. (She has a lower status because she is dark and poor. The film highlights the class status of Kinnu's family who are looked down on because of their business—a liquor store whose clientele are African-Americans.) At the nightclub, Demetrius flirts with Mina to make an ex-girlfriend jealous; despite knowing this, Mina is intrigued and becomes interested in him. Both Demetrius and his friend Tyrone profess an Orientalist attraction for Mina seeing her as exotic and erotic. Mina and Demetrius become involved soon after. South Asian antiblack racism raises its ugly head when the relationship is discovered; the African-American community, despite their Orientalism, in general, is pictured in a more favorable light. Demetrius and Mina are censured by their communities, the former for getting involved with the foreigners and the latter for crossing the color line and dishonoring the family. Consequently Demetrius, perceived by whites as a trouble-making uppity black man who does not know his place, loses many customers and becomes at risk for foreclosure by the bank. Meanwhile, Jay receives notice of his court date in Kampala and returns to manage his case regarding his illegal expulsion and loss of property. Although Kinnu and Mina initially acquiesce to this desire for return, Mina changes her mind and pursues Demetrius, challenging him to let her join him in his business and life. The film closes with Jay in Kampala, having discovered the death of his friend

Okelo and now resolved to return to the United States, and more important to Kinnu, thus forgoing a return to the homeland. Similarly, Mina and Demetrius reconcile, willing to see what the future brings them.

As I discussed earlier, a resurgence of academic scholarship and cultural production in the nineties questioned the relationship between place and subjectivity in seeking to deconstruct the organic connection between race, culture, and nation. The film pursues this line of inquiry in dissecting the valorization of national belonging and the subsequent nostalgia engendered by displacement; it also exposes how the nation and diaspora are consequently gendered and racialized. In *Mississippi Masala,* originally titled *Twice Removed* (Gerstel 6G), the diasporic homeland refers not to South Asia but rather to Uganda. Defying expectations, Mina is an Ugandan-born woman of South Asian descent who has never been to India, and Demetrius is an African-American man who has never been to Africa. This disassociation prevents any simple constructions of essentialist belonging, thus problematizing the ethnonational terms of identity within the film because Mina and her family "originate" not from the expected homeland but from Demetrius's supposed homeland. The notion of a "native" is always attached to the idea of place in what is supposedly an organic and autochthonous relation. The mobility and displacement of diasporas (the African resulting from slavery here linked with the South Asian resulting from colonialism and later forced political exile) create spaces critical of nationalisms and racialized notions of authenticity and purity. The alternative title *Twice Removed* not only evokes issues of national belonging and the convoluted trajectories of diasporic displacement but also the dependency of national narratives on tropes of the family (motherland, fatherland, patria, etc.). This title emphasizes how the film exposes and interrupts the frequent employment of family both metonymically and metaphorically to describe and constitute the naturalized, racialized, heteronormative, and gendered relationships between identity and place in articulations of the territorial nation-state. Liisa Malkki (1992) convincingly argues that the botanical tropes often used to evoke ethnonational identities are seen in the link between family, origin, nation, and land.

Anne McClintock (1995) points out that the trope of the nation as family uses a gendered framework of configuring national belonging while naturalizing those gendered, sexual, and familial relations as ahistorical and natural. It is specifically the gendered and generational desires of Jay, rather than of Mina or Kinnu, that are linked to the material and political sphere of nation-state and citizenship that is held up for questioning in the film. Jay's diasporic and masculine nationalism is counterposed to the domestic and cultural femininity of his wife Kinnu, who invests not in the nation but in familial and financial needs. The film reveals and plays with how the nation-state, both postcolonial Uganda and multicultural America, imagines itself as a racialized, heteronormative, and gendered set of families. The nation's imaginings are gendered with the men bonded in a fraternity, one to which Asian men belong as cousins twice removed and Asian women belong contracted through marriage.[5] This construction of fraternity incorporates an understanding of the ways in which the nation is imagined as a fraternity of men, but more specifically, men who are normatively constructed as heads of households consisting of racially homogenous heterosexual families in which the men are affiliated with the nation-state and women with culture. In the film, Kinnu's affiliations and desires contrast to Jay's, whose longings are for Uganda. Pining for both property and citizenship, Jay's vision of home contrasts with that of Kinnu, who fosters and cultivates a different sense of home, one that is deterritorialized and fluid in diaspora.

Kinnu's lack of affiliation suggests a gendered critique of and disenfranchisement from the nation-state. In the prologue of the film, Kinnu is forced off the bus carrying the departing Asians to the airport and is searched by African Ugandan soldiers.[6] In her baggage Kinnu carries a tape of Hindi film music and a framed photo of Jay in his professional barrister's garb (signifying class position and participation in a classed and colonial political system), symbols of her cultural and familial pleasure and desire. The soldier laughs at the toothless totems. The first totem is music, specifically, the Hindi film song quintessentially associated with diaspora—*Mera Joota Hai Japani:*

> Mera joota hai Japani
> Yé pantalon Inglistani
> Sar pé lal topi Rusi
> Phir bhi dil hai Hindustani.

> Translated as: [My shoes are Japanese
> These pants are English
> On my head a red Russian hat
> But my heart is Indian, for all of that.]

Testifying to Kinnu's Hindustani heart housed in her portable body, the song indicates the proper construction of the Indian diaspora that maintains its deterritorialized cultural and national affiliation. It formulates India as constant, embodied, and portable—the essentialist construction that Rushdie writes against. In this scene, we also can see that not only are diasporic imaginative processes gendered but also that they are performative.[7] Specifically, it is Kinnu's, rather than Jay's, performances that are associated with ethnicity and culture (e.g., carrying music as well as singing hymns and wedding songs) that appear throughout the film. Throughout the film, Kinnu can be read as negotiating through her desires and performances the national contestations that are mapped across her body.

Later in this same scene, the soldier uses his weapon to tear off what appears to be Kinnu's mangal sutra, a necklace symbolizing her marriage and "Indianness" (see Figure 3.1). The scene illustrates the positioning of Asian women in contestations over the multiracial in postcolonial Uganda. Here, the sexual and violent threat of the African male metonymically violates the "purity" of the

Fig. 3.1 Soldier tearing off Kinnu's mangal sutra in *Mississippi Masala*.

Asian bourgeois family. This threat reflects anxieties regarding Asians' social and cultural separation from Africans across the racial, class, and gender divide established by colonial rule and persisting into postcolonial independence. The portrayal evokes a masculine and sexually dangerous African nation-state that is threatening to the vulnerable Asian and feminine racial minority, a violation of the fraternity of the nation—one that is particularly significant to the film.

Race, Gender, and Sexuality: The Family Romance of the Postcolonial Nation

> If the importance of culture rather than biology is the first quality which marks this form of racism as something different and new, the special ties it discovers between race, culture and nation provide further evidence of its novelty.... The family remains a key motif but the multiracial family of nations has been displaced by the racially homogenous nation of families. The nation is composed of even, symmetrical family units.... The emphasis on culture allows nation and race to fuse. Nationalism and racism become so closely identified that to speak of the nation is to speak automatically in racially exclusive terms.
>
> —Paul Gilroy

The force behind the family's "removal" to the United States, via Britain, is Idi Amin's expulsion of approximately 50,000 Asians from Uganda within a three-month period in 1972. Within the film, Idi Amin's postcolonial Uganda illustrates the failures of the multiracial nation-state. Amin's expulsion produces a monoracial national narrative justified, ironically, by the failure of Asians to integrate into the gendered Ugandan nation. The film does not delve into the complex history of British colonialism leading to the presence and expulsion of Asians in East Africa (Uganda, Kenya, and Tanzania) nor into the transnational and colonial racial formations of Asians that lead to the production of the shadow of the color line between Asians and Africans.[8] The failure of the multiracial nation-state leading to the expulsion of Asians remains unexplained in relation to its colonial history in the film, therefore unwittingly, as I argue later, forwarding an American exceptionalism in the possible formation of a multicultural society.

The British colonial system relegated Africans to the bottom of the socioeconomic and cultural hierarchy, placing the heterogeneous Asian groups in mediating middle but precarious layers, creating a racialized bourgeois class that was encouraged to identify not with the indigenous people but with the British. Internalizing colonial relations, many Asians frequently remained socially isolated from Africans, as well as socially isolated among themselves along caste and religious differences.[9] The film notes this presence of South Asian antiblack racism and chromatism (differentiation based on a privileging of lighter skin) as markers of difference in South Asian diasporic communities in Uganda and the United States. In Uganda, the bourgeois and petty bourgeois Asians with British citizenship were positioned as wealthy outsiders in opposition to the Africans, a positioning that led to social friction and ethnocentric feelings of superiority over the Africans who were thought to lack social and cultural values. Robin Cohen (1997, 103) writes that this racial formation of Asians favors colonial powers:

> The dominant elite (colonialists or Africans in power) of the dominant group uses the middleman minority to foster economic development, but turns it into a scapegoat when things go wrong. The subordinate group benefits from the services the middlemen provide, but sees them as competitors or "future-oriented sojourners" who owe no fealty to their society of displacement.

Asians in British Africa were enmeshed in an implicitly colonialist racial hierarchy that became inverted with national independence.

Independence brought the necessity of recasting the socioeconomic and political order in Uganda. Agehananda Bharati (1972) suggests that as postcolonial independence approached, many Asians supported African nationalist movements while nevertheless recognizing their own precarious position as a minority in the changing political climate. In the film, Jay counters African nationalist constructions of Uganda as monoracial, rather than multiracial, with the statement that Uganda is his home and that he has been and is "African first, Indian second" even in the face of censure from other Indians. Many Asians attempted to negotiate political representation for themselves in the newly forming governments, committing their lives as Ugandan citizens.[10] For example, in Tanganyika, Asians attempted to forge a multiracial society in which power was divided into thirds among Europeans, Asians, and Africans (with Africans comprising 98% of the population) (Tandon 1970, 84–85). However, some Asians distrusted the local economic situation and invested their money overseas, often in British banks to which they had access as former British Commonwealth members. Although Asians remained integral to the economy, simple assimilation through naturalization or citizenship was seen as insufficient. The uneven distribution of representation and resources was targeted by African nationalists in the name of forming a socialist state (Ramchandani 1974, 252–54).

It is important to note that the shots in the film that depict Jay inwardly reflecting on Uganda spatially locate him in imperial poses as he usually appears on a hillside looking down surveying the land or is located within his property's compound separated from the street and nameless blacks by walls. After his conversation with Okelo, Jay nobly and tragically stands on his backyard terrace overlooking his domain. The camera zooms out to survey the panorama of Kampala's fertile fields and Lake Victoria from his elevated position. The point of view reflects a gaze with which Jay surveys "his" land—a gaze that indicates class and racial privilege and also loss. In this tragic moment before exile, Jay's own privileged class status as a part of the postcolonial legal system is overwritten by his ethnic oppression. Throughout the film, Jay's class and ethnic position are suggested visually, especially in the contrast between the beautiful home and compound and the dangerous and deadly street. Nostalgia is depicted in the imperialist terms of dominant cinema. Jay mourns not only the loss of his home (property) and country (cultural and state citizenship) but also the "innocent" friendship of his youth with Okelo (national fraternity). Jay's flashbacks counterpose bathing and playing in a stream with Okelo with their later arguments about the fate of Uganda. In addition, Jay's action against the state is the denunciation of Amin on BBC, and thus to the former colonizers. Because we have also seen the photography of Jay proudly garbed in his British legal gown, his critique of the postcolonial nation-state to the former colonizers indicates an ambiguous relationship with the British colonial system and state.

African resentment was not directed only at the upper-class Asians who controlled approximately 20 percent of the gross domestic product (the per capita income of Asians was approximately twenty-five times that of Africans) (Ramchandani 1974, 240–41). Economic, social, and political disparities caused greater tensions for all Asians whose presence was associated with British rule. In the case of postcolonial Uganda, the Asians became scapegoats of fascist African leaders who masqueraded racial policies as indigenization acts, seizing only the property of Asians in the name of creating a socialist state. As conditions became more unstable within the state, nationalist rhetoric of racial homogenization asserting that "Africa is for Africans, black Africans" (Okelo in *Mississippi Masala*) increased. Amin employed further drastic measures including the scapegoating of Asians in the wake of his own failing popularity. The deaths and

disappearances of an estimated 80,000 (primarily African) Ugandans also occurred under Amin during 1971–72 (Ramchandani 1974, 272). In the film, these
deaths are evoked by the disappearance and presumed murder of Okelo soon
after the departure of Jay, Kinnu, and Mina.

Mississippi Masala does little to portray this racial hierarchy and economic
disparity or the failure of the multiracial nation-state as a legacy of colonialism.
Instead, we see the expulsion of Asians from Uganda linked to South Asian–
American antiblack racism, locating the latter as an essentialized and ahistorical
antiblack racism rather than as a produced and constituted by the transnational
circulation and mobility of racial formation due to migration.[11] (Nair herself
appears in a cameo role to comment on the color prejudice or chromatism
within South Asian–American communities. Gossiping about Mina and the
prized male "catch" in the community, she says, "You can be dark and have
money, or you can be fair and have no money. But you can't be dark and have no
money *and* expect to get Harry Patel." This tidbit of gossip succinctly identifies
the complex intersections of class, gender, and color within Indian-American
communities.)

Demetrius labels Jay's objections to his relationship with Mina as racism by
stating, "I know that you and your folks can come down here from God knows
where, and be about as black as the ace of spades, and as soon as you get here you
start acting white—and treatin' us like we your doormats." Demetrius criticizes
the assertion of Indian-American antiblack racism, racial superiority, and white
identification.[12] He does not identify Jay's racial discrimination and privilege in
relation to class or colonialism. But nevertheless, professional-class South Asian
diasporans, whose high incomes make Indian-Americans the second wealthiest
ethnic group in the United States, often distance themselves by race and class
from blacks and other people of color. Jay argues that his detachment results
not from racial and class "prejudice" but from his previous affiliations to and
experiences in the homeland, specifically his friendship with Okelo. In other
words, Jay frames his rejection of Demetrius not as white identification but as the
"betrayal" of Okelo and the subsequent futility of racial solidarity and the failure
of the multicultural nation-state. (Kinnu, on the other hand, does not participate
to the same degree in this racism and classism. In Uganda, her feelings for Okelo
are ambiguous only in the sense that they sometimes appear intimate. In the
United States, she runs a liquor store alone in an African-American part of town.)
Jay's explanation to Demetrius clarifies that he is "protecting" his daughter,
not because South Asian men are restrictive and oppressive but because of his
own experiences of expulsion and exile: "I tried to change the world and be
different. But the world is not so quick to change. Mina is my only child. I don't
want her to go through the same struggle that I did." In response, Demetrius
incredulously remarks on Jay's refusal to acknowledge the parallel histories
of slavery and racism in the United States and colonialism and independence
in Uganda: "Struggle? Look, I'm a black man born and raised in Mississippi.
There ain't a damn thing you can tell me about struggle." Demetrius and Jay's

interaction addresses how the shadow of the color line operates bilaterally—Demetrius indicating in one direction how South Asian isolation and seclusion maintains a superiority based on racial hierarchies, and in the other direction, Jay noting how South Asian racial processes are overshadowed and how South Asians are erased from the nation.

This dialogue occurs between Jay and Demetrius in regard to Mina and her intimate involvement with Demetrius. It is significant that Demetrius comes to speak with Jay (rather than Kinnu) and that Jay effectively refuses Demetrius access to Mina. This exchange echoes earlier Ugandan discourses presented in the film. As further justification for the expulsion of Asians, Amin turned to the gendered and racialized discourse of intermarriage and complained about African men's lack of access to Asian women. In a 1971 speech, Amin declared,

> It is particularly painful in that about seventy years have elapsed since the first Asians came to Uganda, but, despite the length of time, the Asian community has lived in a world of its own to the extent that the Africans in this country have, for example, hardly been able to marry Asian girls. (Ramchandani 1974, 276)

The Asian woman was significant to the national narrative in that the new Ugandan national citizen was configured as an African man, and Asian endogamy was seen as an impediment to the integration of the Asian (man) into the postcolonial nation-state. In fact, Asian women were part of the terrain on which the discourse of multiracial citizenship was negotiated through the idea of "having access to their women." This configuration subordinated Asian and African women to men within patriarchal nationalisms. Consequently, the new nation is imagined through the multiracial heterosexual couple of an African man and newly accessible Asian woman.[13]

This reconfigured multiracial alliance of families is asserted through the trope of the interracial heterosexual romance. The film links the formation of Mina's U.S. adult desire and sexuality with this nationalist discourse through a series of flashbacks of her childhood in Uganda juxtaposed with her sexual liaison with Demetrius in Greenwood. In the setup, Demetrius and Mina spend the night together on the eve of Mina's birthday. The following morning, she asks him to wish her a happy birthday and he sings to her, as she lies cradled in his arms. The film cuts to a flashback of Mina's childhood birthday celebration in which a televised speech by Idi Amin disrupts the festivities. The film features actual footage of Amin's televised speech in which he states that he has dreamed Asians must be expelled from Uganda immediately:

> "The Asians come to Uganda to build the railways; the railway is finished—they must leave now. I will give them ninety days to pack up and go. Asians have milked the cow but not fed it. Africans are poor. Asians are rich. Asians are sabotaging the economy of Uganda. *They have refused to allow their daughters to marry Africans.* They have been here for 70 years."
>
> —*Mississippi Masala*

The younger Mina runs out onto the terrace, devastated with the redirection of the family's attention to the television broadcast. Jay follows her to the terrace where he too cradles her in his arms and sings happy birthday to her. The film cuts to another flashback, this time depicting young Mina innocently playing in the yard until she comes upon a dead African man's body covered in maggots outside her gate (warning of political racial and gendered danger lurking just outside of the bourgeois family home). The film then returns to the present in which Mina awakens from her "dreams." In the context of Uganda and the United States, the interracial heterosexual romance's function is to resolve complex class-stratified and gendered racial hierarchies and the problematic of diasporic displacement.

This scene indicates that Mina and Demetrius's union functions to resolve many of the disjunctures from her childhood in Kampala, especially her movement out of the family compound into the dangerous streets where she may encounter black men's bodies. Her involvement with Demetrius indicates the reopening of possibilities that have been foreclosed in postcolonial Uganda in the colonially overdetermined relationships between Asians and Africans. By interweaving these scenes, the film suggests that Mina's relationship with Demetrius is part of a process of remembering, restructuring, and healing from the colonial legacy of racial hierarchy experienced through gender. Rather than implying that the romance signifies the fulfillment of Amin's scapegoating desires, the film sets up the personal desires and romance as a fulfillment of the political possibilities of multiracial allies. The narrative turns to romance as the solution to the situation of racism in the United States and the history of colonial and postcolonial relations in Africa and as the site of reconciliation of interracial injustices. Furthermore, it suggests that these hybridities, alliances, and mixings are possible (only) within the space of the United States.

Multicultural Gendered Resolutions: Domesticating the Transnational

> Good girls go to heaven; bad girls go everywhere.
> —bumper sticker

In the United States, the trope of the interracial heterosexual romance operates within the national cultural logic of multiculturalism. In the film, the proper corrective to the failure of multiracial Uganda proves to be the exceptional multiculturalism of the United States. Although the film presents identities that are complexly related to place and time, it envisions multicultural racial politics as adequate engagements with the issues of migration, transnationality, and indigeneity. I interrogate the seductive possibilities and limitations of articulating South Asian diasporic racial politics and identities in a vocabulary that resembles and is based on a construction of African-Americanness as authentic, stable, and American, whereby African-American politics are presented as an established and reified site of identification for all racialized Americans inadequately.

Before returning to the film I want to clarify that I am neither arguing against interracial relationships nor against multiracial solidarities and alliances. The relationship in the film indicates, at some level, the possibilities of the social gendered and sexual politics of South Asian communities that go beyond easy lip service to racial solidarities or multicultural alliances as declared by a relative of the family to Demetrius and Tyrone to avoid litigation: "Black, brown, yellow, Mexican, Puerto Rican, all the same. As long as you are not white, means you are colored. United we stand and divided we fall." (Missing in this evocation is a reference to the "red Indian" or indigenous.) Here, the film asserts that the recognition of racial identity in the name of multiculturalism is sufficient and inclusive politics in the United States; it does not acknowledge how multicultural alliances based on race do not necessarily account for the politics of sovereignty and land that are often the basis of indigenous politics, a point to which I will return.

The relationship between Mina and Demetrius addresses the very political nature of intimate relations; in other words, the film suggests that the politics of alliance are located in the intimate details and relations of everyday practices. However, it is important not to simply celebrate such alliances and unions but instead to probe the consequences and investments of such narrative resolutions, especially ones that suggest alliance in the name of sameness and unity. In *Dark Princess,* DuBois ([1928] 1995) also employs the exotic Asian to forge global racial politics. Mullen (2003, 219) comments that the novel "reveals how DuBois's conception of orientalism was wedded to a patriarchal or paternal ideology inflected by conteporary debates about female subalterns in United States and India in particular, and by DuBois's own romantic conceptions of the Asiatic." However, unlike the novel that effectively internationalizes African-American politics, inserting it into conversation with anti-imperialist struggles, *Mississippi Masala* seems to do the opposite—it domesticates diasporic and transnational politics in the name of antiracist U.S. multiculturalism. Furthermore, it does so through asserting a gendered heteronormative narrative that erases other politics and subjects, such as the African woman. In doing so, it erases the connections between U.S. imperialist racism and colonialism.

The film asserts the necessity of South Asians claiming American racial identity and multicultural solidarity by having Mina choose to be with Demetrius. Overcoming South Asian antiblack racism is made possible only by becoming American, which for South Asian migrant women means becoming sexual. In doing so, *Mississippi Masala* highlights how Indian-Americans are inserted into a classed racial classification, which is based on a polarized black and white binary inadequate for understanding the position of Asians who often experience shifting, flexible, and sometimes contradictory racialization processes.[14] The antiracist response to this racialization is often the assertion that South Asians have misidentified with whites and should properly realign themselves as people of color with African-Americans. However, in Asian-American studies, South

Asians are seen as racially aligned in a pan-ethnic political strategy by scholars such as Yen Le Espiritu (1992). Yet some South Asian–American studies scholars have noted the racialization difference between South Asians and other Asian-Americans. Moreover, South Asians are often positioned as either black or white in the dominant binary that structures conceptions of U.S. racial identities.

Within the dominant national imaginary, Asian-Americans are perpetually cast as foreigners or unassimilable aliens, or in contrast, they are positioned as model minorities, those paragons of whiteness and achievement that still deny them access to claims of cultural citizenship. Thus, despite narratives of immigration that emphasize assimilation and incorporation, the racialization processes of Asian-Americans continually mark them as not belonging, as suspended between departure and arrival, or in the words of David Eng (1997 and 2001), "out here and over there."[15] Because of this exclusion, Asian-Americans are positioned in relation to the necessity of claiming national belonging through a cultural nationalism and the necessity of multiculturalism. In addition, Asian-American scholars have been wary of theoretical frameworks that emphasize diaspora, transnationality, and "denationalization."[16] Hence, scholars such as Robert Lee celebrate the conclusion of the narrative as it returns Jay to Kinnu and Mina to Demetrius in the United States to forge multicultural alliances and resolve the problematics of exile, foreclosing the necessity of transnationality and local engagements.

Mina's relationship with Demetrius functions in the film not only as the resolution of historical racial conflict but also as the process of Americanization and racial and cultural identity formation through a subsuming of the transnational migrant woman's narrative by the narrative of multicultural romance and American solidarity. The film forcefully suggests the necessity of alliances between people of color. But my concern is with the teleological emphasis on Mina's "true" position at the "side" of African-Americans and the implied domesticated heteronormative politics of racial solidarity. Here, as in the film, it is an emphasis on Mina's insertion into racial U.S. politics always and already configured as domestic African-American (male) politics.

Gilroy (1993a, 194) writes, "These crises (of home and displacement) are most intensely lived in the area of gender relations where the symbolic reconstruction of community is projected onto an image of the ideal heterosexual couple." Here, the heterosexual relationship is not metonymic for the reconstruction of each of the ethnic communities but rather is thought to indicate the potential of interracial alliances and multicultural nations configured as separate from specific communities. Mina must leave the South Asian diasporic community (as does Demetrius though for different reasons) because her political identity must be articulated in multicultural American terms. Both the African-American and South Asian–American communities are represented as oppressive societies that prevent transracial harmony. However, it is the South Asian–American community's sexually repressed misogyny, antiblack racism, and false commitment to multiracial solidarity that must be overcome to achieve an American identity. The process of "becoming American" (necessary only of course for Asian-Americans) in the film involves separation from the oppressive and repressive community of South Asians and the formation of a heterosexual family unit. Mina's coming of age in America evokes a standard American narrative of becoming sexually active (in the face of generational and cultural disapproval) and freed from her inherently oppressive community. Initiation into America is a racialized and gendered sexual rite of passage. The film constructs a gendered narrative that replicates the logic of the bumper sticker (good girls go to heaven; bad girls go everywhere), arguing that sexual activity (especially with African-American men) mobilizes and nationalizes migrant women.

Demetrius and Mina's romance configures the proper heteronormative relationship in contrast to the other "undesirable" heterosexual relationships that prove less ideal sexually and economically. For example, stereotypes of the hypersexualized black Jezebel and the frigid tradition-bound South Asian woman are opposed to the desirability of Mina. First, *Mississippi Masala* vilifies the African-American woman who is depicted as a scheming and greedy Sapphire ready to jettison her man in her climb to the top. In contrast, Mina is the eager partner for Demetrius, ready to clean bathrooms and carpets. Second, scattered throughout the film for humorous effect are scenes of Anil's attempts to consummate his supposedly arranged marriage with his wife. One such scene is spliced into a scene of Demetrius and Mina engaging in phone sex. Mina, the mobilized exciting "bad" girl, is juxtaposed against Anil's wife, a traditional "good" girl, who is depicted as the nonsexual and repressed domestic South Asian woman. Anil (the effeminate, undesirable, and inassimilable Indian man) and his nameless new bride (the desirable, passive, and silent Indian woman) play the counterpoint to Demetrius (the clean-cut sexual black man) and Mina (the exotic and erotic hybrid).

Mississippi Masala offers the possibility of the heterosexual couple as a site of resolution to the conundrum of national belonging, not only through Mina and Demetrius but also partially through Jay and Kinnu who are "spiritually" reunited in a liquor store. In a subplot of the movie, Mina's father pines for Uganda and mourns his broken friendship with Okelo.[17] At the end of the film, Jay returns to Kampala to reconcile with Okelo and to reclaim his property. He arrives only to find that his friend had been politically executed many years ago. The film then cuts to his wife's liquor store where she reads a letter saying that he is returning "home" to her (the final words of the film "home is where the heart is; and my heart is with you"). In response to the difficult questions raised by the film on diasporic displacement and exile, the narrative resorts to clichés struggling to provide closure within a Hollywood formula. The definition of home has been overtly complicated and deconstructed in the film, and, the cliché marks the inability of resolution to be represented and contained within the Hollywood romance. Jay's longing for the nation as home has now been successfully rerooted and rerouted to the family, that is, Kinnu, who culturally and physically embodies a deterritorialized nation and negotiated citizenship. The heteronormative family in this Hollywood romance solves the conundrum of masculine exile.

The resolution to a diasporic predicament of homelessness or dislocation is both heterosexual and entrepreneurial. Robert Lee (1999, 230) characterizes the ending as "a utopian resolution [which] can only be imagined on the basis of a class struggle through a materialist engagement with history." The ending is more ambivalent and problematic than utopian. Following the logic of a multicultural nationalism that is compatible with global capitalism, the film closes with a Hollywood marriage of romance and entrepreneurship in connection to Kinnu's liquor store and Demetrius's carpet-cleaning business. In both cases, it is the heterosexual couple that provides the labor for economic survival. The film celebrates the "liberation" of self-employment in the service industry along with the interracial coupling, folding the ambivalence of economic disenfranchisement into the "happy" ending. Nevertheless, the independence associated with achieving the American dream is in sharp contrast to the incorporation of the Third World woman into the global economy as fresh labor, cleaning bathrooms and shampooing carpets. The multiracial couple of Mina and Demetrius represents the self-selected and regenerative nation, a multicultural nation in which the interracial couple as family business is the new model.

One more consequence of significance here is the erasure of the African woman. Both film and novel erase her presence and the possibilities of certain feminist politics. (In *Dark Princess*, DuBois ([1928] 1995) conflates his celebration of mother Africa with the Orientalized exotic Asian in the figure of the princess.) The film closes with a gesture that reimagines the national and the transnational through the multicultural alliance, but it attempts to do so by severing Africa from African diasporic politics and the erasure of the African(/)American woman and feminist alliances. In the film, she appears briefly as a dancing spectacle signifying a "global." The final scenes of the film prior to the credits are of Jay standing in the street amidst a crowd and holding a Ugandan child while watching a Ugandan woman dance. The audience gazes, through Jay's perspective, at her black body which is surrounded by African men, dancing in the streets of Kampala. The Ugandan woman is another exotic spectacle, like Mina, to be consumed—an authentic and primitive speechless body. The film's romanticization of the African woman reduces her to a ludic and silent but reproductive body (we assume that the child is hers), outside of the film's narrative of history and politics. She has been absent from representations of the history of postcolonial Uganda and only emerges here as a celebration of the union of Demetrius and Mina and Jay's return to Kinnu. And Jay, swaying to the beat of the drums, holding an African child foreshadowing the coming of his own messianic grandchild and fostering a new multiracial and global family, becomes a sign of hope for renewal and newly reforged reconciliation and connection in his own appreciative gaze of the African woman. The film dangerously evokes and erases African (indigenous) women who are not mobilized by capital to the developed countries, who function as silent representations of authentic culture for the tourist and traveling camera, and who are perhaps most vulnerable to the neocolonial economic and political forces of globalization.

Multiculturalism and Hollywood

> Because we live in a world that is now global in terms of media, in terms of production. We now see India, Africa on our TV. People are ready to talk about multiculturalism. Whereas before, Africa and India were something "out there."
> —Mary Vasudeva (Bahri and Vasudeva 1996, 81)

The presence of a film almost entirely about people of color made by a South Asian woman director in Hollywood is remarkable and historical in and of itself. However, it is important to ask what enables such a film in the first place and what investment there is by Hollywood in bringing such a film to theaters. I want to consider how such a film participates in the immediate translation of the idea that "we now live in a world that is global" into a readiness "to talk about multiculturalism." The idea of Africa and India as no longer out there but located here in the United States illustrates the domesticating tendency of U.S. multiculturalism that forwards that "we are the world." This containing and totalizing concept relies on the idea of representative politics that underlies a noncritical multiculturalism in its most benign form, marketing cultural diversity as classifiable and consumable commodities for white normative American viewers.[18] Attention to the role of diasporic intellectuals and cultural production in this slippage is eminently significant.[19] In "We Are Not the World," George Yudice (1992, 202) remarks that he is uneasy "whenever the impulse to recognize the diversity that constitutes the United States overshoots its mark and self-servedly celebrates 'American' multiculturalism as isomorphic with the world." The call for recent migrants to stand as representatives of ethnic minorities within multiculturalism and of global constituencies stems from internal U.S. identity politics. In this section, I consider how the film participates in this logic in its presentation of culture and positioning of audience.

Scholars like Robert Lee and Gwendolyn Foster who compare *Mississippi Masala* with independent features position the film as a radical text challenging hegemonic constructions of racial identity, interracial desire, and male gaze and subjectivity, especially because it features few white characters. However, closer examination of *Mississippi Masala* might suggest that these readings ignore the context of production and the racial identifications constructed by the film, more specifically the multiple possibilities of white identification. Foster (1997, 126) says that the film is an antiracist diasporic text that criticizes the white supremacy and bigotry of the South, therefore delivering "fresh images of people of color and critical images of whiteness." Although I agree that a critique of racism is central to the film, there are multiple constructions of whiteness that operate in relation to the film. The construction of whiteness as white supremacy does little to displace or challenge the liberal white viewer of multicultural texts such as *Mississippi Masala*. The "critical images of whiteness" are particularly of white bigotry and ignorance, which I argue may not be read as challenging liberal white normativity. Foster (1997, 124) further comments that "the few incidences in *Mississippi Masala* that include white presence depict white Southern folks as mean-spirited, stingy, racist, or stupid in a manner that is designed as a visual shorthand of whiteness that is constructed for the pleasure of Black and Brown spectatorship." Although I agree that black and brown spectators appreciate the humorous portrayal of whiteness, I posit that whiteness is not monolithic, so that it is not only people of color who receive pleasure from the portrayal of Southern white racism. Laughing at the remark "I wish they'd go back to their reservation" about Mina and her family, the culturally aware white audience positions itself as transcending racism, here constructed simply as ignorance.

Addressing U.S. racist national narratives through its setting, particularly Greenwood, Mississippi, the film metonymically identifies racism only as white supremacy and bigotry located in the South. The South in this film, as in other American popular culture works, contains racism. The South functions as a metonym for racist imaginings of America; therefore, it evokes a caricatured national narrative to distance, contain, and dismiss racism. For example, the film depicts the white loan officer as a caricatured "good ole boy" without implying any such systemic or structural racism in other parts of the United States. Racism, although represented as institutional (represented by a loan officer) and individual (represented by the "redneck" Southerners), is nevertheless entirely disconnected from the white liberal viewer who is neither involved nor implicated as a racist. The film only marks whiteness as white supremacy, leaving dominant white liberal normativity unmarked and in place. The film's setting allows white spectators to not identify with the Southern whites whom they read as rural rednecks different from themselves, therefore allowing them to suture their identification processes with the characters of color. This permits a liberal white audience in a nonalienated spectatorship to appreciate the colorful addition of inoffensive and empathetic racial minorities to the American landscape of their imagination without having to rewrite the hegemony of white privilege.

In *Mississippi Masala*, white normativity also remains unchallenged by difference that is constructed as consumable hybridity. The Hollywood multicultural mode of production, distribution, and consumption clearly relies on the circulation and commodification of hybridity within globalization, in which hybridity becomes an appealing mix of cultures that can be packaged and sold (like the movie soundtrack advertised at the beginning of the video). "The whole film is a masala involving several different countries, actors of three nations, and colliding communities. This mixture is reflected in the accents, the politics, the

clothes people wear, the cars they drive, and especially in the blending of traditions within the music. As the movie travels from Uganda to Mississippi and back
again, the music makes a similar journey in cultural rhythms" (CD liner notes
for soundtrack, Nair 1992). Diasporic hybridity in the film is also an individual
ontology or identity—Mina as a self-identified hot and spicy masala (mixture)
rather than as a situated strategic discourse or collective cultural production.[20]
In this case, Mina identifies herself as a masala to make herself attractive and desirable to Demetrius. Although she attempts to relay the historical processes that
render her a masala, ultimately it is her sexual desirability and consumability
that is significant to the film's narrative. This resonates with the casting of Sarita
Choudhury in that the film capitalizes on presenting and selling Choudhury
(and Denzel Washington) as hot and spicy. The viewer's introduction to the
adult Mina is through the image of her hair, which appears as a curtain of long
black tresses that is lifted to unveil her face. In addition, even though Demetrius
chastises Tyrone for objectifying and leering at Mina, the audience sees images
of Mina's sexual activity, replicating the gaze of Orientalist soft pornography.
In one scene, shot in golden orange filters, the camera pans up Mina's naked
legs and hips, fragmenting her body, as she talks to Demetrius on the phone.
The film reviews reveal this consumption of the Orientalized cultural difference: Vincent Canby (1992), the venerable *New York Times* film critic, remarks
that it is Choudhury's "voluptuous presence [that] defines the urgency of the
love affair." It is precisely this eroticizing and exotification of ethnic masala and
hybridity that is at stake in the politics of cultural consumption.

This is not to suggest that Mina's self-identification as masala is not a political
act. Masala has become a powerful and popular metaphor of the South Asian
diaspora to describe hybrid identities and subjectivities. As a constantly varying mixture of spices, masala (as opposed to the British concoction curry) may
make visible its own culturally and historically contextual construction while
attempting to challenge essentialist notions of purity and stasis. However, the
metaphor of masala particularly evokes consumable commodities with their
own hot and spicy (post)colonial history. The desire for tasty, easily swallowed,
apolitical global-cultural morsels or the increasing consumption in the dominant public culture of specifically South Asian diasporic hybridity is a feature of
American (and European) Orientalism that rises in popularity periodically, and
in this case partially undermines Mina's self-naming. Although the film predates
this popularity of Indo-chic literature, fashion, and food, it is still possible to
examine the production and consumption of these phenomena embedded in
racist and sexist political economies, particularly in those packaging the India
"out there" as "over here." The specific consumption of *Mississippi Masala* is
contradictory. In many ways, it challenges (white) normative viewers to imagine nonwhite worlds (Uganda, India, and even Mississippi) that appear ever
so distant, and yet, it also presents such worlds for cross-cultural consumption as familiar and nonthreatening locales. *Mississippi Masala* as a Hollywood

production produces diasporic hybridity as a form of myopic and domesticated multiculturalism that presents the local United States as a microcosm of the global, as a unique multiracial society, as a nation of nations. Hollywood as a global cinema means not just the circulation of U.S. films transnationally but also the representation of the global for U.S. consumption.

Travel, Nomadism, and Westward Wandering

> The nomad is literally a "space" traveller, successively constructing and demolishing her/his living spaces before moving on. S/he functions in a pattern of repetitions which is not without order, though it has no ultimate destination. The opposite of the tourist, the antithesis of the migrant, the nomadic traveller is uniquely bent upon the act of going, the passing through.
>
> —Rosi Braidotti (2000, Web page)

Although I already have discussed how this narrative of racial alliance is gendered, I want to examine now how it also is spatialized. The earlier aphorism "good girls go to heaven; bad girls go everywhere" reflects an American gendered account of mobility. Questioning the relationship between subjectivity, culture, globalization, and space has occurred most productively in recent scholarship challenging the rooted fixity and boundedness of the nation. Appadurai, in his formulation of the postnational, asks us to interrogate and deconstruct the primacy of the nation-state without necessarily discarding it. Yet, Appadurai's work, like *Mississippi Masala,* seems to offer the United States as a privileged location for formulating postnational identities and politics. He (1993a, 806) writes,

> America may yet construct yet another narrative, of enduring significance, about the uses of loyalty after the end of the nation-state. In this narrative, bounded territories could give way to diasporic networks, nations to trans-nations, and patriotism itself could become plural, serial, contextual and mobile. Here lies one direction for the future of patriotism in a postcolonial world.

Although Appadurai's statement clearly forwards postnational politics, it also is haunted by a narrative of U.S. exceptionalism, one that is linked specifically to freedom of movement and mobility. Frederick Jackson Turner (1920), in his infamous 1890 speech on the receding frontier "The Significance of the Frontier in American History," claims that America has been conditioned and determined by the perennial rebirth of the frontier in successive forms, from the Puritan settlements and the California gold mines to the secular spirit that characterizes America as a promised land, expressing its unique history of rugged individualism, endurance, and possibility. He posits this "pioneer spirit" as the embodiment of American success and exceptionalism. In this chapter, I argue that American exceptionalism has taken a new turn through evoking the frontier that creates a narrative of the United States as the ideal multiracial society, a microcosm of the global.

Demetrius and Mina's relationship suggests U.S. exceptionalism by locating the United States, rather than Uganda or elsewhere, as the site for overcoming national identities, a place in which movement is not bounded by national narratives. Yet, national narratives endure in this postnational construction, specifically, the narrative of the frontier that reappears as a space of postnationalism. Unlike DuBois's novel that closes on the Southern coast facing Africa, opening up possibilities of Afro-Asian diasporic postnational affiliations and linking U.S. slave trade and imperialism to colonialism, this film turns away from Africa and especially Uganda, spaces it associates only with affiliations of the nation-state. The film, eschewing the possible transnational politics, moves away from Africa or even the South that faces Africa and ends ambiguously with Mina and Demetrius standing in an empty field as they flee Mississippi. Even when considering South Asians in Asian-America, it is necessary to note the shifting and local inflections of Asian-American as we seek to differentiate between what it means to be such in India (colonial or postcolonial), in Uganda (colonial diaspora), in Britain (refugee), in Mississippi (immigrant), or on the road (migrant domestic labor).

The film closes with its critique of the nation and national identities as Mina and Demetrius find possibilities in routes rather than roots. This narrative of diaspora becomes an antiessentialist but linear teleology of continued travel as displacement in "routes." The binary is inverted, and it is the subordinate mobility rather than Jay's backward-looking longing of exile that is now celebrated. Early in the film, Demetrius and Mina reject this fixed notion of self and home. At an amusement park on their first night together, they sit in a whirligig. Spinning quickly in circles, they cry out that their futures together hold travel—Jamaica, Madagascar, India, and Africa. It is this same desire for travel that they rearticulate at the end of the film. Leaving her family and community, Mina asks Demetrius to take her with him; in return he asks where they will go, to which she replies that they will travel. Mina and Demetrius will travel, though not to the exotic destinations that they have named earlier but to other motels in need of cleaning in a van at the risk of repossession in the service of global capitalism. The film ends ironically with their physical mobility in sharp contrast to their dreams.

Instead of looking "homeward" to the roots of India or Uganda or "settling" in the United States, the film activates the American romance of the frontier and reformulates the diasporic trope of mobility, producing a home on the range in mobility. Although the film carefully interrogates dominant narratives of geopolitical territorial claims, its ending simultaneously disassociates itself from the nuanced specificities of historical context. Since the characters find neither imaginary homelands nor the racist diaspora hospitable, the film presents a vision of constantly shifting and changing homes, of incessant (westward) movement in empty land, and of a semidisenfranchised U.S. nomadism. The myth of the open road leading to the frontier is a U.S. narrative of identity formation for the individual and the national culture. In a post-sixties era, this myth no longer necessarily leads to the frontier or golden land of California but to nowhere, only to more highways and mobility as a new form of migrant labor.

Mobility or westward migration is a trope of U.S. exceptionalism that has been reactivated in postmodern and postcolonial discourses as well. Deleuze and Guattari's (1987) political philosophical metaphors uproot the sedentary and sedimented botanies of modernist thought and capitalist relations in favor of destabilized and minoritized positions. Addressed to Western audiences, their work, like that of feminist Rosi Braidotti, uses poststructuralist paradigms to valorize displacement and marginalization as modes of deprivileging. Braidotti (2000) writes,

> The nomad . . . stands for the relinquishing and the deconstruction of any sense of fixed identity. . . . The nomadic style is about transitions and passages without pre-determined destinations or lost homelands. . . . It is the subversion of set conventions that defines the nomadic state, not the literal act of travelling. But more figurations come to mind, and not only classical ones like gypsies and the wandering jews.

Caren Kaplan (1996) in *Questions of Travel* points to the highly regarded post-modern theories, including those of Deleuze and Guattari, which valorize travel and mobility in opposition to Western modernist values. In this case, it is the migration and translation of these theories into the American frontier and exceptionalism that should provoke caution. The theme of mobility and its problematic consequences in *Mississippi Masala* suggest the necessity of reconsidering nomadic theories and their usefulness for all subjects, especially those who are already disenfranchised and are mobilized in the service of global capitalism. (For example, nomadism becomes a metaphor that mystifies the material and political situations of those who are nation-, state-, or land-less or who are literally nomads, by romanticizing and valorizing them.)[21]

Mississippi Masala jumps from a historical grounding in the exilic displacement of a community to a U.S.-based postmodern celebration of individual nomadism and movement. Coined by Ralph Waldo Emerson, *nomadism* describes a metaphorical American ontological and epistemological state in which one is at home everywhere, where mobility is an adventure fueled by "trade and curiosity" (cited in Peters 1999, 30). Here the political economy driving mobility becomes more clearly visible. In postmodern and diasporic celebrations of mobility, attention to the political and economic conditions that fuel that mobility is paramount; in the case of the film, Demetrius and Mina's pleasure in mobility seems somewhat undermined as it is propelled in the name of the service labor in late capitalism. Mina's mobility, in other words, also can be seen as a form of migrant domestic labor.

The American myth of the frontier is evoked as a space signifying freedom and progress for the rugged individual of the white male citizen choosing to

Fig. 3.2 Demetrius and Mina in the new American frontier in *Mississippi Masala*.

escape the confinements of society. Westward journeys often signify the possibility of renewal and rebirth; mobility into this empty space is valued for the opportunity to define oneself against family or larger social community. In the context of *Mississippi Masala,* the postindustrial frontier is enabled by "trade and curiosity" due to the uneven expansion of capital masked as postmodern self re-creation. Westward migration here can be read as part of late capitalism's postmodern narratives of uprooted mobility and surplus service labor in open but circumscribed space. In the film's conclusion, though Mina and Demetrius's destination remains unnamed (they refuse even the pinned-down location of the West), Tyrone, Demetrius's business partner, departs for Los Angeles. Whether California or the West is the ultimate target destination for the couple is less relevant than their constant movement into an open and ahistorical terrain. In the United States, that space that is uninscribed and can be "traveled" is the West.

The final shot of the film, inserted among the credits, depicts Demetrius (clad in kente cloth) and Mina (dressed in a salwar kameez) standing in an empty and open field (see Figure 3.2). The camera pans around the couple emphasizing their isolation in this empty space. The West is often symbolized by space that is empty and uninhabited to suggest the possibility of movement and expansion, a place where one can remake oneself, an open terrain in which identity is reconstituted, a space waiting to be "worlded." In this case, it is a space that is unmarked by history as well. Echoing McClintock's (1995) idea of anachronistic space, the myth of the frontier is further imagined as a site severed from history, especially the history of slavery and colonialism that is the evoked by the Africa-facing South.[22] This postmodern rewriting of the frontier is evoked by Jean Baudrillard in *America:* "I went in search of *astral* America . . . the America of desert speed, of motels, and mineral surfaces" (cited in Caren Kaplan 1996, 70). Caren Kaplan points out that "Privileging nomadic rootlessness and an evacuation of signification, Baudrillard's *America* imagines a national landscape that emphasizes the disappearance of history" (p. 80). Similarly, in contrast even to the temporary dwelling space of motels where Mina begins and that ultimately prove to be confining and static, the film offers the trope of mobility in the answer of the American open road and field.[23]

In the beginning of the film, the exile of the family from Uganda is depicted by the drawing of a trajectory from Uganda to Britain (though England never appears in the film), continuing to Mississippi and its motels. When this destination becomes unsatisfactory, the migration continues seemingly further westward, away from the inscribed spaces and histories of Africa and the South. The movement westward, or at least into supposedly unmarked terrain, relies on the resolution of flight and escape into new worlds away from inscribed places. For the (im)migrant, this task is different and difficult, because the most viable option is often the struggle to join the nation, to inscribe oneself within preexisting cartography that resists one's presence. Often diasporas attempt to imprint their cartographies on the narratives of the homeland and the resident nation-state. The diasporic inscription in the film's conclusion is of place that is mapped as empty and unmarked. Thus, the closing is premised on two assumptions: that of unfettered, unlimited, and celebratory mobility and that of empty ahistorical space.

The West becomes space, open and imaginary, that can once again be resurrected as occupiable by a new generation. This space is sought as free from the confines of a "home" that signifies a territorial national identity (Ugandan) or a deterritorialized national or diasporic identity (African Asian or British Asian). What is constructed instead is the inscribing of space by the movement of the globally mobile individual. Mina and Demetrius, displaced by the nation's exclusionary narratives, reactivate the possibility of America as a temporary and transient space inscribed with the narratives of global cowboys.

Cowboys and Indians in the *Wild West*

> Whoever the last true cowboy in America turns out to be, he's likely to be an Indian.
>
> —William Least Heat-Moon[24] (1999, 174)

Mississippi Masala rejects the exilic nostalgia for homeland in favor of "a home on the range." We must pay attention when Indians play cowboys (see

Fig. 3.3 South Asian-Americans as cowboys and Indians in *Mississippi Masala.*

Figure 3.3). What does it mean for South Asians to participate in this version of multicultural America? What diasporic politics are proposed and foreclosed in the film? By contrasting the Hollywood *Mississippi Masala* with the British *Wild West*, it becomes possible to locate and articulate diasporic politics in their local, national, and transnational contexts.

Wild West, written by Harwant Bains and directed by David Attwood (1993), satirizes the American response to diasporic homelessness and displacement through travel. The film's plot centers around three Pakistani brothers who are disenfranchised urban youth in Thatcher's England (the oldest, Zaf, played by Naveen Andrews who later stars in Nair's *Kama Sutra* and *My Own Country*) and who form the country and western band the Honkytonk Cowboys in Southhall (see Figure 3.4). They struggle with neighborhood thugs, underemployment, and institutional racism for much of the film. Because no one seems to want an Asian country and western band, only when a battered Asian wife, Rifat (also played by Choudhury), joins their group do they achieve any form of success. Finally, she alone, because her "dusky looks" present a possible "angle," is signed to an American country and western label. "You, I can really sell," says the record manager, in terms of commodifying her exotic and erotic look for a white audience. The music company, however, sees the brothers as

Fig. 3.4 Zaf entering the frontier of Southhall, England in *Wild West*.

unmarketable except perhaps to a "fringe" or "leftist" label. In disgust, the brothers decide to leave racist Britain, selling their house and purchasing plane tickets to the United States. Thus, gendered Orientalism marks Rifat as commodifiable and desirable by a multicultural capitalist market and marginalizes Zaf and the other members of the band, thus forcing their mobility. Unlike *Mississippi Masala*, this film is conscious of the configuration of nonthreatening and commodifiable diasporic production—the band is acceptable only if they play bhangra, and Rifat is marketable because women can be exoticized. It self-reflectively comments on the multicultural economic conditions in which culture is produced. The movie closes with the Asian Honkytonk Cowboys dressed in their cowboy hats and boots, carrying their guitars, and accompanied by their dog on a plane bound for Nashville, Tennessee, already experiencing, as the video cover suggests, "Nashville [which] is just a state of mind" (see Figure 3.5).

The departure for Nashville, the performative home of American country and western music, functions as a sign parodying essentialized identities and making oneself anew without the burden of colonial history. In this film, as in *Mississippi Masala*, liberation (for the male protagonists at least) is sought (and one imagines "discovered") through travel westward, away from locations

Fig. 3.5   Zaf the disenfranchised Asian cowboy in Thatcher's Britain in *Wild West*.

marked by histories of racialization. However, in *Wild West*, the westward migration of the band is a complex and playful sign blurring the distinction between the West (First World) and the West (American frontier). Although the film moves westward to find a home on the range, it also is very aware of the irony of this final gesture. Therefore, its choice of cowboys as self-determining subjects is an ironic acknowledgment that there is no self or home to imagine outside of inscribed space of global capitalism and history of colonialism. The film does not close with romance as redefining diasporic homeland. Instead, *Wild West*, unlike *Mississippi Masala*, foregrounds the mobilization of capital and the capitalization of mobility. It also playfully pokes fun at American exceptionalism and imperialism that engenders myths of the frontier and self-reinvention. In *Wild West*, the West is a camp site, the terrain of ironic play with no fixed authentic meaning—it is a nomadic diasporic strategy of playful and mimetic repetition. Preventing any celebration of mobility or any sort of closure suggesting that subjectivities can be remade outside of history and capitalist cultural inscription, the whimsically ironic film poses that repetition of representation with a difference is central to diasporic cultural production and that irony may be central to diasporic spectatorship (the subject of the next chapter).

Wild West pinpoints the ways in which certain postmodern discourses of diaspora and travel intersect and reiterate previous tropes, here in particular, those of cowboys on the frontier. *Wild West* relies on camp to problematize mobility and escape, even at the level of language. "Indians" (substituting for South Asians) incongruously and imaginatively become postmodern and transnational cowboys but at the same time evoke the history of U.S. colonialism and "misnomer" of indigenous Americans as Indians. This playfulness evokes the absence and erasure of Indians necessary to the trope of cowboys and U.S. imperialism. Thus the positionality of the South Asian migrant becomes connected to the U.S. history of colonialism and imperialism, a history and politics of alliance that remains perennially undertheorized in postcolonial, Asian-American, and South Asian diasporic studies. *Wild West* emerges from the space of British cultural politics that has already married the postcolonialities of Asia, Africa, and the Caribbean to forge alliances articulated as black identities. On the other hand, although its prologue generates a connection between Africa, South Asia, and then later the United States, *Mississippi Masala* imagines alliance only in the space of U.S. multiculturalism, unable to link further South Asian transnationality, African diaspora, and U.S. colonialism. Moreover, within the U.S. context, African-American cultural nationalism dominates other transnational political discourses so that the narrative of the necessary alliance between people of color that is available is that of the recuperated family with the black male head of the heteronormative household. Unlike *Wild West,* which proves its distant and ironic detachment from the myth of the cowboy and the commodification of gendered ethnicity, *Mississippi Masala* overlooks a critique of U.S. multiculturalism and the significance of transnational and indigenous politics.

Mississippi Masala illustrates the dangers of diaspora becoming a celebratory mobility. Although the film supports the useful critiques of modernist constructions of subject, place, and nation, it does not consider those discourses within the context of postnational American studies or indigenous politics that are imbricated with other categories of social difference. By considering both DuBois's novel and *Wild West,* the erasures and gaps of *Mississippi Masala* and its diasporic discourses become more visible. With this comparison, it becomes easier to see how feminist transnational politics critiquing not only the nation and racism but also colonialism, heteronormativity, and liberal multiculturalism can be constructed. The link between U.S. Indians and South Asian Indians indicates more than word play at the end of this chapter; it poses links that are crucial to dissolving the binary opposition between diaspora and indigeneity and dismantle any simple notion of migration and multiculturalism that does not account for issues of space and place. Moreover, it is a history that is essential to diasporic and feminist politics, especially in light of indigenous politics and rhetoric of rootedness in relation to land and territory that is in contrast to nomad, travel, and diasporic discourses. This particular formulation about

nationality, ethnicity, authenticity, and cultural integrity may have strong implications for cultural criticism and cultural history.[25] If we are to have a nomadic
diasporic politics of location and mobility that destabilizes and denationalizes
national (and territorial) identity, it must be one that also is specifically an-
chored and attentive to complex and simultaneous multiple relations, in this
case, of colonialism, slavery, indigeneity, capitalism, and heteronormativity.

The film raises questions regarding the meaning and possibilities of the "postcolonial" in the United States in seeking to understand the legacies of European
colonialism that are linked to the history of the United States. The silences and
disjunctures of *Mississippi Masala* remind us of the need to formulate politics
that account for race and (post)colonialism within the United States. It is essential to U.S.-based postcolonial critique to bring to the foreground the failures of
U.S. multicultural nationalism in relation to the enduring narratives of exceptionalism that portray the United States beyond race, history, and ideology by
erasing its gendered and sexualized histories of colonization, imperialism, and
migration.

The critique of colonialism and imperialism in Asian-American studies is
crucial. Considering U.S. imperialism in the Philippines, Iraq, and Afghanistan,
the necessity of a complex understanding of the "Asian" in Asian-American studies is apparent. This is not to suggest that Asian-American studies needs to extend
the survey of its domain in relation to its object of study, but rather that Asian-
American critique must shift to address the complex ways in which militarized
capital connects and constructs the geopolitical space of "Asia." The necessity of
reformulating Asian-American critique is a much broader question of knowledge production and politics than the simple inclusion of Asian-Americans
into the fold of multiculturalism or the addition of Arab-Americans to the panethnicity of Asian America. Seeking to continually reformulate Asian-American
critique in regard to the shifting relations between "Asia" and "America" suggests
political possibilities that extend beyond nation-claiming projects to emphasize
imperialism and decolonization. This formulation of Asian-American critique
works against the coherent and singular notions of Asian-American subjectivity that are forwarded by cultural nationalism and liberal multiculturalism,
suggesting instead that Asian-American subjectivities are heterogeneous and
characterized by difference.

4

Reel a State: Reimagining Diaspora, Homeland, and Nation-state in Srinivas Krishna's *Masala*

There's dancing
Behind movie scenes
Behind the movie scenes
Sadi Rani
She's the one that keeps the dream alive
from the morning
past the evening
to the end of the night
Brimful of Asha on the 45
Well it's a brimful of Asha on the 45

And singing
illuminate the main streets
And the cinema aisles
We don't care bout no
Government warnings,
'bout their promotion of a simple life
And the dams they're building
Brimful of Asha on the 45
Well it's a brimful of Asha on the 45

Everybody needs a bosom for a pillow
Everybody needs a bosom
Mine's on the RPM
                —"Brimful of Asha" by Cornershop
(song about Hindi film playback singer Asha Bhosle)

Sung by the pop British musical group Cornershop, the lyrics of "Brimful of Asha" evoke not only the complexities of Bollywood cinema but also the complicated politics of diaspora and diasporic cultural production and spectatorship.[1] Singing "everyone needs a bosom for a pillow, and mine's on the 45," the group narrativizes the playback singer Asha Bhosle's evocation and embodiment of the homeland to nostalgic diasporic listeners. Suggesting that films and film music construct and satisfy structures of feeling identified as nostalgia for the homeland, the lyrics affirm that "dreams" of home, comfort, and belonging are kept alive by the musical recordings of film musicians and singers such as Asha Bhosle and Lata Mangeshkar. These female singers are personified in the Hindi film song industry as maternal figures of the absent motherland, not only as fleshy bodies but also as cultural commodities of exchange. In most discourses of diaspora, nostalgia, longing, and loss are central themes that define diasporic subjectivity and identities. Moreover, displacement from an original homeland, also a defining feature, is seen to produce these effects. In the previous chapter, I examined how these original homelands are constructed and imagined through political exile. In this chapter, I pursue this line of inquiry, further deconstructing the (imagined) relationship between diaspora and homeland, in this case, tackling the idea of homeland as a given point of origin and as an original and consequently, diaspora as a copy rather than as a citation.

In examining the South Asian Canadian film *Masala* by Srinivas Krishna (the first of three Krishnas associated with the film), in this chapter I interrogate the relationship between diaspora and homeland, and specifically the most common paradigm assuming that diasporas and diasporic cultures duplicate homelands and their authentic cultures. What is significant about this film, in part, is that it interrogates the relationship between homeland and diaspora at the same time it challenges any simple identification. It does not take diaspora and homeland as a priori. Like *Mississippi Masala, Masala* produces a diaspora that is not based on the idea of return to a place of origin that has been lost. More important, it explores the relationship between diasporas and homelands in South Asia, foregrounding contradictory constructions of homeland as a stable homogenous site of origin. By evoking the colonial and postcolonial nation-state of India as one that has produced multiple diasporas (in this case Hindu and Sikh), the film complicates not only the simple nostalgia often associated with diasporic belonging but also the idea of the production of diaspora as constituted simply by displacement. Instead, the film suggests that it is diasporic identification processes and performativity that inflect and dialectically produce homelands.

Masala

The Canadian national cinema negotiates not only Hollywood but also its own history of colonialism and colonization, thus representing within its own cultural production the fracturing, renarrativization, and reimagining of the nation. Made within the auspices of the Canadian state-supported film industry, *Masala* functions as part of, but also is critical of, this state-sanctioned multiculturalism in its own processes of disidentification. Following the interrogation of liberal pluralist multiculturalism in the discussion of *Mississippi Masala,* in this chapter I query the politics of state multiculturalism in Canada. *Masala* works at multiple levels, shifting from issues of the nation and national culture to diasporic politics and global processes. The film recognizes the ways in which cinema is itself enabled by capital and the state, attempting to reside in interstices while providing a critique of the conditions of its production. The title *Masala* locates the film in these interstices, marking itself as mixture and hybridity and positioning itself in relation to local, national, diasporic, and global cultural politics.

Opening with the explosion of an airplane (the unnamed fictionalized depiction of Air India flight 182), *Masala* interweaves the stories of several families in a Toronto Hindu community during the late eighties.[2] In this diasporic hybrid film, interspersed are fantastical dream sequences or musical numbers from the perspective of various characters, as well as dialogues with the god Krishna through the VCR. The film balances its tragic plot lines with a comic tone and farcical characters. One of the storylines centers around the upper-middle-class couple Lallu (Saeed Jaffrey in one of three comic roles) and Bibi Solanki as they search for a wife for their medical student son Anil. The Solankis' lives are turned upside down by the appearance of Bibi's leather jacket–clad, ex-junkie nephew Krishna, whose nuclear family died on the plane. The Solankis also court the Canadian minister of multiculturalism in an attempt to gain power as political representatives of the Indian community. They, in turn, are approached by Bahuda Singh, a Sikh taxi driver and radical, who wants to store contraband in their shop basement. In exchange for hiding what they assume to be arms for the separatist Sikh struggle (but what turn out to be cases of toilet paper), the Solankis accept a bribe of $500,000 and conspire to monopolize the Canadian and Sikh sari trade. But carefully laid plans go awry when the incompetent Mounties interfere.

Interwoven with this story is that of Lallubhai's poorer cousin Harry Tikkoo (also played by Jaffrey), a stamp-collecting postal carrier who lost his wife in the bombing of the flight and lives with his two daughters Sashi and Rita, son Babu, and mother Shanti (played by Hindi film and theater actress Zohra Sehgal). When their house is at risk of foreclosure, the family responds in different ways: Harry resigns himself to fate and his stamp collection, Babu absorbs get-rich quick infomercials and scrutinizes over the details of no-money-down real estate, and Shanti asks the deity Krishna (Jaffrey again), who appears on her VCR, to intervene and save her family from foreclosure. The deity Krishna obliges by placing in Tikkoo's possession a valuable and historical Canadian stamp later valued at $5 million. Predictably, the government attempts to procure the stamp in the name of "Canadian cultural heritage," a claim that avid philatelist Harry Tikkoo meets head-on with litigation. The situation is resolved only by wheeling and dealing compromises between his politically savvy daughter Sashi and the minister of multiculturalism. The protagonist Krishna further ties together the two families—he is Bibi Solanki's nephew and the lover of Tikkoo's daughter Rita. This mortal Krishna searches for meaning and location within the community and his identity, as he alternatively accepts and rejects Lallubhai's offers of a home, job, and money. Although he finally aligns himself with the

Tikkoo family and larger South Asian community through his relationship with Rita, he is killed in a racist hate crime while protecting Tikkoo's son.

The opening of the film forwards the centrality of cinema to constructions of diaspora and homeland. The film does more than draw attention to the cinematic apparatus through self-reference. *Masala* introduces and links through montage what it proposes as the central constitutive element configuring the dominant relationship between homeland and diaspora—the chronotope of the plane in cinema (including television, film, and video). It also establishes a complex understanding of spectatorial (dis)identification through its manipulation of the gaze. Thus, the opening sequence crucially situates the viewer in multiple, ambivalent, and complex processes of identification that are significantly linked to diasporic positionality and subjectivity, setting the tone for the rest of the film.

The opening sequence of the film cuts back and forth from (1) the outside of a flying airplane to (2) the interior of plane with its passengers and video monitors and (3) the video setting of the video monitors depicting the god Krishna à la televised religious serial. Evoking both mythological films and religious television serials, the "video" scenes are filmed in the conventions of the genres that are familiar to many diasporic viewers: bright garish and saturated colors, a closely defined and narrow interior setting, and long close-ups. These scenes contrast with the more natural lighting of the interior of the plane depicting real time and space. The first scene depicts the rear exterior of the airplane as it flies above gray clouds into unknown dark space away from the viewer who is thereby gazing from a diasporic position rather than a homeland position. The film then cuts to an interior scene of the Lord Krishna (in full blue makeup) seated on a divan next to a dancing girl whom he kisses as music and appreciative comments indicate some out-of-sight audience. These scenes of establishing shots locate the viewer first to the outside of the plane, then within cinema, and finally in the real-time space of inside the plane. The spectatorial gaze is part of this admiring audience and is also simultaneously more intimate (a devotional point of view I discuss later). Switching from the video setting to the interior of the plane, the music provides continuity and is uninterrupted as the film cuts to consecutive close-ups of the protagonist Krishna's sleeping father, brother, and mother. The music, indicating that the scene with the deity Krishna is being watched as a film within the film, continues under the dialogue when the mortal Krishna's brother asks his mother why Krishna does not come with them to India. The mother looks sadly into the distance and gives no answer as the music plays. The camera then shifts to frame a video monitor in the plane where we recognize the ongoing scene of Krishna the deity. Notably, the dialogue continues as the camera cuts back to the interior of the plane and pans the video monitors and dozing heads of the passengers. This time, the video scenario conversation disrupts the space and time of the viewer, but we soon realize that the internal "audience" in the plane cannot hear this asynchronous conversation. The director

Krishna splits the internal viewer from the external one. The external audience is made simultaneously aware of their similarity to the viewers within the film and their position outside of the film. However, the viewer inside of the plane is not privy to the nondiegetic conversation foreshadowing tragedy. The external audience has a more complex understanding of the situation. The camera zooms back into the video interior to a close-up of the deity Krishna resignedly accepting his fate and directly addressing the external audience in a full frontal shot, lamenting, "Why can't a god be simply a man?" Immediately the camera cuts back to the first shot of the film of the exterior of the retreating plane as the entire jet explodes.[3] The credits begin as a red sari falls through space.

In this chapter, I want to suggest that *Masala* foregrounds a diasporic spectatorship that challenges the idea of nostalgic and passive consumption of homeland cultural products and forwards the diasporic imaginary as the site performing and defining the relationship between the diaspora and the homeland. Furthermore, the film overturns the idea that diasporas are constituted by the language, religions, or culture (cultural productions) of the homelands; *Masala* contests framing diaspora as a replication of an authentic original homeland and instead suggests that they are dialectically constituted.

Camp as Disidentification Strategy

In the opening scene, Balarama cautions Krishna to remember, "This is not a comedy; it's a tragedy." Krishna despondently responds, "Why must innocent people die?" Balarama replies, "After all these years, you complain the world is unfair? . . . Little brother, if the world was fair, people would have no need for gods. Man needs you to explain what he cannot." Despite Balarama's reassurances, religion and gods explain little in *Masala* and the film shifts back and forth from comedy to tragedy. It uses comedic strategies such as camp, however, as a mechanism to recognize, salvage, and reproduce meanings that challenge dominant constructions. At the same time, it becomes a tragedy to mark the limitations of those comedic strategies. In this next section, I evaluate cultural critiques and strategies, such as camp and resistant spectatorship, employed in diasporic cultural productions that seek to challenge dominant narratives. More specifically, I examine how diasporic texts and spectators articulate identification and disidentification processes from contested and contradictory spaces and in doing so produce diasporic cultural politics. José Esteban Muñoz (1999, 31), describing a similar form of cultural production and reception as disidentification, writes,

> Disidentification is about recycling and rethinking encoded meaning. The process of disidentification scrambles and reconstructs the encoded message of a cultural text in a fashion that exposes the encoded message's universalizing and exclusionary machinations and recircuits its workings to account for, include, and empower minority identities and identifications.

Hence, disidentification processes exhibited through camp mimic and parody, reconstructing dominant culture into hybrid productions in the interest of non-dominant politics.

In discussions of camp, the tendency is to discuss it either as style encoded in the cultural products or as the mode of reception by the viewer. This discussion, however, attempts to encompass both production and reception as a strategy of disidentification in *Masala*. More important, camp has been discussed primarily by scholars in relation to white gay males and more recently to feminist cultural politics. Susan Sontag (1986) and Esther Newton (1972) were some of the first scholars to examine the politics of camp, the former arguing against its potential politics and the latter citing its possibilities. Sontag, who locates camp both in the viewer as a sensibility and in objects themselves, argues that camp is easily depoliticized. More interested in the dominant culture's reception of camp than the production and use of camp by nondominant subjects, Sontag focuses on camp from the position of a white bourgeois heterosexual spectatorship. She argues that relying on theatricality and exaggeration for effect, camp is often consumed and reabsorbed by dominant audiences whose political sensibilities remain unchanged by what they perceive as spectacle. Similarly, in reference to the material and power conditions enabling camp, Caryl Flinn (1999, 437) poses that camp depends on a highly prosperous bourgeoisie "first to provide the ideological center whose margins camp inhabits and secondly to supply the economic surplus, leisure time, and wealth needed by camp for sustenance." Newton traces the origins of camp to theatricality in the anti-Puritanism of the Elizabethan and Restoration theatrical scene and the underground world of prostitution, and poses, in contrast, that camp offered safe social space and the possibility of the imaginary for nondominant communities. Newton's emphasis is not on the likelihood of camp's ability to transform dominant modes of perception and analysis but that it is, the site of disidentification processes that mark nondominant communities. Like Bakhtin's carnival, a space of alternative order, plausibility, and belonging, theatrical camp allows the possibility of cultural critique within a circumscribed arena, and more important, it signifies the ability to disidentify with the dominant as a community.[4]

Ethnic humor and kitsch have been employed as camp's corollaries to describe oppositional or negotiated engagements and re-presentations of dominant cultural discourses within ethnic and racial minority, as well as nonbourgeois, communities. Camp, ethnic humor, and kitsch have been linked together primarily because they share humor as the strategic mechanism of critique to disarm dominant discourses. Comedy provides a critique of dominant ideologies at the same time, as it remains intimate with the cultural discourses it interrogates. Kitsch is often seen as the (postmodern) strategy of racial and ethnic minorities, whereas camp connotes an urban white bourgeois gay male sensibility. Celeste Olalquiaga (1992) examines Latino cultural kitsch, particularly religious artifacts and objects, formulating kitsch as a process by which Latino artists recycle

Latino religious objects (hence revamping dominant Latino not Anglo objects) as a postmodern aesthetic of loss. Thus, Olalquiaga's consideration of kitsch as a form of postmodern nostalgia resonates with the work of Fredric Jameson who too suggests that camp is connected to pastiche, postmodernism, and late capitalism. Jameson further argues that camp lacks the satiric impulse of parody and "equalizes all identities, styles, and images in depthless ahistorical nostalgia" (1991, 65). Therefore, on one side of the writings on camp Jameson and Olalquiaga dismiss camp as cultural critique for its affiliation with loss and nostalgia. On the other side, scholars such as Pamela Robertson and Muñoz have tried to rescue camp from charges of depoliticization and ahistoricity by attempting to build on its queer politics.

Similarly, in my employment of it as a cultural critique forged in South Asian diasporas, I posit camp as a historically and geopolitically located cultural strategy that may evoke not only queer politics but also racial and feminist politics in regard to transnational cultural production. Moreover, I emphasize camp's politics as deriving from poststructural challenges and deconstructions of fixed essential categories. Camp in its postmodern reincarnation is associated with a critique of authenticity: "If you can't be authentic (and you can't), if this doesn't feel like real life (and it doesn't), then you can be camp" (Bartlett 1999, 182). In Bartlett's conceptualization of camp, like Judith Butler's (1993 and 1999) theory of gender performativity and Homi Bhabha's (1994) theory of mimicry, reiteration functions as citation of an original that does not exist. Offering drag as an example, Butler (1999) finds that although the performance cites that which is authorized as the original and therefore gains authority from the reference, it also rewrites and dismantles the originality of the original. In Bhabha's theory of mimicry, the citation never quite resembles the original because it is repeated with difference in a form of ambivalent or oppositional negotiation. It is this aggrandized gap between original and copy that I suggest is probed and exploited by camp as mimicry, especially in critiques of the authentic and the original.

Camp and postcolonial diasporic mimicry become strategies to contest racial, gendered, sexual, and class politics within the film. Therefore, camp can possibly be harnessed to analyze ironic performances of gendered national and racial identities that are connected to a diasporic politics of home and identity. In contrast to Jameson's and Olalquiaga's focus on nostalgia, the film employs camp as a productive antidote to nostalgia that reverently remembers without representing homeland and homeland culture as sites of authenticity, origin, and loss. Thus, Robertson (1999, 267) suggest that camp redefines and "historicizes these cultural products not just nostalgically but with a critical recognition of the temptation to nostalgia, rendering both the object and the nostalgia outmoded through an ironic, laughing distanciation." In *Masala*, camp can be seen as parodying the dominant construction of the relationship between the homeland and the diaspora and as questioning the authenticity and authority of the "original." Therefore the relationship between diaspora and homeland is not one of a copy to the original but one of a copy to copy. In *Masala,* it creates repetition with difference, not in some apolitical postmodernism but in the specificity of its material, political, and historical conditions.

Although *Masala* plays on many political aspects of camp, such as gender, race, sexuality, and class, it is the combination of these associated with diasporic politics that I examine here.[5] Following these revamped discourses of camp, I read *Masala* as producing a mode of camp that subverts dominant Indian cinema and Canadian cultural apparatus as originals. This mode of camp works through rather than rejects these cultural forms. The film is intimately familiar with, engaged with, and invested in the subject of its critique. Krishna uses two popular genres of diasporic consumption—the masala film and the mythological serial epic (which I discuss shortly). Masala films are the intertextual films of Bollywood often with familiar structure, plot, sequences, and stock characters. Although masalas develop and shift, the films are recognizable by their combination of romance, family drama, melodrama, and musical numbers. Viewers also recognize the actors who play certain character types and follow the actors' lives very much like ongoing productions themselves. To satirize and remobilize dominant Indian cultural production, the film camps the masala films of Indian cinema, using recognizable characters and plot (i.e., estranged hero reunited with community by heroine) and structural elements (e.g., music and dance sequences separate from the realist plot structure).

Although I do not have the space to discuss fully the history, significance, and function of musical sequences in Hindi cinema, I want to discuss briefly their nondiegetic role in *Masala.* In masala films, the musical numbers, though often external to the plot, are integral to the exegesis of the film and expound on fantasies and desires. In addition, musical numbers make visible the material production of the film against the conventions of the social realist melodramatic plot; therefore, these extravagant and expensively costumed scenes are often shot in settings that are removed from the location of the plot, in places such as Switzerland, Britain, and the United States. Yet, although Bollywood musical numbers are often set in the West, until recently they have seldom depicted desires identified as diasporic. *Masala'*s musical numbers function in the mode of Hindi cinema, as sites of fantasy and desire but reiterated with difference. In *Masala,* Krishna mimics and reformulates the form of the musical numbers from Bollywood cinema (in addition to Western musicals and music videos)—Hindi and English lyrics, dance sequences with elaborate costume changes and backup dancers, lip-synched performances by the characters, and explicit expressions of desire. Three nondiegetic musical inserts occur in the film, the first focused on Rita, the second on Lallu Solanki singing his own version of "My Way," and the third on Anil Solanki.

The first dance number features Rita dancing with Anil while she is dressed in country and western garb, in a courtesan outfit, and then in aviation gear

Fig. 4.1 *Masala's* Rita and Anil in a hybrid Hollywood-Bollywood musical number.

flying a plane. The daydream sequence, an homage, satire, and remake of the musical sequences in masalas complete with costume and location changes, focuses around the idea of flying in three different segments. The first segment, set in a Western carnival, reflects American country and western culture and music sung in English; the second segment features an interior scene in which Rita sings in Hindi dressed in courtesan or nightclub dancer garb; and the third part, also sung in English, is a hybrid (third) space of a plane. The musical sequence evokes the masala and the Western musical, à la *Seven Brides for Seven Brothers* in ways that do not allow non-Bollywood viewers to immediately dismiss the film for its musical numbers (see Figure 4.1). The film, though primarily evoking a Bollywood convention, slyly comments on the presence of musicals in Hollywood and Western cinemas. Thus, when the number switches to Hindi and the more ambiguous interior scene, the film firmly identifies Bollywood as a site of familiarity and intimacy. The final section of the song most strongly articulates the hybrid desire of diasporic subjects and the hybrid space of diasporic cinema. Rita finds the mobility she seeks flying among the clouds in her own plane as Anil floats by, persuaded by her English and Hindi beckonings to fly with her. She sings to Anil (and the audience) "to listen to your body, take charge of your life, and fly with the sky as our own." Although the first two sections (via Hollywood and Bollywood) feature Anil as the object of her desire, the third section shifts the focus of Rita's desire. In the final segment, her desire is more complicated as she seeks escape and (upward) mobility through flying lessons and romance.

In *Masala*, the musical sequences reflect the various desires of characters: romantic escape and physical mobility through flying for Rita Tikkoo, financial and political power as well as fame through monopoly capitalism for Lallubhai Solanki, and the simultaneous fulfillment of patriarchal and bourgeois privilege in the form of a hypersexualized arranged marriage for Anil Solanki. More generally, the musical numbers indicate the ways in which the diasporic characters form the grammar of their desires from homeland, particularly Bollywood narratives. Rita's fantasy, for example, is triggered by a television announcement on the upcoming broadcast of a Hindi movie starring Amitabh Bachchan and Rekha. However, *Masala* presents diasporic subjects in the process of negotiating and rewriting these narratives, simultaneously critical of and complicit with these productions. The musical numbers, therefore, repeat with a difference these desires, not as the copy of some original desire but rather as the recycled and remobilized dreams located in particular historical and cultural contexts.

The film's narrative challenges the desires presented in the musical numbers. In this sense, the film campily and ambiguously undermines identification processes and desires. Though the performances mimic the performances of Bollywood cinema, they are also undermined and ultimately fail for several characters. For Rita, her desire to escape the consequences of her intersectional positionality as a woman of color (experienced through the family, economic hardship, marginalized employment) and find happiness remains unfulfilled within the film, especially as her lover Krishna is killed in a racial hate crime. Less tragically, Anil is rejected by the arranged marriage candidate Saraswati with whom he has had sex, though he has renewed potential in his new position as youth wing leader in the ministry of multiculturalism. His father Lallu Solanki is left without control of the sari trade, but has ample opportunities for further profit. Rita's ambivalent ending portrays her without desire for either flying lessons or romance. Rita, neither mother nor wife, neither pilot nor leader of the youth wing of Asian multiculturalism, is poignantly displaced at the end of the film. *Masala* refuses to resolve diasporic displacement by redefining home through the heterosexual romance or upward mobility, as is typical of Hollywood and Bollywood cinema. All romances are terminated as possible conclusions to the film. Rita is unable to access upward mobility in her relationship with Anil, nor is she able to reincorporate Krishna into the community to rejuvenate and restabilize the community. The film rejects these heteronormative, nationalist, and gendered resolutions to diaspora wherein women and their bodies become the sites of negotiating home.

Instead, the critical diasporic viewer is left critiquing the heterosexual, nostalgic, and individualized subjectivities forwarded by dominant bourgeois homeland and diasporic narratives to fill the absence of representation in the racist nation-state. *Masala* not only provides a feminist critique of diasporic patriarchy (Sashi comically criticizes Indian patriarchy and castrating racism as producing Indian men who are "limp-dicked chicken shits") but, more important, unlike *Mississippi Masala*, it also forecloses the (interracial or intraracial) heteronormative (and same-sex) coupling as resolution to diaspora. In this sense, although the film does nothing to denaturalize or denormalize heterosexuality, it does not predicate national and diasporic belonging simply on marriage and heterosexuality. Through its queer-affiliated politics of camp, the film challenges the normative romantic narrative.

The film provides the means for its own dissection and critique of camp and disidentification as cultural strategies. Although the film balances the excesses of camp with the tragedy of death, it more importantly leaves Rita without desire or identification. At the end of the film, as Krishna lies bleeding to death as a victim of a racial hate crime, he ironically utters, "This was not supposed to happen." Yet, throughout the film, Krishna's position has been as the "bad" subject rejecting the South Asian community and resisting Canadian assimilation in opposition to Anil's "good" subject who identifies with almost all aspects of dominant Canadian and Indian cultures. Reflexively undermining the character's masculine bravado and incredulity, Krishna the director wisecracks about the ending of the tragicomic film. But the film does not conclude there with the death of the hero; it continues beyond tragedy and comedy to the dilemma of the heroine. In this sense, *Masala* monitors and marks the limitations of camp and its dependence on mimicry, reiteration, and performance to resolve, the issues raised by the films narrative exploring the possibilities and limitations of disidentification most clearly at the end through Rita. Furthermore, it reaches beyond the limitations of a white-normative camp through a repeated revealing of the violence of racial ideologies and practices. Alive, but without desires, she is neither the good nor bad subject. Though the final shot is of Shanti the grandmother in the kitchen, it is in the character of Rita that *Masala* ends ambiguously and ambivalently. The viewer is left with uncertainty in seeing Rita as unable to transform her position as she is temporarily immobilized without identifications or desires. No longer seeking to escape or capitulating to normativities, Rita is brought to disidentification through the cultural politics of camp.[6]

Diasporic Spectatorship

Masala highlights the ways in which cultural productions become commodities within transnational markets for spectators who make meaning of the films in a variety of ways. Films exchanged as part of transnational telecommunications and culture industries produce economic, cultural, and social connections between the Indian homeland and its diasporas. *Masala* compels an analysis of the global trade and flow of (cultural) commodities, exploring the economics that enable these technological innovations to change the nature of diasporic relationship to the homeland. In addition, the film, therefore, investigates the ways in which diasporas receive, consume, and make meaning of South Asian cultural production. In addition to the films themselves, extravagant and profitable variety shows starring prominent film performers travel to major cities in the diaspora, bringing Bollywood to the diaspora.

The film and culture industry participates in (re)presenting the homeland to the diaspora in a supposedly one-way relationship in which dominant cultural narratives are produced in the homeland and passively consumed by the diaspora. The films are seen as providing comfort or familiarity as emblems of national homeland culture. (In the opening scene of *Masala*, the viewers doze and sleepily watch the videos.) However, audiences do make "meaning" of the films in contradictory, negotiated, and sometimes oppositional ways. Diasporic viewers, for example, may position Bollywood or Indian vernacular cinema in opposition to dominant Hollywood and Western national cinemas or may subvert representations of India or diaspora to their own purposes. Most important, cinema significantly contributes to processes of diasporic identity formation and thus is central to thinking through pleasure and power and how they affect subjectivity.

Film scholars have highlighted the necessity of understanding spectatorship in relation to subjectivity. Christian Metz (1975) relates the response of the spectator and the "look" produced through the film apparatus to processes of identification. Influenced by Metz as well as Lacan and Althusser, feminist film scholar Laura Mulvey reconceives these discussions through gender, postulating female spectatorship within film theory and asserting concepts such as the male gaze. Her formulation places the female spectator in the masochistic position of identifying with the female victim or in a cross-identified position with the male protagonist observed through a male gaze. Thus, Mulvey's (1975) essay "Visual Pleasure and Narrative Cinema" denies agency or desire to the subject, constructing the female spectator with the "choice" of identifying with the dominant male gaze or with the victimized and passive female, suggesting that only rejection of cinematic pleasure would forestall (heterosexual and patriarchal) complicity. Later, Mulvey (1981) redefines this proposition to assign the spectator a sense of agency in the process of viewing, but still operating within the Lacanian framework of dominant gender relations. Subsequently, feminist and queer studies scholars such as Chris Straayer (1996), Kaja Silverman (1992), and Teresa de Lauretis (1989) argue for appreciating and delineating the multiple ways (including cross-gender or bisexual identification and oscillating mobile identification) in which women and queer spectators can subvert, negotiate, undermine, as well as be interpellated by the spectatorial positioning and gaze of the film.

Meanwhile, cultural and ethnic studies scholars like E. Ann Kaplan (1997), Jacqueline Bobo (1995), and bell hooks (1992) have tried to mark the multiply and socially differentiated spectator who is distinguished by more than gender and sexuality.[7] More generally, they assign historical specificity to the spectatorial position by accounting for different kinds of positioning and spectatorship. Bobo and hooks argue that black female spectators often construct an oppositional gaze, one that strongly critiques gender and racial representations. Similarly, feminist theorist Michele Wallace (1993, 264) posits,

> It seems important here to view spectatorship as not only bisexual but also multiracial and multiethnic. Even as "The Law of the Father" may impose its premature closure on the filmic gaze in the coordination of suture and classical narrative, disparate factions in the audience, not equally well indoctrinated in the dominant discourse, may have their own way, now and then, with interpretation.

Wallace's formulation posits not only the intersectionality and multiplicity of relevant differences but also the negotiated, ambivalent, and ambiguous readings that are possible by nondominant spectators. Her formulation neither sees resistance everywhere (as some reception theory and studies of popular culture do) nor assumes the capitulation of the spectator to the dominant discourse encoded in "classical narratives."

Stuart Hall's (1980) theory for encoding and decoding dominant cultural texts from a nondominant position suggests that texts are encoded with denotative and connotative meanings that can be read in a variety of ways in relation to the dominant systems of representation. He offers three modes of decoding: (1) the dominant mode that reads dominant products following the dominant logic with which they are encoded, (2) the negotiated mode that operates by recognizing the constructedness of cultural products without necessarily challenging their authorial power, and (3) the resistant or oppositional mode that demystifies, deconstructs, or critiques dominant cultural production. The viewer, not bound to any one fixed position, therefore may slip and shift from one mode to another. Consequently, Hall's schema provides a paradigm for discussing the multiple and contradictory practices of engagement. Importantly, in Hall's work this paradigm is not established to suggest that each viewer has infinite agency and constantly displays resistance. I, in turn, do not employ this model to suggest simply that spectatorship is always negotiated and conflicted but rather to examine how and when those shifts and negotiations occur.

Bollywood cinema can be seen to encode a national gaze, one in which the (deterritorialized) spectator aligns himself as part of the national narrative. The dominant mode in this case encodes and decodes national belonging in a form of citizen spectatorship along such lines as religion, gender, class, caste, and sexuality. This dominant mode is the only mode in which diasporic spectatorship is currently imagined and discussed. However, audience members, building on Hall's propositions, may construct differing relationships with these national narratives, adopting dominant, negotiated, or resistant modes of decoding in relation to (dis)identification processes. The diasporic spectator decoding dominant national narratives of Indian culture industries may acquiesce to the dominant mode, performing the role of displaced culturally different citizen (as nonresident Indian for example). In contrast, and like black or female spectatorship, negotiated or resistant diasporic spectatorships may challenge the narratives of longing and belonging, opposing, resisting, and in *Masala*, literally talking back to the films. The film parodies the nostalgia that is associated with dominant diasporic spectatorship, marking diasporic spectatorship as sometimes ironic, oppositional, and active. Krishna interjects the possibility of an active and adaptive diasporic spectator who does not disrupt the steady unidirectional transnational flow of Indian film distribution but complicates consumption. Diasporic viewers do not eagerly and passively consume ideologies and products exported by the homeland nation but actively produce meanings through translation, negotiation, and adaptation.

Masala probes, prods, and transforms the position of the diasporic spectator of dominant national narratives in negotiated and resistant modes of decoding. *Masala* obviously refers to Indian cinema and in particular masala films through its title; in addition, the text also evokes the religious mythological film or serial through a fond satirical portrayal of the god Krishna as a campy and ineffectual deity. The live performance of religious drama has an extensive and diverse history throughout the subcontinent and consequently has led to development of the religious genre in cinema and television that owes many of its characteristics to these various dramatic traditions. (See Philip Lutgendorf [1990] on the development of the televised serial *Ramayan* in India and its relation to traditions of dramatic performance.) Hindu religious epics, especially the *Mahabharata* and the *Ramayana*, are incredibly popular televised serials in India and, as Marie Gillespie (1995) and Purnima Mankekar (1999b) discuss, often watched as a mode of worshipping.[8] In the film, the video deity Krishna from the opening scene reappears later when the grandmother Shanti Tikkoo prays and then worships by watching a video. The scene opens with Shanti praying to an idol of Krishna at a homemade altar. She pops in the video *Krishna* as part of her religious observations. His appearance through the VCR parodies Hindu émigrés' nostalgic attempts to recapture their national ties and to reproduce their cultural roots, as well as portray worshipping, through repeated viewings of the video epics.

It is significant that *Masala* references Krishna (and therefore more loosely the *Mahabharat*) rather than Rama (and the *Ramayan*). The latter serial was critiqued as communalist by many scholars, activists, and critics who saw it as furthering Hindu nationalism, whereas the former was seen as more inclusive and less hegemonically Hindu. The *Ramayan* (a variation of *Ramayana*), first telecast in 1987 on the state-run television channel Doordarshan and directed by the well-known Ramanand Sagar, received unprecedented ratings—an estimated astounding 80 to 100 million viewers (Lutgendorf 1990, 136). (Non-Hindu religious minorities such as Sikhs and Muslims also watched the serials, though Purnima Mankekar (1999b) in her ethnography on television viewing

argues they made different meanings of them.) The *Ramayan,* supposedly constructed out of multiple versions of the epic, nonetheless produced a Hindutva
nationalist narrative of Lord Rama as noble king and Sita as dutiful wife.[9] The
serial's evocation of Ram Rajya (the rule of Rama) encodes the Hindu nationalist discourse of a contemporary Ram Rajya through the achievement of a pure
Hindu national culture and a Hindu nation united by its devotion to Rama.

Directed by the famous Bombay film director B. R. Chopra, the epic serial
of the *Mahabharat* (the Doordarshan version of the *Mahabharata*) was seen by
more than 200 million viewers. In contrast to *Ramayan,* however, *Mahabharat*
questions the corruption of state power and its protection of its citizens along
with praising devotion to Krishna. The story of two warring branches of a family,
Mahabharat ponders actions and their motivations through dialogues between
the Pandavas and the Lord Krishna.[10] In general, emphasizing politics, from state
politics to family politics, the serial addresses national narratives of the "private"
and "public" within a liberal framework. Instead of either a Hindu nationalist
Rama or a politically Machiavellian Krishna, *Masala* features a playful and flirty
deity who demands devotion but whose national identification is disruptive.

The deity Krishna appears on the VCR as Shanti begins to watch and worship
with the *Krishna* videotape. Viewing the videotape constitutes acts of prayer
and pleasure in narrative. Gillespie (1995, 363) comments that for some faithful
Asian British, in addition to providing entertainment, "viewing is thought to
bring the gods into you and if, after watching, you can bring the gods into
your dreams then it is considered to be like a divine visitation where blessings
are bestowed and requests can be favored." Mankekar (1999b, 226) concurs
that many viewers in India watched the religious serialized epics, especially the
Ramayan, as if participating in a religious ritual. (Ironically, one might note
that although *Masala* circulated in India to a limited but receptive audience,
some fundamentalist and conservative Indians in Canada saw it as a sacrilegious
portrayal of Krishna. Responding quite in the dominant mode, these diasporans
condemned the movie on charges of religious blasphemy for its portrayals of
the hybrid deity.)[11]

In *Masala,* Shanti's viewing of the video thus represents not only a diasporic
spectatorship but also a different relationship between the devoted spectator
and the deity. As the scene continues, the camera cuts to the VCR and video and
zooms to the TV, in which Krishna the god chants "Shanti Shanti." She (and
the audience) soon realizes that he is addressing her to grant her a boon for her
devotion. Though the dialogue that follows is satirically inflected by diasporic
hybridity, the request and transaction are familiar tropes. Krishna, who deems
himself "master of the airwaves" is a media-savvy diasporic hybrid sighing "oy
vey" who later dons hockey gear (see Figure 4.2), but who nonetheless faithfully
appears to reward devotees. Not to be outdone in hybridity, Shanti replies to
his grant of a boon: "My son is a dreamer. He has lost his ambition and collects
stamps. We are outsiders here. Make it like it was before we came to this country

Fig. 4.2 The Canadian avatar of Krishna performing diasporic hybridity in *Masala*.

of no money down and supply side economics." Krishna apologizes that he cannot help because he is outside of his jurisdiction but promises to intervene to eliminate the risk of foreclosure. Krishna's appearance does not seem shocking or unnatural to viewers who are familiar with Hindu narratives in which gods materialize to grant rewards for devotion or *bhakti*. Mankekar (1999b, 199) suggests that bhakti, "the personal relationship of surrender and absolute devotion between a devotee and the subject of her worship," is a prevalent mode of engagement with the television productions. Mankekar and Lutgendorf both comment on the actual act of *darsan* carried out in relation to the televised serials. Darsan, most simply defined, is the "visual perception of the sacred" (Eck quoted in Mankekar 1999b, 200).

In *Masala*, the relationship between the viewer and the deity begins in the dominant mode of the devotee and the deity in the Hindu process of darsan; moreover, the darsanic gaze operates in the film in multiple ways. Furthermore, the viewing of religious serials raises questions about spectatorship and processes of identification as well. Thus, at another level, we may want to consider the darsanic gaze as a prevalent component of spectatorial looking in Hindi cinema. Finally, the darsanic relationship also can be considered metaphorically to describe the relationship between the diasporic spectator and the homeland culture.

Considering political, cultural, and material specificities, dominant Hindi cinema and television may construct different spectatorships than those of Hollywood cinema. Marxist postcolonial scholar M. Madhava Prasad (2000, 74) argues that the spectator of Hollywood cinema, an individualized position of voyeurism that is identified with a figure in the narrative, is not typical of Hindi cinema. Instead, he sees the darsanic gaze as a model for spectatorship of Indian cinema in general. This scopic relationship is different from Western ones theorized in feminist film scholarship, for example, which assumes a spectator constituted by identification processes that desire to be and identify with the object of the gaze. In this scopic relationship between the deity and devotee,[12] the deity bestows darsan on the devotee who receives it.[13] Prasad writes that the "practice signifies a mediated bringing to (god's) presence of the subject, who, by being seen by the divine image, comes to be included in the order instituted and supported by that divinity" (p. 75). Therefore, desire and identification in darsanic positioning are not based on the wanting or wanting to be like the object of the gaze. Prasad characterizes darsan as one in which "the devotee's muteness is a requirement of the entire process. The devotee's look, moreover, is not one that seeks to locate the divinity. . . . It is not a look of verification but one that demonstrates its faith by seeing the divinity where only its image exists and by asking to be seen in turn" (p. 75). Although I am hesitant to characterize the Hindu darsanic gaze as a predominant and primary structure of spectating in Hindi cinema as does Prasad, I nonetheless recognize its potency in describing the scopic positions of the diasporic and religious spectator.

The darsanic relationship metaphorically describes (and differs from) the dominant mode of diasporic spectatorship. It seems possible to employ the darsanic relationship as an analogy for the diasporic spectator who gazes in devotion at the purity and splendor of the authentic national culture of the homeland that is mutely revered and worshipped as pure and sacred. The spectator's darsan therefore enacts the performative aspect of national or nostalgic diasporic identification processes. However, unlike the darsanic relationship that does not center on identification processes (i.e., symbolic identification), the diasporic relationship is an imaginary one in which the diasporic spectator desires and aspires to be like and imitate the original upon which it gazes. The spectator not only desires to be recognized by the authentic but also to resemble and perform it.

Thus far, I have for the most part discussed the representations that depict what Hall might characterize as the dominant and negotiated modes of decoding texts. I turn now to the more resistant and oppositional modes. Attesting to the resistant modes of diasporic spectatorship, the director Krishna transforms the VCR from an instrument of passive viewing to an interactive hybrid apparatus

Fig. 4.3 Shanti's oppositional and resistant spectatorship in *Masala.*

that positions the diaspora as more than peripheral and passive. Shanti is at
first surprised that Krishna begins to address and converse with her as she sits
down to pray. But her interactions with Krishna quickly move from those of a
mute, devout, and obedient devotee to those of a quick, confident, and tech-
nologically savvy spectator (see Figure 4.3). Shanti freezes the deity in a pause
when the doorbell rings, and she is displeased with his handling of the situation. Diasporic Shanti is able to manipulate and control the representations
produced by the homeland, and her ability affirms the dialogic rather than unidirectional relationship between the diaspora and the homeland. Although she
is framed by the cinematic apparatus as the devoted subject within the framework of dominant narratives, as diasporic spectator Shanti literally interrupts
the constructed gaze reformulating the intersubjective relationship. In contrast
to the silence associated with darsan and the mute devotee looking only to be
seen, this diasporic devotee calls forth and talks back to the god, challenging
his power and authority. Later, when Shanti has mastered control of the darsan,
beckoning Krishna when she pleases, Krishna complains, "Ever since you discovered the video, I've had no peace." Shanti, an articulate diasporan, retorts
that she's "had no justice." Here is diasporic spectatorship of dominant texts
at its most resistant and oppositional. The film evokes the power of diasporic

consumption and spectatorship in its ability not only to negotiate, resist, and oppose narratives but also to rewrite them.

Of course, not all diasporic viewers resist or rewrite narratives in the same way. Shanti is a Hindu spectator and her negotiations and resistances differ from that of a resistant Sikh spectator position that challenges the Hindu-normative narration of the secular postcolonial Indian nation-state. When Krishna appears in all his adorned and armed glory in front of Bahuda Singh and Rita Solanki, who are trapped in the sari shop by the Mounties, he is dismissed by Singh. Singh deflates Krishna's bravado as out of place and time in diaspora and modernity. This second diasporic oppositional spectatorship allows us a different view of Shanti's spectatorship, which can now be critically reevaluated in light of its Hindu normativity and bourgeois cultural nationalist associations. The darsanic relationship between diaspora and homeland is reformulated by Singh, who does more than talk back to homeland narratives; he writes them, therefore not only challenging the construction of diasporic spectatorship and consumption but also of diasporic cultural production and circulation, thus further probing the a priori relationship between diaspora and homeland.

Diasporic Chronotopes: Planes and Houses

Bakhtin introduces the idea of the chronotope (literally time-space) to explain the entrance of history into the space of the novel, suggesting that chronotopes locate the specific historical and material conditions within the text. In other words, they link the time-space of the text with (representations of) historical processes. Gilroy (1993a) mobilizes the chronotope of the slave ship to mark the time-space of the emerging postmodern subjects of the Black Atlantic.

> The ship provides a chance to explore the articulations between the discontinuous histories of England's ports, its interfaces with the wider world. Ships also refer us back to the middle passage, to the half-remembered micro-politics of the slave trade and its relationship to both industrialization and modernization.... For all these reasons, the ship is the first of the novel chronotopes presupposed by my attempts to rethink modernity via the history of the black Atlantic and the African diaspora into the western hemisphere. (p. 17)

Thus, the ship of the Black Atlantic functions as a crucible of transnational space and history of African diaspora. Cinema scholars also have found the idea of the chronotope useful to thinking about filmic genres. Vivian Sobchack (1997) sees chronotopes as characterizing the literal time-space of the narrative and the characters. The film noir, she argues, is defined by its contrasting chronotopes—the removed, discontinuous time-space of the nightclub or hotel versus the protected private space of domesticity. In her analysis, the oppositional chronotopes express the economic, political, and cultural conflicts characteristic of the postwar film noir.

An analysis of the chronotopes present in this text provides us a way to understand the ways in which time-space is constituted in diaspora. In the case of diaspora, displacement from the space of the homeland is often projected onto the temporality of diasporic loss. In doing so, the time of the homeland evoked through history, memory, and nostalgia is represented by crossings of space, land, and territory. Within the time-space of South Asian diasporas and the diasporic films, airplanes and houses function similarly to Gilroy's ships and Sobchack's hotels and homes as chronotopes. Airplanes, like Gilroy's ships, evoke not only the displacement of migration but also the possibility of return to places and territories of origin. Houses or real estate are private spaces of capital-purchased domesticity whose rooted stability compensates for the displacement of diaspora. The contrast between the time-space of the airplane and the house, like that of the film noir's hotel and home, is useful in exploring the theoretical tensions of diaspora and diasporic cinema. In the film, both chronotopes are camped and satirized so that the defining features of diaspora including loss of the homeland expressed through nostalgia and displacement are interrogated, undermined, and denaturalized.

Airplanes are clearly associated with mobility and, more pronouncedly, the spatial mobility and displacement of the postcolonial South Asian diaspora within the moment of late capitalism or globalization in the film. Unlike the slave ship, they are ambivalent and ambiguous vessels that indicate a contradictory relationship to modernization and post-Fordist industrialization. In this case, airplanes run amok, uncontrollable by those who seek refuge in escape. Free and unencumbered mobility of any type is impossible in *Masala*. Planes explode, break windows, and become abandoned dreams of escape. From the very first moments of the film, as I have described already, planes are the setting of a suspended time and space, of a displacement from the normative identifications between territory and history for characters. The film infuses the space of diaspora with the time and history of diaspora. Though *Masala* does not directly identify the exploding plane as Air India flight 182, the reference to this postcolonial diasporic event is clear. Thus planes evoke mobility (space) but also memory and history (time). As a constant reminder, airplanes materialize throughout *Masala,* appearing in at least five additional scenes; most often they fly overhead as various characters grapple with diasporic displacement and are reminded of their loss.

The chronotope of the plane ironically functions to complicate the concept of displacement and return within diaspora. In one significant scene, Uncle Lallu arranges for Krishna to work at a travel agency. The owner of the agency walks Krishna around the agency and into a room with a huge table at the center. On the table is a model airport with a toy plane harnessed to a rod and spinning in circles taking off and landing on a runway. During the scene as Krishna inquires about the position, the owner of the agency demonstrates the model.

Fig. 4.4 *Masala's* chronotope of diaspora—the dangerous and uncontrollable plane.

Uncontrollable, even in the hands of a travel agency owner, the plane flies loose from its clasp and barrels through the room. The camera angle and focus shift at this moment in the scene from Krishna's perspective to a point of view located just behind the plane's tail (see Figure 4.4). The audience sees blurry figures dodging this life-size vehicle as it flies full-speed through the room. The camera angle and perspective relay the disorientation and instability of mobility. Finally, free from its moorings, the plane is liberated through an open window. The scene in the travel agency demonstrates the unpredictability and uncontrollability of diasporic mobility. This same irony is at play later as Krishna attempts to handle travel plans for Pinky, a well-to-do matron in the community. All of his attempts to create an itinerary according to her stipulations backfire as he sits helplessly and incompetently negotiating the computer software. Krishna fails to harness the technology to provide her the freedom of unencumbered mobility that is accessible with her wealth.

The film's interrogation of mobility, in addition to a critique of displacement, through the chronotope is multifold. *Masala* recognizes the desire for travel that infuses *Mississippi Masala* and *Wild West*. It, however, rejects not only diasporic return to homeland but also travel as escape or resolution to diasporic displacement. Like *Mississippi Masala*'s Mina, Rita also desires to escape through mobility. The daughter of the mild-mannered postal worker yearns not to go to medical school as her father wishes but to take flying lessons for which she earns money by laboring at the travel agency. Krishna regards her "conformity" with disdain and asks if she always plays by the rules; she answers no, that she wants flying lessons. He disbelievingly asks her, "Is that a revolution?" with her reply, Rita indicates that she, unlike Krishna, provides financial and emotional support to her family and that rebellion and revolution also are gendered. Her income is necessary to supplement her father's civil servant salary and therefore inadequate to purchase the freedom of movement of pilot lessons. Neither can a rejection of family and community come so simply, especially in the absence of a mother. Like Anil, Rita is circumscribed by her father's desire that she attend medical school. She feels the pressure of the recent immigrant's desire for upward mobility as well as a gendered form of duty.

Mobility seems necessary to the masculine process of self-awareness as it plays out in the character of Krishna. For Rita, however, alienation from the community is not the primary issue. Rather, it is achieving a balance between commitment to family and community and mobility. The first-generation desire to produce a second and third generation that is purely and authentically Indian applies the most pressure to women, who often become embodiments of tradition and therefore must replicate Indianness. However, despite the potential mobility symbolized by the planes, the film portrays how marriage is often the primary (fantasy) vehicle for women's escape. Rita romantically believes that her self-chosen relationship with Anil will adequately fulfill her dreams if he opposes his parents' wishes for a good financial match by marrying her. *Masala* exposes the naïveté of her fantasy. As Krishna and Anil's female counterpart, she presents a femininely gendered challenge to the perceived rigid rules and demands of the community and family. Rita's desire to escape by learning to fly, however, is also an ambivalent one, especially as we assume that Rita's mother has been killed in the explosion. Planes appear here as associated with not only violence, loss, and death at the beginning of the film but also, at the same time through Rita's eyes, as a symbolic hope for transcending the servile service jobs and economic difficulty of women's immigrant life. Rita's ironic desire for flying lessons is an attempt to wrangle, literally, a space outside of the gendered service position at the travel agency and the upwardly mobile but overly determined option of medical school or marriage; the film suggests that Rita's attempt to locate herself in this space, however, is futile. Furthermore, Rita's desire to fly is in contrast to a desire for home; in the case of the woman in diaspora, the space of domesticity itself may be dangerous.

Within the film, the protagonist Krishna becomes mobile only to recognize the futility of escape, hence returning to the Indian Canadian community. It is only when not home, that he can realize what home is—home becomes a place in the memory where he is not—and it is the time-space of the plane that most evokes this "defining" characteristic of diaspora. After finally collecting his $800 from a former girlfriend, Krishna plans to escape his uncle's home and the Indian Hindu community in Toronto and find a new home. But he disembarks from the bus before it arrives in Vancouver, too involved and connected to leave his community. Unlike in *Mississippi Masala,* this westward movement does not resolve the characters' issues by producing some new unwritten space. Instead, Krishna confronts his own alienation from the community, overcomes his fear of flying to board a propeller plane piloted by the deities Krishna and Balarama, and heads back to Toronto to keep his date with Rita for the rathyatra. Krishna, unlike Nair, returns the (male) protagonist back to community and family, thus critiquing travel as a mode of escape. But his mobility becomes a male rite of passage in which he gains vision and desires to reconnect, to seek the elusive home in the heterosexual union. Rita, circumscribed by domesticity and the institution of the family, seeks mobility, only to find it an unachievable form of escape; simultaneously, she functions as Krishna's attempted method of resolving his identity through reconnecting with the community. In fact, Rita serves as access to domesticity and ethnic community that are emblematic of diasporic cultural identity as I have discussed earlier.

The gendered home, configured as houses and real estate, are counterposed to the chronotope of the plane in general. As sites of refuge from not only diasporic displacement but also from economic impoverishment, homes and houses are desirable, though also satirized, in the film. In contrast to Rita, in her younger brother Babu we see the grooming of the young minority capitalist who yearns for a foreclosure-free home. Babu's desire is fueled by paid televised advertisements for the Canadian dream—middle-class homes through no-money-down real estate. He watches these televised narratives of desire as a way to plan his family's "escape" from foreclosure and racist hate crimes. He echoes in words outweighing his age, but not his migrant minority experience, formulas to financial success. As real estate and private property become the imagined protective refuge from the violence of exclusion and discrimination, Babu imagines a future in which class mobility can purchase a sense of belonging not too different from the one desired by Bahuda Singh. Similar to her grandson Babu, Shanti too wishes for a foreclosure-free home, but with an appliance-loaded kitchen like Bibi Solanki's in which she can make the perfect (authentic?) masala. Shanti yearns not for a homeland, as expected for a first-generation elderly woman, but for bourgeois private property complete with luxury commodity goods. The last shot of the film depicts Shanti in charge of the kitchen at the newly established heritage center, surrounded by her desired appliances and ordering the service workers in Hindi. The film closes with Shanti's gleeful and ludic laughter as she gestures upward chanting "Krishna Krishna" to the redeemed deity who has satisfied her wishes. Her desire, like that of Harry Tikkoo's ironic attachment to and desire for the colonial stamp, is one of the few satisfied within the film. (Harry is made curator of the newly built cultural heritage center that will house his precious stamp.)

Masala continually juxtaposes the house and plane as chronotopes of postcolonial diasporic time-space. These repeating images evoke the ambivalent postcolonial history of diasporic displacement and formation in the contemporary moment of late capitalism. In the film only material homes, nonmortgaged houses and real estate, are achievable forms of home. *Masala* systematically examines several diasporic definitions of home and suggests that in lieu of a resolution—a completion to the problems and desires of defining home within global modernity—there are only disjunctures and contingencies in which the diaspora narrates displacement, desire, and homeland.

Contesting Narration: Sikh Diaspora and the Necessity of a Homeland

Masala challenges the fettering of diaspora to homeland as an attachment to a site of origin and authenticity. As a consequence, rather than assuming diasporic longing and belonging as natural and a priori, it becomes necessary to examine under what conditions they are produced and narrated. South Asian diasporic films focus on politics of national belonging and cultural hybridity. Though these narratives may feature travel or migration, they explore mobility and hybridity as liberating rather than debilitating. But *Masala* is critical of these discourses of diaspora and focuses on mobility but does not resolve diaspora into a state of nomadology or interminable travel.

Unlike other narratives that depict diasporic longing for homeland, *Masala* complicates the teleology of assimilation. Whereas *Mississippi Masala* and *Wild West*, for example, depict diasporic desire to return as a first-generation issue, *Masala* forwards that generation may be misused to explain differences in Asian-American communities. *Masala* evinces that generation does not and cannot adequately explain affiliation to homeland; within the context of the film, none of the characters, first or second generation, long for or nostalgize the homeland. In other words, generation neither correlates with nor adequately explains attachment to the homeland. Longing and nostalgia associated with physical displacement have been used to overexplain the relationship between diasporas and homelands, as in the case of Sikhs; further inquiry into other explanations and mechanisms is required.

This complex rendering of attachment is best illustrated in the interactions between the Solankis and Bahuda Singh, in which the former express no attachment to the homeland and the latter expresses extreme desire for it. Lallu is at first resistant to the idea of accepting the money for storing the contraband until Bibi convinces him that the profit is greater than the risks and consequences. Though her sister dies in the plane crash, she ironically rationalizes, "What do we care if innocent people are killed; it is in the hands of god." Bibi denies a connection between her potentially storing arms, the loss of her sister,

and the possibility of other deaths. The Solankis' relationship to India is depicted as a purely economic one in which the homeland is a source of trade
and capital to diasporans who re-turn to India in to gain further power and
prestige in the diasporic place of residence. Thus, the Solankis express no diasporic longing or transnational affiliation as is expected. Through them, Krishna
slyly parodies and deconstructs the dominant homeland construction of the
nonresident Indian, one who is naturally invested (literally and metaphorically)
in the homeland due to nostalgia and nationalist identification processes. The
film also implicates Hindu Indians who villianize Sikhs for violence and terrorism without interrogating their own complicity in furthering tensions and
exploiting their privilege and sense of entitled belonging.

Furthermore, as first-generation immigrants, they campily and lucratively
perform Indian Canadian identities, profiting from migrant bourgeois and political status, exploiting their class privilege to become representatives of the
Indian community in Canadian multiculturalism. (For example, in contrast to
Krishna's mother who is presented in sari and mangal sutra, Bibi is clad in "Indian" clothing [a sari] only when the Solankis are entertaining the multicultural
set. Bibi Solanki is associated with a display of ethnicity solely as a marker and
commodity of exchange in multiculturalism.) The Solankis are not interested
in issues of racial or material inequality; instead they divest themselves entirely
of interest in the homeland and only involve themselves in diasporic issues
when politically and economically advantageous. In contrast, Bahuda Singh's
relationship with the homeland is clearly not for profit but stems from a desire for affiliation.[14] But none of these characters configures a homeland as a
place of origin from which they have been displaced and to which they long to
return.

The Sikh diaspora within *Masala* offers the opportunity to examine not only
nondominant South Asian diasporas but also the normalization and dissemi-
nation of concepts such as homeland. Displacement from the homeland in this
case is not the primary narrative of the Sikh diaspora. (Thus it is hardly the
plane that functions as the chronotope of the Sikh diaspora.) The Sikh diaspora
here illustrates the ways in which most theorizations of South Asian diasporas
take the Hindu from India as the normative subject. Often diaspora is taken as a
homogenous given that is singularly defined as a displaced national culture that
is determined by religious traditions and precolonial social practices. *Masala*
satirizes any simple construction of diaspora and diasporic longing and return;
instead, it suggests that involvement and engagement with places marked as
homelands are based on complex colonial and postcolonial histories in South
Asia.[15]

Framed by the explosion of Air India flight 182, the film lampoons the
stereotypes of all Sikhs as militant and violent terrorists as it is revealed that this
"contraband" for the Sikh struggle for statehood and homeland is toilet paper
inscribed with the narrative of Sikh history (see Figure 4.5).[16] The transient

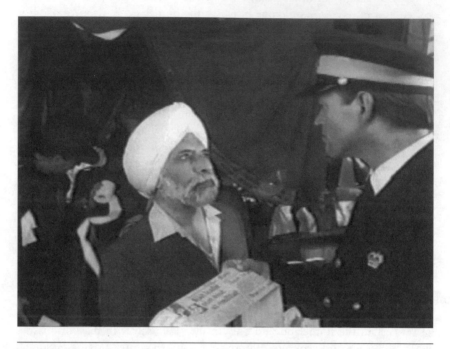

Fig. 4.5 The nation narrated on Singh's contraband toilet paper in *Masala*.

toilet paper can be read self-referentially and self-mockingly as reels of film that narrate this particular history of the nation and the diaspora.[17] The rolls of toilet paper evoke the significant contemporary and historic production of Sikh diasporic communities, in Punjabi and English, in desiring and narrating the nation and homeland from within the diaspora. Dominant Indian media work primarily and predominantly with a Hindu, not Sikh, normative subject. The film campily questions the function of diasporic production (and cinema) in English, where it is presumably a luxury that is consumable as toilet paper to the substantial middle class. The necessity of diasporic (cultural) politics for Sikhs as minorities in India can be seen in the contrast between access to videos and reels of films on one hand and rolls of toilet paper on the other. Hence, the rolls of toilet paper being sent from the diaspora to the homeland also attest to the marginalization of Sikhs in the Indian nation-state.

In the film, Bahuda Singh, the only visibly Sikh character with a speaking part, describes himself to Lallu Solanki as "a victim of necessity." He explains, "Other Sikhs don't agree with my methods. I was a professor of modern Indian history before the temple was destroyed. . . . This country is not mine. I am not looking for vengeance, but for justice, the ability to worship our own god." His gentle earnestness counters the image of him as a terrorist storing arms. Krishna is careful to disassociate Singh from separatist terrorism; Singh is not portrayed as involved in a militant and violent struggle for the territorial sovereignty of Khalistan. His nationalism is not a call to arms for the establishment of a Sikh state based on some anterior connection to Punjab ("Sikhs belong to the Punjab; the Punjab belongs to the Sikhs.") Singh's need for a nation here is not some autochthonous connection to a territory but rather current historical needs arising out of a search for justice. Instead, Singh asks for religious freedom and to live with justice. His desire for a homeland is articulated in terms of contemporary South Asian politics.

The discourse of Sikh claims to Punjab, contends Harjot Oberoi (1994), is recent, a colonial discourse produced by the partition of India when Sikhs felt themselves to be "victims of necessity" in need of a "communal" group identity. Oberoi also poses that Sikh identity and the Sikh desire for a homeland (in Punjab or a separate Khalistan) are recent phenomena. In other words, Sikhs have not always demanded a Khalistani nation-state separate from India; some have asked instead for a homeland in India.[18] Until 1984 and the Indian state's storming of the Golden Temple, the struggle for Khalistan was a minor Sikh discourse. In the past decade, especially since subsequent attacks on Amritsar and the Hindu riots against Sikhs after the assassination of Indira Gandhi by her Sikh bodyguards, there has been a rise in Sikh activity in support of Khalistan. The violence following Indira Gandhi's assassination led to the death of an estimated 10,000 to 100,000 in Punjab. Some Sikh scholars, including Oberoi and Axel, point to these events as ones that have mobilized and consolidated Sikh discourses of nationalism and Khalistani separatism. They argue that the desire for a separate homeland has regenerated narratives and histories of Sikhs as a nation.

Moreover, this increasing desire for a sovereign homeland separate from India has been greatly fostered within the Sikh diaspora. Prior to the events of 1984, the Khalistan movement was primarily an isolated emigrant endeavor. Since then, Khalistani sympathy has grown in the diaspora. Recent calls to statehood in the diaspora have been made by migrants such as Jagjit Singh Chauhan, a British resident and leader of the National Council of Khalistan and self-professed president of the land of Khalsa, and Ganga Singh Dhillon, U.S. citizen and president of the Sri Nankan Sahib Foundation. Increased Sikh nationalism in diasporic communities is a factor that separatist militant Sikh organizations have come to rely on with economic and political support from the diaspora, through the production of constitutions, documents, and Web sites. Like the toilet paper, these diasporic productions forge links among different places of residence, creating a Sikh diaspora. Axel (2001) argues that the fetish for this production often has been the tortured male body. Images of the bodies documenting, witnessing, and attesting to Sikh victimization function as spatiotemporal sites linking the porous body of the subject to the larger diaspora and homeland. Nevertheless, the Sikh body located elsewhere also is referenced by the presence of the toilet paper. The toilet paper then can refer to the porosity of those bodies, here satirized in their scatological rather than tortured modes. Nevertheless, the reviewer is returned repeatedly to evocations of death through violence—hate crimes, state persecution, and terrorism that appear throughout the film. *Masala* foregrounds the ways in which the nation and state perpetuate and permit violence against minorities, but, it does not seek nationalism (either cultural nationalism or state sovereignty) as a solution to the status of minority.

The narrative of Sikh history inscribed on the toilet paper is the history of the nation written in the diaspora. Krishna satirizes not only the activity of Khalistan separatism but also the very construction and narration of that nation. The imagined community is narrated neither in novels (Brennan 1990) and newspapers (Anderson 1991), nor in film and mythological epics (Shohat and Stam 1994), but rather on toilet paper. Furthermore, here the imagined community is quite different from the idea of imagined implied by Rushdie, as I mentioned earlier. Although Rushdie offers that South Asian diasporas create imaginary cities of the mind, his construction of imaginary homelands are those that are anachronistically created out of memory and nostalgia. Instead, in the case of the Sikh diaspora, the nation, diaspora, and homeland are created not from memory or nostalgia, which are considered the common mechanisms of recalling the homeland, but from constitutive discourses and everyday practices. Although Krishna recognizes that desire for a homeland and national affiliation is perhaps a "necessity," he simultaneously undermines the preexistence and naturalness of the homeland that is desired and written into histories. What is captured, then, is the diaspora in the process of dialectically constituting the nation and homeland. Thus, I am not only arguing that history is constructed, or that traditions are invented, but, more important, that these are generated in the diasporic imaginary. As Axel (2001, 209) writes, "The production of knowledge of *displacement,* which apparently defines diaspora *as* diaspora, effectively collapses that place into the temporality to which I have been referring as an anteriority, positioning the homeland within a time prior to the diaspora's emergence." Axel too argues that homelands are mutually constituted by diasporas. Moreover, he suggests that the space of the homeland then becomes a marker for the anteriority and existence of the subject in diasporic displacement. It is this anteriority that the toilet paper reveals.

Even though historical narratives of Sikh history often deploy affiliations to Punjab as justifications for posing Punjab as the potential Sikh nation-state, Singh's narrative of Sikh history never claims Punjab in the film. He only proposes that Sikhs as a nation share a language, history, and culture and are in need of a place to worship. In an age when the discourses of nationalism and territorial sovereignty are not easily avoidable in claims of representation and identity, and of power and justice, what are the alternatives? Oberoi writes,

> Having derived sustenance from the stories of territoriality, the Sikhs are now
> trapped in the depths of a classic dilemma: if they pursue its resolution, they
> are faced with a situation similar to that of the Basques, the Kurds, and the

Palestinians (which are fellow ethnoterritorial communities), but if they abandon this newly constructed emblem they undermine an element of their own identity. One possible way out of the labyrinth would be gradually to invent new myths. (cited in Dusenbery 1995, 35)

Masala attempts to acknowledge and promote Sikh justice or nationhood without demanding Khalistani statehood. A neat narrative of nationalism—producible in mass quantities, exportable, and absorbent, like toilet paper—leads to this dilemma, which is lampooned in the film. But more important, the film marks the toilet paper as narrating the nation and a luxury that Sikh diaspora must afford for legitimacy in geopolitical and postcolonial power systems. An alternative to the discourse of statehood is difficult to construct and hardly conjures the power that is afforded to the nation-state. As a people, nation, and diaspora, you must have a state to be real.

Masala depicts the character of the Canadian Minister of Multiculturalism (an actual post) as an opportunistic, slick, hypocritical civil servant—a symbol of the ineffectual and elaborate bureaucracy designed to appease Francophone separatists and "visible minorities" through tokenism that does not disturb the racist power structure.[19] The oversimplified construction of the pluralist nation in multicultural policy unravels and exposes the inadequate model that homogenizes the multiplicity of South Asian diasporas to one ethnicity classifiable as East Indian, based on country or nation of origin. The bureaucratic government is not the only one prone to this homogenizing and lumping; the film illustrates the ways in which the Canadian popular imaginary does not distinguish between Indian and Pakistan, Sikh and Hindu. Krishna's junkie former girlfriend continuously addresses him derogatorily as Paki and suggests that he begin his own import business of good drugs with his connections in Pakistan. To this helpful advice Krishna responds with frustration, "I am from India, not Pakistan. I am Indian!"

At the same time, the Canadian state differentiates Sikhs from other Indians, marking them as threatening, but nevertheless represented by the category of Indian within multiculturalism. *Masala* clearly illustrates the ways in which Sikhs have become associated with violence, not so much by the Indian nation-state as discussed previously but by the Canadian nation-state. Bahuda Singh's activities are immediately seen as suspicious by the Mounties. The Mounties constitute the Sikh diaspora as a threat to the Canadian nation-state and as the target of state surveillance. Portrayed as a victim not only of Indian state oppression, Singh is also victimized by Canadian multiculturalism. We see in the film that it is Sikhs who are targeted by the Mounties and Hindus who are courted by the Ministry of Multiculturalism. Thus, Sikhs are differentiated from other Indian Canadian citizens but are nevertheless identified and categorized as Indians. One imagines, however, that Sikh subjects may feel unable or refuse to claim Indian identities in the same way, especially after the events in the past few decades. Multiculturalism undoubtedly constructs the Sikh homeland as India, not Punjab or Khalistan. However, multiculturalism, taking no note of these contested identities, is not only a national-based politics with its limits of representation but also a local-based politics, one that privileges the local over the transnational and global.[20]

The tendency of Canadian ideology to clump all South Asians together as East Indians has resounding effects. Upon the diversification of immigration, with an increase in regional, religious, cultural, linguistic, and class differences, this label provides a homogenizing effect in its desire to identify those from the same nation of "origin" as having similar configurations of identity. Sikhs marginalized by postcolonial Indian nationalism constructed as Hindu in diaspora and South Asia leads to increasing desire for separatism. The marginalization of Sikhs in the representative state politics of multiculturalism in Canada is clearly depicted in the power relations of the film in which the minister of multiculturalism interacts only with a certain elite Hindu community. The logic of this pluralistic multicultural nationalism as a model requires the categorization of peoples into communities that have or claim sovereign territorial rights in relation to a homeland that is a nation-state.

Verne Dusenbery (1995) suggests that participation in homeland politics also is often influenced by several factors besides "longing" and disenchantment with and disenfranchisement from the diasporic place of residence. He suggests that "psychological" explanations are factors but also that this diaspora participates in a discourse about homeland and statehood because of its marginalization in the place of residence. This multiculturalism predicates Sikh identity in national rather than religious terms, thus imposing Western assumptions about the primacy of race and ethnicity. In the case of Canadian multiculturalism and Sikhs, religious identity is then recalibrated to an ethnonational metric. Darshan Singh Tatla (1999, 206) states,

> Many leaders point out that, year after year, issues of religious authority have risen in almost every country: justification for the turban and kirpan; provision for Punjabi in schools, on radio and on television.... A large number of leaders believe that many such issues would not have arisen, or would have been more easily soluble, if the community had had an independent state.

Thus nation is the most authenticating of identities. Without recognition as a nation, a diaspora loses legitimacy and faces (forced) assimilation into a dominant Indian identity or a Canadian one.

Conclusion

In this chapter, I have considered diasporic culture as merely duplicating the national homeland culture. I have reformulated paradigms in which the diaspora is taken to be an impure copy of the authentic original through a discussion of camp and resistant diasporic spectatorship as strategic critiques of dominant culture in diasporic cultural production. *Masala* poses possibilities of disidentification from and with dominant cultures (in this case Indian and Canadian) for diasporic subjects. As camp and satire, the film offers few satisfying resolutions and closures. Instead, *Masala* suggests that in lieu of a resolution—a completion to the problems and desires of defining home within the displacement of global modernity—there are only disjunctures and contingencies in which diasporic subjects identify and disidentify. Among the various modes of escape envisioned by the characters, only the security of real estate, material possessions, and political power are achieved. For women who are often outside of or have ambivalent relations with the state, Krishna portrays the domestic as a site in which Shanti displays ludic laughter in the face of state policy. Diasporas appear as sites of negotiations and dislocations articulating nondominant cultural politics. Disidentified subjects who perform identities with difference reshape transnational cultural politics within the space of diaspora. In doing so, they embed their critiques and strategies within discontinuous and multiple fields of power that authorize dominant narratives.

Masala deconstructs these diasporic resolutions to question the very formation of the question of displacement, challenging the normative narratives of diaspora that assume that they are formed from the act of displacement from a given homeland. It questions the anterior time of that construction and formulates diasporas and homelands as mutually and dialectically constituted. In doing so, the film, of course, undermines the logic of multiculturalism that assumes that identities and peoples are associated with the fixed sites of the homeland nation-state with "natural, primordial, and organic" connections between identity and place. The implications lead us to begin to reformulate diasporic and transnational studies, concentrating not on how diasporas replicate but on how they produce and consume homelands and cultures. Finally and most important, *Masala* examines the relationship between nostalgia and cinema, suggesting how the cinematic apparatus may function in diasporic processes of (dis)identification and in nostalgic viewing that imagine community.

5

Homesickness and Motion Sickness: Embodied Migratory Subjectivities in Gurinder Chadha's *Bhaji on the Beach*

Body-feeling, "that queasy sense of being inside/outside the officially designated places of home, state, and public—does not transcend space but more deeply connects body to place without demanding a fixed—or even any—identity as a conduit for being recognizably 'citizen' (however plural the faces)."
—Cindy Patton 1997, xiii

Bollywood and Diasporic Nostalgia

One of the most popular Bollywood films of the nineties, *Dilwale Dulhaniya Le Jayenge* (*The Lover Takes a Bride*), opens with the actor Amrish Puri feeding pigeons in London, gazing into the distance, nostalgic for the mustard fields and untainted culture of Punjab. *DDLJ*, as the film is commonly known, is a significant film in Bollywood cinema because it is the one of the first to signify the diasporic subjects as Indian national subjects rather than as corrupted Westerners. The "Indian and his family" can and have remained intact despite its transplantation abroad argues the film. More specifically, it suggests that despite their vulnerability to Westernization, gendered and sexualized normativities can also exist in the diaspora. The popularity of the film transnationally attests to the pleasures and desires associated with such a narrative of belonging.

Focused on the lives of nonresident Indians, the film was significant in its depiction of the shifting relationship between the diaspora and homeland in light of globalization processes including the political and economic liberalization in India. Constructing the ideal diasporic subjects, *DDLJ* counterposes the deterritorialized national subjects of the heroine (Simran played by Kajol) and the hero (Raj played by Shahrukh Khan) with the pained patriarch who reminisces simultaneously about the productive land and the fertile maidens of home. The film opens with Baldev comparing the search for sustenance by the homeless pigeons with his own experiences of migration; his monologue articulates his alienation in and from a land where only the pigeons know him:

> Where have you come from, why have you come here? Half a life has gone by, and yet this land is so strange to me and I to it. Like me, these pigeons too have no home, but when will I be able to fly? But someday, surely, I too will return. To my India, to my Punjab.

Here "home" is produced not only as a territory, community, nation-state, and place (rural and pastoral Punjab as metonym of India) but also as a structure of feeling associated with a particular time (in psychoanalytic terms as the canny—experienced as a past that is familiar and unforeign). Meanwhile, the balm for this suffering is the desire and dream to return to India, especially his Punjabi village. Although quite a bit more can be said about the nostalgia in this passage, suffice to say the contrast between London and the Punjabi village visually encapsulates an entire host of implicit comparisons within the film. More important, although the visual foregrounds the object of nostalgia, the home of Punjab, the dialogue prioritizes the subject of nostalgia—Baldev, who experiences nostalgia as a response to displacement and disenfranchisement. Like *Mississippi Masala*, the film associates diasporic nostalgia and desire for return most strongly with the (disenfranchised) male migrant.[1]

In *DDLJ*, it is the patriarch who longs for the homeland and finds the West threatening in terms of contamination and corruption; in contrast, for Baldev's daughters, diaspora is home. In this film, men are the subjects and women the embodiments of nostalgia. The displaced patriarch, emasculated and disempowered by race and class in the postcolonial metropole, consequently produces an overcompensating iron grip on his family. His loss of home is a consequence of displacement but also of the resultant destabilization of the patri-archal and heteronormative formulation of family. In particular the daughters, as the metonymic embodiments of Punjab (like the frolicking peasant women) and the metaphoric emblems of homeland, become the objects of heteropa-triarchal surveillance and law manifested in the institution of marriage and conducted as an exchange with homeland patriarchy. Not surprisingly, Simran and her sister do not express or experience nostalgia. Moreover, rather than experience nostalgia and desire for the homeland or the past, they embody it.[2]

Baldev's oldest daughter Simran secures permission from her father to travel to Europe prior to her engagement and marriage. The travel to the continent provides the space and place for Simran to fall in love with Raj, a fellow British Asian. Vijay Mishra (2002, 253) in *Bollywood Cinema* argues that Simran's tem-porary mobility away from the domestic and national (English and Indian) with the "grand tour" of pastoral Europe creates the possibility of romance. However, it is Baldev's desire that Simran marry Kuljeet—a son not only of India but also in India. Kuljeet the willing groom turns out to be scheming and opportunistic with a passion that is stronger for settling abroad than it is for Simran. The true son of Hindustan proves to be the British Asian Raj who is honorable and loyal; Raj is shown to be more than capable of maintaining his "Indian values and culture" though residing abroad. In the end, Baldev (and consequently his wife and also youngest daughter) remain in Punjab, having returned to the much-desired homeland, while Simran and Raj head "home" to England. *DDLJ* thus rewrites the narratives of earlier films such as *Paurab aur Paschim* (*East or West*) that configure deterritorialized national subjectivity within the framework of a binary of Western or Indian, but as always already Westernized. In such films, diasporic female subjects are consistently configured as good Indian girls who have been contaminated and corrupted, that is, as vamps complete with miniskirts, cigarettes, and blonde wigs.

The British film *Bhaji on the Beach* also attempts to write these dominant narratives and thus shares some striking similarities with *DDLJ*. Both films strongly depict the experiences of British Asians as ones that are confronted by racism and displacement. Likewise, both films narrate this experience from feminine points of view. *DDLJ* and *Bhaji on the Beach* also view mobility and travel as significant to the agency of gendered diasporic subjects. However, the differences may be more notable than the similarities; unlike *DDLJ*, *Bhaji on the Beach* is a British film. *Bhaji on the Beach* is more critical of the patriarchal family structure and endogamous rules of heteronormativities, for example, in its critique of domestic abuse and its support of multiracial relationships. Chadha's film, unlike *DDLJ*, does not dichotomize subjective experience and embodiment in regard to nostalgia; in other words, women are more than the surfaces of the inscription of nostalgia in the film that refuses to force a dichotomous division between the subjective experience and embodiment of nostalgia.[3] Moreover, *Bhaji on the Beach* is a film that does not offer the heroine as the female figure of identification to represent a singular and homogenized version of diasporic experience; it instead presents a multiplicity of female characters who are heterogeneous in their depiction of gendered migratory subjectivities. Most important, although *DDLJ* retains the binary of West and East and poses that the East can retain its essential cultural difference even in the West, *Bhaji on the Beach* seeks to work against the binary of Indian/Western in framing itself in terms of multiple and fragmented British Asian hybridity. Hence, it constitutes itself more through an understanding of racial politics of Britain than it does with the deterritorialized national politics of *DDLJ* (specifically, a call to and claim on India as a homeland).

The film comments that diasporic construction of women as motherland and family as nation creates women's bodies as the terrain of diasporic struggle. The film's closing marks not the resolution of new nation building but rather the formation of community outside of the nation and state. The films discussed earlier—*Mississippi Masala, Wild West,* and *Masala*—do not specifically attend to issues of the body and embodiment as they skirt around the cultural politics of the somatic.[4] Chadha's film, on the other hand, explicitly portrays the diasporic heteronormativity (e.g., pregnancy) and displacement (e.g., sickness) as somatic experiences that are located in relation to complex and intersecting social differences. In doing so, it allows us to explore a fuller understanding of the meanings of migration and diaspora in terms of the body.

Bhaji on the Beach not only offers a complex interrogation of how British Asian women are positioned by racial, sexual, and gender oppressions but it also poses alternative modes of understanding phenomena associated with migration that differ from dominant Bollywood cinema. Multiple generations and classes of women suffer in the film from illness such as vertigo (displacement and disorientation), domestic abuse (women as cultural producers of the home and nation), unplanned pregnancy (women as reproducers of home and nation), and dizziness (motion sickness due to overconsumption as a response to racism and ethnic insularity).[5] *Bhaji on the Beach* focuses on understanding these bodily processes and somatic experiences within the gendered context of a diverse community of women. In my reading, I seek to understand what I am calling homesickness—the gendered embodiment and subjective experience of nostalgia—by linking together understandings of nostalgia, home, and cinema in relation to the somatic.[6]

I do this by examining two salient and related discursive and material diasporic constructions, home and mobility, on diasporic female embodied subjectivities. Clearly, nostalgia becomes (en)gendered through constructions of home and the domestic, however, seldom have conversations on nostalgia ventured to ascertain an understanding of how migration and diaspora produce embodied subjects. Pursuing this line of inquiry, the first part of the chapter forwards that such an analysis can lead productively to understanding how homesickness is a significant concept-metaphor for gendered embodied subjectivity located in racism and heteropatriarchy. More specifically, it elaborates on the idea of homesickness—social and physical illness that is the production of and desire for "homes" within diasporic contexts, including, but not limited to, heteropatriarchal constructions of nostalgia.[7] In the film, homesickness signifies the condition of migratory embodied subjectivities located in relation to heteronormativity, racism, Orientalism, and displacement. My analysis here emphasizes two different homesicknesses—dis-Orientation and domestic abuse. The concluding part of this chapter explores the movement away from the space of the "domestic and private" to analyze the embodied and subjective experience of women's agency and mobility or motion sickness. I propose that the women individually and collectively resist these power relations through seeking (temporary) mobility away from domestic spaces; nevertheless, their agency and mobility is accompanied and characterized by an embodied ambivalence.[8]

In this chapter, I forge a conversation between previously disparate areas of inquiry including feminist theories of the body and agency, understandings of nostalgia, and migration and diasporic studies. First and foremost, within feminist theorizing of the body and embodiment, there has been little discussion of migration and diaspora. Importantly, in this chapter I posit that feminist and queer theories of the body need to be embedded and understood within the specific and material frameworks of transnationalism and diaspora with special attention to the heteronormative imperative implicit in these constructions. In addition, I endeavor to establish how the concept-metaphor of homesickness collapses the private/public distinction that is associated with gendered space and the female body, thereby exploring psychoanalytic understandings of subjectivity in relation to race, gender, and migration. Finally, I ask for us to consider the consequences and impact of gendered mobility as a mode or strategy of agency in relation to embodied subjectivity.

British Asian Representation of Diasporic Women

The film focuses on a group of Asian British women on a day trip to Blackpool (a holiday sea and entertainment resort associated predominantly with working-class white English, a point to which I return later) for leisure and consumption (including the eating of *bhaji* or snacks). It weaves together the stories of the various members of the Birmingham Saheli Women's Center—Ginder (and her son Amrik) who has left and is divorcing her husband Ranjit because of his abuse, medical-student-to-be Hashida who has just discovered that she is pregnant by her Afro-Caribbean British boyfriend Oliver, brash and sexually curious Ladhu and Madhu who are teenagers out looking to meet boys, middle-aged mother and newsagent Asha "Auntie" who is experiencing dizziness and hallucinations, her wealthy socialite friend Rekha who is visiting from Bombay, the elderly and formidable shop owner and housewife Pushpa, the group organizer Simi, and the middle-aged shop assistant Bina. The ensemble cast functions as a method of suggesting the heterogeneity of British Asian women with regard to differences such as sexuality, religion, class, education, and age.[9]

The women escape for one day of leisure, but they cannot leave behind their difficulties. They are followed by Ranjit (and his brothers) who plans to persuade or force Ginder and Amrik to return home with him, and they are also followed by Oliver who wants to find Hashida before she makes any unilateral decisions regarding the pregnancy. At the beach, the older generation of women is perplexed and shocked upon discovering Hashida's pregnancy, resulting in an open confrontation between Hashida and Pushpa. Meanwhile, Asha continues to experience dizziness and disorientation, finding herself "rescued" by an elderly Orientalist fellow named Ambrose who regales her with his knowledge of *Gunga Din* and other colonialist films during a tour of Blackpool. Ladhu and Madhu pair up with two burger-flipping lads who accompany them on amusement rides and to a pub. They all rendezvous at the women-only club Manhattan at the end of the day. At the club, a host of male strippers who pluck Pushpa and then Ginder from the audience to dance with inadvertently reveal the bruises on Ginder's body.

Bhaji on the Beach is Gurinder Chadha's first feature-length narrative film, and Chadha is Britain's first Asian woman director. Chadha, a self-identified Punjabi born in Kenya, migrated to England at an early age and settled in Southall in the sixties. Her previous work includes shorts and documentaries, including the critically acclaimed *I'm British But. . . .* (1990), *A Nice Arrangement* (1991), and *Acting Our Age* (1992). She began her career as a BBC reporter, later working at Channel Four, which eventually financed *Bhaji on the Beach* for about

1 million pounds (1.5 million dollars). Her latest film, *Bend It Like Beckham*, has been hugely popular, as I have discussed earlier.

Bhaji on the Beach was written by Meera Syal (author of *Anita and Me*, 1996, and *Life Isn't All Ha Ha Hee Hee*, 2000, as well as screenwriter for Andrew Lloyd Webber's *Bollywood Dreams*, 2002) and produced by Nadine March-Edwards (producer of Isaac Julien's *Young Soul Rebels*, 1991). Chadha emerges out of a historical moment in the eighties British (post)multicultural scene in which artists, intellectuals, and activists challenged conceptions of British/English identity around issues of race, class, and gender. Unlike the more experimental and deconstructive style of the collective and workshop films, *Bhaji on the Beach*'s narrative is more informed by the British and Indian cinema of the sixties and seventies. Nevertheless, like the films made by the collectives (such as *Passion of Remembrance*) it articulates itself, not as torn between two cultures but as located in the third space of minority identities in England as both British and Asian.

The character of Simi (the organizer of the women's group in the film) most directly articulates the politics of the film (and perhaps the filmmaker) when she declares, "It's not often that we women get away from the patriarchal demands made on us in our daily lives, struggling between the double yoke of racism and sexism." Yet within the film, her statement is met with puzzlement, silence, and dismissal by the other day-trippers. This moment seems a self-reflexive one in which Chadha suggests that although black and feminist politics undergird the film, these are not explicitly the terms by which they are understood by the characters in their everyday lives. This strategy seems to be one that Chadha employs to make a "populist" rather than "avant-garde" film in her terms in that she is more interested in exploring how racism and sexism structure the labor, leisure, and desires of Asian women's lives (Chua 1994, 18–19). The scene also indicates the ways in which humor figures centrally as a mode to disrupt expectations regarding black cultural production. In this way, Chadha's film is located centrally in relation to conversations on black British filmmaking, but it does not shy away from defining the cultural and social milieu of her films as Punjabi and Asian. Because of this, though it is often compared to *Mississippi Masala*, Chadha's film is differently located in that black coalition politics precedes the film, and therefore the film is not apologetic for the Asian community. Its depiction of the Asian/Afro-Caribbean relationship is not defensive.

Overall, *Bhaji on the Beach* seeks to produce such an understanding through its content and form. First of all, the dialogues are multilingual in English, Hindi, Punjabi, and Urdu. The film incorporates aesthetic elements of British cinematic and Indian cinematic productions, the latter particularly through the use of music, dance, and quirky editing cuts. The British song "Summer Holiday" features prominently to reflect the very English day trip undertaken by the women in the film, but here it is transformed with Punjabi lyrics. Evoking not only trips to Britain's sea resorts, the use of "Summer Holiday" alludes to the film of the same name and its plot of a young white woman seeking to escape the control of her mother. Similarly, other aspects of the British humor of films such as the early *Carry On* series as well as Tony Richardson's *A Taste of Honey* (1962) and Ken Loach's *Up the Junction* (1965) are used as comic counterpoints throughout—vomiting from the Ferris wheel or the cakes shaped like breasts (O'Shea 1995, 8). Bollywood song numbers, specifically a parodic reference to *Paurab aur Paschim,* seek to undermine the ways in which Bollywood films constitute diasporic subjectivity but simultaneously acknowledge the seductive and significant power of these narratives and forms within British Asian cultural production.

Unlike Bollywood films, *Bhaji on the Beach* does not configure the women's situation as being engendered by some conflict between East and West or being caught between two worlds. Nor does it replicate the simple notion that those from India are "backward" and less Westernized than those who live in England. Instead, the film uses class as a marker to distinguish the "modern" Western Bombay socialite Rekha who appears in the film in a rosy suit, sunglasses, and high heels from her more conservative and "Indian" salwar-kameez and sari clad compatriots. Thus, Rekha vibrantly stands in her stiletto heels and bright suit in contrast to the middle-aged sari-clad women who are British but who appear more "traditional" than she does. All of the women are implicated in British Asianness in the film as Bhattacharyya and Gabriel (1994, 59) point out in their analysis. *Bhaji on the Beach* refuses such easy binaries and identifies more complicated negotiations of the ways in which the perceived conflict between West and East is played out on the embodied terrain of domesticity, marriage, femininity, and pleasure. Rather than suggesting that the family is merely the site of patriarchal control in Asian communities, a position that plays directly into white dominant discourses of repressive Asian culture, I argue that these are particular sites around which power struggles coalesce in relation to the nation-state and migration.[10]

Embodiment

The body has been a site of feminist interrogation by theorists with diverse interests and investments. Although many scholars seek to understand the body through the development of corporeal feminisms (Elizabeth Grosz, 1994, for example) based on the idea of the reproductive body, they do so often through the frameworks of language and psychoanalysis. These discourses of psychoanalysis have been helpful in thinking through many aspects of embodied experience. (They have not, however, sought to understand the racialized body that undergoes migration and displacement.) Feminist theories of the body have not only forwarded the corporeality of subjectivity but also have striven to understand it within the (supposedly oppositional) frameworks of materiality and discursivity. Foucauldian theorists have attended to the ways in which the body is not only produced in discourses but also is disciplined by everyday practices. Specifically, they have examined how the body and embodiment are immersed in and the site of contested power relations and are marked by disciplining, resistance, contradictions, and transgressions. Using multiple and blended frameworks, scholars such as Elaine Scarry (1985), Rajeswari Sunder Rajan (1997), and Bibi Bakare-Yusuf (1999) have theorized the body in pain in various conditions such as torture, postcolonial nationalism, and slavery, respectively. However, the conditions of slavery and torture are significantly different from the condition of diaspora; this area of research is underexamined. In this study, it is the lived materiality of the body in pain (or one that is suffering "sickness") due to diasporic displacement and configured through racial, gendered, classed, and sexual discourses that is placed at the center of analysis.

Working from a queer and intersectional position, I take race, class, gender, and sexuality as frameworks for theorizing postcolonial migrant women's embodiments, particularly to ask about the ways in which the political and social meanings of embodiments are formulated in postcolonial diasporas.[11] I emphasize the relationship between subjectivity and embodiment to signal a refusal of the mind/body dichotomy that characterizes much of Western theorizing about the body. Embodiment, in the work of Rosi Braidotti (1994), for example, implies multiple sets of situated positions that are located in contradictory and complex discourses about the body and consciousness. Thus, I read the film not for constructions of the migrant, postcolonial, or black/Asian British woman's body but for multiple embodiments that attempt to exceed the totality of representation. *Bhaji on the Beach* does not simply assert the impossibility of representing the South Asian woman but rather marks the ways in which these embodied positions are produced and performed among the multiple and shifting presence and performances of multiple bodies. In particular, the analysis foregrounds the narratives of homesickness and motion sickness—disorientation and dizziness, wife battering, morning sickness (arising from a concealed pregnancy in a multiethnic relationship), and vomiting (due to alcohol consumption and amusement park rides).

There is a dearth of theory relating embodied subjectivity to mobility and migration in feminist theories of the body. Despite the ubiquity of the body in transnational migration, theories of the body have either taken no account of such processes or metaphorized them into some disembodied nomadism. For feminist theories to engage seriously with the processes of globalization, they will have to develop numerous paradigms for contending with these complex and shifting corporealities. If bodies are produced and constituted through social discourses imbricated in networks of power, as poststructuralist theorists such as Judith Butler have argued, then pursuing an understanding of the materialization of the body as it occurs at multiple levels from the local to the transnational is a necessary endeavor in feminist studies. Conversely, if feminist theorists seek to understand migration within the context of globalization, they must ask what constructions of the body are produced by these social contexts and what interests they serve.

Nostalgia

Homesickness encapsulates an analytical method for understanding the gendered and sexualized embodiment of migratory subjectivities. Postcolonial scholars such as Partha Chatterjee (2001) and Dipesh Chakrabarty (1997) argue that the nineteenth-century Indian nationalism was not a rejection of the West but rather a way to produce an Indian modernity by using selective understandings of European modernity but that is marked by cultural and spiritual distinction. The spiritual, home, and Indian were gendered feminine, and the material, public, and Western as (an unmarked) masculine. The modern was identified by nationalism's derivative discourse as those masculine traits associated with Westernization and the material (Partha Chatterjee 1993). In opposition, tradition was written into the feminine domain of the native and spiritual, hence the space of cultural difference. Chatterjee argues that this anticolonial nationalism distinguished itself from its Western counterparts through this rewriting of the public-private divide.[12] Sexuality too was mobilized by anticolonial nationalism in the name of family, motherhood, and purity (marked as tradition), in contrast to the Western modes of romance and love (signifying the modern). Consequently, women's interests were collapsed with the interests of the heteronormative family and the home. Women have somatically represented the nation itself and have been figured as the mother of it. Thus, during the early part of the century, the family emerges with the consolidation of the middle classes as an institution that reproduces national culture through representations of women's bodies.

Within the colonial and national context, national independence marked bourgeois women as home, nation, and spirituality. Furthermore, in (neo)colonial discourses, the burden of sexual and gender oppressions is laid at the feet of patriarchal and feudal "traditions" (of religion, marriage, and heterosexuality) located within the "Indian" family. Since then, the deterritorialized nations of diasporic communities have similarly gendered and configured cultural nationalism. Anannya Bhattacharjee (1992) poses that bourgeois cultural nationalist constructions of the ethnonational formulate women as home because the bourgeoisie lose the ability to be ex-nominated due to ethnic and racial difference. Therefore, migrant and homeland bourgeoisie construct the West as modern through material consumption and East as home of spiritual and cultural difference. However, the public-private distinction that is theorized by feminists such as Catherine MacKinnon and by postcolonial scholars such as Partha Chatterjee is transformed in the case of Asian immigrant women. Bhattacharjee suggests that in the United States, South Asian immigrant women are associated with spaces identified as the space of home and the private, but they are actually already public and under the scrutiny of the state and circumscribed by law. Thus, public-private is a false dichotomy that shores up and masks the privilege of white bourgeois heterosexual women as normative citizen-subjects, especially in relation to immigrant women of color.

Frequently, home is defined in opposition to those spaces marked as public, political, and unsafe.[13] Home is constructed not only as the private (space of the patriarchal family or homogeneous ethnocultural community) but also as a site of consumption and (re)production, of domesticity and familiarity, as a womb of safety and containment. In addition, home is created through the productive and reproductive labor of women. In the film, women seek to interrupt the labor required to produce homes and to destabilize constructions of home based on embodiment. (Illnesses related to consumption are discussed further in the mobility section, because leisure and consumption within the film suggest double-edged desires.) In particular, *Bhaji on the Beach* exposes how home that is constructed as the site of the domestic is conflated with the home of diasporic cultural belonging that is associated with nostalgia. Here, I expand on my previous line of inquiry regarding the gendered and sexualized home of diasporic cultural belonging as I investigate how nostalgia is related to embodiment and illness. Although nostalgia has been clearly associated with cinema and even with spectatorship, as in my previous discussions, very few discussions have sought to understand how these are linked to somatic experiences. If nostalgia is such a central component of postmodernity and migration (whether in the form of exile, diaspora, or immigration) as scholars have argued, then it seems fruitful to understand its relationship to cinema and embodiment.

Nostalgia, derived from the Greek "nostos" for return and "algos" for suffering, suggests the pain of yearning for return. The term *nostalgia* was coined in 1688 by the Swiss physician Johann Hofer who was interested in the frequent emotional disturbances among Swiss mercenary soldiers abroad and hence defined it as "a sad mood originating from the desire to return to one's native land" (McCann cited in Kimberly Smith 2000, 509–10). Hofer included in its description symptoms such as anxiety, melancholia, fever, and insomnia and listed its cure as a return home. During the colonialism and imperialism of the eighteenth and nineteenth centuries, nostalgia became a psychological medical condition with physiological characteristics (*Oxford English Dictionary* 1989). Medical discourses produced the condition of nostalgia as a gendered phenomenon during this time period. In English, this yearning has been termed homesickness, and in German *heimweh*.[14] During this time, nostalgia and homesickness became intertwined in the English language, and nostalgia became understood as an illness that linked spatial displacement with the experience of loss, which resulted in physical and psychological pain.

Homesickness and nostalgia were associated with military and imperialist projects and therefore most often considered a male disease.[15] However, cases of nostalgia also were associated with class as in the case of female domestic servants according to Kimberly K. Smith (2000).[16] Moreover, acts such as setting fire to the employer's house by some young servant women were categorized as criminal behavior and were explained as consequences of the medical disease nostalgia according to Smith. Here is the beginning of a different understanding of nostalgia, one in which rebellious acts against the servitude of domestic labor are medicalized and criminalized but can be read to speak in regard to multiple forms of alienation experienced by the female subject laboring within bourgeois domesticity.

In subsequent centuries, the connotative meaning of nostalgia has shifted from medical discourses to more psychological ones and also has shifted from associations with physical displacement to associations with temporal ones. In psychoanalysis, *heimlich* (canny) refers to the familiar or homey, while the *unheimlich* (uncanny) refers to the unfamiliar, fearful, and unknown. Hence, the uncanny can evoke that which has been unknown or hidden, which is marked as the return of the repressed. My use of homesickness, like Bhabha's concept of the unhomely, is meant to resonate with but expand this meaning. Some Freudian analyses further temporalized the meaning of nostalgia, suggesting that it was rooted in the Oedipal conflict and hence the time of childhood. Popular cultural evocations of nostalgia, such as Proust's infamous text, characterize nostalgia as a pleasant and universal experience that is bittersweet in its experience of loss. Thus, the popular understanding of nostalgia as universal emotional and natural temporal yearnings is a recent phenomenon. Scholars of postmodernity, such as Jameson, identify nostalgia and irony as central features of contemporary cultures in late capitalism. In particular, Jameson (1991, 18) critiques what he calls the "nostalgia films," which stylistically present the past as a spectacle for consumption: "Nostalgia films restructure the whole issue of pastiche and project it onto a collective and social level, where the desperate attempt to appropriate a missing past is now refracted through the iron law of fashion change and the emergent ideology of the generation." [17] For Jameson (1990, 85), nostalgia films are inauthentic "celebrations of the imaginary style of a real past." [18]

Although nostalgia is pondered as a universal experience, that is, a structure of feeling that is naturalized so that any subject's experience of displacement from a past time and place is categorized as the condition of nostalgia, we may seek to differentiate between different productions of nostalgia, such as the patriarchal deterritorialized national nostalgia of *DDLJ*, the anticolonial nativist nostalgia of Negritude, the colonial nostalgia of Raj, and the postmodern nostalgia associated with late capitalism. [19] Therefore, postcolonial diasporic nostalgia in *Bhaji on the Beach* differs from the nostalgia described by Jameson as associated with the logic of postmodernity. Hence, homesickness can be differentiated from the idea of postmodern nostalgia. Rosemary George (1996, 175) writes that homesickness

> can cut two ways: it could be a yearning for the authentic home (situated in the past or in the future) or it could be the recognition of the inauthenticity or the created aura of all homes. In the context of the immigrant novel it is the latter that usually prevails.

The argument here, while recognizing the "inauthenticity" of all homes, is more concerned with the consequences of creating such homes and nostalgia.

Homesickness I—Dis-Orientation

Within the film, Asha's homesickness is experienced as nostalgia in the form of hallucinations and headaches, that is, dis-Orientation. Asha is depicted as dis-oriented by her attempt to reconcile gender and sexual normativities. These normativities, in particular, weigh on her as they signify the maintenance of cultural "authenticity" and "difference" in the British Asian communities. The first scene of the film is a single take of the camera starting on a street corner and panning down the block past shop windows, graffiti (of a swastika), produce, posters for Indian films and videos, and advertisements for newspapers until a blackout occurs, after which Asha's hallucination begins. The film opens from the perspective of Asha amidst a hallucination as she labors in the family and the shop. Her dis-Orientation builds as a huge and looming statue of a Hindu god tells her to know her "place"; as Asha performs an *aarti* (prayer) for the god, a booming voice extols the virtues of womanhood (i.e., for wives and mothers)— beauty, honor, and sacrifice. She wanders lost in the dream-space surrounded by outsized versions of commodities and products in her life, including monumental videocassettes (see Figure 5.1). Overwhelmed, she drops her aarti tray,

Fig. 5.1 Asha's dis-Orientation amidst Bollywood videos and other commodities in *Bhaji on the Beach*.

returning to "reality"—the cries of her family's demands and the arrival of the white newspaper deliveryman dropping off the day's tabloids whose headlines scream "They Curried My Baby." It is this site of women's labor, displacement, and dis-Orientation through which we enter the film. These moments of hallucination return several times throughout the film, as Asha experiences memory loss, disorientation, and headaches.

It is telling that the film begins in a shop. From the opening, *Bhaji on the Beach* links the migration and experience of Asian women to women's insertion into capitalism and colonialism. The collapse of the shop into the site of the domestic family business and therefore as the site of women's labor ensures the extraction of capital and wealth based on immigrant women's labor. In the case of Asha and Pushpa, these are not the bodies of Third World women laboring for multinational corporations but rather bodies whose labor in terms of housework has now expanded to ensure security and mobility as the petty bourgeoisie. Their productive and reproductive labors are the subjects of the film.

The hallucinations function as moments of anxiety regarding the normative role of women. The second hallucination occurs after she discovers that Ginder is joining the women on the trip to Blackpool. Asha, Pushpa, and Bina discuss disapprovingly Ginder's "abandonment" of Ranjit and his family. Contrasting Hashida with Ginder, one woman announces that "at least some of our girls we can be proud of," as another of the women gossips that Ranjit's family is such a nice family and that poor Ranjit's mother has heart trouble. Feeling ambivalent, Asha drifts off into another vision; in this one, a brazen and rude Ginder disrespects Ranjit's family as she serves dinner, resulting in the mother having heart trouble. As the family rushes to her side to provide her comfort and medicine, Ginder pulls to the side laughing maliciously and deliberately neglecting her mother-in-law, spilling a pitcher of water, and thus denying her mother-in-law a glass of water with her pills. Asha's hallucination reflects her anxiety about how Ginder does not comply with the exhortation to duty, honor, and sacrifice, especially in regard to the domestic labor and the demeanor that is required of her. Asha's internalized expectations of Ginder as the laboring docile daughter-in-law and wife lead her to participate in disciplining her. Ginder's transgressions and resistance against this normativity snap Asha out of the hallucination, resulting in her complaints of a headache and visions.

Asha's disapproval of Ginder is soon followed by her shock upon discovering not only Hashida's illicit relationship with her Jamaican British boyfriend Oliver but her pregnancy as well. In her third hallucination, Asha imagines a scene straight out of *Paurab aur Paschim* with Hashida playing the Westernized and corrupted heroine who parades around in a temple dressed in a red miniskirt and blonde wig, while lighting a cigarette and sitting on the altar. Her lack of decorum and respect are represented by her drunken disregard as she knocks over pundits and idols. This rhetoric of good and bad Indian is played out within the film's narrative and is even repeated by the characters who first praise Hashida for being a good girl as a successful receptacle of her parents' desire for her education and upward mobility, then later scold and admonish her. As Asha walks away, the women's argument over Hashida echoes in her head, and she begins to experience another hallucination. In this fourth hallucination, Asha once again sees the statue of a Hindu god looming over her as she beseechingly asks him what to do. When she comes to, Asha finds herself shoeless and knee-deep in water being rescued by the elderly white gentleman Ambrose. These visions not only indicate the level of anxiety experienced by Asha in regard to the "morals" of the community women but also indicate her own internalization and enforcement of the gender and sexual normativities.

Asha's hallucination scenes employ allusions to religion and Hindi cinema, both of which provide dominant narratives regarding gender and sexual normativities that she seeks to reconcile with the contradictions of her everyday life. From the oversized and looming videocassette boxes to the allusions to *Paurab aur Paschim*, Indian films function as sites of cultural authenticity that are central to constructing and deconstructing diasporic existence. *Bhaji on the Beach* cites the influence of these films in the ossification of "Indian" culture that is produced in British Asian communities. As Asha and Pushpa lament the loss of morals from "back home," Rekha reminds them that they are experiencing nostalgia for a home that they have not been to in twenty years, and that, in other words, "home" is a fiction.[20] The realness of home for Asha and the other women, however, cannot be debated, because it is a sustaining and productive imaginary for them, and, it is Bollywood cinema that provides the narrative for home and family. Though Asha and Pushpa act as the wardens of the collective memory, authorizing particular narratives of what is authentic and what is not, Asha also recognizes that her nostalgia is constructed from her needs and that it is not fully aligned with the present.

Chadha's film offers the possibility that if home is fiction, it can be written and rewritten. *Bhaji on the Beach* strives to redefine home, in the words of Chandra Mohanty (1993, 353), "not as a comfortable, stable, inherited and familiar space, but instead as an imaginative, politically charged space where the familiarity and sense of affection and commitment lay in shared collective analysis of social injustice, as well as a vision of radical transformation." Unlike Baldev, Asha does not prescribe to the return-home theory as a cure for homesickness. However, like Baldev, she and Pushpa perpetuate constructions of home that nonetheless reproduce home as a space of surety and safety, of fixed identity and culture, following the binary logic of anticolonial nationalism. Ultimately, Hashida's pregnancy and the abuse of Ginder persuades the women that the heteronormative and patriarchal fiction of home is based only on a narrative of diasporic women's duty, honor, and sacrifice.

Homesickness II—Domestic Abuse[21]

Elaine Scarry's (1985) treatise *The Body in Pain* theorizes the tortured body, the body at war, and the body as artifact in Marxism and Christianity. Scarry's text emphasizes the making and unmaking of the subject through the body in pain. Scarry sees the body in pain beyond language, a point that seems questionable in light of much poststructuralist and postcolonial theories. Bibi Bakare-Yusuf (1999, 314) suggests that what is unspeakable about the enslaved body is "the experience of violence against human flesh wherein the body-surface registers and transmits nothing but pain, a pain that produces nothing but horror.... The conflation of the body and the unspeakable draws us into an awareness of our physical mortality and the erasure of the human voice." Bakare Yusuf further argues that Scarry's articulation of the pained body as refusing to speak relies on a binary in which pain is associated with the body and language with the mind, reifying the mind-body split, and she offers instead that pain resists "everyday speech" and thus is not beyond representation (p. 314).

The pained bodies in the film are neither enslaved nor tortured; nevertheless, we may want to think about certain homesicknesses (such as domestic abuse) as bodies in pain.[22] The postcolonial nation-state's subjects in pain are distinguishable from each other (i.e., the widow in sati, the subaltern tribal or peasant, the tortured male Sikh, and the victim of dowry death) and from those in diaspora where one of the most common figures is that of the abused wife.[23] Feminist discourses on heterosexual domestic violence are marked by the language of speech and visibility as they emphasize the "voices" of those who are abused and make "visible" the abuse in communities. This emphasis on "speaking the pain" is one attempt at dismantling the inhibitions and prohibitions about representing this gendered pain within heteropatriarchal power relations. But what does it mean, then, to go beyond a simple denouncement of pain or worse to naturalize it as always already existing prior to language, especially in the case of the postcolonial or Third world migrant or racialized woman's body?

Domestic violence is never directly spoken about or named in the film.[24] Hence, the film reveals the body in pain not through enunciation or articulation but through the visual display of marks on Ginder's body. The film's signification of this absence of enunciation emphasizes the difficulty of naming abuse and abuser within a racist nation-state. Frequently in South Asian diasporic communities, domestic violence services are dependent on and derived from Western models and hence often focus around the individual. As feminist scholars such as Bhattacharjee have argued, this individualized approach often limits the collective and individual responses that could be mobilized against domestic violence. In fact, the individualized approach of many domestic violence organizations inadvertently protects the batterers in many cases and at times silences the naming of abuse and abusers. Furthermore, in this approach, it is the women who are removed from their homes because of immediate dangers, and when they do become visible, they are stigmatized and vilified. But batterers themselves remain unnamed and within the home and community, protected by their privacy. It is this notion of the private that has shrouded and plagued "domestic" violence, demarcating it as separate from the "public" and the possibility of collective action. Echoing this social pattern, the film portrays how Ranjit's access to articulation in the public sphere of the community overpowers Ginder's and negates the ability for her pain to be heard—for example, Asha listens and speaks kindly to Ranjit when he approaches her to discuss Ginder's whereabouts, whereas the older women in the film, including Ginder's own mother, refuse to listen to or hear her. This renders Ginder a subject whose articulation of pain and abuse is not read or heard in everyday acts of speech. As Scarry argues, an assault on her body is also an assault on the language associated with embodiment. It is only the visual spectacle of the marks of Ranjit's brutality that are made visible on the surface of her body that speak for her experience of terror and pain.

The enforced silence around the abused body in pain has been addressed by many feminists who seek to "voice" experiences of abuse, domestic violence, rape, or harassment to make them visible. Bhattacharjee's (1992) essay on the habit of ex-nomination among the diasporic bourgeoisie provides insight into why the public visibility of this specter (along with the gay and lesbian South Asian) figures so strongly in the cultural politics of South Asian diasporas. Bhattacharjee illustrates the ways in which the bourgeoisie, in order not to be named, silences bodies and acts that seek to name and represent violence. Filmmakers such as Chadha and Nair who depict these particular embodied experiences of violence rely on the visuality of the cinematic apparatus and its significant role in diaspora. The visuality of film provides a site of intervention according to the filmmakers. As I discuss in the next chapter on *Fire*, the visual spectacle of the film does significantly affect the discourses of the public sphere in tremendous ways. Ranjit's ability to articulate his power functions throughout the film, because it is always he who is allowed to speak about why Ginder has left their home. He discusses Ginder's flight with his parents, brothers, uncle, and Asha while Ginder is rebuked and silenced by her mother Asha and Pushpa. It is in this manner that Ginder becomes persona non grata at the hands not only of the family she is married into but also at the hands of the older British Asian women.[25] Thus, we can read the women in the film as participating in this ex-nomination by not only supporting but also perpetuating gender and sexual normativities through many kinds of speech and silencing. Significantly, the text attempts to ambiguously position Ginder's silence about her abuse as a withholding of information (an expression of displeasure and resistance) and as a forced absence.

In regard to the inability of the wife to name the husband as the perpetrator of violence, Rajeswari Sunder Rajan (1993 and 1999) argues that though there is a prohibition of speech that renders assaulted women silent and unheard, reversing the dominant term of the silence-speech binary will neither resolve nor correct the situation. *Bhaji on the Beach* clearly foregrounds how the abused woman is silenced, and it is only the physical bruises on her body that are allowed to speak for her. The scene in which Ginder's bruises are made visible very carefully depicts the gazes and the responses of the other women (especially Pushpa and Asha) as well. Pushpa sits looking disapprovingly at Ginder as if she were stripping, equating the status of a divorced woman with those of other sociosexual deviants such as the sex worker. When the male strippers grab Ginder from the audience and force her to dance with them, they teasingly begin to remove her jacket and in doing so reveal the large bruises that are stamped across her arm and shoulder. The scene "reveals" the bruises from the point of view of the audience and then reverses the shot to illustrate the reactions of the previously critical Pushpa (with the empathetic Simi), distressed Asha, and shocked Bina (with Ladhu and Madhu who rush over to Ginder in concern). This intercutting of scenes suggests that the visibility of "physical evidence" is required for the (older) women and consequently for the audience to believe Ginder's abbreviated testimonies. *Bhaji on the Beach* emphasizes how visible pain and its traces on the body of the abused postcolonial migrant woman are required as evidence when the woman herself is continually not heard or is silenced. If the body is not enough, the day-trippers all witness Ranjit's verbal and physical abuse when Ginder talks back to him and refuses to return.

Ginder first responds to Ranjit that it might be possible to reunite, but only if he listens to her (a statement that she repeats several times) and is willing to make changes, beginning with leaving the extended family. His response indicates his unwillingness because to do so would result in a loss of face within the family and community. She talks back when he orders her to get in the car, insisting that she has "come too far now." Ginder states again that he needs to listen to her for her to choose to return, at which point he yells at her to "shut up," slaps her, and seizing Amrik runs away to the car. His younger brother refuses to let him enter the car. As the now abject Ginder pleads with him to return Amrik, Asha steps out from the gathered women to grab Amrik out of his clutch, yelling "put that boy down now" and "do you want him to grow up like you!" Ranjit turns and attacks the women, blaming Simi for inciting Ginder (attempting to deny Ginder's agency) and pushing Ladhu and Madhu. Pushing Ginder to the ground, Ranjit taunts her, suggesting that no one will want a woman dishonored by divorce, except him.[26] It is at this point that Asha pulls him off Ginder and slaps him several times, cursing at him and shaming him for his abuse (see Figure 5.2).[27] As the women gather up Ginder and Amrik to leave, Ranjit crumples to the ground while his older brother eggs him to respond and retaliate. It is, of course, significant that it is Asha, rather than Simi or Ginder, who physically strikes Ranjit.

Asha's performative enunciation functions not only to reconfirm the resolution she has reached in regard to gender and sexual normativities undergirding

Fig. 5.2   Asha as the moral force of the community strikes Ranjit in *Bhaji on the Beach.*

women's roles in marriage but also to assert her action as essential to her own redefinition of those roles.[28] Furthermore, physical confrontation is possible because Asha (or perhaps Pushpa) as middle-aged mothers and wives are attributed with moral authority. It is when Ranjit posits that Ginder's value and subjectivity are defined only by her relationship to him through marriage that Asha steps in to stop him. The physical slaps that Asha gives are a significant counterpoint to the binary of speech and silence that operates in this scene. While Asha yells at Ranjit, it is the three blows that transform the situation. Moreover, it is the publicness of the retaliation and rescue that disempowers Ranjit.[29]

Two points here are especially significant in relation to the proposition that the body in pain is beyond language. First, the proposition relies on the unstated opposition between speech and silence that features prominently in liberal feminist discourses that equate speech with having subjectivity and silence with total victimhood (which is a status that is often reserved for Third World or postcolonial women or women of color). Ginder's repeated statements to Ranjit to "listen to her" indicate not a silence on her part but a silencing of her. Therefore, it is necessary not only to reevaluate the ways in which Ginder's agency is circumscribed by power relations but also to name and demarcate the conditions and determine the impact and effects of her resistance.[30] Second, the public display of Asha's slaps suggests one possible reframing of the silence-speech binary, not because (her) action is outside of language but because of the significance of visibility to performative enunciation. The transformation of the older women's perspectives is based on physical evidence rather than testimony. In this manner, the publicness of their actions is essential, especially as much of the feminist response to domestic violence is based on the principle of "privacy."[31] Procedures to maintain the safety of women from violent men are, of course, tantamount. But as the film suggests, this sequestering of survivors also prevents collective action. The film collapses the distinction between the public and private, making visible the patriarchal heterosexist space of the family within the community. Home, a clear site of intervention, can no longer be demarcated as private.

Motion Sickness

As I have discussed earlier in regard to *Mississippi Masala*, feminist discourses often employ metaphors of space (containment, captivity, and immobility) to describe gendered oppression in the sphere of the private and the domestic. Often in these discourses, the space away from home (either nature or the public sector of labor) functions as the space of liberation. Liberal bourgeois feminism assumes that women are confined to the home and that mobility engenders escape and liberation and thus provides agency to female subjects (as in the feminist road film). Moreover, in these discourses, Third World and migrant postcolonial women are constructed as without agency and spatially confined, frequently as trapped in the domestic, in contrast to the bourgeois woman who is "liberated" by her insertion into the workforce. Instead, postcolonial and black feminist scholars have sought to differentiate modes of travel and mobility and the subjectivities associated with them. Carole Boyce Davies (1994, 37), for example, distinguishes a migratory subject from a nomadic subject as one who moves "to specific places for definite reasons." She further argues that mobility and confinement may need to be reconsidered in the case of black women's narratives:

> If we open the category "Black woman," from its monolithic assumptions, then this identity may contain multiple narratives of confinement, but it could also leave room for other narratives of escape and agency.... If we continue to read Black women only as doubly contained because of the implications of race and gender oppression and therefore further distanced from the possibilities of flight, then whatever agency is implied in physical mobility is too easily erased. (Pp. 134–35)

Like Black women, South Asian diasporic women are read as doubly confined by race and gender. This double or multiple confinement is further attributed to "cultural difference" by Western liberal feminism. In Davies's (1994, 37) work, mobility is significant to articulations of black feminist migratory subjectivities:

> Employing a variety of meanings of subjectivity, I want to pursue the under-standing of the resisting subject and apply it in different ways to the diasporic elsewheres of a radical Black *diasporic* subjectivity. As elsewhere denotes move-ment, Black female subjectivity asserts agency as it crosses the borders, journeys, migrates and so re-claims as it re-asserts.

Similarly, by focusing on the gendered travel to a beach resort by the British Asian women, the film also is preoccupied by the insertion of women in space and mobility, specifically in terms of their agency.

Like *Mississippi Masala*, *Bhaji on the Beach* imagines the possibility of women's agency through mobility, but unlike Nair's film, it does so not as individualized diasporic nomadism but through circulation to and from the domestic sphere as the women embark for a day of leisure at the beach. Even within the trip to Blackpool, the women move together (to the beach and night-club) and individually (e.g., Asha on her tour with Ambrose or Hashida to the museum), hence there is not simple narrative of liberation through or un-derstanding of mobility that is possible. Both films examine alternative modes and possibilities of travel for women, however, *Bhaji on the Beach* offers more contradictory and conflicted associations between mobility, migration, gender, and agency. Although there are multiple modes of mobility referenced in the film (Ginder's inhabiting a shelter awaiting a divorce, Hashida's imminent de-parture for medical school, and Rekha's transnational visit), most predominant is the travel referenced in the title of the film, a trip to Blackpool for a day of tourist leisure and consumption. Importantly, the mobility engendered in the film is propelled by British Asian feminism, because it is a British Asian women's organization that provides the mode and context of mobility.

Overall, travel to Blackpool signifies a respite from productive labor for many of the women. In this case, travel to Blackpool illuminates (literally as the famous lights of Blackpool appear at the end of the film) the women's bodily pleasures and desires. Blackpool functions as a space of "female friendly time" for the women (like it does for the white working class), focused on consumption and leisure tourism rather than on production and reproduction. The women eat bhaji and chips (doctored with spices), play arcade games, enjoy amusement park rides, wade in the water, meet boys and men, view an art exhibit, walk down the boulevard, visit music halls, get makeovers, and watch male strippers. In *Bhaji on the Beach*, the act of eating is not only about gendered embodiment but also about racial and ethnic embodiment. (In the café, Pushpa and Bina are yelled at by the woman at the counter for eating their "foreign foods" in the shop.) Ironically, many of the local "sights" have an Orientalist theme, because these seaside resorts functioned to consolidate British identities for the white working class through tourism based on experiencing the exotic "other."

Fig. 5.3 Cosmopolitan Rekha amidst the Orientalist markers of British leisure in *Bhaji on the Beach*.

The town is filled with Orientalist markers of pleasure (i.e., men dressed in gaudy Aladdin-like outfits with kohl-rimmed eyes and pythons draped around their neck and arcade games of camel races that feature hawkers clad in Orientalist garb) (see Figure 5.3). But in *Bhaji on the Beach,* it is a desirable destination associated with pleasure and leisure that reminds cosmopolitan socialite Rekha of Bombay with its bright neon lights, food stalls, and amusement rides and sideshows.

Although the film marks mobility as the site of women's agency, desire, and pleasure, it also illustrates the ambivalent and complex impact of their consumption, pleasures, and agency. For example, Hashida's romantic pleasure results in the mixed result of homesickness and motion sickness. Similarly, Madhu also experiences conflicting desire and pleasure. At Blackpool, Ladhu and Madhu spend most of their time with the two young men whom they encounter who are flipping hamburgers. Madhu, in particular, experiences motion sickness as she vomits when riding the Ferris wheel after gorging herself on fast food, alcohol, and her new friend Paulie. She is unable to ingest fully the ambivalence that accompanies her desires and consumption.

When Ladhu asks her why she attaches herself to any white boy that comes along, Madhu answers that all the Asian boys have taken up with white girls. Her

Fig. 5.4   Asha's fantasy of desire and escape á la Bollywood in *Bhaji on the Beach.*

affection for Paulie is thereby undermined as the gendered, sexual, and racial politics of her desires are revealed. In the last scene of the film, Rekha reminds the women of this ambivalent embodied pleasure (i.e., libidinal and gustatory) as she presents them a cake in the shape of a pair of breasts captioned "Blackpool or Bust"—a reference to the female body and its consumption, and the desire for mobility. The women demonstrate agency in seeking to pursue their conflicting and contradictory desires associated with the day trip to Blackpool that results in motion sickness. For the women, travel produces space that is not categorizable as public or private but rather is a space in which these distinctions are collapsed, circulating and reformulating information and social norms and power.

Finally, Asha's fifth hallucination is actually a fantasy of desire and escape as mobility and romantic rescue become interlinked. While touring Blackpool with Ambrose, Asha imagines a romantic fantasy where, clad in beautiful saris, she dances around trees with Ambrose, who is dressed in kurta pajamas and brown face (see Figure 5.4). Ambrose's flirtation with Asha allows her to confront her dissatisfaction with her own life, particularly with the gender and sexual normativities of duty, honor, and sacrifice that she attempts to square with her own desires. However, her desire for romantic rescue as performed in Hindi cinema is interrupted and disrupted by Ambrose's own Orientalist and racist

Fig. 5.5   Ambrose in brown face is unmasked in Asha's hallucination in *Bhaji on the Beach*.

Raj nostalgia. As the water literally unmasks him and removes his brown face, Ambrose is revealed as another white man with an overdetermined discourse about Asian women (see Figure 5.5). Disillusioned by the disruption of her rescue fantasy, Asha stands on the music hall stage with visions of her family and a Hindu god facing her own frustrated desires: "I went to college. I wanted to study." Asha temporarily and ambivalently reconciles these desires recalling her family and the pleasure she receives from them before she returns to the group of women. Though the film rejects the heteronormative narrative of fantasy of home, it does not do so fully. Not only do we find Hashida and Oliver and united but Asha also recuperates her faith in family. The closing of *Bhaji on the Beach* momentarily resolves the homesickness for all of the women. Nevertheless, these resolutions are temporary and provisional respites that can be read as ambivalent and complex in relation to the women's motion sicknesses.

Bhaji on the Beach does not romanticize women's resistance but rather catalogs the impact and consequences of mobility and agency. *Bhaji on the Beach* interrogates the gendered production of space, especially that space associated and categorized as the home and private. The film attempts to transform our understanding of space defined as public-private by showing the two to be mutually constituted and implicated in the interests of the bourgeois patriarchal family. *Bhaji on the Beach* offers us new ways to think about these spaces and the possible interventions in those spaces by challenging these kinds of distinctions.

In *Bhaji on the Beach,* the issue of motion sickness also signifies another site of inquiry into understanding gendered agency within postcolonial migration. By attending to the illnesses that result from women's strategic deployments of mobility, consumption, and general resistance, in this chapter I present the position that motion sickness is also a concept-metaphor that registers and reveals the consequences of women's agency, marking its negotiations, mediations, compromises, and limitations. Hence, it presses feminist scholars to seek detailed examinations of not only the modalities and contexts of resistance and agency but also the manifestations of the consequences. Women's varied attempts at escape and flight are always circumscribed by diverse and shifting conditions with forces the press back. As agency is often unknowable or unretrievable, we may read against the grain of failure to find and foreground traces of motion sickness that mark the embodied subject.

Conclusion

Location in a diaspora has not meant an escape from the nation-state for the diasporic woman; instead, she has become the site on which postcolonial and metropolitan nation-states are configured and reconfigured. Spivak (1997, 251) comments on the location of the diasporic woman in transnationalism:

> Her entire energy must be spent upon successful transplantation or insertion into the new state, often in the name of an old nation in the new. She is the site of global public culture privatized: the proper subject of real migrant activism. She may also be the victim of an exacerbated and violent patriarchy which operates in the name of the old nation as well—a sorry simulacrum of women in nationalism.

According to Spivak, the diasporic woman is positioned by multiple nationalisms, contested citizenships, strained patriarchies, and the expansion of capital in the new nation-state; furthermore, she is called forth by myopic multicultural national politics to represent all transnational women. Diasporas maintain and consolidate connections and imaginings of the homeland through performing national identities on and through women's bodies. In this way, I suggest that homesickness experienced by the social body of a diaspora is made manifest in the bodies of women. They are also the site of state control through policies on immigration and the family and further positioned as fresh and cheap labor by forces of economic globalization. Many of these gendered discourses are domesticated or privatized in that they are marked as distinct from concerns that are public. Therefore, the migrant woman in the new and racist state often strives to shift the struggles against economic exploitation, racism, and patriarchal nationalism from the private and domestic to the public and political. Chadha's film *Bhaji on the Beach* depicts South Asian diasporic women's mobilization to reformulate identity and community by shifting homesicknesses from the invisible and private space of the domestic to the visible and public political arena of ethnic community. Within the film, mobility is a crucial strategy that enables and enacts this shift, thus partially redefining mobility and political possibilities; motion sickness, on the other hand, attempts to illustrate the consequences of agency and transformation on embodiment.

In this chapter, I seek to rewrite the scripts through which women's agency and resistance is understood. By attending to the formulations of gendered embodiment within the film, I suggest possible interventions in the current feminist debates about speech and silence, as well as home and travel. The attempt is not to pathologize female diasporic subjects but rather to identify and name the specific conditions that determine our understandings of agency, embodiment, and community.

Homo on the Range: Queering Postcoloniality and Globalization in Deepa Mehta's *Fire*

Precisely because culture in our postmodern era of what Fredric Jameson has called "late" capitalism has been especially burdened with managing the contradictions of the nation-state, it is often on the terrain of culture that discrepancies between the individual and the state, politics and economics, and the material and the imaginary are resolved or, alternately, exposed.

—David Eng (2001, 33)

It is not simply a matter of locating indigenous or local sexuality, whether in Asia or in Asian America, and identifying an appropriate lexicon of sexualities. Perhaps even more so than in other areas of inquiry... the terms by which the sexual-political economy gets defined is both local and global at the same time. Given the instantaneous transmissions of information that defy both time and space as constraints, the changes in travel and patterns of diaspora determined by multinational capital and commodity exchange, and the ways that the particularities of AIDS are fashioned into international tales of mortality and morality of somatic economies, it is neither possible nor desirable to insist upon some *pure* local episteme: we must consider the *circuits of desire*.

—Yukio Hanawa (1996, viii)

Exposing many cultural discrepancies, Deepa Mehta's film *Fire* provoked conflict in India in 1998 as Hindu nationalist Shiv Sena members not only attacked and closed theaters but also repeatedly condemned and attempted to communalize the film for its "deviancy." These events surrounding the film are part of the postcolonial nation-state's complex histories and power relations. *Fire* illuminates how contemporary postcolonial and transnational cultural discourses articulate racialized, classed, sexualized, religious, and gendered forms of social regulation and normalization.

In the first half of this chapter, I focus on how anticolonial nationalist formulations of gender and sexuality inflect the contemporary construction of heterosexuality producing sanctioned and nonsanctioned sexualities. Consequently, I examine the possibilities and failures of the film in forging a queer politics based in its production of nonheteronormativities. In the second half of this chapter, I interrogate the various transnational, diasporic, and national discourses surrounding Mehta's *Fire,* with specific attention to how normativities and identities are mobilized with the circulation of the film. I begin with its Western reception and trace through the Shiv Sena attacks, Mehta's defenses, and finally, lesbian and diasporic responses. In the conclusion, I locate *Fire* within diasporic film production and also address how these responses and the distribution of the film raise questions regarding the context and the reception of such "diasporic" films within globalization. Overall, I argue that the resultant discourses of normativity, like the film itself, expose not only negotiations between the subject and the nation-state but also between the politics and economics of transnationality in postcolonial diasporas and globalization. Reading the film and the responses, it becomes possible to examine the shifting discourses and meanings of diaspora, transnationality, and globalization by using contestations over sexualities and related normativities and the competing class struggles over cultural citizenship in the postcolonial nation-state.

Written in English, the film was conceived as part of a trilogy (*Fire, Earth,* and *Water*) focusing on women in India in three different decades. Mehta resided in Canada and India while writing the film, which was financed jointly from North America and India. It opened at the Toronto film festival in 1996. *Fire* is thus part of Canadian, South Asian diasporic, and Indian cinemas. It then continued to play for several years to high acclaim and full audiences at many festivals and theaters in the United States and Europe, including Asian American and gay and lesbian film festivals, garnering multiple international awards, before it ever opened in India. In November and December 1998, *Fire* ran for several weeks to full audiences in India in English and Hindi, until members of the Shiv Sena, a Hindu supremacist group, vandalized and closed the theaters, identifying the film as lesbian and stating that lesbianism was not Indian. In response, feminist, celebrity, lesbian, anticommunal, anticensorship, and antifundamentalist groups and citizens mobilized to counterprotest Shiv Sena's violent acts. The most attention by the media was paid to Mehta (in her role of author and authority) and to the Shiv Sena but also focused on the issue of censorship or sensationalized lesbianism and therefore marginalized the issues of heteronormativity and queerness.

The film's plot revolves around a middle-class joint family (and its associates) in New Delhi. Sita (whose name is changed to Nita in the Hindi version) is married to Jatin, the younger brother of a joint family who operates a video rental business in contemporary Delhi.[1] Ashok the older brother practices Gandhian celibacy and runs a take-out business with the help of his wife Radha, Sita, and Mundu the servant. Jatin has a Chinese girlfriend who refuses to marry him, preferring the "hunt" to domestication in a joint and extended family. He agrees to marry Sita to please Biji (his mother who though mute and paralyzed due to a stroke observes everything in the household) and his brother. Ashok follows the teachings of a guru to give up earthly desires, including sexual ones that he tests by having Radha lie next to him as the object of his temptation. Radha, because of this practice and her infertility, has retreated from desire, until the arrival of Sita. As desires are flamed, the two sisters-in-law fall in love. Mundu the servant too is in love with Radha but has little or no access to the pleasures (or their denial) that are available to the two middle-class brothers and sisters-in-law and must resort to masturbating, which he does in front of Biji to Jatin's pornographic videos. Confined to the domestic sphere like Biji, Mundu becomes aware of and exposes Radha and Sita's secret to the shocked and titillated Ashok. Upon discovery, Sita and Radha make plans to flee and meet at the shrine of Nizamuddin (a Muslim Sufi poet) where Sita will await Radha, who wants to speak with Ashok before leaving. Humiliated and emasculated by Mundu's knowledge and divulgence, Ashok dismisses him and then goes to confront Radha. Ashok desires and condemns her, demanding her forgiveness. In the kitchen as she refuses to beg pardon, her sari accidentally catches on fire. Ashok leaves her there and walks away, rescuing Biji. Radha survives the fire and joins Sita at the shrine.

Fire is a South Asian diasporic film and also part of South Asian cinema. Diasporic films in the 1990s returned to South Asia as a site of connection rather than nostalgia as the directors re-turned their cameras to the homeland in a moment of globalization. Mehta's camera returns to explore the changes in cultural processes in urban middle-class culture in South Asia. As I discuss in the next chapter, the middle class in India is an audience eager for more cosmopolitan depictions of Indian middle-class life outside of the Bollywood mode. As I discuss later, *Fire* reflects the significance of Bollywood and Indian cinemas not only through referencing particular films through its dialogue, plot, and music but also through its form and aesthetics, employing melodrama and the family social drama as significant.

Not since Salman Rushdie's (1989) *The Satanic Verses* has a diasporic text and artist produced such debate.[2] *Fire* and *The Satanic Verses* are significant case studies of metropolitan postcolonial migrant cultural production within the context of globalization and postmodernity. However, *Fire*, unlike *Satanic Verses* whose central theme Spivak (1993, 219) characterizes as the "postcolonial divided between two identities: migrant and national," takes place entirely in India and thus the divided postcolonial appears not in the text but in its context. The postcolonial nation is divided here by a different contestation, one that is characterized as tradition and modern, but is actually about shifting bourgeois interests in the postcolonial nation-state. Furthermore, the division between the postcolonial national bourgeois and the postcolonial diasporic bourgeois also has consequently shifted and is a contradictory and uneven relationship; therefore, the text and the responses to it (through para-texts) evoke the postcolonial as divided between the migrant and the national. Although I pay attention to both in my analyses of *Fire*, in this first section I examine the critique and possibilities of the film as text in understanding postcoloniality and nationalism.

Text

> Modernity is disavowed even as it is endorsed; tradition is avowed even as it is rejected.... In Bombay cinema, although the narrative form locates itself in tradition, textual ideology is firmly grounded in modernity.
>
> —Vijay Mishra (2002, 4)

Fire is most frequently read as suggesting that (arranged) marriage privileges men and suppresses women's desires and that the ill treatment of women, more than the compulsory heterosexuality, results from the oppressive nature of Indian traditions such as religion. Women, caught within the repressive structure of the family, can seek only solace and love in each other for lack of a better alternative. Women can seek an alternative now only because the bourgeois family is changing and enables "choice" or "transformation" because of the "modernizing" shifts occurring in India. The tendency in reading *Fire,* like films of Hindi cinema, is to participate in delineating the line between tradition and modern, arguing over its placement and the subsequent gender roles and sexualities within the family. For example, the director's own authorial reading frames Radha and Ashok as tradition, in contrast to the modern Sita and Jatin. Mehta states,

> The women's relationship represents modern India itself.... Radha is tradition-bound and just waiting to blossom, but can't because of the absurdity of tradition and duty. Sita is modern India, desiring independence over tradition. Yet it's not as if she can speak her mind. She's simply a catalyst, so when she walks into the house, she makes things happen just by her presence. (interview by Ingrid Randoja, 1996)

Sita is configured as modern for uttering statements such as "duty is overrated," for cross-dressing and playing the vamp, for kissing the always sari-clad Radha, and for questioning religious practices and female domestic labor. Ashok and Jatin are seen as charted along these lines as well; the former is traditional for his religious devotion and the latter is an undesirable modern for his extramarital affair and pornography business. Some, such as Madhu Kishwar (1998) and Uma Parameswaran (1999), accuse the film of vilifying tradition.[3]

Alternatively, as many postcolonial scholars have pointed out, it is more significant to delineate how and in whose interest tradition and modernity are manufactured rather than to identify what is modern and tradition. The film, while employing the tradition-modernity binary, also mobilizes tradition in complex ways so that the same-sex relationship between the women is not configured in the name of modern and Western homosexuality or lesbianism but rather through homosocial practices of everyday domestic life. For example, it is Radha (instead of Jatin) who feeds and blesses Sita after her fast on *karva chauth.*[4] And when Radha oils Sita's hair and Sita massages Radha's feet, the film takes familiar homosocial intimacies of the middle-class joint family and eroticizes them differently.

Postcolonial theorists, Kumkum Sangari and Sudesh Vaid (1989), and Partha Chatterjee (1986), have persuasively described how in this history of colonialism the binary of tradition and modernity is (en)gendered by the project of modernity in anticolonial nationalisms, often through the tropes of the material and spiritual. By employing the hegemonic binary of modern and tradition, a disavowal of modernity through the idea of maintaining cultural difference could simultaneously enable and coexist with modernist projects of nation building. "Modern" was identified by nationalism's derivative discourse as those masculine traits associated with Westernization and the material (Chatterjee 1986). In opposition, tradition was written into the feminine domain of the native and spiritual, hence the space of cultural difference. Sangari and Vaid, and Chatterjee elaborate how middle-class women in Bengal were constituted as good Indian women through the tropes of home, spirituality, family, and domesticity (in opposition to the masculine public space of the nation). Consequently, women's interests were collapsed with the interests of the family and the home. Thus, during the early part of the century, the family as an institution that reproduces national culture through women's bodies emerges with consolidation of the middle classes. Within the colonial and national context, national independence marked bourgeois women as home, nation, and spirituality. Furthermore, in (neo)colonial discourses, the burden of sexual and gender oppressions is laid at the feet of patriarchal and feudal "traditions" (of religion, marriage, and heterosexuality) located within the "Indian" family. Sexuality, too, was mobilized by anticolonial nationalism in the name of family, motherhood, and purity (marked as tradition), in contrast to the Western modes of romance and love (signifying modernity). This overdetermining binary continues to configure centrally national (and cinematic) discourses and institutions of gender and sexuality.

Currently, the construction of tradition and modernity intersects with discourses of class, caste, religion (communalism), and gender, in addition to those of anti-imperialism (or anti-Westernism). The growth and impact of South Asian diasporic communities transnationally and the particular moment of globalization also have revitalized this discourse, more specifically, the anticolonial nationalist trope of modern and tradition gets evoked when there are central material and political shifts occurring in the nation. Since economic liberalization and globalization, the burgeoning of a new middle class that has developed with its increased consumption of material goods and services has triggered the remobilization of the tradition-modern binary along spiritual-cultural and material lines. In particular, the middle-class Hindu woman has had a materially privileged position that is policed by heterosexist, communal, classed, and gendered discourses. Because of these contemporary shifts (particularly the formation of a "new" middle class in India), the discourse of tradition and modern is mobilized in contestations over the nation by communal and class interests.

Writing from a Marxist framework on the ideologies of Hindi cinema, M. Madhava Prasad (2000) proposes that anticolonial nationalism was ushered in by an uneven alliance between multiple classes but without ever establishing bourgeois hegemony of the nation.[5] Partha Chatterjee (1986 and 1993) asserts that passive revolution (a Gramscian term describing the formation of a bourgeois state without the consolidation of bourgeois hegemony) well describes the formation of twentieth-century postcolonial nation-states. Based on this articulation of capitalism and the postcolonial nation-state, contemporary examinations of the bourgeois class, the nation, and cultural production must consider the impact of globalization and the developing hegemony of what is now termed the "new middle class" with its increasing ties to global capitalism. M. Madhava Prasad (2000, 237) speculates that Hindi cinema centrally articulates this rising hegemony or hegemony-to-be in its ideologies of family and romance:

> Capital is breaking out of the impasse of the ruling coalition, emerging into complete dominance. It is no longer necessary to artificially prolong the life of "tradition," that alleged entity which was modernity's own invention, its preferred rendering of the adversary's profile. The ideology of formal subsumption, which insisted on the difference between the modern and traditional, and the need to protect that difference, resulted in the protection given to the feudal family romance as the appropriate form of entertainment for the masses.

Although M. Madhava Prasad's argument is persuasive in marking the shifting class relations due to globalization, *Fire* and its responses suggests that tradition and modernity remain as vital accompaniments to global capitalism's presence in the postcolonial nation-state. As a corrective to this arm of his argument, I want to suggest that a reading of Hindi cinema and its ideologies of the family and romance cannot ignore the significant influence and impact of diasporic transnational cinema that provides particular insight into the cultural logic of transnationality.[6]

Fire does not present the relationship between Radha and Sita as some form of lesbianism imported from the West nor does it assert some traditional Indian same-sex relationship traceable to the kama sutra. Radha and Ashok do not represent some ahistorical tradition of Indian sexuality but rather represent specific articulations of dominant Hindu anticolonial bourgeois nationalism; likewise, Jatin and Sita do not signify conceptions of the modern couple, but they do signify competing bourgeois discourses of family and marriage. It is more fruitful to link the shifting definitions of tradition and modernity with current processes of globalization and negotiations over hegemony in the nation that are restructuring contemporary Indian class and gender formations within postcoloniality.[7]

Configuring Heteronormativity through Tradition and Modernity

Various formations of (non)heteronormativity are presented complexly in *Fire*. Rather than suggest that all nonheteronormativities are equal or identical, the queernesses in the film are carefully delineated by other differences such as class and gender. Through the characters of a joint household representing differences of gender and class, the film criticizes the self-justifying masculinist practices and ideologies of Gandhian celibacy and the self-serving male overconsumption of the new patriarchal bourgeois class, which is fortified by gendered discourses of tradition. The film illustrates how bourgeois female interests and working-class male interests provide space for a critique of the heteropatriarchal construction of the bourgeois family. However, it also portrays how these interests conflict in relation to gender and class privileges, resulting in a failure to produce a more substantial queer politics.

There is an anticolonial and postcolonial critique of middle-class masculinity and male sexuality in the film: anticolonial masculinity is embodied in Gandhian nationalism in Ashok and the more modern cosmopolitan masculinity of the new bourgeois man is embodied in Jatin. I want to first explore how celibacy (as a form of regulated rather than repressed sexuality) is mobilized by Ashok in a moment of familial and therefore national crisis (namely, the inability to reproduce). Ashok, the figure of Gandhian nationalism and celibate sexuality, evokes a particular discourse of nonheteronormativity associated with the formation and independence of the Indian nation-state. On the advice of his swami, Ashok pursues a life without desire within the sexually charged field of the family. His quest for freedom from desire is tested by employing Radha as his temptation. This practice, associated with Gandhi among others, is strongly linked to masculine and patriarchal narratives of the nation. Writing about earlier proponents of celibacy as part of nation building, Mary John and Janaki Nair (1998, 16) note, "Celibacy received a fresh lease of life with Vivekananada's call to sexual abstinence for building a nation of heroes, one which anticipated in many ways the more publicized embrace of celibacy by Gandhi." Thus, this often upper-caste Hindu valorization of celibacy was revitalized by Gandhi in anticolonial nationalist politics. In ultimately Foucauldian terms, Gandhi's incessant and obsessive discussions of male genital sex and confessions of desire and denial in abstinence constituted, controlled, and regulated a masculine and (hetero)sexist discourse associated with nationalism.

> Its very repudiation demanded that sexual desire be talked about endlessly and confessed to at the slightest sign of its arousal, displaced onto other practices, food habits and relationships, and vigorously policed in everyday life. Here was a "technology of the self" by which the male libido could be repeatedly named and reviled as "poison," "the enemy within," and so on, in order that Gandhi might become the subject of the nation. (John and Nair 1998, 16)

As the subject of the family and the nation, Ashok, like Gandhi, harnesses moral authority through the technology of trial and denial as the celibate male, constructing sexuality through the rhetoric of repression. In *Fire*, this sanctioned nonheteronormative and patriarchal practice emerges within the context of Ashok controlling the family as the eldest son and moral and economic force. In addition, he requires Radha to serve as the object and mechanism of his desire. Ashok here, too, like Gandhi, needs Radha not only as an embodiment and projection of his desire but also as the "proof of his successes in the cause of celibacy, . . . capable of inciting male lust even when desire was absent" (John and Nair 1998, 17). Ashok patriarchally regulates his sexuality through the incitement and then suppression of Radha's desires. The film's logic deems this valorized anticolonial nationalist celibacy anachronistic and misogynistic within the context of the middle-class family. (This celibacy and its associated piety are criticized by Sita, who quips that Ashok, like other wives, should fast for his swami during karva chauth.)

Jatin's relationship with Julie (the Chinese Indian hairstylist) is also nonheteronormative.[8] The role of Julie in the film is fascinating, because she provides an example of female desire that is not circumscribed by the institution of marriage and family. Julie's sexuality, however, is clearly linked to capitalism and consumption, not only by her profession but also by her desire to speak American-accented English (the accent of capital) and desire to travel to Hong Kong. Their relationship is deviant not only because it is interethnic but also because Julie does not desire marriage as the culmination of the relationship. Jatin is willing to marry Julie and comply with his family's wishes, but he simultaneously understands that Julie does not desire to join a Hindu joint family. It is significant that Julie's objection is to the joint and extended family, because it indicates her perception that there is no space for female libidinal desire within that particular institution. (This is, of course, ironic because the joint family is exactly the space of Radha's and Sita's desires for each other.) Jatin marries Sita as a form of "duty" and for the privilege it conveys to him. He, unlike Sita and Radha, can exercise some modicum of choice as he marries Sita while loving Julie after his wedding. Jatin's failure, according to the film's logic, is his lack of struggle against the heteronormative push into marriage and, consequently afterward, his deployment of male privilege in continuing his affair with Julie. In this sense, the film points out the double standard within the nonheteronormative practices within the film: both couples are, for lack of a better word, "nonmonogamous," but Sita and Radha's relationship is transgressive not only because it is same-sex but also because it is specifically between women and therefore disrupts the bourgeois family. The latter is the real deviance, as the film points out.

In the postcolonial Indian context, Anand Patwardhan's (1994) film *Father, Son, and Holy War* suggests that masculinity and male virility are very much entangled in communalist discourses that normalize Hindu middle-class male heterosexuality and make deviant other male sexualities, especially those of Muslims and lower class males. *Fire* attempts to interrogate this classed heterosexuality in the character of Mundu, the servant. An unvalorized and unauthoritative celibacy is forced onto Mundu, indicating the ways in which class plays a significant role in marking sanctioned and deviant sexualities, even within heterosexuality. Mundu watches Western pornography in the film (one video is ironically titled *Joy Fuck Club*). His circumscribed sexuality is confined to the domestic sphere, because he is kept in a feminine position of servitude without the class privilege entertained by Jatin or Ashok. Mundu's class exploitation prevents the formation of his own family, because his emasculated presence and domestic labor are required by the bourgeois family. In addition, though Mundu may labor in the video and take-out business, he is not the appropriate subject of consumption. Although he may participate in the circulating of transnational cultural products such as pornography, he may not desire them. Thus, his crime (against the institution of the family) of unsanctioned sexuality is masturbating to pornography in front of Biji, because of a lack of privacy, and he is excused by absolution from the swami. Significantly, the film depicts Sita with her middle-class sensibilities responding to his infraction by calling him a "rat." As a lower class man associated with animalistic and uncontrolled sexual desires, he is dehumanized by her more readily. Her class privilege allows her to harbor romantic bourgeois conceptions of love and sexuality that confer social and sexual respectability on her while pathologizing him as sexually deviant. She also imagines exercising middle-class privilege by throwing him out if he were to reveal their secret (which is ironically exactly what Ashok does after Mundu exposes Radha and Sita's relationship). Hence, while Ashok, Jatin, and Mundu exhibit nonheteronormative behaviors, the film foregrounds that they do not disrupt the bourgeois heterosexual family as do women.

Importantly, the film explicitly links the sexuality of the lower class male servant to the "deviancy" of the women. Mundu's greater crime and the reason for his dismissal, however, is not his viewing of pornography but rather his witnessing of Radha and Sita's sexual activity and his relation of it to Ashok. It is the violation of the middle-class man's honor by the gaze of the lower class servant that is violated in this case.[9] Furthermore, his banishment from the family is the beginning of the disintegration of the family. As the servant, Mundu enables the bourgeois family structure but at the same time is witness to the ensuing crises. This tension of needing and being threatened by his presence indicates the contradictory and complex constructions of the home within the national imaginary. The film openly acknowledges the ways in which nonheteronormativites are not only nontransgressive but also located within the dominant sexual order of the bourgeois family. Radha's explicit linking of the women's desires with those of Mundu indicates queer possibilities (ones that link nonheteronormativities); however, the film simultaneously hints at the failure of those queer politics.[10]

Like Mundu, Radha garners neither power nor authority through celibacy. As John and Nair (1998, 17) comment, "It is not virginity that is upheld as an ideal for women so much as the notion of the chaste wife, an empowered figure in myth who functions as a means of taming or domesticating the more fearful aspects of the woman's sexual appetite." Although earlier Gandhian nationalism deployed male celibacy as an ideal method of regulation, the contemporary Hindu right mobilizes (female) celibacy and male virility in its demonization of non-Hindu male sexual powers and sexualities. Likewise, Amrita Basu (1995) argues that three of the Hindu right's women leaders (Vijayraye Scindia, Uma Bharati, and Sadhvi Rithambara) are celibate, and their chastity is valorized and associated with purity, nonmateriality, and selflessness, enabling them to enter into the political sphere in the name of serving the people in maternal roles. In contrast, this position is unavailable to Radha not only because chastity is forced onto her but because she is infertile. Neither the self-sacrificing manufacturing of sexuality under chastity nor the sanctioned and normalizing mode of female sexuality in the form of sexual reproduction is accessible to Radha, causing her to become cast in the role of the chaste and victimized wife as compensation. For Hindu middle-class women, it is as mothers and reproducers of the nation that the figure of the woman was most frequently mobilized by anticolonial and postcolonial nationalisms. Thus, Radha's forced celibacy complements her barrenness and places her in a different position than that of the chaste wife, sanyasin, or mother of the nation. (Radha fails to become mother of the nation or sanyasin; with globalization however, she can be an assistant in the service-providing family business.)

Significantly, in Hindu mythology, the married Radha embodies a sexualized and feminized relationship as a human consort and shakti (female power) of the god Krishna. Radha, though married to someone else, is the primary lover of Krishna and thus symbolizes love, desire, and sexuality that are not within the heteronormative narrative of the family or marriage. In this manner, Mehta's film evokes a female sexuality and desire that is not activated by dominant discourses in regard to compulsory gender and sexual roles for heterosexual women.[11] In contrast to Sita and Savitri being most frequently evoked as sacrificing and dutiful wives, Radha stands in sharp contrast as a significant figure of heterosexual desire located outside of marriage and the family.[12] Therefore, it is particularly significant that the film opens with the extradiegetic (memory and history or fantasy) of Radha's, and not Sita's, childhood. The film's first scene does not begin neoorientalistically at the Taj Mahal (as suggested by some scholars) but with the child Radha and her parents in a field of mustard flowers. Gazing into the distance, Radha's young mother laughs fully and heartily when Radha says she cannot see the ocean, a symbol of accessible desire and choice (within the film's logic). This scene in its different repetitions in the film evokes a setting that is not exoticizing but that evokes the memory of desire and possibility. In this case, rather than allegorizing Radha as tradition (and Sita as modern), the text provokes a more complex configuration in which Radha is evoked in association with desire. Although the film suggests that it is the institution of marriage, heteronormativity, and mobilized discourses of tradition that are mechanisms of power, these scenes of memory and fantasy also foreground the necessity and possibility of female desire and fulfillment (either within the heterosexual Indian as in the memory of Radha's parents or within the same-sex relationship between Radha and Sita).

In contrast to Radha, the mythic figure of Sita in dominant Hindu discourses is evoked as the ideal traditional wife, one who follows her husband into exile, is later banished for imagined impurities because of sexual improprieties, produces and gives up sons for patriarchal lineages, and disappears back into the earth from where she first appeared once having proven her purity so as not to sully her husband's honor. *Fire* thrice repeats the reference to *agnipariksha* (trial by fire) from the *Ramayana* in its critique of the dominant discourse on Sita. However, the film reverses the characters so it is Radha, rather than Sita, who undergoes and survives the fire. The film's Sita wryly comments that duty is overrated, dishing out a critique of the long-suffering ever-sacrificing woman. (Of course, for Western viewers, the overloaded symbol of fire conjures dowry deaths, sati, and now tests of purity as stereotypes of the destruction of the Indian woman by Hindu religion and culture. I will return to the issue of how the film is read in the Western metropolitan centers in the next section.) My primary interest is in Sita in relation to the binary of tradition and modernity rather than pursuing the many different representations of Sita in dominant and resistant discourses as evidence of antihegemonic possibilities within Hinduism.[13]

In the film, Sita first appears outside of the Taj Mahal with Jatin on her honeymoon. As they approach the monument linking tradition, romance and cinema through nation and family, she attempts to engage Jatin in a discussion about cinema, in particular, her favorite—"classical" romantic Hindi cinema. This almost self-referential comment about cinema supports my earlier suggestion that cinema is a central site for discourses of sexuality. As the properly interpellated middle-class female subject of the nation, Sita's ideology of marriage and sexuality is configured in cinematic terms. As a new middle-class bride on a honeymoon, Sita evokes not only the rhetoric of exotic and middle-class Indian tourism associated with the Taj Mahal but also the cinema that has disseminated this romance to Indian viewers and associated it with the bourgeois consumption and tourism of honeymooning. (The nuclear heterosexual couple is accommodated by the joint family in this case by the presence of the honeymoon trip to Agra.) Like Radha's earlier memory in the field of flowers, Sita's question positions her as a gendered and classed subject desiring to enter and participate in the sexual economy sanctioned in the bourgeois heterosexual family. Jatin's response of Hong Kong kung fu films to her question of what kinds of films does he enjoy signifies his masculine misconfiguration of cinema, modernity, love, and marriage within Sita's (and the film's) logic. These martial arts films represent the misaligned interests of the new (South) Asian family due to globalization and transnationalism, one desired by Julie. Rather than the mobile and violent hero separated from the family, Sita seeks the intimacy associated with the romance of the heterosexual married couple and the family.

Sita's desire for love and romance are configured contradictorily through the terms of tradition and modern in relation to the institution of the family and marriage. For example, in one of the most discussed scenes of the film, Sita dons

Fig. 6.1   Sita in (vamp, western, and cross-dressing) drag in *Fire*.

Jatin's jeans, pretends to smoke, and lip synchs to Hindi film music; scholars have read the scene either in terms of cross-dressing or in terms of Westernization (see Figure 6.1). Madhu Kishwar (1998) seems to suggest that putting on pants is a form of Western liberal feminism, in which feminist is equated with being (like) a man. More persuasively, Gayatri Gopinath (1997) posits that for Sita donning jeans is an act of cross-dressing (as opposed to the more ambiguous drag) that allows her to claim temporarily male freedom and privilege as she crosses the threshold as the new bride in a joint family. Gopinath's reading emphasizes the links between Sita's performance here and her later cross-dressing and dancing with Radha who is dressed as a Bollywood heroine (see Figure 6.2).[14] Suggesting that these scenes reference the familiar Western queer trope of cross-dressing but invest it with different meanings, Gopinath explores the queer politics associated with the codification of dress, gender, and sexuality.

Nevertheless, it seems that most readings do not pay attention to the ways in which discourses of modernity are gendered or the ways in which dress and clothing itself becomes a marker not only of gender but also of gendered and sexualized modernity. In anticolonial nationalist rhetoric, Gandhi used the fig-ure of Sita as a nationalist who dressed in *swadeshi* (home goods) as opposed to imported cloth. This appeal in the name of Sita to forgo fine foreign silks and cottons for *khadi* (homespun cloth) and therefore to maintain purity was directed to middle-class women in the name of the nation. (In contrast, men can wear jeans or other Western clothing without being read as Westernized and antinational.) Significantly, Sita putting on jeans no longer necessarily sig-nifies a colonial Westernization, though it does signify partially modernization

Fig. 6.2 Sita and Radha perform in Bollywood drag in *Fire*.

under liberalization. Importantly, this scene of Sita putting on jeans follows her exclamation of her fondness for Hindi cinema and thus references many of the newer Bollywood films that feature heroines dressed in jeans and other "modern" clothing. Cinematically, the distinction between the corrupt Western and pure traditional woman has usually appeared in the oppositional characters of the vamp and the heroine identifying formative and trangressive gender roles. The vamp figure in Hindi cinema often has represented the corrupt Westernization and modernization of the Indian woman whose sexual impropriety, greedy consumption, and immodest clothing (such as jeans) mark her as the counterpoint to the chaste, selfless, sari-clad woman of tradition. As film scholars have argued, the vamp character now has been collapsed with the figure of the heroine so that female lead often represents a woman who is modern and traditional with appropriately channeled and expressed desires. (However, Julie can be seen as functioning partly in the role of the vamp in the film as she eschews marriage and family for flirtation and sex, speaks English with an American accent rather than an Indian, and wants to leave India for the Westernized Hong Kong.) Sita's performance, however, conveys her desire to be the new heroine of the cinema in the postcolonial moment of economic liberalization, one that incorporates the figure of the traditional heroine and the vamp into the newly married middle-class woman, one who may wear either saris or jeans, the modern woman of India. Her performance and cross-dressing are queer and trangressive whether one reads as performing femininity or masculinity.

Economic "liberalization" and globalization have affected the institutions of family at various class levels, but in particular the new middle class. This is the site where woman as wife must be configured as traditional and modern in a balance that allows for the modernization of India (through her labor and consumption) but that maintains national identity, which is located within the family. For example, because women's participation in the formal workforce is necessary for increasing middle-class consumption, the ideal of womanhood in the context of a globalizing economy has shifted from the social reform's educated-yet-traditional woman to a distinctly different figure, the urban, English-educated, upper-class New Woman (Srilata 1999). Scholars have pointed out that it is often Indian middle-class women who are targeted as the new consumers of the growing market of food, beauty, appliance, and household goods. Furthermore, the new middle-class woman should not only consume modern products but also be modern. As one magazine puts it, "Some women feel that their wifely duties cease at being a good cook and a housekeeper. No, it does not. The modern husband is much more demanding. He wants an intelligent, beautiful and smart mate who will walk proudly by his side, take interest in his work and share his interests" (Podder cited in Srilata 1999, 68). Romantic love and equal partnership are now demanded of the good married Indian wife as the new woman mediates, negotiates, and modulates between good tradition and good modernity. The production of the new avatar of the balance between tradition-modern (as well as local-global) is the new woman. However, the new woman as wife also is caught by the collusion between national (and transnational) patriarchies and capitalism.[15] Thus, in the film, the joint patriarchal family becomes the ideal setting for a take-out food and video (including pornography) business, in which the women's labor as domestic labor can be used to support businesses that supply services and products for the growing consumption of the middle class and their disposable incomes.

Fire's feminist politics suggest that it is the modern bourgeois woman as wife who desires and deserves more choices than those "traditionally" open to her but that already are available to middle-class men. In the film, the structure of the joint family appears ideal as a means to provide labor for a take-away business. However, the film also depicts the joint family as being unable to accommodate or contain the ideological shifts in the family and conjugal couple emboldened by these same economic processes. Neither the self-absorbed celibate Gandhian (nationalist) character of Ashok nor the philandering, self-absorbed modern character of Jatin are adequate. This brand of feminism, as other scholars have commented, hardly does more than situate the women as seeking each other out because men have failed to satisfy them. Mehta's comments that the film is about choices, rather than about lesbianism, resonate with the rhetoric of a new middle class. Within the logic of the film, it is "choice" that is lacking in the women's marriage and therefore they choose each other (as second choice). This ardor for choice also was echoed in the words of many cosmopolitan twenty-somethings on Indian MTV on Independence Day. These middle-class youth enthusiastically defined freedom most frequently with the simple word—*choice. Fire,* in this political and economic context, resonates more as about the possibilities of the liberal economic market than about the gendered possibilities of agency and subjectivity within the postcolonial nation-state. The same-sex relationship functions as a metaphor for the condition of middle-class women during the major transitions taking place across India during global-ization. Therefore, new women produce modern families and seek to enter the revitalized public space promised by capitalism and the secular postcolonial nation-state. The nation-state's articulation of the heterosexual family locates the woman as the site of consumption. Therefore, it also is heterosexuality that bestows family and women, as consumers of products and providers of labor and services, citizenship of the postcolonial capitalist nation-state.

This new space of the nation draws women from the domestic sphere into a particular formation of the secular national at the end of the film. Secularity is part of the vocabulary of the film as it opens with the music from Mani Ratnam's *Bombay,* which is associated with all of Radha's fantasy-memory scenes, attempts to secularize the Taj Mahal, and closes at the Nizamuddin shrine. *Bombay* was a significant Hindi film that employed the trope of inter-marriage as anticommunal resolution to the crisis of religion in a multicultural (i.e., multireligious) nation. This popular and controversial film asserts anti-communal liberal politics through the family consisting of a Hindu man, a Muslim woman, and their twin sons.[16] *Fire* maps the same-sex love between women through an analogous politics. The film tries to imagine itself out of the construction of Hindu tradition as nation by having the women flee to the *dargah* (shrine) of the Sufi Muslim poet Hazrat Nizamuddin. The shrine known as a refuge for the destitute as well as for poets figures in the film as the space of liberal secularism outside of the domestic space of the home. Though it is not openly queered or alluded to in the film, Nizamuddin's works include ref-erences to same-sex love and desire for poet Amir Khusro. Instead, the woman at the end of the film leave the home generated by heterosexual Hindu nation-alist and transnational capitalist class discourses to make a home using their new gendered and classed experience—they flee to a non-Hindu shrine and, though deprived of the labor extracted from the underclass servant, hope to open a take-out restaurant. Thus, the film argues that same-sex couples also may be modulated into the modern, middle-class, consuming, and laboring family, reformulating a new secular nation.

The legacy of anticolonial nationalism and the rhetoric of liberalization continue to animate the binary of modern and tradition in India; in its con-temporary articulations, gender and sexuality are transformed with the rising hegemony of the middle class in the postcolonial nation-state. Therefore, the rising hegemony of the new middle class may be seen not only in the control of state policies focused on biopower (reproduction, marriage, etc.) but also within discourses of marriage, tradition, and modernity in cultural production, especially films. In addition, with increased transnational economic, political, and cultural flows between diasporas and South Asia, particularly in the cosmopolitan transnational class, diasporic discourses and cultural productions will strongly affect the formulations of cultural citizenship in the postcolonial nation-state. Sexuality centrally configures cultural citizenship through transnationalism, diaspora, and national identities. Furthermore, the film indicates the possibilities and limitations of queer solidarities based on nonheteronormativity. Because sexuality is imbricated in and articulated through other differences, attention to the simultaneous productions of difference are necessary not only to feminist, queer, anticommunal, class, and anti-imperialist politics in the postcolonial nation-state. In this mode, a queer reading of the film exposes how productions of difference in transnational cultural production are the contested site of negotiation for the postcolonial female subject located in the unstable nexus of the politics of globalization, postcolonial nation-state, and modernity.

Context

Attending to the context means engaging the para-texts of the film through an analysis of media representation, ethnography, and archival information. Looking at the responses by Western film reviewers, Shiv Sena, Mehta, and lesbian activists to the film, we can see multiple struggles over author-ity in regard to the regulation of women's bodies and sexualities at a variety of scales and locations.

Western Discourses

The reception in the United States and Canada indicates an inability (1) to locate the film as part of a national cinema (it was not seen as Canadian), (2) to understand its gender and sexual politics as contemporaneous (*Fire* was deemed protofeminist and pregay), or (3) to identify its aesthetics and genre (it was read as an unsophisticated melodrama or a soap opera). I argue that all three neocolonial responses suggest that South Asian (diasporic) cinema, politics, and sexualities are read as part of an evolutionary process in which South Asia slowly follows the linear progress of the Western nations in developing its national politics and cultures. In such a reading, this Western logic delineates a paradigm in which postcolonial sexualities are like Western normative ones, with the added oppression of Third World cultural difference. This critique parallels the one made by Chandra Mohanty (1991) of Western liberal feminists who construct Third World women as similar to Western women but with added Third World cultural differences.

Fire was not identified as a Canadian film by the Canadian Telefilm guidelines requiring Canadian settings and actors (as the film was shot in New Delhi with primarily Indian actors). These guidelines forced Mehta to seek all funding for the $1.6 million film from private sources. Nevertheless, in 1996 the Toronto festival considered *Fire* Canadian enough to assign it the opening spot of its "Perspective Canada" program and award it a festival prize. Even after this further acknowledgment of its "Canadianness," the video, though distributed in thirty countries, was bought last by Canadian distributors. These events indicate that Canadian national cinema's project of nation building through multiculturalism is challenged by such a film because the nation-state configures multicultural-ism as the process of assimilated immigration and heteronormative settlement and does not accommodate the project of diasporic or transnational cinema, hence diasporic or transnational queer and gendered subjectivities. Multicul-turalism assumes that immigration is a teleology of progress in which the Asian immigrant modernizes and joins the Western (Canadian) nation, never to seek to return or re-turn to the homeland. Furthermore, the position in the festival also indicates a contradictory desire and attempt to incorporate and contain the transnational film within the narrative of multiculturalism.

Following neocolonialist tropes, other Western critics had trouble locating the film's politics through a denial of coevalness and placed the film and its contents in a space marked as prefeminist or pregay politics. Daniel Lak (1998) of the BBC Online News comments,

> The fact that *Fire* passed the tough Indian censorship process without a single cut could be seen as recognition that this is a serious film that has chosen its scenes and story line carefully. Or it could be taken as an indication that society remains ignorant or unaware of the sexual options before women.

Lak suggests that India in its backwardness has no conception of sexuality and has not developed enough along the teleology of liberalism to have knowledge of lesbianism, therefore the censors will not even "recognize" the women as lesbians.[17] Here, the assumption is that (Western) gay and lesbian identities and politics are the defining mode of political and social transformations; this for-mulation posits a universal and ahistorical framework of reading all sexualities and sexual identities. Furthermore, his commentary presumes that Indian soci-ety is more prohibitive and repressive because of "tradition," rather than seeking to understand the political and historical contexts in which these discourses are produced, for example, recognizing that Indian censorship code is derived from British code during colonialism. Typically, then, the controversy was portrayed as an issue of censorship rather than as political and cultural power struggle. The video also is marketed under this logic, (falsely) suggesting that the film is taboo breaking and banned in India.[18]

Even when feminist politics are identified within the film, they are presented under teleological ideologies. Lawrence Van Gelder (1996, C16) reviewing the film in the *New York Times* writes,

> Perhaps bold and novel in India, its feminist messages seem dated by American standards, and *Fire* would be easier to take more seriously if throbbing drums, didn't underline its images of passion, if a devastated husband didn't slump beneath a soda machine reading "Crush" and if a sampler inscribed "Home Sweet Home" didn't lay such emphasis on the contrast between the stitched sentiment and the miseries and tensions that motivate the characters under this particular roof. Now for the Jackie Collins part.

When the film's politics are recognized as feminist, they are easily read within the narrative of passive Indian woman oppressed by her undeserving Indian husband. Another review in the *New York Times,* and one of the most favorable, goes as far to suggest that these Indian men are undeserving of their beautiful wives, seeing them as cads and fools (rather than as symbols of patriarchal discourses), and thus remobilizing the colonial trope that the Western (re)viewer would better appreciate Indian women's beauty and sense of duty (Bearak 1998, A4). Furthermore, according to Van Gelder, this lowbrow, feminized, and undeveloped cinema has yet to achieve aesthetic standards (i.e., the proper style and genre of social realism required by Hollywood conventions). Its fourteen awards from various international film festivals of course belie a lack of consensus.[19] Mehta herself comments on the expectations of neocolonialist Western audiences: "I think it was very important to have a picture of a contemporary middle-class India, not a starving India, not an exotic India" (Mehta cited in Wilkinson 1997, 38+). Nonetheless, the film does not easily thwart the neocolonialist readings of these critics as it produces commodified gender and sexuality for transnational consumption.

Hindutva and Liberal Responses

In India, the English version of *Fire* was submitted to the censor board for review on May 13, 1998, and on June 8 it was approved with an adult certificate. In August, the Hindi version was approved after it was determined that Mundu the servant does not masturbate while watching the Hindu epic serial *Ramayana* and after the name Sita was changed to Nita in the film. Because the figure of Sita is highly esteemed in popular Hindu culture, the name was most likely changed to avoid offending Hindu sensibilities. *Fire* opened in mid-November, playing in theaters to full houses (80 to 100 percent full) without any disruptions until early December. Women-only screenings also were well attended.[20] Reviews of the film were mixed, some considered it breathtaking and moving, others found the sex scenes boring. Most discussion of the film as lesbian, feminist, or diasporic was shuffled aside by the attacks on the representation of same-sex love in the film. The debates around the film featured the Shiv Sena naming it a lesbian film, with the liberal transnational director backing away from such a position, leaving lesbian activists without many recourses or resources. The following account has been assembled from articles gathered from various newspapers in India (including *The Times of India, The Indian Express, The Hindustan Times,* and *The Asian Age*), from the Campaign for Lesbian Rights (CALERI) report, and by a timeline created by a member of the lesbian organization Sangini in New Delhi.

In late November 1998, a small group (Jain Vahini Samiti) in Mumbai asked the state minister for culture of Maharashtra to ban the film. This demand was followed in early December by a similar request by the Shiv Sena women's group Mahila Aghadi Sena, who deemed the film morally offensive because

Fig. 6.3   Shiv Sena attacked and closed theaters showing *Fire*.

of its lesbian scenes. On December 2 in Mumbai, approximately 200 men and women of the Shiv Sena vandalized and closed theaters where the film was playing (see Figure 6.3). Theaters were forced to refund ticket money and cancel future showings. The following day, theaters in several cities in northern India (including Pune, Surat, and New Delhi) were threatened or attacked. In New Delhi, Shiv Sena activists stormed four theaters (Regal, Satyam, Priya, and Anupam), forcing them to close on the last day of the film's showing. Despite their high visibility, very few of the attackers were arrested (only twenty-nine out of the two hundred in Mumbai, and only one of the several dozen in New Delhi). Media attention to the attacks caused a resurgence of interest in the film and audience numbers rose in some cities where it continued to play. The press primarily covered the attacks, though many editorials were printed that supported the film.

The federal government was involved at this point, as a minister of state requested a private screening. Nevertheless, the film was sent back to the censor board by the Maharashtra state minister of culture, Pramod Navalkar who reasoned, "If women's physical needs get fulfilled through lesbian acts, the institution of marriage will collapse, reproduction of human beings will stop" (CALERI 1999, 16). The deputy minister Naqvi concurred: "Lesbianism is a pseudo-feminist trend and is not part of Indian womanhood. . . . Some people create a controversy for marketing films in foreign countries, while foreigners give more prominence and prizes to such kind of distorted version of Indian culture" (CALERI 1999, 16). Attacks continued throughout different cities into late December and mid-January.

Although many of the spokespersons for these events were men, women played in an important role in assaulting and closing the theaters and leading the Hindutva movement. Amrita Basu (1995, 158–60) argues convincingly that lower class and lower-middle-class (upper caste) Hindu women have become active and respected figures in the Hindu nationalist Bharata Janata Party (BJP) through their roles as protectors of Hindu culture from Western imperialism and victims of Muslim sexual violence. In addition, women have been able to gain power and achieve status with the use of Gandhian anticolonial nationalist rhetoric of celibacy because women are seen to be responsible for the moral, spiritual, and cultural elements of the nation. Therefore, claiming women's moral and cultural standpoint, women protestors of *Fire*, the Miss World Pageant, and Valentine's Day, sanctioned by patriarchy to participate in the political sphere, object to the contamination of India and Indian womanhood by Western imperialism.[21]

Response by various communities to these two days of attacks and this state interference was quick. Appealing to the state, friends of Mehta (including Dilip Kumar and Shahbana Azmi's husband Javed Akhtar) submitted a petition to the Supreme Court charging the Union of India, the state government of Maharashtra, Chief Minister Manohar Joshi, and the head of the Shiv Sena Bal Thackeray with violating articles of the Constitution. The petition stated that the rights of the filmmaker were strangled by the shutting down of the film and demanded that the state probe these acts of violence and bring those guilty to trial. On behalf of the transnational subject, the cosmopolitan nation challenged the ways in which the legal apparatus was employed by Hindutva citizens in an assertion of state sovereignty; this petition to the court contested the Shiv Sena's right to represent the interests of the nation through state structures. This appeal to the state to assert its sovereignty in its protection of traditional Indian norms reflects an ambivalent relationship with the highly valued members of the deterritorialized nation—the South Asian diaspora located in North America. A counter-petition also was filed a few days later by the Janakpuri Welfare Council calling for an apology by the filmmakers suggesting that they had hurt the sentiments of a large (i.e., Hindu) section of society. The Supreme Court, though upset by the appeals to the media by the petitioners, scheduled a hearing date for December 15, the following week.

Activists also gathered at theaters to protest and to prevent other closings (in Calcutta, for example, counterprotestors were able to keep open the Chaplin theater in the face of an attack by the West Bengal Hindu Mahasabha and the Shiv Sena). In New Delhi, just four days after the Regal theater was closed, a coalition of thirty-two organizations (including lesbian, feminist, and gay activists) staged a peaceful protest in show of support for the film, Mehta, and producer Bobby Bedi. The posters approached the film from many positions: "Indian and Lesbian," "No more agni pariksha,"[22] "Lesbianism is incidental," and "What we are fighting for is the right to express ourselves." The last poster was by the activist women's group Jagori and attests to the refusal of lesbian politics by a feminist organization. Jagori, like other women's groups, was forced to confront their own heterosexism and dismissal of lesbian sexuality and rights, as well as incorporate a stronger engagement with heteronormativity into their politics. The first poster garnered much media attention and was featured in almost every photo of the protests; it also triggered Mehta's ire as she saw it as an attempt to "hijack the film." Many feminist activists were vocally supportive of the film, including Madhu Kishwar and Mary E. John, though Kishwar later severely criticized the film in *Manushi*.

Progressive groups often presented the issue as a case of civil rights and freedom of expression, arguing that the censor board had already approved the film (as did those who petitioned the state). Not many actually questioned the role and function of the censor board or the censor code; instead, they suggested that state-approved films must be protected. (The issue of censor board clearances is a perennial topic in contemporary Indian cinema. For example, when I was conducting my research on this film in India, simultaneously, director Shekhar Kapur (1998) was battling the censor board to release *Elizabeth* without cuts.) The press and several state officials reported favorably in regard to this line of argument, suggesting that "After all freedom of expression is the heartbeat of a democratic society" (Thapar 1999).

Press releases also were quickly assembled by many groups, including lesbian activists. A joint press release written by the lesbian groups Sangini (Delhi), Sakhi (Delhi), and Stree Sangam (Mumbai) iterated the position that lesbians exist globally (including India) and historically (evident through lesboerotic sculpture and yogini temples); most important, the press release asserted lesbian civil rights in relation to the nation-state. Also, activist groups began to label the general state of crisis a "cultural emergency," playing on the state's suspension of civil rights called the "Emergency" under Indira Gandhi. In Mumbai, in addition to counterprotests, a group of activists including lesbians printed twenty thousand posters in an attempt to mobilize the city against the Shiv Sena's management of social and cultural norms. The text of the poster stated, "They have broken a masjid, ruined cricket pitches, burned paintings, choked music concerts and stopped a film from being screened. Mumbai just sits back and watches?" Getting the posters made was in and of itself an ordeal, because printers refused to make the posters from fear of retaliation by the Shiv Sena. (All posters are required to have the name of the printer and publisher by state law.) Furthermore, contractors also refused to put them up, and two activists were arrested illegally by police as they postered. These references are to the Hindu right's actions of communal violence including the destruction of a mosque in Ayodha, the cancellation of India-Pakistan cricket matches, and the burning of Muslim painter Hussain's nude portraits of Hindu goddesses. A primary argument that was forwarded by these activists was the civil rights of individuals as citizens. They linked together the choice to watch the film and other cultural and social events with a critique of the hegemony of Hindu religious right in defining the Indian nation.

The Shiv Sena, too, increased their activity, leading a protest of men in their underwear outside of the home of Dilip Kumar, which Bal Thackeray justified saying, "as long it was peaceful there can be nothing objectionable in that if people cannot tolerate party activists stripped down, how can you put up with scenes of nudity in the film *Fire*" (cited in Raghunatha 1998, 15). Approximately twenty people were arrested and released the same day. In response, a candle-light gathering of more than one hundred people was well attended outside of the home of Union Minister L. K. Advani (who had declared such films should be made in the West as lesbianism does not suit India). As a cautionary measure, the Supreme Court directed central and Maharashtra state governments to provide security to Dilip Kumar and other petitioners.

In mid-December, the Shiv Sena's Bal Thackeray followed their first line of attack in deeming the deviant material "foreign" to India by attempting to attribute the deviancy to Muslims, hence communalizing the situation. Thackeray suggested that if the names in the film were changed from the Hindu names Sita/Nita and Radha to the Muslim names Saira/Najma and Shabana, he would find the film acceptable. (Shabana is the name of the actress who plays Radha, and Saira is Dilip Kumar's wife's name.) "The whole exercise is to suggest that we will show rapes only in temples and not in masjids," Thackeray further reasoned (Raghunatha 1998, 15). In response to these attempts to "taint" the film Muslim, a little-known Islamic group Tanzeem Allahu Akbar also called for a ban of *Fire*. Finally, Thackeray alleged that Shabana Azmi and the Minister for Information and Broadcasting Sushma Swaraj influenced the censor board into releasing the film hastily; this accusation implied that the clearance might have resulted from some "friendship" (i.e., sexual relations) between Azmi and Swaraj. (Swaraj later replied that she knew nothing about the film until early December and that she found it offensive.) Angered by the accusations, head of the censor board Asha Parekh (former film star) threatened to resign from her BJP-nominated position.

Meanwhile, in the Rajya Sabha (a house of Parliament), various members "defended" the film, some forwarded it simply as a cultural censorship issue, while others attempted to dismiss it altogether as trivial and therefore as a waste of state resources. (This latter position also followed a relativist logic suggesting that all opinions have equal exposure whether depicting lesbians or assassins, as in the controversial play *Mee Nathuram Godse Boltoy* about Gandhi's assassin, thus linking lesbians and murderers and deeming neither worthy of state attention.) Individual communalizing attacks followed these debates as well; for example, in an attempt to cast Muslim Dilip Kumar's reputation as an Indian in doubt, Shiv Sena member Sanjay Nirupam labeled Kumar a "Pakistani" (more or less equivalent to labeling Kumar a traitor during contemporary escalated tensions between India and Pakistan).[23] The Rajya Sabha was adjourned due to the resultant discord. (The Congress Party's Sonia Gandhi finally joined the game in late January, criticizing the Shiv Sena and BJP-led coalition government.)

Early January marked the emergence of articles on lesbian and gay issues in the popular presses in unprecedented numbers. But it was not until mid-February that the censor board re-cleared the film without a single cut. The film was rereleased on February 26, and by March 6 was removed from most theaters due to low turnout and continuing fear among theater owners in some major cities. In Mumbai, the names of both protagonists were dropped altogether from *Fire* as producers made a "slight change" upon a demand by Thackeray. That same month, Valentine's Day was celebrated by young heterosexual Indian couples by purchasing heart-shaped objects, signing the world's largest Valentine's Day card, and attending entertaining venues with evening programs for couples only. Protesting nearby, women members of the Shiv Sena decried the Westernizing and imperialist gesture of the holiday. In New Delhi, the CALERI formed and began to implement a strategy for increasing the visibility of lesbian rights.

Although the Shiv Sena clearly saw *Fire* as a lesbian film, the positioning of the film as "lesbian" raises several issues. First, the naming of "lesbian" as a Western category emerges in the Shiv Sena's attempts to claim cultural specificity of the term, but it does so in denying any history of heterosexuality or same-sex desire in India. This logic unfortunately willfully (mis)uses theorizing about the social construction of sexuality that has helped locate the emergence of sexuality and sexual identities. Following Foucault, David Halperin makes the argument that (homo)sexuality has a history and should not be treated as a foundational category. In his work, Jonathan Ned Katz (1997) forcefully suggests that homosexuality and heterosexuality are social and historical constructions emerging recently in Western discourses. Transhistorical references and arguments regarding lesbianism and homosexuality can therefore be seen as political and problematic projects. Considering geography and history, Evelyn Blackwood and Saskia Wieringa (1999, 12–19) note that women

> in different historical and sociocultural constructions engaged in same sex practices . . . cannot be unproblematically classified as "lesbian." . . . Making "lesbian" a global category is problematic because it imposes the Eurocentric term "lesbian," a term usually used to refer to a fixed sexual identity, on practices and relationships that may have very different meanings and expectations in other cultures.

The assumption that lesbianism exists globally is ethnocentric in its assumption that same-sex practices transnationally are identifiable by Western constructions and norms (a point to which I will return as I discuss diaspora and queerness). More important, it operates on the logic that sexualities engendered by the project of modernity occurred everywhere the same. The Shiv Sena's heteronormative appropriation of this argument is framed around the idea that homosexuality is Western, whereas heterosexuality is unquestionably natural and Indian. The fact that the film (through Sita) suggests that there is no word for what the women are to each other in their language indicates a refusal or reluctance to identify the women as lesbians, but it also facilitates Shiv Sena and Western readers to assume that same-sex desire is only Western. Although the film deftly explores the multiple modalities of heteronormativity, it does not clarify the social construction and histories of heterosexuality, homosexuality, or otherwise in India.

In India, the political setting of these events was the ongoing culture wars waged by the Shiv Sena and, at that moment, its waning power in its alliance with the BJP. Earlier in the year, the Shiv Sena protested against the Indian cricket team playing the Pakistani team. The BJP, asserting its own power, had supported the match. Snubbed by the central government, the Shiv Sena struck out once again. The Shiv Sena's Bal Thackeray claimed the authority to define the national narrative on sexuality by asserting that homosexuality was not Hindu (therefore not Indian). Mobilizing in the name of the Hindu nation, Thackeray and the Shiv Sena sought to "protect" the threatened nation from homosexuality constructed alternatively as an outside Western contagion (diasporic cultural production and economic globalization) and as an internal pollution (Muslims). Here, the Shiv Sena substituted lesbians for Muslim men as threatening to Hindu women and men in their Hindutva rhetoric. Mary E. John (1998, 372) argues that the BJP and other Hindutva groups in the 1990s actively sexualized art, figures, films, and images to condemn them, clearly making cultural production the terrain of political struggle. Therefore, the rhetoric on *Fire* varied from attempts to communalize the film by marking it an attack on Hindu culture to suggesting that lesbianism, like AIDS, is a transnationally transmitted disease infecting a vulnerable Indian nation (particularly and implicitly Indian women and femininity).

In the case of *Fire*, it is not just the general category of homosexuality but also lesbianism and lesbian identities that prove particularly threatening. The specificity of lesbians as women-identified women who may implicitly challenge compulsory heterosexuality and heteronormativity provokes anxiety. Jai Bhagwan Goel remarks, "What do you gain by showing lesbianism? As it is, the institution of marriage is breaking down. This will make it worse" (CALERI 1999, 16). Lesbianism or female same-sex desire challenges sexual and gender norms; in particular, the critique of the heteronormative institution of marriage endangers the (Hindutva) nation. Similarly, conservative BJP member Malkani (1998, 15) describes an anxiety about the increasing impact of globalization on the postcolonial nation-state, claiming moral authority through the rhetoric of anticolonial nationalism:

> Obviously, all this is part of the current rage for "modernization," "globaliza-
> tion," "emancipation." . . . Any rational being will concede that homosexuality is
> unnatural. . . . However, there was always a strong aversion to these perversions.
> When an Indian king was defeated by Mahmud Ghazni, he was invited to em-
> brace Islam or face death. He said he could become a Muslim to save his life, but
> only if he was not made to eat beef or sleep with a boy. When that did not work
> out, he chose to immolate himself. . . . The presiding deities of globalization are
> already thinking in terms of work for 20 percent and dole for 80 percent; more
> profits, fewer jobs. In this situation the unemployed majority will have nothing
> else to do but to entertain themselves with sex—any sex. In the words of Zbigniew
> Brzezinski, former US national security chief it will be "tittytainment." In the
> words of French president Jacques Chirac, the dictatorship of the world market
> will be "the AIDS of the World economy," with joblessness leading to divorces,
> abortions, murders, and worse. . . . The Swadeshi Movement in India, therefore,
> is not just a movement for our own goods and services. Even more than that, it
> is a movement for the health and integrity of society, for safeguarding the body,
> mind, and soul of mankind. . . . It is this death wish that has gripped millions in
> the US—and that threatens to engulf all societies that go American.

Heteronormativity here becomes a constant and natural presence that historically always requires protection from external threat whether it be Muslims
or globalization. In Malkani's anti-Muslim Orientalist formulation, the threat
of sleeping with a boy (even more deviant than sleeping with a man) proves
the historical danger requiring the valorous Indian (meaning Hindu) king to
immolate honorably himself rather than suffer contamination by performing
this deviancy. Heteronormativity is positioned as the embattled terrain of postcoloniality, modernity, and globalization for the nation-state. Malkani in his
pronouncement further poses AIDS as a contemporary marker of the contagion of Westernization. AIDS and homosexuality are seen as the cultural and
political menacing threats that accompany economic globalization and are the
domain of the Hindutva movement to address the rhetoric of anticolonial nationalism. The Shiv Sena and the BJP have appropriated the cultural national
project in the name of communalism, and simultaneously often have developed ambivalent positions on the cosmopolitan new middle class and Indians
identified as nonresident Indians in diaspora. On one side, the Shiv Sena claim
the space of speaking for a unified Hindu nation based on communalism and
anti-Westernization of the diaspora and nation, while on the other side, the
state (including the BJP) attempt to negotiate and manage late capitalism and
the processes of globalization. Although late capitalism and globalization have
been significant to the Hindutva movement, they also are necessarily disavowed
by Hindutva members who employ anticolonial and anti-Western rhetoric to
mobilize and control those who are being marginalized and exploited by nationalism and globalization. We can see here that Hindutva movement is very
interested and invested in processes of globalization that they employ in the

service of exclusionary discourses of the nation. In particular, they maneuver against those who can be marginalized in multiple ways: women, Muslims, queers, and marginalized members of the diaspora.

Deepa Mehta

In many cases, the performance of the director or writer becomes foregrounded in contestations over meanings; in these situations, the enunciations of the author become more relevant in discourses of authority. Though writing before the current discourses on globalization in India, Gayatri Spivak (1993), discussing Salman Rushdie and *The Satanic Verses* as postcolonial migrant cultural production, makes a similar argument by suggesting that religious faith used as a counternarrative within the colonial context was revitalized within the postcolonial context and became the means by which a strike could be taken against the West by anti-imperialist Muslim fundamentalism.[24] Furthermore, in a moment of national crisis, the Indian postcolonial nation-state concerned about its own internal unity sacrificed the postcolonial Muslim migrant by banning the book in the name of the minority (i.e., Muslim) vote. "The narrative of the State and the narrative of religion overdetermined the rumored book into a general mobilizing signifier for crisis" (Spivak 1993, 228). However, unlike *The Satanic Verses, Fire* is different in that it was not attacked in the name of Muslim minority nor in the name of the Muslim vote but rather in the aid of furthering Hindu normativity through communalism and fortifying Hindutva power. At stake is the control and power of the national culture identified most clearly as a threat to the institution of marriage by the Hindu nationalist in the face of globalization. Economic liberalization and growing power of the diaspora as well as the development of a cosmopolitan middle class (especially in Mumbai) create a crisis in the Hindutva-generated nation.

Furthermore, the shifting economic and material conditions have revitalized the anticolonial (now anti-Western) discourse splitting the material and the spiritual in the construction of the Indian nation. Although the Hindutva appear ambivalent about globalization's impact on India, they have been quite active in the liberalization of the Indian economy and wooing of nonresident Indian investment. At the same time, they have found it necessary to distinguish and secure their own position, especially with the rise of a cosmopolitan class that benefits even more greatly from the liberalization of the economy, and to consider diasporic cultural production and producers contaminated by the West. Thus, it is the contested field of the nation between stratified middle classes that is at stake, and, it is the nonresident Indian and his remittances and investments, along with his Western taint, that must be negotiated.

Like Rushdie in relation to the Ayatollah Khomeni, Mehta wrestled to occupy the position of author-ity in relation to the Shiv Sena's Bal Thackeray. Therefore, she was forced to occupy continually contradictory and shifting positions about the film. I want to examine this positioning, not to judge the inconsistency or truth of her statements but to emphasize the ambivalent position of the diasporic cultural producer who is framed as native informant in the West and in the postcolonial nation-state and who must vacillate between national celebrity and contaminated Westerner. Mehta's shifting positions as a postcolonial migrant make more clearly visible the postcolonial nation's contradictory and uneven hailing of diaspora and modernity.

As a diasporic cultural producer, Mehta is caught in the neither-nor of diasporic (dis)placement; however, her cosmopolitan transnationalism also provides her citizenship (cultural and state) within the postcolonial nation-state. On one side, as I have already discussed, Mehta's status as a Canadian is questioned. Similarly, Mehta as a diasporic intellectual playing native informant is interrogated by South Asians (critical and supportive of *Fire*) in regard to her alienation from, and lack of intimacy with, the homeland. On the other side, her ability to reside in Canada and India attests to the privilege of access to flexible state and cultural citizenships. However, in both locations, her transnational cultural production provokes inquiry on the basis of cultural authenticity (the neither-nor dilemma of diasporic location). At the same time, the film is able to titillate multiple audiences (the both-and paradigm of cosmopolitan transnational positioning). Mehta responds to these queries, "I have spent half my life in India. I grew up in Delhi. But do you have to live in India to be insightful about India? A lot of people talk about this issue of being in or out. It may have to do with insecurity" (cited in Ansari 1998). (Similarly she responds that one does not have to be gay to make a gay film.) However, the role of class privilege in challenging the logic of cultural citizenship further complicates our analysis of the politics of cultural production.

Eschewing diasporic belonging as the basis for evaluating work, Mehta also inadvertently dismisses the significance of responsibilities and liabilities of diasporic positioning associated with transnational cultural production. She comments, "Yes it is going to create a lot of controversy when it is released in India in February 1997. It is not your average film. It makes people think" (cited in Aruna Gupta 1996, D-8). Upon opening at the film festival in 1997, she maintained that her desire was to elicit a response from the Indian audience.

> It was insane. . . . One group was actually saying "We are going to shoot you because what you have done is something not in our culture." The other group was saying it was about time someone held up a mirror to us. . . . At least it started a dialogue. That was our intention. . . . It is amazing that a film that explores choices, desires, and the psyche of people who are victims of people who are victims of tradition, would cause such an uproar. But perhaps I was naïve. (Zeitgeist Web site, www.zeitgeistfilms.com)

It was not until the Shiv Sena disruptions that Mehta's positions became more contradictory as she was forced to defend lesbianism and homosexuality outright at the same time as her diasporic positioning brought her author-ity into question. Her statements varied from naming *Fire* as a lesbian film to claiming it is about women's choices to suggesting that lesbians were hijacking the film. Mehta early on reflects that lesbians appreciated the film because it was not about the politics of sexual preference (or identity) but about falling in love. Concurrently, she suggests that unlike *Go Fish*, it is not a lesbian film, a category she finds narrow and limiting. This heterosexism allows her to mobilize same-sex desire as a metaphor in the film for the transformation of (heterosexual) women's roles. As Mark Chiang (1998, 388) writes, "Homosexuality (especially in films by producers/artists who are not gay) may be visible only as an ideological mirage of transnational capital and is therefore implicated in a process of globalization in which the nation-state is complicit and which the return to nationalism seeks to disavow." Mehta's defensive self-proclamation of heterosexuality affords her the privilege of disavowing her queer-y of the nation; she participates in what Chiang describes, while the film more critically provides a queer challenge to this formulation.

Although she began in early and mid-December to address the Shiv Sena's assertion that lesbianism is not Indian with examples from literature, paintings, and sculpture, she later asserts, "Lesbian relationship is part of the Indian heritage and the film brings into the public domain the hypocrisy and tyranny of the patriarchal family, the issue of women's sexuality, and makes a strong statement about women-women relationships" ("Elite Film Personalities" 1998, 1). "Lesbianism is part of our Indian culture. Take Kajuraho, the Kamasutra, or even Konark, the evidence is all there"; Mehta later did not sustain this position (cited in "Is the Smoke" 1998, 19). (CALERI in a report on *Fire* and lesbian activism posits that the first quotation on Indian heritage is actually a misattribution and originally appeared on a press release signed by a group of more than thirty organizations.) By the end of December, Mehta complained, "I can't have my film hijacked by any one organization. It is not about lesbianism. It's about loneliness and choices" and later, "If you ask me do I believe in it [lesbianism], my answer is 'no.' In case I support it then I would say my film is about a lesbian relationship, which I deny" (cited in Jain and Raval 1998, 80). Mehta also replied that she would be shocked if her daughter came to her and revealed that she was a lesbian. Shahbana Azmi voiced her disagreement with Mehta's lashing out: "When there is a spontaneous demonstration of support, you cannot distance yourself from some of the demonstrators even if their position originates from a source different from yours" (CALERI 1999, 15).

Mehta assumes the shifting author-function, posing alternative interpretations one after another from her diasporic positionality.[25] Shiv Sena Bal Thackeray as gatekeeper to the gates of the cultural nation, however, begins to occupy that role, questioning her cultural authenticity. Mehta's statements about the film are contradictory and shifting, suggesting, not that she is irrational and inconsistent or even conniving and shrewd as others suggest but that Mehta's role as author(ity) continues to shift as Mehta negotiates multivalenced power relations and discourses. In particular, Mehta is attacked as a gendered postcolonial migrant, one for whom raising the discourses of gender and sexuality are immediately seen as threatening the nation from the corruption that is particularly difficult for (male) Muslim, like Salman Rushdie, and (Hindu) women, such as Deepa Mehta and Mira Nair. The events around *Fire* and Mehta's (in)ability to control the discourse attest to the significance and (lack of) power of diasporic and transnational gendering within the nation. In addition, it signifies the complex and ambivalent engendered relationship of diaspora to the nation.

Lesbian Activism

In contrast to the claims of the Shiv Sena as guardians of Indian traditions, feminist and lesbian activists, like Mehta, also are forced to articulate their own claim to the nation positing not only the film as a lesbian film but lesbianism as an ancient Indian tradition.[26] Lesbian activists are cornered into defending the film as a lesbian film, though many identified the film as about same-sex relationships not lesbianism. But, these differences of opinion are overshadowed by the Shiv Sena's labeling of the film and Mehta's defensive denials. In addition, lesbian activists (like scholars such as Giti Thadani) are positioned to frame Indian lesbianism as an indigenous sexuality to be retrieved, as some essential cultural artifact that can be excavated. Lesbians have to claim to exist prior to colonialism to justify that they are not the results of Western imperialism but are "native" and therefore Indian. Thus, these discussions are framed and overdetermined by the discourses of nationalism and (neo)colonialism. Nayan Shah (1993, 113) warns that this reliance on history may force "too much of us today into the past. We may trap ourselves in the need of a history to sanction our existence." Shah's comment reminds of the dangerous repercussions of engaging in the battle over inventing traditions, one that at one level may not be avoidable and at another level binding. These events illuminate the ways in which sexualities are (being) constructed by new transnational sexual economies and overdetermining discourses, rather than being unearthed from their precolonial tombs. *Fire,* as a diasporic text, entered lesbianism into the public discourse in unprecedented ways and affected (at least) middle-class discussions of sexuality, though clearly not on the terms of feminist and lesbian activists.[27]

Challenging the commodification and usurpation of lesbian issues, CALERI released a report titled *Silence! The Emergency Is On: Lesbian Emergence* in New Delhi in August 1999. (A full discussion of the report, a powerful and detailed account of the group's political actions and engagements including protesting the closure of the film, distributing leaflets, performing street plays, and organizing public forums, is beyond the scope of this chapter.) Written by the collective to assert lesbian rights in the public sphere, articulate a relationship with the women's movement, and explicate its differences from the gay men's movement, the report uses the trope of the state emergency to describe the state of siege against lesbian rights by the nation-state. CALERI draws an analogy between forced sterilization and the criminalization of homosexuality as it foregrounds the violation of rights as citizens and the regulation of sexuality by the state.[28] Reflecting on the shifting discussions on lesbianism during the *Fire* controversy to the following months, the report astutely comments on the way that the film and protests enable space in the public sphere for lesbian visibility but simultaneously regulate and control the terms of discussion (e.g., through Mehta's insistence on framing the film as about "choice"). CALERI carefully outlines their strategies for asserting a different agenda of cultural citizenship, outlining the complex ways in which the group questions (hetero)sexuality and heteronormativity, queers the nation, and thus negotiates the political possibilities opened up by the film.

Diasporic Responses

In diaspora, similar discourses force gays and lesbians to seek originary and returning narratives of sexuality. A diversity of transnational articulations, rememberings, and identifications suggest multivalenced and contradictory connections between diaspora and homeland. For example, the desire to claim histories in Asian cultures and seek representations of Asian "lesbians" (i.e., traditional Asian homosexualities) in teleological narratives beginning with the Kama Sutra and ending with contemporary Asian-American lesbians is driven by a form of self-validation and assertion of authority often by the double denial of home resulting from postcolonial diasporic positioning and queerness. Queer studies and diasporic communities have been concerned with the formation and construction of the nation-state as home, albeit in different ways. Displacement in queer studies often is configured through the paradigm of sometimes losing family and home, coming out, and gaining a new family, community, and home, ones that are aligned with the acceptance of identities based on sexual practices. Within this configuration, Gloria Anzaldúa (1987) in *Borderlands La Frontera* has written about defining homophobia as her fear (as a Chicana lesbian) of going home. Asian-American and queer studies scholar David Eng (1997, 32) writes,

> Traumatic displacement from a lost heterosexual "origin," questions of political membership, and the impossibilities of full social recognition dog the queer subject in mainstream society impelled by the presumptions of compulsory heterosexuality. In this particular ordering of the social sphere, to "come out" is precisely to never *be* "out"—a never ending process of constrained avowal, a perpetually deferred state of achievement, an uninhabitable domain. Suspended between an "in" and "out" of the closet—between origin and destination, and between private and public space—queer entitlements to home and a nation-state remain doubtful as well.

It is precisely these suspensions that drive many glbt (gay/lesbian/bisexual/transgender) South Asian diasporic narratives of identity as well, and correspondingly, engender claims of *Fire* as an Asian-American or queer text and fuel desires to seek Indian lesbianism. (*Fire* played at numerous Asian-American or queer film festivals throughout the United States. These festivals, like literary anthologies, for example, imagine communities and therefore narrate nations. As scholars have argued, the politics of Asian-America have in part been characterized by a paradigm of cultural nationalism, which has arisen within the American historical context of the exclusion of Asians from membership to the nation-state. Asian-American politics has been marked, therefore, by a need to claim home within America.)

A reader of *Trikone* (a queer South Asian diasporic magazine) recently asked, "Where is our *Go Fish*?" (Malhotra-Singh 1999, 10). The response indicates that we cannot have our *Go Fish* because we have not had our Stonewall yet. Following logic similar to that of Western film reviews, the comments though they may indicate that cinematic production is significant to political status and citizenship also indicate a hegemonic teleology of sexuality that marks India as insufficient to warrant lesbian sexualities, identities, and cultures. As Mark Chiang (1998, 386) writes, these movements "risk subsuming heterogeneous forms of sexuality under a gay identity that is implicated in a specifically Western and bourgeois construction of subjectivity, with its themata on voice, visibility, and coming out." In the case of the individual narrative, it is the process of coming out and claiming a lesbian identity that is valorized. For the group, Stonewall (as a marker of the beginning of the gay and lesbian movement) becomes a required stage in the teleological paradigm of sexual and gender liberation leading to the lesbian community depicted in *Go Fish*. More important, the idea of "our Stonewall" claims a linear and continuous connection between India and its diaspora, but one that is inattentive to differences (such as class and gender) and political and economic contexts.

Not all diasporic queers have fallen prey to the logic—in contrast, the South Asian Lesbian and Gay Association (SALGA) sought to support CALERI and other groups in India by protesting in New York against the Shiv Sena's attempts to equate a right wing Hindutva platform with the terms of Indian values. SALGA, however, also was careful to note and respect the differences in resources and political context between their location in diaspora and CALERI's and other queer groups in India. Similarly, Gayatri Gopinath (1997 and 2002) in her reading of *Fire* offers the possibility of a queer diasporic home located in the relationship between particular queer diasporic audiences and cultural texts such as *Fire* and Shyam Selvadurai's (1994) *Funny Boy*. Gopinath's strategic reading attempts to negotiate the marginalization of racial or queer citizen-subjects in South Asia and South Asian diasporas but operates within the context of diasporic politics only. Although I am empathetic with her project, I am wary of the ways in which diasporic cultural production dominates transnational flows between diaspora and the homeland because of resources, sometimes without attention to repercussions of power and resources. Diasporic queerness seems to demand an engagement not only with diasporic positioning and displacement but also with the political flows between the postcolonial nation and diaspora under the processes of globalization (i.e., a consideration not only of how the nation narrates diaspora but also of how diaspora narrates the nation).

Conclusion

Within the postcolonial nation-state, among the nonsubaltern classes, there are struggles over the deployment and promotion of globalization as various groups seek to mobilize and harness global processes to serve their own interests. In the case of Hindutva groups, although they seek to benefit from the expansion of global capitalism in India, they simultaneously seek to mobilize and control those who are being marginalized and exploited by this expansion by deploying anti-Western and antiglobalization rhetoric. Popular culture has been a significant site of contestation and engagement for these groups who have found it possible to deploy anticolonial nationalist rhetoric of swadeshi, purity, and pure cultural difference in relation to different forms of cultural production. Moreover, these groups have consolidated power by targeting groups that are nonnormative—diasporic or the transnational elite, women, and queers.

Foucault (1986) in *The History of Sexuality* seeks to dismiss the theories that locate power in the repression of sexuality that are forwarded by Marx and Freud and instead to forward sexuality as a productive site of power. In her work on Foucault's theories of sexuality, Ann Laura Stoler (1995) convincingly argues that though he linked class and race, to a lesser extent, to sexuality, he inadequately addressed colonialism as essential to the emergence of sexuality in modernity. In her corrective argument, Stoler forwards that the colonies were the laboratories of modernity and extrapolates that we cannot understand sexuality without understanding empire and colonialism. From what I have argued previously, it may be clear that contemporary discussions of sexuality continue to be imbricated in the histories of colonialism and its legacy of anticolonial bourgeois nationalism. Conversely, I have begun to demonstrate how contestations within the postcolonial nation-state around issues of globalization and diaspora by forces such as Hindutva occur through the production of social differences that can be identified as a form of biopower. Sexuality is the site of the reformulation of the postcolonial bourgeois subject in globalization. Furthermore, in this chapter I begin to unravel how postcolonial technologies of sexuality sustain and support technologies of the West (whether diasporic, Asian-American, or metropolitan).

In this prolegomenon on diaspora, nation, and queerness, I have tried to ascertain how transnational cultural production engenders complex political positions and discontinuous processes of identifications, ones that move beyond simple identity politics and engage with the (im)possible articulations of home and belonging that challenge queer and diasporic studies. One can argue that a diasporic relationship with the homeland can be a queer one, and conversely queerness can be form of displacement, both of which can call into question the very foundations of home, nation, and citizenship. In the words of Mark Chiang (1998, 389), "The politics of sexuality in the global system, then, cannot be directly extrapolated from within the nation." In particular, this project raises questions about how to think about sexuality within globalization from diasporic and transnational positions when homosexuality has become a sign of the global. Eng calls for an analysis of the nation and home that queers diaspora and diasporizes queerness. With attention to the intersections of multiple differences (gender, sexuality, geopolitical location, class, etc.), Eng (1997, 41) suggests that not only does queer problematize certain claims to citizenship and formations of the nation but that the nation-state itself can be queered. This will allow us queer methods and politics that not only require us to queer-y at the levels of the local, national, and transnational but also link our critiques of heteronormativity to our understandings of other social normativities, with special attention to narratives of desire and longing. We may need a political economy of queerness that recognizes the interrelationships of political, economic, and cultural structures and their traffic in normativities and nonnormativities that simultaneously considers the nation-state, postcoloniality, and globalization.

7

Sex in the Global City: The Sexual and Gender Politics of the New Urban, Transnational, and Cosmopolitan Indian Cinema in English

Within the context of transnationalism and globalization, diasporas have been conceptualized as deterritorialized nations, unbounded from the nation-state. Postcolonial diasporas located in the economic North, for example, often act as transnational agents integral to globalization processes in the economic South. Transnational communities play significant roles in influencing and supporting the political economy of the homeland nation-state through strategies such as remittance, investment, and lobbying.[1] In the case of India, billions of dollars have been invested by NRIs (nonresident Indians). South Asian diasporic communities located in the West or economic North, including the Brown Atlantic and Australia, have had such a strong impact on South Asian nation-states that India, for example, has increasingly sought to develop state apparatus dedicated to its relationship with its diaspora.

In turn, diasporas are increasingly recognized and beckoned by South Asian nation-states. From the development of state councils on NRIs and a center for the study of the Indian diaspora to the prevalence of NRI characters in Bollywood cinema, the nation-state advances its interest in diasporas in different modalities.[2] Probing how the nation-state recognizes and empowers diasporic communities, bestowing on them legitimacy and membership, further illuminates the relationship between diaspora and the nation-state. In the case of India, the state has sometimes sought to disenfranchise those who might otherwise claim national membership, while in other cases it has cultivated transnational citizens under categories such as NRI and Person of Indian Origin. In some cases, the state identifies certain members of diaspora as desirable and deterritorialized members of the nation (as NRI) to invest in government bonds, technology industries, and the development of nuclear capabilities.[3] (Those transnational subjects who may be migrant workers, exiles, or refugees need not apply for state or cultural citizenship as deterritorialized nationals). Since the structural adjustment policies of the eighties and nineties requiring India to "liberalize" its economy by devaluing its currency, opening its markets to transnational and foreign corporations, and continuing to increase its debt, the ideal diaspora is one that responds to the hail of the homeland with its economic and technological investments in exchange for membership and citizenship in the nation-state.[4]

Often, the ideal diasporic subjects are imagined as those privileged elite interested in infusing investments for the economic and technological development of India. Through the media, academia, and governmentality, the nation-state registers and communicates its interrogation of diasporic relations. For example, newspaper advertisements sponsored by the Indian government promote various investment opportunities and benefits targeted specifically to NRIs. In her study of Chinese diasporas, Aihwa Ong (1998 and 1999) describes these transnational subjects with political and economic privilege and with cultural if not state citizenship in multiple places as elite flexible citizens. Bollywood cinema eagerly depicts the deterritorialized citizen-subject as global elite subject who desires a homeland in films such as *Kabhi Khushi Kabhie Gham* (K3G) and *Yaadein*. Again the trope of the family is employed to reproduce national narratives of belonging to satisfy diasporic desires. Multiple valances of desire (e.g., longing, belonging, and (af)filiation) are eroticized as the heteronormative romance and framed within the Indian family and marriage (between the male NRI protagonist and the homeland heroine). In most films, the heroine is a pure virgin who is unsullied by Westernization and embodies Indian "culture" for the male NRI, thus reuniting the wayward capital of the male NRI with the proper object of desire.

The transnational cosmopolitan class, made wealthy by recent globalization and liberalization, also has emerged in South Asian metropolises. This urban transnational cosmopolitan class overlaps with but is not identical to diaspora or the new Indian middle class. In her study of love and romance in modern India, Rachel Dwyer (2000) investigates the rise of this elite transnational class and the new middle class in urban centers, particularly in Mumbai, the cultural and economic capital of India.[5] She links together these classes and contrasts them to the older bourgeois who are the dominant class of the nation and have often hegemonically defined middle India while unnaming themselves and their privilege.[6] Dwyer describes the new middle class with its own structures of feelings and ideologies distinct from the previous colonial and postcolonial dominant bourgeoisie. In addition to fluency in and frequent use of English, consumption of material leisure goods and services (including food, fashion, travel, and other high-priced commodities) defines this new middle class as well as the cosmopolitan transnational class. This new middle class is in the process of naming and contesting the old bourgeoisie and its values. Though different from diasporic subjects, this new middle class also is affiliated with the consumption and display of luxury and especially Western commodities.

The youth (16–26 years of age) of this class have come of age during the emergence of these economic and political shifts due to globalization, including increasing consumption of media, fashion, music, and mobility. New businesses and services have emerged to cater to this new class of youth, and dominant

Indian cinema has registered these shifts, exhibiting the "taste" and cultural capital of these classes. However, this new middle class in India has also engendered other cultural production in the formation of its own public sphere, in particular cinematic productions in English foregrounding its own articulation of Indian culture. Moreover, these groups share cultural capital and advance cultural and social values that often contrast to those of the national bourgeoisie, challenging conceptions of aesthetics, language, and culture.[7] More important, as I discuss later, this cosmopolitan class employs sexual politics as the sign of its difference from the older bourgeois classes. For example, the film *Mango Soufflé: A Metrosexual Love Story* by Mahesh Dattani (2002) describes ambiguous sexualities in contemporary urban and cosmopolitan India as metrosexualities; technologies of sexuality here signify class difference through cultural and social capital.

I have so far concentrated on how transnational films produce and represent diasporas and homelands. In this chapter, reversing the gaze, I consider how diasporas and homelands are constituted in the emerging transnational and cosmopolitan cinema in English from India by focusing on the conflicting class interests of the postcolonial bourgeoisies. I examine a recent spate of films made by and marketed for this developing cosmopolitan class, focusing on its constructions of diaspora. I also emphasize the significance of transnationality to the bourgeois national and cosmopolitan cultures and communities, especially in the formation of their new public cultures. Finally, I discuss the gendered and sexualized logics of transnationality at work within these films, arguing that sexuality is most often the site marking and negotiating these class interests. I do this because the proliferation of discourses on sexuality and gender are as much as part of globalization as are transnational corporations.[8] Consequently, I argue that these emerging films mark the increasing centrality of diaspora and the transnational class to the postcolonial nation-state due to the deterritorialization of the nation and other global processes. Notably, these films rarely if ever depict conflict with the West. In other words, in none of these films is there any open confrontation with the West. Instead, as I discuss, it is wealthy NRIs as diaspora, rather than encounters with the West, that configure negotiations and constructions of exploitation, contamination, and privilege, but not modernity. In this case, modernity is not positioned as foreign to the global city of Mumbai, which positions itself as connected and closer to a transnational network of global cities than with the postcolonial nation-state. In their critique of NRIs and other global citizens, these cosmopolitan elite position themselves as protecting the postcolonial nation from these outsiders and hence deploy a contradictory and conflicted affiliation with the postcolonial nation-state.

New Wave Cinema

A new low budget "independent" cinema characterized by such films as *Bombay Boys, Split Wide Open,* and *Hyderabad Blues* depicts the interests of a shifting middle class, whose interests have supposedly been unmet by Indian national cinemas.[9] The filmmakers assert that these films challenge the aesthetics and content of dominant Indian cinemas. Kaizad Gustad the director of *Bombay Boys* explains:

> What started to happen in 1998 was that a lot of young Indian filmmakers had gone abroad and came back to India and figured Bollywood just didn't do it for them, perhaps because they were urban people and wanted more representation through a cinema that speaks their language. So in 1998 we had a series of films that came out of all this and bucked the trend. They had low budgets and dealt with entirely new stories with an entirely new set of values. (cited in Kay 2001)

Gustad's comments most clearly foreground his perception of the inadequacy of national cinemas in expressing the cultural values of the new middle class and the transnational cosmopolitan classes.[10] Although Gustad frames the difference of this group demographically in terms of age (youth) and residence (urban), he clearly refers to the new middle class that is searching for its interests (new set of values) articulated in its own public sphere (cinema that speaks their language). Moreover, Gustad stresses that the transnational travel and experiences of this class are essential to the emergence of the new cinematic productions. Ironically, the transnational mobility seemingly engenders the possibility of expressing new Indian cultural values and experiences resulting from dissatisfaction with the conventions and ideologies of national cinemas. For example, Gustad, a graduate of New York University film school, internationally financed *Bombay Boys* through friends, family, and credit cards.[11] Gustad took four years to complete his first full-length feature film *Bombay Boys,* with shooting in Mumbai and postproduction in London. The low value of the rupee in relation to British, Australian, and U.S. currencies allows low-budget filmmakers to garner venture capital internationally for cinematic production in South Asia. Thus, many of the artists (for example Kaizad Gustad, Nagesh Kukunoor, and Rahul Bose) work or seek funding outside of India.

Notably, the language of these recent films is English. Although Indian literature in English has a long history because of the legacy of colonialism, popular Indian films in English are a more recent phenomenon.[12] Similarly, although vernacular language films in Hindi, Tamil, Telegu, Malayalam, Punjabi, Gujarati, and Bengali are present in Indian cinema, English films have not developed a large audience. Although South Asian diasporic films in English have received some crossover attention in India (from Merchant and Ivory productions to the films of Deepa Mehta, Mira Nair, and Gurinder Chadha), these films are nevertheless often viewed as diasporic films in terms of subject, financing, and production. The liberalization of the Indian economy (and globalization processes in general) has led to increasing use of English, not only as the language of science and technology or transnational economy and culture but also (mixed with vernacular languages) as part of everyday practices for the new transnational and middle classes in the urban centers. English used in conjunction with vernacular languages, especially Hindi, in this case functions not only as a marker distinguishing the economic status of the new middle class but distinguishing its cultural status as well, suggesting ease in code switching from English to other Indian languages. This multilingual literacy is prevalent in many of the cinemas—in Bollywood with the use of English words peppered throughout, and now in English films with multiple Hindi, Gujarati, or other vernacular usage. For example, in *Split Wide Open,* the protagonist code switches from Hindi to English and back again, depending primarily on the class of his addressee; so he directly addresses not only the NRI characters but also the audience in English, while speaking Hindi with his "sister," a homeless child.

Released in 1994, *English August* directed by Dev Benegal and adapted from Upamanyu Chatterjee's novel is the first of the major English language films. Although it was not a box office smash, the popular film was critically well received and set the stage for expressing urban dis-ease in the "real" India with its depiction of an urban cosmopolitan (played by Rahul Bose) in the civil service sent to the boondocks where he must survive provincial bureaucracy, corruption, ennui, and flies. It depicts the newly emerging middle-class man of India with his urban "modern" sensibilities confronting the reified "backwardness" of nonmetropolitan India, in the words of the promotional materials as a "foreigner in his own country." Its popularity seemed to indicate the emergence of a certain new urban young bourgeois audience invested in cultural production in English expressing its own interests and experiences.

Split Wide Open (1999), Benegal's second film, also starring Rahul Bose centers on the impact of globalization on various characters in Mumbai. Written by Benegal and Chatterjee, produced by Anuradha Parikh-Benegal, and adapted to screenplay by Farrukh Dhondy, the film loosely weaves together various "untold" stories of Bombay.[13] Focusing on Kut Price (KP) a former villager who is now a Bombayite who tries to eke a living from water trade (from charging for access to municipal water supplies to doling out cases of Evian to NRIs and diasporic elite), the film touches on his relationships with Didi (sister) a ten-year-old flower seller who becomes a child sex worker to a wealthy NRI, with a diasporic Londoner who hosts an anonymous sex discussion talk show, and with a Christian priest who has same sex desires and taught the abandoned child KP English and survival skills.

Portraying the contrasting and simultaneous worlds in which designer spring water and cell phones coexist with a lack of potable water and exploited children, the film probes contemporary contestations of social and sexual mores, seeking to expose the bourgeoisie's and underworld's sexual and economic exploitations of the lower classes in Bombay. Furthermore, in Benegal's film, predatory diasporic characters meander through Mumbai with the power to expose, exploit, and purchase. For example, the vehicle for these sexual "exposures" and confessions, the anonymous sex confession and talk show titled *Split Wide Open* is hosted by an ambitious NRI Nandita (Laila Rouass) whose insider-outside role enables the show and her career climbing. It soon becomes apparent that her probing questions about the sexualities and sexual practices of her guests are based on Western conceptions of confession, truth, and repression. Her understandings of culture, sexuality, and India are repeatedly exposed as inadequate and ultimately only useful in advancing her own career. Undercutting her authority, the guests of the show, the residents of Mumbai, blatantly tell her "You don't know anything." The show is popular because the audience and the guests seem to have a different assessment of the show's topic and the possibility of transgressing and challenging social gender and sexual normativities. Although her naïveté in exposing the stories of Mumbai is justified as the ability to use the power of television and the press, the show's guests are much savvier in their use of the media, confession, and power. A servant, who has been involved with his employer and his wife and was released from service by his employer's father, is reunited with the shame-faced employer after the show. Ironically, the film, like the television show, focuses on the sexual exploitation of the poor, sporadically interweaving discussions of other forms of exploitations. Nandita's own understanding of her role changes when a guest on the show attempts suicide on air and the show does not stop; confronted with her own use and exploitation of others' suffering as well as the impotence of talk-confession and television, Nandita eventually quits the show, only to be replaced by Leela, the NRI daughter of a "pedophile."[14]

More severe and perverse exploitation occurs at the hands of an NRI man posted to Bombay by a multinational corporation whose wealth and political power enable him to kidnap and sexually abuse preadolescent female street children; his pedophilia is discovered and then revealed by his NRI daughter on the show. When the common Indian man KP goes to rescue Didi from the lair of the pedophile, clutching her Toblerone box in one hand, she dismisses him, asking if he can provide her with a television, food, and shelter, not to mention imported candy. The sexual predation by the diasporic elite upon the vulnerable populations of Mumbai (children, women, poor, abused, etc.) becomes a trope for many forms of exploitation in general. A similar take on the gendered and sexual logics of transnationalism is presented in Mira Nair's *Monsoon Wedding*, which also presents the older and rich NRI male character as predatory, exploitative, and dangerous to the daughters of the homeland. In this manner, these films employ this concept-metaphor for the economic, social, and political impact of globalization, personified by the NRI transnational elite of the economic North, on the postcolonial nation-state as gendered and sexualized. (This is not to suggest that the cosmopolitan elite and underworld of Mumbai are not exploitative.) However, the most egregious abuse occurs by those with political immunity, patriarchal power, economic wealth, and a detachment from the family and nation, by those harbingers of globalization—the diaspora and NRI. I return to the issue of the concept-metaphor of sexual abuse in the next chapter.

Fig. 7.1 *Bombay Boys* Xerxes, Ricardo, and Krishna return to the homeland.

Emerging around the same time as *Split Wide Open,* Kaizad Gustad's *Bombay Boys* and Nagesh Kukunoor's *Hyderabad Blues* surprised the film industry with their popularity in urban theaters.[15] Originally scheduled to play the early afternoon matinee in Mumbai theaters, *Bombay Boys* by word of mouth and guerrilla publicity managed to secure top evening slots in a number of theaters within a few weeks of opening. The satirical and campy film features three NRI Indian men returning to the homeland, searching for fame, fortune, family, and fulfillment in Mumbai (see Figure 7.1).[16] Formerly Goan Christian Ricardo Fernandez (Rahul Bose) has come from Sydney to find his brother but finds romantic love instead, Hindu Krishna Sahni (Naveen Andrews) has come from New York to find fame and fortune or at least an acting career in Bollywood, and Parsi Xerxes Mistry (Alexander Gifford) has come from London to further his music, if not his sexual identity. The three men are thrown together in the film as representatives of diaspora in the form of the transnational cosmopolitan NRI, suggesting that diasporas in the West all resemble each other regardless of location, history, class, and so forth. Unlike films such as *Mississippi Masala, Masala, Wild West,* and *Bhaji on the Beach* that portray the political, social, and historical specificities of diasporas in the United States, Canada, and England, *Bombay Boys* constructs a general and universal diaspora defined only by its neglect, exploitation, and ignorance of the homeland. Gustad, himself a transnational cosmopolitan who grew up in Mumbai but traveled and lived throughout Europe, Australia, Asia, and North America, nevertheless seems to distinguish himself from his ignorant and naive diasporic and NRI protagonists who are chewed up and spit out by Mumbai. In the case of Ricardo who becomes involved with Dolly (Tara Deshpande), the moll of mafia don Mastana (Nasruddin Shah), he is forced to depart from Mumbai by Mastana for his trespasses; similarly, Xerxes decides to return to England after he is arrested for public displays of same-sex desire. Ultimately, all three boys flee their homeland, forced away by their inability to handle the law, the underworld, or the city itself.

Atlanta resident Nagesh Kukunoor, the director and star of *Hyderabad Blues,* creates a wistful narrative of a young NRI's return to see his family after twelve years. The film centers on his coming to terms with his inability to accept social "traditions" and practices such as arranged marriages that he confronts upon his return to Hyderabad. The film revolves around his expectations and behaviors upon meeting a Hyderabadi doctor with whom he falls in love. Kukunoor's (2000) second production *Rockford* is a coming-of-age narrative in which a young boy recounts his trials and tribulations of his first year at boarding school. Both *Bombay Boys* and *Hyderabad Blues* focus on the return of diasporic Indians or NRIs to their homeland. In the former film, the treatment is campy, emphasizing an ironic but empathetic critique of this return, further employing the diasporic men as mechanisms to reveal the sentimental, sordid, and sinister underbelly of Mumbai and its film industry. In the latter film, the narrative mobilizes the binary of modern and tradition, producing a denial of coevalness resulting from the displacement experienced in returning to Hyderabad. *Bombay Boys* avoids such evocations, painting Mumbai as a cosmopolitan global city, albeit with its own logic and practices around sex, drugs, alcohol, and culture. Moreover, Bombay as a global city is tied to other global cities such as London and New York, sometimes more so than to the nation-state. Hyderabad, in comparison, functions as every city in India (despite its emergence as a center of technology in India) and is circumscribed by class, caste, gender, and family practices that are critiqued from a neoliberal Western vantage. I return momentarily to this topic.

Although these films do not constitute a cinema in and of themselves, they nevertheless are seen as initiating a new Indian cinema and have been grouped together as a coherent category. The films *English August, Bombay Boys, Hyderabad Blues, Split Wide Open,* and *Rockford,* along with *The Godmother* (a Hindi film starring Shahbana Azmi in a fictionalized depiction of a real Gujarati widow who replaces her husband as mafia don), toured together as an international film festival under the title Filmi Fundas (Film Fundamentals) in England and Australia. The popularity of the films created the possibility of imagining a new market, audience, and spectator for such films. *Hyderabad Blues* bills itself as the highest grossing small budget film in India; the film played to audiences in Mumbai for more than seven months and in other cities like Hyderabad and Delhi for more than six months. The financial success of *English August, Bombay Boys,* and *Hyderabad Blues* enabled the possibility of low-budget "independent" films to be made and marketed in India. Gustad comments on the popularity of the festival and the films:

> The point is these films captured the imagination of the public. Suddenly everyone wanted more, it was a new wave, a new understanding, a new cinema. Of course we also had our detractors and imitators but the point is that two years later there are 20 films like this in production in Bombay, in English and each for under $340,000. "Fantastic! This is what the festival is all about." (in interview with Caroline Smith)

The group of films showcased as Filmi Fundas also led to the development of a manifesto. The text of the Filmi Fundas Manifesto is as follows:

> Filmi (adjective): Referring to the Indian film industry.
> Fundas (adverb): What's the agenda? What's up? What's hot and what's not?
> Filmi Fundas is a movement of filmmakers who have a common vision for the creation of a new Indian cinema.
> Our manifesto is a simple one: set after 1947 (partition); director of Indian origin or content of Indian origin; no Bollywood, parallel, or art house; no gratuitous songs, dances, or foreign locations. Fiction: short or long contemporary. Original. Any medium. No script, no shoot. No slow pans, and the director retains final cut. Currently the filmmakers are Dev Benegal, Anuradha Parikh-Benegal, Kaizad Gustad, Elaphe Hiptoolah, Nagesh Kukunoor, and we keep our doors open to other filmmakers who share the ideals of our manifesto.
> Filmi Fundas is a formal association that represents the interests of independent filmmakers from India. The idea is to develop, produce, promote, and acquire films that create a new culture of cinema in India that is independent of the mainstream and parallel ideologies.
> Filmi Fundas aims to set up a commercial film fund that will serve as a one-stop shop for the development and creation of a new cinema in India and the promotion of this cinema worldwide. Our aim is to acquire and/or produce at least five feature films a year and to find means of distributing and promoting these films ourselves.
> Filmi Fundas: By filmmakers. For filmmakers. For a new Indian cinema.

The Filmi Fundas Manifesto outlines the ideologies and guidelines of alternative cinematic production in India, more specifically emphasizing "independence" from the film studios and industries. The Filmi Fundas directors categorize themselves as independent filmmakers, creating low-budget movies initially financed by the filmmakers themselves rather than by film industry; elsewhere they have noted the difficulty in acquiring venture capital to establish vertical integration to avoid the monopolies in the film industry, specifically, control of the film from production to distribution. However, in the sense that independents also rely on the distribution and production networks of major studios and companies, they are hardly independent of the economic sphere of the Indian film industry. The films have had difficulty in acquiring distribution outside of India and are available thus far only through Bollywood distributors such as Eros International. For example, *Bombay Boys* is available in its dubbed Hindi version with English subtitles; ironically, extensive advertising follows the film with excerpts from the "extraneous" song and dance numbers critiqued by the manifesto. In this manner, even independent films are highly dependent on the preestablished networks of exchange and as the manifesto states the filmmakers realize their dependence on the dominant film industry from production through distribution. This financial independence, the filmmakers argue, will provide the means to create low-cost films ($25,000–$1,000,000) that avoid the homogeneity and high cost of Bollywood cinema.

These filmmakers attempt to distinguish themselves from the hegemony of Bollywood and vernacular cinema and what they call parallel or art cinema. The manifesto elaborates its antidotes to what it identifies as the Bollywood formula of national Indian cinema—loosely scripted films with rehashed stories, high production cost, extradiegetic musical sequences, and an overabundance of slow pans typical of melodramas and epics. Moreover, the specified topical and aesthetic precepts target the most frequently cited characteristics distinguishing popular Indian cinema from Western cinema (the melodrama, the extradiegetic scenes set in foreign scenic locations, and the musical sequences), suggesting the influence of Western cinema on these filmmakers. The manifesto also emphasizes that the control of production remains with the director (rather than by the financiers and producers), attempting to ensure that new stories are told without compromise. Simultaneously, the filmmakers eschew the social realist narratives or docudramas associated with parallel and even diasporic cinema, especially those depicting colonialism or the Raj. Evoking their sensibilities as those of a new middle class to whom extradiegetic song and dance numbers are signs of catering to the lower classes and older generations, these directors claim to tell new stories, presumably ones that relay the interests of the young new middle or transnational cosmopolitan class.

Notably, the manifesto collapses the distinction between diasporic and transnational Indian, requiring only that the director or content be of "Indian origin." In doing so, diasporic films and filmmakers are incorporated into the body of "new Indian cinema." Yet, the manifesto while distinguishing between this cinema and national cinemas also differentiates itself from other diasporic productions, such as Merchant and Ivory productions, which often focus on the Raj, as well as Deepa Mehta's *Earth* and Mia Nair's *Kama Sutra*, both of which take place before or during independence.[17] These filmmakers posit their texts as Indian and therefore within Indian cinema, thereby forwarding their challenge to other constructions of the nation (especially by those of the bourgeoisie and the diaspora). Furthermore, many of these filmmakers travel, work, and live abroad, as well as in India, blurring the line between the diasporic and the transnational. Nevertheless, as I discuss later, the films frequently interrogate the relationship between national, diasporic, and the transnational. Despite the simple opposition declared by the manifesto, its politics are quite complicated in relation to diasporic filmmaking. *Fire* does meet many of the requirements for being included in this collection of films (except of course its mode of production), but in many ways it had a greater impact as a marginalized film. In other words, it is interesting to note that these films including *Bombay Boys*, despite their potentially controversial topics, have not garnered the kind of response that *Fire* did. This is in part due to, as I argued in the previous chapter, the way in which Mehta, in contrast to Gustad, is located as a diasporic woman in the nation. Thus, films such as *Fire* call for a complication of the manifesto as working against certain aspects of the nation and Bollywood.[18]

Vertical integration of the film industry results not only in difficulty in acquiring wide distribution in theaters and sufficient visible screen time but also in garnering publicity and exposure for the films as well as "positive" reviews. Furthermore, contesting the aesthetics and content of Indian national cinemas also may result in confrontations with the state that is invested in protecting bourgeois cultural sensibilities and ideologies and other groups seeking to represent the nation. In the case of *Bombay Boys*, Gustad had difficulty getting publicity for the independent film, resorting to graffiti and postering in Mumbai. Being media savvy, he also spread the rumor that the film had been denounced by a right wing women's group whose members threatened to immolate themselves at theaters and assassinate the director. In this case, the transnational cosmopolitan director whose familiarity with the confrontations faced by diasporic films such as *Fire* and *Kama Sutra* (with the middle-Indian interests of the state censor board and with Hindutva nationalists) creates a tongue-in-cheek campaign that satirizes both from an ironic distance.

The tongue-in-cheek campaign proved to be prescient and the film was eventually protested by the Shiv Sena and faced difficulty with the censors. As in the case with *Fire*, the Shiv Sena's Pradeep Bhavnani of the Mumbai Youth Association wrote to the Union Home Minister Lal Krishna Advani objecting that the film crossed all forms of vulgarity in its portrayal of homosexuality, drugs, and alcohol, as well as in its use of profanity. Despite the director's coolness and irony, the censor board also objected to segments of the film, more specifically to its use of offensive language, its depiction of animal abuse, and its explicit sexual context both heterosexual and homosexual. Cited for its lewdness, one of the requested cuts paradoxically was the clip of a Bollywood film that had previously been cleared the censor board. In the film, the New York University film school–trained actor Krishna (played by Naveen Andrews) goes to the theater to study Bollywood cinema for his upcoming part in a B movie. In the theater, he watches a song and dance sequence featuring Govinda and Karisma Kapoor as they simulate sex while dancing. Krishna sits among the lower class male audience members who boisterously sing and gesture along with the movie. Despite Gustad's defense that the board had already previously approved the original Bollywood scene seven years before, the Bollywood excerpt was now deemed too explicit and provocative by the censor board that required it cut from *Bombay Boys*.

Also challenged was a later scene in which the Parsi Londoner Xerxes goes home with a Mumbai boy he has met in a nightclub. The censors cut the scene in which they begin to strip and kiss, allowing only one, rather than both, of the actors to be seen shirtless. The scene abruptly ends as the second shirt is in the process of being removed. Both scenes were cited as being too explicit. The clip though previously approved is now deemed to be too explicit due to change in context; Gustad's use of the Bollywood clip satirizes the ways in which sexual and explicit is defined by the Indian censor board. The state censors' acceptance of the heterosexuality depicted in Bollywood cinema was originally normalized by bourgeoisie respectability and the institution of marriage. That same heterosexuality when reframed as extramarital especially from the vantage point of the lower class male audience's gaze is then deemed pornographic by the censor board. Normative sexuality, therefore, functions as the terrain of contestation between the lower middle class (Shiv Sena) and the national bourgeoisie (state censor board) on one side and the transnational cosmopolitan class on the other—conflicts indicating the lack of hegemony and struggle for power within the nonsubaltern classes in India.

The contradictory responses of the popular presses also reflect the conflicting class interests and tensions between cosmopolitan urban and bourgeois national ideologies. The postmodern ironic parody of Bollywood and vice-ridden Mumbai are characterized alternatively as a deceptive and heartless "cold-blooded snake" (Vijayakar 1999) and as a fresh and funky depiction of new Indian values (Kay 2000) by various critics. These responses reflect the struggle for representation in the national imaginary between an English-based, cosmopolitan, upper-middle-class audience in opposition to the audiences of the Hindi dominant Bollywood cinema.

Sexual Orient-ations

With its quick edits, campy humor, and farcical plot, *Bombay Boys* incorporates romance, drugs, sex, films, and music in a staccato cut-and-mix narrative to portray the fast-paced and modern life of Mumbai as a world city. Its satirical tone critiques the Orientalist ways in which travel to India is a spiritual journey in search of the self and the abandonment of family and cultural values in the homeland by diasporans. The first is articulated through the character of Xerxes and the latter through Ricardo; both Ricardo and Xerxes together illustrate the ways in which diasporic desires become eroticized.[19]

The trope of the family also is employed here in suturing diaspora to the homeland nation territory, marking the desertion of the nation by diaspora. Accusations of being forgotten and abandoned are put forth by the nation (family and neighbors) and the state (the police officer). These accusations hound Ricardo as he searches for his brother Roger, who after falling in with "bad company" and drugs, has died alone and almost forgotten in the city. During his search, Ricardo is censured by Bombayites for abandoning his brother and his homeland. Their chastisement reflects a criticism of diasporic neglect and abdication of filial responsibility: "You leave the country with your family, and come back looking for him. Why did you go away in the first place? Wasn't it fun out there?" The criticism suggests that while diasporas hail the homeland through nostalgia and return, they do so at their convenience. The homeland nation's heralding of diaspora has little to do with the everyday lives and interests of the nonelite classes who are clearly critical of and ambivalent in regard to diaspora. The state in the form of the police too admonishes Ricardo: "So you forgot him. Know why people are lost? I think it's because we forget them. Completely." The barrage of criticism inevitably indicates a resentment and recognition of the ways in which diasporic economic, cultural, and political capital operates in power relations with the homeland. The broken family, in particular, becomes the trope of the deterritorialized diaspora's neglect of the homeland nation, particularly its most vulnerable members.

At one level, *Bombay Boys* reasserts and maintains the Bollywood trope of the family and the heterosexual romance as significant modes eroticizing and domesticating diasporic desires. At another level, in contrast to the reunited family of Bollywood cinema, Ricardo proves himself inadequate because he lost his brother and the object of his love Dolly. In the end, he must flee Mumbai, abandoning the romance he has begun and leaving Dolly in the clutches of Mastana. Thumbing its nose at Bollywood romantic fantasies of the NRI hero rescuing the Indian damsel in distress, *Bombay Boys* subverts the narrative closure of the happily ever after between the wealthy masculine diaspora and the poor feminine nation-state. Although the heterosexual relationship still serves to suture the masculine diaspora back to the feminine nation, it does so in complicated ways. The romance between Ricardo and Dolly hardly resembles those of dominant Bollywood cinema. In *Bombay Boys*, this relationship is satirized, because the heroine is not the chaste and innocent Hindu maiden but the vampy and sassy Christian actress Dolly who is the mistress of a Bollywood mobster producer Mastana. In the film, Mastana ropes Ricardo and Xerxes into shooting the ending of his film *Mumbai Banditos* with Krishna. The three, mounted on horses dressed as Parsi, Hindu, and Christian cowboys, dispose of all the evil henchmen à la Clint Eastwood before they ride off into the sunset.

As in my discussion of *Mississippi Masala* and *Wild West*, here once again displaced diasporic Indians become cowboys, nomadic and without women, home, or state. These three Indian cowboys, however, are hardly heroic; in fact, they prove incapable and self-preserving, suggesting that they are far from the Indian value-spouting heroes of Bollywood cinema who would gladly risk their lives to prove their commitment and attachment to their families, loves, and homelands, thus demonstrating their true Indianness. The film eschews dominant Bollywood narratives that usually forward the NRI male as retaining Indian values. In this film, the NRI men prove to be inadequate Indians and Bombay boys, as all (including Ricardo) choose to leave Dolly to her fate in Bombay and Bollywood. (However, during the credits, we see Dolly holding a plane ticket presumably from Ricardo.) Most often, the heroine provides the mechanism for inspiring and reasserting his Indianness or cultural authenticity. Although the film forwards a critique of the dependency of the nation on the diaspora, it does not make Dolly's escape contingent squarely on Ricardo. In fact, Dolly proves capable of protecting herself. Not the virgin maiden representing Indian tradition in the national imaginary, Dolly suggests a different formulation of the feminine homeland nation, albeit characterized as the romanticized prostitute with the heart of gold; nevertheless, she provides a space of critique in regard to the heteronormative narrative that sutures and reunifies the diaspora and homeland nation through the tropes of family and marriage.

Dolly in part represents a different aspect of the Indian nation. Rather than returning to the fertile fields of a Punjabi village symbolizing the traditional culture and soil of the nation, a common trope of Bollywood cinema, the return in *Bombay Boys* is to the world city of Bombay or Mumbai. In dominant Indian cinema, the West marks the space of contamination and vice. Films have consistently and repeatedly emphasized this theme. Bollywood film romances and "happy endings" indicate the preservation of cultural values and authenticity despite the dangers of diasporic and Western contamination. Mumbai functions in contrast to Punjabi villages as a site already filled with vice and corruption. In this film, it is not Westernization that has sullied India. It is the cosmopolitan city itself, which is a playground of capital, sex, alcohol, and violence, one that is decidedly Indian. In this case, it is not the Western-residing protagonists who contaminate Indian values and traditions; in fact the boys prove overwhelmingly incapable and inadequately prepared for their return to India. Mumbai is no longer and never has been the site of unchanging Indian culture and traditions that welcomes with open arms weary travelers from the West who have come to seek fame, fortune, and themselves in its Oriental mystique.

Bombay Boys satirizes this travel from West to East (usually the Punjabi fields of the cultural heartland or mystical and spiritual Orient) through the inability of the three protagonists to negotiate the space of India—Mumbai. However, although other films have handled the topic of colonial and neocolonial tourism, the difference in *Bombay Boys* is that all three characters are South

Asian diasporic or NRIs. Although the South Asian protagonist cannot travel to the mystic East to find himself, the diasporic Indian still has the possibility of doing so.[20] In a series of ongoing exchanges, Pesi the boys' gay Parsi landlord (played by Roshan Seth) admonishes Xerxes and all desi "foreigners" for their exploratory trips to the exotic East.

XERXES: I've come to India to discover myself. I wanted to see a new place too. I had never been outside London all my life. So I though, what better a place than India could there be? My forefathers are from here, too. But it's a brand new world for me, man.

PESI: A brand new world, huh? . . . Are you happy with India?

XERXES: No. . . . Where are the elephants and monkeys?

PESI: In the zoo, where else? Where do you keep the in London? No wonder India has all the filth in the world. You whites [foreigners][21] have found a convenient place to wash your dirt. If you don't know if you're straight or gay, go to India. If you don't know who you are and what you want, go to India. This is the place the sinners have found to discover themselves. Know what your problem is? You're too cute to be tough, and too scared to be gay. You can't decide to be AC or DC. Nothing wrong, actually. It's just that you're not being able to decide.

Pesi's criticism makes no distinction between Xerxes and other foreigners. Both come to India for orientation. But Pesi is not the only Indian national to criticize Xerxes for his dalliances.

Soon after this incident, Xerxes is arrested after a homophobic barroom brawl. Although his Bombay boy lover and the others escape, Xerxes is taken to the police station where he attempts to bribe the police officer. In contrast to Xerxes's expectations, the police officer not only refuses but also is indignant at the affront. The officer records the crime and chastises him: "You think you bloody Indians settled abroad can buy everything in this country. . . . If I were you, I'd save that money to find a competent Indian lawyer, someone who could save me from prison. You're going to need the money." In this manner the postcolonial nation-state expresses its resentment at its dependent relationship with diaspora and especially NRIs. Both the nation (Pesi) and the state (the police officer) chastise the diaspora for its audacity and entitlement, the former for the inconsistent and "mixed" signals to overtures of desire and the latter for attempting to brandish its economic and political power in circumscribing the law. Of course, Xerxes's expectations are not unreasonable. Certainly other aspects of the state emphasize the privileges accorded to NRIs who may circumvent legal restrictions that bind resident Indians. The state is clearly not homogeneous here, but multiple and at many levels. Components of the state court NRI tourism, investment, and development, offering economic, political, and cultural benefits in exchange. However, in this case, the legal apparatus enforces state policies on social and sexual normativities. The ambivalence of state is in regard to the power and privilege purchased by NRIs on the territory of the nation-state. Although the state may be willing to close an eye to other criminal activity, in this case, the taint of sexuality and NRI economic power are unpalatable to the nation, and the state is able to reassert its authority over social normativities.

A miffed Pesi later chides Xerxes after bailing him out of jail: "What you don't know is that homosexuality is illegal in India. You'd have been imprisoned forever.... At least we know your preferences now?" Thus, "we know" Xerxes's preferences only because the state (the law) has identified them as such. It is the state marking and enforcing of social normativities that pronounces practices and produces identities. In other words, it is the law of the postcolonial homeland nation-state that discovered Xerxes and his sexuality, not his desire for self-knowledge gained from Orientalist transnational mobility and diasporic return. Although Xerxes hopes to Orient himself sexually by discovering his ethnic and familial roots, ironically it is the law based on nineteenth-century colonial British code (India's laws on sodomy derive from its colonial statutes) that recognizes and outs him. (He identifies himself as such only to "prove" to Mastana that he could not be Dolly's lover because he is gay.) The gay/queer cultures that are depicted portray Mumbai as a hip, transnational, and cosmopolitan city like other world cities including London and New York.[22] But within the film's context, it is not Mumbai's transnationality and cosmopolitanness but its colonially derived legal codes that identify Xerxes's sexuality, which is not waiting to be discovered but is produced in his interactions with the nation and the state. (Of course, Xerxes would hardly have to travel to India to be arrested for violating British-derived sodomy laws; he could have stayed in London as well. But the journey arises for Xerxes more importantly because of the unique place occupied by India and the Orient in the global and diasporic imaginary.)

Although India has functioned in the Orientalist imaginary as the site of spirituality, it has done so in contrast to the materiality of the West. In evoking Mumbai as a world city (an urban cosmopolitan metropolis albeit with disparities between poverty and wealth), the film upsets that binary. In this case, India does not function as escape from the excess of the West, because drugs, sex, money, and vice too are rampant here. The film argues that any expectations of an idyllic and holy experience are out of place (and time). This is the new Mumbai. In fact, Ricardo's quest for his brother and involvement with Mastana's moll Dolly exposes the underbelly of the cosmopolitan city, a city that challenges social normativities beyond the naive expectations of the diaspora. Transgressing sexual and social normativities is entirely possible in Mumbai, which thwarts all Orientalist expectations as a land of tradition and repression. But deviancy results in consequences that surpass the boys' capabilities. Finally, hounded by Mastana and overcome by their run-ins with the law, the boys decide to leave Mumbai: "We'll have to go away or this city's going to kill us." They seem unable to stomach this modern global city.

Despite Mumbai being a global city, despite the boys being global citizens, despite the supposed neutralization of space and distance in hypermobility, place still seems to matter according to the film. While Saskia Sassen argues in *The Global City* (2001) that these global cities connected in a system or network may be more aligned with each other than with their particular nation-states, *Bombay Boys* suggests that these nodes are not identical and that postcolonial nodes in particular may have complex and contradictory relationships with (citizens of) other global cities and nation-states. In other words, these cities are not interchangeable and place remains highly significant with its multiple connections at many levels.

Conclusion

In different degrees, the NRI men in *Bombay Boys* trace the class, gender, and sexual ideologies; political economy; and power relations between diaspora and postcolonial nation-state located in the global city. As *Bombay Boys* establishes, global processes are not only economic but also inextricably imbricated in local negotiations of the social, cultural, and political that may not appear to have anything to do with globalization per se. Sexuality is one node in which local and global processes are instantiated and embedded. Hence, the Third World woman doing sex work, while not mobilized, is nevertheless incorporated into sexual global economy in the global city. The film portrays the possibility of disempowered subjects emerging as actors and gaining a presence in relation to each other in the global city.

Since the bourgeoisie achieved power with dominance and not hegemony in Guha's (1997) understanding of the nation, it is significant that the bourgeoisie now try to align themselves with the subaltern through their opposition to the diasporic or transnational class that are privileged. In the films, as in transnational arranged marriages, it is often the economic wealth of NRI men that engenders and enables access to the Indian girl-woman and nation. *Bombay Boys* and *Split Wide Open*, in contrast to Bollywood cinema, portray these relationships as exploitative and predatory, ones in which the feminine nation is taken advantage of by the masculine diaspora in the form of the male NRI; thus, these films critique the NRI for his mobility and privilege in removing himself from the consequences of actions and responsibilities. The unheroic diasporic characters are hardly the cowboys they are painted to be. In contrast, the unnamed elite of the city, suggested by Mastana, Pesi, and Xerxes's lover, maneuver through Bombay with similar interests but with greater ease and grace, while the nonelite suggested by Ricardo's brother and Dolly are either lost or continue to survive. Many of these recent films in English characterize the vulnerability of the Indian nation through the figure of the (often sexually exploited) female. In contrast to the figures in diasporic films made by women (such as Nair and Mehta) in the following chapter, it is quite striking that although many of these English films concentrate on the exploitation of women, they are made by men.[23] In

Split Wide Open, the figure is the homeless girl-child who is paid in candy and clothes by the male NRI; in *Bombay Boys*, it is the romantic mobster's moll with the heart of gold who sells herself in hope of making it big in Bollywood and is abandoned by her NRI lover; and as I discuss in the final chapter, in *Monsoon Wedding*, it is the girl-child who is molested by her rich NRI uncle, the patriarch and sugar daddy of the family. Although some of these figures emphasize the unequal power relations of these exploitations, others emphasize the increasing sexual agency of women. It is these gendered relationships that challenge the heteronormative narratives of Bollywood, suggesting cracks and fissures in the relationship between diaspora and the homeland nation. These films, less interested in wooing overseas markets than their Bollywood counterparts, provide a critique of the power of diasporic transnational capital that suggests there are alternative narratives of diaspora and nation that require attention.

Bombay Boys and the new Indian cinema provide a critical perspective of diaspora from the position of the global city in homeland nation-state, particularly from the new middle and transnational cosmopolitan classes. Its perspective relays the shifts in the formation of world cities such as Bombay in the postcolonial nation-state due to expansion of global capitalism and especially to NRI participation in the liberalization of the economy encouraged by the Indian state. Some of these films continue to stress the exploitation and economic power of relations between the diaspora characterized as the elite NRIs and the homeland. Most important, these critiques are located in relation to the gender and sexual politics that operate within the cultural logics of transnationality that are specifically located in the global city. This critique of diaspora emerges from a particular classed (and gendered) location in the homeland nation-state, namely that of the cosmopolitan urban elite. The emerging Indian cinema in English articulates the nationalist claims of a dominant but nonhegemonic class in India, one that is struggling to establish its own public culture in the global city. It is discourses on diaspora, gender, and sexuality that most strongly configure modernity and the nation for these urban classes in the films. Simultaneously legitimating themselves while remaining unnamed (and almost invisible as the films feature very few cosmopolitan urban characters), the new middle class not only challenges the hegemony of the postcolonial urban bourgeoisie (symbolized in these discourses by the state and Bollywood) but also highly regarded diaspora hailed by the "liberalized" postcolonial nation-state in structural adjustment and globalization.

8

Conclusion: Migrant Brides, Feminist Films, and Transnational Desires

Nostalgia is not simply a reaching toward the definite past from a definite present, but a subjective state that seeks to express itself in pictures imbued with particular memories of a certain pastness. *In film,* these subjectively pictorialized memories are there for everyone to see: nostalgia thus has a public life as much as a purely private one. The cinematic image, because of its visible nature, becomes a wonderfully appropriate embodiment of nostalgia's ambivalence between dream and reality, of nostalgia's insistence on seeing "concrete" things in fantasy and memory.

—Rey Chow (2001, 215)

Produced in a capitalist (if alternative) mode of production, the accented films are not necessarily radical, for they act as agents not only of expression and defiance but also legitimization, of their makers and their audiences.

—Hamid Naficy (2001, 26)

This chapter, is after all, one woman teetering on the *socle mouvant* of the history of the vanishing present, running after "culture" on the run, failure guaranteed.

—Gayatri Spivak (1999, 359)

I began this book with a discussion of my own pleasure in seeing brown skins on the silver screens, and after more than fifteen years, my pleasure has hardly decreased. These films continue to provide the sense of presence and present that I described earlier coupled with a better understanding of the construction of my pleasure, the architecture of its satisfaction and homely-ness. Certainly, my own enmeshed investment in the success (in the many ways that success can be understood here: commercial, theoretical, and political) of these films is always palpable to me. But during these years, I also have learned that the closure of one narrative is the foreclosure of another, that every representation requires access to the means of production. From this materialist and deconstructive methodology, I have learned to search for the failure in every success.[1] What I mean here is not the failure of inaccurate or negative representation, but the impossibility of completing or "getting right" the project of representation at all, focusing instead on the context and means of representation.

As a first step, the successes of the recent films by Deepa Mehta, Gurinder Chadha, and Mira Nair must be identified. These films are first and foremost attempts to present a feminist reckoning of South Asian diasporic cultural production and politics. The multiple successes of the films are not only interlinked but also intimately related. The commercial success of films such as *Bend It Like Beckham* and *Monsoon Wedding* is entirely connected to their political and topical engagements, namely in this case, with the idea of feminism and sexual agency. Although Bollywood and diasporic films seek to attract dominant (white) audiences in the West, transnational and multicultural filmmakers such as Mehta, Nair, and Chadha hold the distinct advantage of producing films that will be most accessible to cross-cultural viewers. Notably, it is the focusing on issues of gender and sexuality that has produced commercial successes in the past five years. In this final chapter, though I briefly overview *Bend It Like Beckham* and *Bollywood/Hollywood*, I focus on *Monsoon Wedding* to discuss how diasporic films by transnational cosmopolitan filmmakers employ feminist narratives that seek to challenge and rewrite the sexual agency associated with the heterosexual female but simultaneously foreclose queer sexualities and nonheteronormativities.

All of the films endeavor to contest the construction of South Asian and diasporic women as passive victims of heteropatriarchy. Each of the films stresses some challenge to the construction of Third World women as without sexual and social agency. In this sense, the films valorize the much maligned sex worker, the sexually active single woman, the sexually abused woman, and the athletic woman with the interracial lover. These are all of course "good" feminist projects in that they assert women's agency in the realms of work, marriage, and sexuality. Not only do the films provide pleasure but they are laudable for their assertion of their feminist scripts: women should play sports, including soccer, consent to marriage, be respected even if their occupation is sex work, and be protected from and supported in terms of sexual abuse. These political assertions are successful within the films because, at some level, they are accepted within the framework of liberalism. Much of the feminist work in these films seeks to supplement the victimization of women in these areas (i.e., heteropatriarchal control of sexuality, embodiment of aspirations of class mobility, racial heteronormativity) with representation of women's agency as they seek to invert these overdetermining dominant narratives. Writing against narratives of victimhood, the films target narratives of sexual agency to multiple audiences simultaneously, including one that is Eurocentric liberal feminist.

My Big Fat Sikh Wedding—*Bend It Like Beckham* and *Bollywood/Hollywood*

Chadha's most recent film *Bend It Like Beckham* (see Figure 8.1) interweaves the story of a young British Punjabi woman's dream of playing soccer with a multiracial heterosexual romance. Mehta has most recently released *Bollywood/Hollywood*, a romantic comedy that plays with the forms of both cinemas in the familiar narrative of the hooker with the heart of gold. Nair, also pursuing the nexus of these two cinemas, has created *Monsoon Wedding*, a luscious

Fig. 8.1 "My Big Fat Sikh Wedding" in *Bend It Like Beckham.*

and lush story of a Punjabi wedding in Delhi. The popularity of these films has propelled Nair and Chadha, in particular, into dominant culture. Gaining access to Hollywood, television, and Broadway, Nair and Chadha are poised on the brink of elaborate projects. Chadha is seeking to film a version of *Pride and Prejudice* (titled *Bride and Prejudice*) combining Bollywood and Hollywood (and starring Aishwarya Rai and Martin Henderson). Similarly, Nair is currently working on simultaneous projects including an adaptation *Monsoon Wedding* for Broadway, a Hollywood production of *Vanity Fair,* and a television serial about a Punjabi motel-owning family.

Monsoon Wedding met with commercial and critical success to become one of the highest grossing foreign films in the United States, the winner of the Golden Lion at the Venice Film Festival, and a nominee for a Golden Globe Award as best foreign film (but lost the Oscar nomination to *Lagaan*).[2] Nair having observed and experienced the difficulties faced by diasporic filmmakers in India, has delicately created a film that few will find politically objectionable. Carefully skirting controversy, Nair's film attempts to challenge overtly and safely some unspoken subjects (e.g., child sexual abuse) in contemporary cinema as it focuses on sexual power and politics of the bourgeoisie. While *Monsoon Wedding,* like *Bend It Like Beckham* and *Bollywood/Hollywood,* seeks to provide cross-over appeal, we must ask to whom and why it might be appealing. Is Nair's film a Bollywood wedding film like *Hum Aapke Hain Koun* (*HAHK*) (*Who Am I to You*)? Or is it a Hollywood film set in an exotic location with a colorful plot? Clearly this opposition is a false one in that the film is both and neither. What remains to be seen is what kind of hybridity *Monsoon Wedding* produces and to whom does that hybridity appeal.

These films (as well as the Andrew Lloyd Webber musical *Bollywood Dreams*) hinge on the heterosexual romance narrative infused with a feminist focus on female sexual agency and supported by the eclipsed queer subjects of the film. The films attempt to disrupt South Asian gender normativities of heterosexuality through challenging the dominant gendered ideologies such as female chastity and virginity, multiracial romance, and arranged marriages. The popularity of these films is based on the accessibility and familiarity of these narratives to cross-over viewers. Non-South Asian viewers may find these challenges not only nonthreatening but also familiar and comfortable. Furthermore, the deployment of the queer characters (effeminate boys, gay men, and drag queens) as contrast to the feminist heterosexual figures also refocuses attention to the centrality of the heterosexual narrative, but it provides a familiar marginalization of nonheteronormative sexualities in the service of consolidating an acceptable understanding of feminist agency.

In *Bend It Like Beckham,* the most intimate and obvious relationship is not immediately recognizable as the one between the Jesminder (Jess) and the Irish coach Joe but rather between the two soccer-playing pals Jess and her English friend Juliette (Jules). Repeatedly, the relationship between the two women is sexualized and queered despite the overwhelming narrative of heterosexuality and female competition for male attention that is emphasized in the film (see Figure 8.2). In one of Jules's first appearances, the film creates parallels between her watching Jess and other women watching the male soccer players; Jules's observing and tracking gaze of Jess is ambiguously sexual as it is intercut with the ogling of the shirtless Asian men by the benchful of young Asian women. Similarly, Jess announces to her family, "It's not like I am sneaking around seeing someone" just as Jules enters the scene. Upon seeing the two women together, friends of the family assume that (Jules is a man and) the women are lovers as they intimately touch and laugh together at a bus stop. However, Jess's nuclear and extended family are able to deny the possibility that Jess has been with a lover once she announces that she was with Jules who is a woman; they can, instead, chalk it up to gender deviance: "Those English girls have short hair." The impossibility of an Asian queerness is repeated throughout the film not only through the denial of its presence by the older generation—"What is lesbian? She is a Pisces"—but also by Jess, who responds to her best friend's announcement of his same-sex desire for men with an incredulous "You're Indian!" Further undermining his declaration is his willingness to play Jess's fiancé so that she can gain her family's permission to travel to the United States to play soccer as

Fig. 8.2   Jules and Jess embrace and kiss in *Bend It Like Beckham.*

an engaged woman. Male same-sex desire within Asian British communities in the film, if it is named at all, can only be named to be disavowed, while female same-sex desire is denied altogether.

The link between lesbianism and sports is integrated into the film's plot that attempts to waylay any audience anxiety through comic relief any time there is intimacy between the two women. The anxiety around this same-sex desire is portrayed through Jules's mother Paula, who worries that her daughter and Jess are lovers. Her attempts to normalize Jules to white bourgeois notions of femininity and her fears about same-sex desire appear humorous to the audience who is informed about Jules's desire for Joe. The audience readily laughs at Paula when she "misinterprets" a conversation between Jules and Jess (regarding Joe) about the betrayal experienced by Jules when Jess and Joe become involved; Jules say to Jess "You don't know the meaning of love. . . . You betrayed me." The film ridicules Paula's observations and fears about the women's sexuality, because she also is framed as being racist, ethnocentric, and invested in gender normativity. At the same time, the film proposes that the viewer would accept a same-sex relationship between Jess and Jules but does not have to because the viewer is already always in the know about the platonic nature of their relationship. Hence, the film does not have to deny the possibility, but merely to disavow its accuracy.

Both families are concerned with the ways in which sports may disrupt gender and sexual normativities; for Jess's family, this challenge is framed through the scheduling conflict between the final soccer championship (complete with a visiting American scout) and Jess's sister Pinky's wedding. In both cases, soccer, like feminism, is shown to be disruptive to heteronormativity but reclaimable through a rewriting of women's heterosexual agency. Hence, the queer moments of the film are quickly overwritten by its foregrounding of heterosexual female agency of the Asian woman; although the film challenges heteronormativity in relation to multiracial relationships, it does so by sacrificing and disavowing same-sex desire in white British communities. Again this suggests that white British communities are more open and progressive, in that soccer, feminism, and lesbianism at least enter the public sphere. As a film advocating women playing sports, *Bend It Like Beckham* proposes an engaging narrative that has been immensely popular. Finally, the film concludes with the celebrated migration of Jules and Jess to the U.S.

In *Bollywood/Hollywood*, the heteronormative and patriarchal pressure to marry is the target of the film. The film presents the sexual escort (a familiar figure in Hollywood films such as *Pretty Woman*) initially as the sign of woman's agency in opposition to the heteronormative family and (arranged) marriage. Sunita (Sue) is hired by Rahul to pose as his fiancée after the death of his first fiancée (a white Canadian) and in response to his own family's pressures to marry. Despite her profession, Sue proves herself to be an appropriate bride-to-be at Rahul's sister's wedding, the ultimate test site of her gender normative performance and ethnic authenticity. To overcome the impropriety of her life as an escort, the film forwards the feminist script that she must be accepted on her terms. However, *Bollywood/Hollywood* proposes that this is because she should not be misjudged for "choosing" her line of work. The film reveals that not only is Sue working class and Sikh but also that she has taken up escorting only after the egregious matrimonial mismatch arranged by her parents. Paired with a bodybuilding television wrestler, Sue is driven into to her occupation by the lack of "choice." Sue is befriended by the Rocky chauffeur (played by Ranjit Choudhry) who leads a double life as a drag queen (see Figure 8.3). His dutiful role as the friend and adviser of Rahul is literally replaced by Sue in the ending of the film as the lovers are reunited with her playing the role of the chauffeur. The feminist contestations of dominant South Asian and diasporic discourses in *Bend It Like Beckham* and *Bollywood/Hollywood*, like *Monsoon Wedding*, require further attention.

Bollywood Wedding Films—The Return of the Bourgeoisie

Monsoon Wedding relies on a complex interplay of nostalgia, pleasure, and feminist politics in its depiction of a large bourgeois family wedding. Set in the contemporary moment, the film is nostalgic in its employment of the genre of the wedding film to propel a heterosexual narrative of family, community, and

Fig. 8.3 Rocky as a drag queen in *Bollywood/Hollywood*.

belonging. However, the film offsets the narrative of sexual agency of women in patriarchal heteronormativity with the figure of the sexually abused girl-woman. The film attempts to reconcile an arranged marriage to an NRI with the sexual agency of the modern Indian woman. Consequently, I investigate the meaning of the material and metaphorical meanings of weddings in regard to the suture of diaspora and nation. Weddings function in many ways, evoking nostalgia for different audiences: for some audiences, weddings are most frequently evoked as markers of the idealized relationship between diaspora and the homeland nation-state that is mapped onto heteronormativity, as I discussed in the last chapter. Weddings serve not only as signs of heteronormativity but also as the object of the transnational and cross-cultural gaze.

Nair's film is a hybrid in that it mixes many forms and genres, but most important here is its use of the Bollywood wedding film. While love, marriage, and family are common themes of many cinemas, in Indian cinema, in particular, it was the emergence of *HAHK* in 1994 that rejuvenated a certain kind of nostalgia for the joint bourgeois family. Not laden with the violence or sadism that was associated with commercial Indian cinemas at the time, *HAHK* presents a sentimental and idealized view of two North Indian Hindu bourgeois families, from the engagement to the birth of the first child, as they prepare for a wedding.

The film features fourteen songs and made a record 600 million rupees (1 billion rupees adjusted) at the box office, making it one of the highest grossing films in Indian film history. Its popularity spanned India (in rural and urban areas—it played continuously for two years in one Bombay theater) and South Asian diasporas (e.g., it played three months in theaters in Fiji).[3]

HAHK aggressively reinscribed cinemagoing as a middle-class phenomenon. Previously, the middle class had retreated to its private viewings of films on video and television cable channels. For middle-class viewers, HAHK suggested to many that it was safe to return to the theater as the lowbrow and vulgar taste of the working class had been momentarily, at least, vanquished. In an era when liberalization and globalization are transforming social relations in the postcolonial nation-state, the film in many ways displayed nostalgia for a utopic "traditional" joint bourgeois family. As Patricia Uberoi (2001) comments, many viewers admired the film precisely because it was perceived as a "clean" film, one that did not display the vulgarity that is associated with commercial cinema for the working class in India, instead portraying the romances as wholesome and moral.

It also was commended by viewers for its depiction of how families could be—untainted by greed, power, or conflict. As Uberoi (2001) reports, the film achieved its appeal to bourgeois tastes through several strategies, including an explicit avoidance of the violence associated with commercial Hindi cinema of the eighties and a highly visible display of consumption and wealth. These features were combined with an emphasis on representations of social and family practices that were sanitized and normalized so that "offensive" or "vulgar" material was removed (e.g., the frequently bawdy, transgressive, and sexually expressive wedding songs sung by women became less risqué, obscene, and offensive) in order to present the film as appropriate for the middle classes. Not surprisingly, considering its themes of families and marriages, the film was extremely normative, especially in terms of its gender and sexual codes. Though there are moments of eroticism between family members (e.g., the sister of the bride and brother of the groom are in love) and ruptures that open up nonnormative moments, the film is perceived by many as depicting the idealized sanctioned and chaste relations appropriate to a joint family. Significantly, the joint bourgeois family in this case functions as a microcosm of the nation in that it is able to absorb and manage difference. The film features North Indian Hindu families in large homes complete with cars, servants, and other signs of affluence. But the servants within the family are to be considered less markers of wealth and more like members of the family. HAHK pointedly foregrounds the family's inclusion of and trust in the servants in suggesting that class is not an important feature of social relations because the bourgeois family is generous, kind, and considerate of other classes.

Although I am arguing for the centrality of weddings to these films, oddly enough what I am referring to here is not the actual religious ceremony but its attendant cultural practices. In other words, the popularity of HAHK is because of its employment of the wedding and its associated practices that center on interactions between families, rather than on official ceremonies as the site of desire and fantasy. *HAHK* presents an idealized version of wedding practices that many viewers in South Asia and South Asian diasporas nostalgically associate with their own experiences. The film's excessive consumption and elaborate displays of wealth are justified in the narrative through the event of the wedding and other ceremonies. But most important, the film, contrary to expectations, does not focus on the Sanskritized wedding ceremony itself but rather on the social practices of weddings associated with bourgeois social formations and consumption such as applying mehndi, women's songs, and exchanging of gifts. For example, in *HAHK* the actual Hindu ceremony in which the bride and groom are married is less central than the North Indian Hindu cultural practice of the bride's sister hiding the groom's shoes, which are returned only in exchange for money. A long sequence of the narrative as well as a song and dance number are dedicated to this event. In addition, in another scene, the families are brought together during the women-only *sangeet* (song session) in which the women sing about the forthcoming marriage and sexual relations. I shall return to this topic in relation to *Monsoon Wedding* momentarily.

HAHK is important to Indian cinema and diasporic cinema because of the ways it reasserts the family as and in the space of national culture. It does so not by depicting the family as threatened by social, economic, or political forces of modernity but rather by depicting the family as the site of tradition that has been unsullied and unmarred by urbanization, liberalization, globalization, or Westernization. The one tragic event in the film occurs only by chance, as Puja, the older married sister, falls accidentally down a long flight of stairs to her death. Here, there are no social, political, or economic forces at play; in the world of the film, everything is about family, and good bourgeois families can be and are protected from harsh social and political forces by the upholding of traditional family values (i.e., sacrifice and duty). In other words, the film asserts that the family, specifically the joint Indian family, has withstood and can withstand these onslaughts by indigenizing modernity in the Indian nation. Patricia Uberoi (2001) in her essay on *HAHK* poses the formation of the narrative of the "arranged love marriage"—a relationship based on love, but one that must also garner familial approval. Hence, the film provides pleasure in satisfying narratives of romance and family simultaneously.

Universal Heterosexuality, Cultural Difference, and Nostalgia

Monsoon Wedding exposes the many disturbing issues brewing underneath the silence that is imposed on the self-proclaimed happy Indian family in Bollywood films, but it also develops a narrative of nostalgia and fantasy regarding familial relations and cultural practices amidst global processes of late capitalism, transnationality, and modernity. Specifically, it makes visible the economics of such production of culture, linking these familial celebrations of heterosexuality with larger macroeconomic frameworks of the national and global economy. The film romanticizes some aspects of globalization and migration, employing the wedding as a trope of fantasy and desire. While *HAHK* seeks to show that Indian cultures, values, and families have remained and can remain traditional having incorporated modernity into the family through gender and sexual normativities, *Monsoon Wedding* proposes that these are modern transnational formations, albeit with "traditional cultural practices," in the process of transformation due to female sexual agency. Its feminist representations of women's heterosexual desire and practices are offered as the strongest evidence of the changes due to modernization and cosmopolitanism in liberalized India. Hence, what makes the film travel well is its appealing heteronormativity and liberal feminist politics, particularly its interpretation of tradition and modern (in ways similar to and different from *HAHK*) through its depiction of individual feminist agency and bourgeois family consumption.

As Chrys Ingraham (1999, 88) comments, "The way that heterosexual imaginary works is by making use of both fantasy and nostalgia. The effect is a masking of the very real, contradictory, and complicated ways institutionalized heterosexuality works in the interests of the dominant classes. Through the use of nostalgia, romance renarrates history and naturalizes tradition." In the case of India, *HAHK* promotes and provokes a nostalgia for the traditional folk practices associated with an idealized joint family that become the site of fantasy in (post)modernity and postcoloniality. Similarly, in *Monsoon Wedding* the focus is not on the wedding ceremony but rather on the cultural practices surrounding the ceremony that emphasize the bonds between families, in this case, despite the distance of transnational kinship. Like *HAHK*, *Monsoon Wedding* emphasizes the sangeet (the singing of bawdy songs by women) prior to the wedding; however, *Monsoon Wedding* explicitly marks this as a traditional space of female (hetero)sexual agency and expression (see Figure 8.4). The sangeet section of

Fig. 8.4 The sangeet as feminist space of heterosexual expression in *Monsoon Wedding*.

HAHK includes a possible moment of queer identification and pleasure as a cross-dressing woman dances with the heroine during the sangeet before she is literally replaced by the male protagonist.[4]

Wedding films may evoke and invoke nostalgia for viewers and filmmakers alike. *Monsoon Wedding* is informed by Nair's Punjabi background. In a recent interview, Nair recalls going to see *HAHK* and thinking that it was a wonderful experience in terms of family, but that she wanted to make a film that depicted what "real" families experience. Like the director Sooraj Barjatya who authenticates *HAHK* by suggesting that it is based on his own experiences, Nair too articulates a claim to Indian social practices, validating her memories of Punjabi weddings and families. Interestingly, Indian films have increasingly featured Punjabi characters and locations; Vijay Mishra (2002, 260) suggests that Punjab is becoming the dominant setting of Hindi cinema. He attributes this shift as partially due to the significance and wealth of the Punjabi diaspora. He also suggests that the Punjab functions in the Indian imaginary as the site where cultural values have been maintained, where Indianness has been preserved unsullied. Nair's version of Punjabi culture is, of course, not in Punjab but in Delhi, a site that she (like Mehta) identifies as a hybrid of tradition and modernity.

The nostalgias associated with Bollywood and diasporic cinema and produced by viewers are complex and not necessarily identical. Weddings in diasporic and multicultural cinema often testify to the ability to survive and thrive by "ethnic" groups through "maintaining" traditional familial structures and practices despite displacement. In films such as *Moonstruck, My Big Fat Greek Wedding, Monsoon Wedding,* and *Bollywood/Hollywood,* weddings function as signs of community and ethnic belonging constituted through heteronormativity. In other words, wedding films, by naturalizing and stabilizing heterosexuality, reassure ethnic audiences of the possibility of cultural tradition and allow viewers to fulfill narratives of desire, belonging, and community. Several second-generation South Asian–American viewers in my forthcoming study on the consumption of Indian cinema reported that the films function performatively and pedagogically in that they teach rituals, traditions, and social practices as well as identifications. These films are ethnographic and pedagogical for multiple audiences. In addition to Western viewers, South Asian diasporic viewers also may view these films as documents recording South Asian or Indian cultural practices. Watching films is identified as pedagogical in these viewers' method of learning about India and Indian culture, what it means to be Indian; it is also a lesson in how to be good consumers, as some commented on how they watch films to get ideas about the latest fashions in India. In this manner, visual media, especially cinema, functions as a significant site in constructing and disseminating discourses on weddings and marriage, family, and culture.

The dominant viewer inhabits the space of insider and outsider that allows her to identify with the construction of heterosexuality propounded by the film, while consuming the ethnographic spectacle of cultural tradition and diversity.

In their constructions of culture, tradition, and ethnicity, these films simultaneously offer dominant viewers a nonthreatening spectacle of otherness that at the same time can be absorbed into the narrative of universal heterosexuality: as one viewer responds, "Mira Nair's *Monsoon Wedding* may not be as broadly comic as that other well-attended wedding in town (that Big Fat Greek one), but it is every bit as universal in its observations and appeal" (Internet Movie Database, February 20, 2003, http://www.imdb.com). Cross-cultural consumption of wedding films relies on the rejuvenation of an anthropological desire for knowledge of and intimacy with the other. Weddings have been a site of fascination in anthropology and the ethnographic film. Illuminating the patterns and practices of kinship, cultural tradition, and the political economy of gender and sexuality (the traffic in women), Western (feminist) fascination with the authenticity of the other coalesces around wedding films such as *Monsoon Wedding* and *My Big Fat Greek Wedding*. In particular, white ethnicities such as Greek and Italian particularly signify a very safe way to multiculturalism, because they favor foregrounding ethnicity and culture while sidelining racist inequalities.[5] *Monsoon Wedding* also can avoid the issues of race and racism as well as the context of global capitalism as engendering transnational migration. These films are often "whitened" by viewers who are eager to absorb South Asian diasporic films into the dominant mode. One online reviewer calls the film "Greek Wedding in a sari": "If you enjoyed *Greek Wedding*, you'll like *Bollywood/Hollywood*. . . . Darker and more exotic than *Wedding*, *Bollywood/Hollywood* is equally funny. The musical scenes—a staple of the Bollywood melodramas this film spoofs—are a treat for ear and eye" (Internet Movie Database).

These films provide the means of pleasure not only through negotiating intimate positions of heterosexual identifications but also through recognizing the familiar trajectory of the Third World's development into modernity. Like *Fire*, *Monsoon Wedding* also contends with the overdetermining narrative of India's backwardness. In contesting this formulation, the film forwards a familiar "modern" world that creates spaces of identification for the dominant culture viewer who seeks images of the India that is modern like us. As one reviewer surmises,

> Nair makes sure that the India we see in this film is no technological or cultural backwater. It is, instead, a modern, vibrant land filled with cell phones and golf carts, disco music and high minded TV talk shows. In much the same way, the people we meet in this large extended family struggle with the vicissitudes of life common to us all. There are good, well-meaning parents wanting to do what's right for their children, but not always knowing how to cope with the uncertainties of a modern world. (Internet Movie Database)

My point here is not that the viewer is ethnocentric in his review but rather that the film functions to satisfy the desire for representations that modulate imperialist understandings of modernity. *Monsoon Wedding* thwarts this dominant paradigm in that it upholds the arranged marriage as one site of difference. In this regard, there are complex negotiations of tradition and modernity in the film in that it does not simply offer romance and choice as the markers of modern marriage and love. The arranged marriage is an ambiguous sign of the tension between modern and tradition in the film that can be read differently by viewers. For example, in comparing *My Big Fat Greek Wedding* and *Monsoon Wedding*, one reviewer explains, "In the latter film, the arranged marriage actually serves as an anchor holding the family in place in a time of rough seas and uncertainty. . . . The difference in attitude between the two films arises, I imagine, from the fact that one is American in origin and the other Indian" (Internet Movie Database). *Monsoon Wedding*, in this viewer's eyes, poses the arranged marriage as a site of tradition and stability (similar to the ways *HAHK* does) in the sea change of globalization and modernity; simultaneously, the viewer also isolates this possibility by establishing its difference from the United States through geopolitical cultural distance (not here, but over there). This simultaneous claiming and disavowal is central to the film's crossover appeal.

Sexual Agency

In one strand of the narrative, the bride's teenage cousin Ayesha assertively pursues her attraction to Rahul, an NRI from Sydney who is visiting India after an absence of five years. Ayesha befriends Rahul as she practices a dance performance for the wedding celebration with Aditi's effeminate brother Varun. Astounded by Ayesha, who challenges his assumptions and recollections about young Indian women, Rahul struggles to understand the shifting rules of acceptable heterosexuality in contemporary India; he eventually meets the challenge by dancing along with Ayesha's performance. This is one example among many, suggests the film, of modern Indian womanhood—bold, assertive, sexual, and self-assured. Set in the capital city of Delhi, rather than the global city of Bombay, *Monsoon Wedding* nevertheless signifies India's modernity through the sign of the sexually active female.

Aditi, the bride of *Monsoon Wedding*, has agreed to an arranged marriage with Hemant, but she is hardly a chaste and demure bride-to-be. Gambling on her decision to accept the arranged marriage proposal once she realizes that her married lover and former employer will never leave his wife, Aditi declares herself ready to try something different. Nevertheless, apprehensive about and underprepared for her upcoming marriage and transnational migration, she returns momentarily to her former lover Vikram just prior to the ceremony. (I will return to the possible anxiety associated with migration momentarily.) However, the film establishes this relationship and her choice of Vikram as questionable. As the police interrupt their late night tryst, Vikram abandons her to answer a telephone call from his wife as she is harassed by the police officers; adept and resourceful Aditi resists and flees, deserting Vikram by taking his vehicle. In contrast to the self-chosen lover Vikram, the film frames as the arranged-for groom Hemant as the better of two options; moreover, Aditi and her modern female sexual agency are seen as problematic and critical of the idea of "choice." An engineer from Houston, Texas, Hemant eagerly seeks to create an arranged-love marriage by getting acquainted with Aditi amidst the wedding preparations. Aditi "confesses" her trespasses to him and, no longer recalcitrant, appears adequately prepared for marriage. The couple's reconciliation reconfirms the stability of the arranged-love marriage as a traditional-modern institution, appropriate to the sensitive modern heterosexual NRI man and the sexually active heterosexual Indian woman. In contrast to *Bollywood/Hollywood* and dominant Western discourses that frame arranged marriages as denials of choice and an antithesis to love, *Monsoon Wedding* delivers a complex portrayal of its contemporary mode; in contrast to expectations, Hemant, for example, stands out is the most appealing avatar of masculinity in the film. As Aditi "matures" into the appropriate bride, her sexual agency too is channeled into appropriate forms; in other words, upon meeting Hemant, Aditi refines her sexual freedom that allows her to negotiate the dangers and drawbacks of heterosexuality to come to resolution and select the one proper mate.

Although lavish and excessive in its display of affluence at the wedding, the film explicitly foregrounds the expenses associated with such spectacles. Significantly, the film illustrates the concerns of the bride's parents Lalit and Pimmi in financing such an opulent affair that must display excessive consumption for the national and transnational elite. The lavish wedding requires the services of the wedding coordinator P. K. Dubey who organizes the construction of massive tents, illuminated maidans, and marigold-covered structures for the event for significant profits.[6] Furthermore, when the groom is from the United States, even more is at stake, because the bride's family must prove themselves worthy of such a "catch." Lalit, though an international trader, experiences a cash flow difficulty and must borrow to finance the cost of the wedding, dowry, and trousseau, until his shipment to Macy's is complete. This detail of the film again evokes the question of political economy between India, its diasporas, and the West, a pressing and visible concern recently of the Indian nation-state. However, although the film remarks on this aspect of the political economy, it delights nevertheless in the pleasures associated with the display and consumption. Furthermore, we are to feel that in the end the cost is justified by the happiness that is achieved, especially in (re)joining families, especially those that are fractured overseas; hence, weddings (re)unite diasporas with their homelands.

In *Monsoon Wedding*, counterposed to the figure of the celebrated figure of the modern sexually active bride-to-be is the abject specter of the sexually exploited young girl-child. As I commented in the last chapter, many of the recent Indian films in English center on the abused female; here, I turn briefly to this issue seeking to understand how the figure of the molested girl-child functions as a concept-metaphor in *Monsoon Wedding*. In this reading, I attempt to consider a reading of the sexually exploited girl as a literal and allegorical figure. The film reveals that Aditi's cousin Ria has been molested as a child by her powerful and wealthy NRI uncle Tej. Like in *Split Wide Open,* the molested girl-child is a victim of sexual abuse because of her status as female and her status as an Indian child. In other words, she is located not only in gendered but also in economic power relations. The uncle, unlike the heroic males, returns to the homeland to exploit his economic and social power. Ria's divulges her secret during the wedding preparations only when she sees a younger girl at risk. Dismissed by several relatives who suggest that she is lying, Ria leaves the fete. Upon convincing her to return the next day, Lalit accompanies her back to the celebration where he forces Tej to leave.

Ria's agency in exposing her abuser is not to dismiss or punish her abuser but to protect another child from molestation. The film poses voice and visibility as motivated by prevention, not as a means of justice or empowerment. Nevertheless, Ria's statements have exposed a rupture in the fabric of the family that require either disavowal or attention. However, the power of punishment and banishment is reserved for the patriarchal figure of the family who as male head of the household takes responsibility for action.[7] In this case, Lalit is forced and empowered to act on behalf of Ria and the embodied collective (see Figure 8.5). The film portrays Lalit's decision as difficult because he feels in debt to Tej's financial contributions to and patriarchal leadership of the family; at times, Tej's economic power has been wielded to consolidate the family despite transnational dispersion. Nevertheless, Ria's agency provokes Lalit to seek justice on her behalf, not through the law or state but through his role as guardian and parent. The film does not allow Lalit to abdicate his responsibility as parent-guardian

Fig. 8.5   Lalit banishes Tej from the celebration in *Monsoon Wedding.*

of Ria as he not only banishes Tej from the wedding but also asks Ria's for-giveness. This feminist script in particular enacts a transformation from the dominant discourses surrounding sexual abuse, rape, and incest in many South Asian and diasporic communities.

However, rather than rendering the power of the transnational elite up for analysis, *Monsoon Wedding* recuperates the bourgeois family and heterosexual-ity through the feminist reconfiguration of female heterosexual agency and the arranged love marriage. This recuperation occurs in the service of a feminist rendering of heterosexual female agency as the film rescues Ria from the status of abject undesiring and undesirable victim and transforms her into a bride-to-be. In the final scene of the wedding, as the cathartic rain falls, one last NRI male arrives, this time from Britain, and makes a beeline for Ria. Here again is a significant feminist turn; the primary discourse around sexually violated women in commercial Indian cinema is the impossibility of their recuperation. This turn in the film is opposed to the possibility of banishing or disposing of the victim of sexual abuse as the marker of shame and contamination. The strength of the heteronormative romantic narrative is suggested by its ability to overwrite the gender normative narrative in which the raped woman of pop-ular Indian cinema must die. The material and metaphorical aspects of sexual violation in the narrative gesture toward male power, not heterosexual desire, hence the ability to incorporate Ria into the heteronormativity of the wedding in the final scene of the film.

The figure of the domestic servant Alice is an incredibly rich site of analy-sis and investigation in relation to the issues of gender, sexuality, and political economy. The Christian Alice is depicted in primarily romantic terms. Her sweetness and simplicity render her an idealized and remote subject in relation to the other modern women. Although a more full discussion of her romance and marriage with Dubey is outside of the scope of this discussion, I propose that she functions as a counterpoint to the other women explicitly because of her portrayal as simple, charming, and innocent, that is, traditional in contrast to their more sexually explicit cosmopolitanism. As the urban domestic worker, the film continually presents her from the perspective of someone else; unlike the other women whose subjectivities are established through intimate conver-sation with other women, family members, and their partners, Alice is observed almost entirely from the voyeuristic gaze modulated through Dubey. Offer-ing few opportunities for processes of identification, the film barely establishes Alice's character outside of her relationship with Dubey—she has no family or friends that we ever see. Therefore, unlike the other women, she is continually portrayed only in relation to heterosexuality and labor; Alice appears only in relation to the bourgeois family and the heterosexual male (see Figure 8.6).

The one figure that is not reintegrated into the narrative is that of the nonnormative son Varun. With his penchant for cooking shows and choreog-raphy and lack of interest in cricket, Varun's lack of gender normativity marks

Fig. 8.6   Alice and Dubey as the romanticized couple in *Monsoon Wedding.*

him as proto-gay (because of his age and because gay identity is not always associated with same-sex desire in India) in the film. Varun's belonging to and participation in the festivities is depicted as partial and contradictory; he is often depicted at the margins of the affair, for example, sitting with the women as they sing bawdy wedding songs, his age and queerness allowing him entrance into, but not active participation in, the women-only event. His moments of active participation, as in the case of his dance with Ayesha, are displaced by the arrival of his heterosexual replacements. In the middle of rehearsal when Ayesha flirts with Rahul by dancing provocatively in front of him (see Figure 8.7), Varun cries "come on didi—not more interruptions." But his belonging is consistently characterized by heterosexual interruptions by which he is thrust aside. His desires remain unaccommodated; once the heteronormative couplings are achieved, the queer character and nonheteronormativities are brushed aside to make way for the real subjects of the film. In this way, *Monsoon Wedding,* like *Bend It Like Beckham* and *Bollywood/Hollywood,* forwards the feminist retooling of heterosexual female sexualities, acknowledges but contains male queer sexualities, and unequivocally denies female queer ones.

Like the films discussed in the previous chapter, *Monsoon Wedding* suggests that gender and heterosexuality are the primary terrains and tropes of the cultural, social, and economic politics between the diaspora and homeland nation-state. But unlike *Bombay Boys,* whose cowboys are unheroic, *Monsoon Wedding* recuperates the figure of the male NRI. Significantly, each of the young women in the film (Ayesha, Aditi, and Ria) is ultimately paired with a heterosexual NRI

Fig. 8.7 Indian Ayesha seduces NRI Rahul to Varun's chagrin in *Monsoon Wedding.*

male from Australia (and the Gulf), the United States, or Britain. The large wedding, the ultimate but not the only enactment of the relationship between diasporic men and homeland women, functions as a way to suture the deterritorialized nation together. It becomes a symbolic and material act in which the deterritorialized nation is made stable through the heteronormative transnational arranged love marriage. This wedding also functions to prove that the arranged love marriage that is forged at the wedding is stable and invulnerable to social, political, and economic forces despite migration or displacement.

Conclusion

> What we still narrate in the language of immigration and ethnicity, I would argue is actually a series of processes having to do with the globalization of economic activity, of cultural activity, of identity formation.... Understanding them as a set of processes whereby global elements are localized, international labor markets are constituted, and cultures from all over the world are de- and re-territorialized, puts them right there at the center along with the internationalization of capital as a fundamental aspect of globalization. This way of narrating the large migrations of the post-war era captures the ongoing weight of colonialism and postcolonial forms of empire on major processes of globalization today, and specifically those processes binding countries of emigration and immigration.
>
> —Saskia Sassen (1998, 17)

Although they serve as the site of feminist rewritings of heterosexuality, wedding films function to suture and soothe in complex manners in relation to processes of globalization. They are framed as not only consolidating transnationally dispersed kinship networks and maintaining cultural practices and traditions but also serving as mechanisms of reassurance for women and their families who experience hope and anxiety in relation to the vulnerability of transnational brides due to separation and isolation. Wedding films also pacify Western audiences anxious about the consequences of increased global migration while providing a nostalgic comfort in the possibility of life less transformed and ruptured by modernity. The nostalgia for family and kinship intimacy (lost in a past time) is satisfied in seeing the possibilities contained in other cultures (across cultural space). At the same time, the mobilization of the emancipated sexual agent in the form of the transnational bride is a familiar and comforting narrative to Western feminist audiences in that it properly deposits the modern woman in a teleological trajectory in the West where her feminist self belongs. From the very opening of the film, the Western feminist viewer is made ready for the departure and arrival of the newest member of the sisterhood.

Recent feminist scholarship recognizes how migration alters gender practices, sometimes to empower simultaneously women and render them vulnerable.[8] The migration of the bourgeois bride is marked by a set of contradictory relations to imperialism, the nation-state, and the global economy. For middle-class women of the South, transnational migration may occur through the institution of marriage rather than through incorporation into the feminized industrial economy or international domestic service. In other words, they may be inserted into the global economy through the heterosexual household. This arrival is always already a departure that is predicated on problematic notions of mobility and containment—that is, it is often predicated on the subject not in migration. Furthermore, as Lisa Lowe (2001, 274) writes, "Within a global cartography in which capital is consolidated in the North through the exploitation in the South, the third world bourgeoisie becoming migrant in the West is a narrative of the consolidation of capitalism." Every arrival is more than a departure, it is also the nondeparture (but not necessarily the immobility) of a different subject and position. These films and the bourgeois migrant woman defy and legitimate. Scholars, in turn, must fully consider these implications and complications in their representations and theories of migration. Furthermore, we must be vigilant to the problematic and singular deployments of feminism within these multiple and fragmented contexts, attentive now to the consolidation of imperialism, capitalism, and heteronormativity and to sexual agency, political economy, and nation-states. Brown-skinned cinema and its politics of the "beyond" is central to the narration of postcolonial migration in globalization. It clearly traffics with and amidst these local and global processes, back and forth, departing and arriving, always in transit and in between as we attend to its successes and failures.

Notes

Chapter 1: South Asian Diasporas and Transnational Cultural Studies

1. Discourse refers to not only cultural productions and texts but also to social practices.
2. The scholarship of M. Jacqui Alexander (1994), David Eng (1997 and 2001), and Kobena Mercer (1994), for example, are exceptions to this criticism.
3. One can therefore argue that the specter of India needs to be considered in discussions of South Asia.
4. The context and route of migration often determine whether one is considered to be a member of diaspora, an exile, a refugee, and so on. Emigrants to the Middle East are hardly ever referred to as a diaspora, often because of their temporary status. Myron Weiner (1986, 47) in "Labor Migrations as Incipient Diasporas" writes that

   > a new class has emerged in many of the world's industrial and oil-producing economies: the foreign workers. Foreign workers are not immigrants. They are not entitled to become citizens. They are allowed to remain in their host country only to work, and can be forced by the government to leave. Except as allowed by the government, they cannot bring their wives and children, and may not be entitled to the social benefits or political rights given to citizens.

   Because these workers are seen as surplus labor and are likely to remit funds to the homeland, there is little interference by the homeland government into their status while others are actively recruited for dual citizenship status by the nation-state. Similarly, not all persons of Indian descent will be eligible for citizenship status—those from Pakistan and Bangladesh, for example, are not included.
5. See Gayatri Spivak's (1999) *A Critique of Postcolonial Reason.*
6. Various scholars such as Aijaz Ahmad (1995), Stuart Hall (1996), Jenny Sharpe (1995), Ella Shohat (1992), Anne McClintock (1995), E. San Juan Jr. (1998), and Gayatri Spivak (1991 and 1999) have debated the term *postcolonial*, many critiquing it based on arguments about depoliticization, economics, and temporality.
7. Inderpal Grewal and Caren Kaplan (1994, 15–16) comment that *postcolonial* "can serve as a term that positions cultural production in the fields of transnational economic relations and diasporic identity constructions. It is particularly useful in projects that delineate fields of reception *in the West*" (italics mine).

8. In other feminist critiques of the nation, such as those by Anne McClintock (1995), women (as handmaidens or mothers) are identified as the reproducers of national culture. They embody the traditions and perform the rituals that are narrated as the cultural roots of the community. In these movements, women's rights often are seen as secondary to the national struggles, resulting in the subordination of women's issues to anticolonial nationalism. Thus, the exclusions and inadequacy of the gendered nation-state have been forwarded as central features of many feminist postcolonial theories.

9. This bourgeois postcolonial subject is proficient at using discourses of cultural difference within the economic and multicultural North to claim the position of native informant of postcoloniality.

10. A United Nations Council on Trade and Development (UNCTAD) study estimates that a qualified doctor who leaves to settle elsewhere represents a loss of $40,000 to India and a scientist represents a $20,000 loss. The United States, however, gains $64,800 for each foreign-trained doctor and $23,600 for each scientist. It is estimated that between 1961 and 1972, India lost $144 million because of emigrating physicians alone. In the 1960s, an estimated one-quarter of all engineers and one-third of all doctors trained in India left the country. India loses 24 to 30 percent of its graduate doctors and engineers, according to Arthur Helweg (1986, 120).

11. See Lisa Lowe (1998a), *Immigrant Acts.*

12. By hybridity I do not mean some simple apolitical mixing nor some mediated form of assimilation to dominant forms but rather the "formation of cultural objects and practices that are produced by the histories of uneven and unsynthetic power relations" (Lowe 1998a, 67).

13. See the work of Fredric Jameson (1991) and David Harvey (1989).

14. Deterritorialization does not indicate here the irrelevance of place in global processes but rather the displacement of national politics from the specific territories of the nation-state.

15. The terms that I generally employ here, *North* and *South,* refer primarily to the uneven economic and political relations between northern and southern hemispheric nation-states, respectively; this pair functions, like *core* and *periphery* and *First World* and *Third World,* to describe uneven economic distribution within geopolitics, without the implicit hierarchy of these other terms. Here, I use several different forms of nomenclature to refer to epistemological approaches to dividing and categorizing global relations. Although *North* and *South* are preferable to describe the economic and political power relations between nation-states, I also use *First World* and *Third World* at times. I employ *Third World* primarily as a descriptor for the racialized positioning of people and culture from the economic South (e.g., I refer to a character as a Third World rather than a Southern woman).

16. "Racial formation" is employed by Michael Omi and Howard Winant (1994, 61) to refer to "the process by which social, economic, and political forces determine the content and importance of racial categories, and by which they are in turn shaped by racial meanings."

17. Lowe comments on the racially homogenous state but does not expand the discussion to examine the ways in which nonheteronormativity is facilitated by capital as well, which is in contradiction with the needs of the nation-state. Chinese American migration, for example, was the subject of not only racial but also gendered and sexualized contradictions in relation to the nation-state.

18. Diasporic nostalgia is different from postmodern nostalgia, as I discuss later.

19. In "Diasporas in Modern Societies," William Safran (1991, 84–85) defines *diaspora* as sharing several of the following characteristics: (1) dispersal of a "people" from an original "center" to two or more peripheral or foreign regions, (2) the presence of a collective memory or myth about the homeland, (3) a belief that the diasporic people cannot be fully accepted into the hostile host society, (4) the homeland as the true, ideal home to which the diaspora should eventually return when conditions are acceptable, (5) a commitment to the maintenance and restoration of the homeland, and (6) a continuing relationship with the homeland and a sense of ethnonational consciousness.

20. In South Asian diasporas, the homeland is narrated, mythologized, and imagined by many, but returns to the homeland vary. For example, although many people plan to migrate temporarily, patterns of duration differ for diasporic communities due to the historical specificities of mobility and migration. In the Middle East, the sojourn is often "temporary" for Indian, Pakistani, and Bangladeshi guest workers who are not allowed permanent resident or citizenship status. Alternatively, the separatist Sikh diaspora maintains that it lacks an

established homeland nation-state to which it can return, as Khalistan remains a contested dream of a minority of Sikh diasporans (although some Sikhs often travel back and forth between Punjab and diaspora). On the other hand, in the older nineteenth century diasporas, many African-settled diasporans returned to South Asia after the railroad was completed, though many Caribbean emigrants remained and only imagined India as the homeland.

21. I do not want to suggest that Gilroy and Hall are the first to profess diaspora as a mode of intervention in black studies. Focusing on their scholarship allows us to examine how diaspora has become a discourse about race and nation in traveling theories of cultural studies.

22. Diasporas are overlapping and hybrid contact zones rather than pure entities. In the case of the South Asian and African diasporas, there are overlaps and similarities. Of course in British racial politics there is a delicate coalition held together by the term *black,* much in the way that *people of color* functions in the United States. Unlike *people of color,* which is further fragmented into Asian-American, African-American, and so forth, *black* indicates an alliance between Afro-Caribbean, South Asian, and African migrants, each group with multiple overlaps (Indo-Caribbean and Indo-African, for example). This is based not only on a history of racial oppression but also on colonialism. This coalition has been increasingly differentiated in the past decade to recognize the differences between these ethnic groups.

23. Political economy here means less a strict adherence to the homogenous narratives of Marxism than it does attention to the multiple and uneven modes of capitalist expansion and their effects. Recognizing capitalism as heterogeneous, it may be necessary to attend even more closely to the inequalities it exploits in its uneven expansion.

24. The framing of "transnational" as a new paradigm presents a monolithic history of Asian-American studies and the Asian-American movement, erasing earlier frameworks and rewriting previous politics. Asian-American students who linked their struggles with and identified as Third World people demanded the establishment of ethnic studies at San Francisco State University and at the University of California–Berkeley in 1968–69. Protesting U.S. cultural and economic imperialism and internal colonialism, the Third World–student strikes were connected to black civil rights and power movements such as the Black Panthers and anti–Vietnam War struggles (see William Wei, 1993, for a detailed history of Asian-American movements and studies). Although much of Asian-American identity has been based on establishing the difference between Asian and Asian-American (see Wei 1993 and King Kok-Cheung 1997), Asian-American groups protesting against the Vietnam War often strategically and transnationally aligned themselves as Asians, as did those who linked U.S. racism (as a form of internal colonialism) to global imperialism. This transnational perspective worked to retain a commitment to U.S. politics at two levels: one identifying international struggles with local ones (U.S. imperialism as internal colonialism) and the other linking the local to the global (the relationship between the Vietnam War's dehumanizing of Asians as "gooks" and anti-Asian-American racism); the latter, in particular, was used not only to understand U.S. racism but also to act against U.S. military action in Asia. Therefore, Asian-American critique was able to destabilize and mobilize both halves of the term *Asian-American* to position itself as internal and external and as local and transnational in its politics, ideologies, and actions.

25. Several factors have contributed to the recent interest in diasporic perspectives in Asian-American studies. Criticisms based on feminist, queer, and class theorizing have challenged the primary emphasis on the bourgeois and masculine cultural nationalist project in Asian-American studies (see the work of King-Kok Cheung 2000, Elaine Kim 1987, Shelley Wong 1993, and David Eng 1997), thus, shifting the attention away from claiming America.

26. See David Eng (2001) and Laura Hyun Yi Kang (1997) for similar arguments. Peter Feng (2002a), on the other hand, argues that the hyphen configures Asia and America as distinct and discrete entities, indicating a past in which these spaces (like all spaces) were mutually exclusive. Consequently according to Feng, "Asian Americans, on the other hand, situate ourselves in history by calling attention to the temporal and spatial migrations that brought us here as well as the discursive power of concepts such as 'nation' to define who, where, and when we all are" (p. 18). See Kang (2002) and David Palumbo-Liu (1999) for discussions of Asian/American as well.

27. Many of these objections to diasporic and transnational paradigms have come from Asian-American studies scholarship focusing on East Asian–Americans. The ambivalent and complicated location of South Asian–Americans in Asian-American studies has been suggested by numerous scholars, most concisely in the edited collection *A Part, Yet Apart: South Asians in*

Asian America, Lavinia Shankar and Rajni Srikanth (1998). Although South Asian-Americans participate in the pan-ethnic coalition of Asian-America, this participation does not preclude the necessity of other frameworks for understanding and analyzing race and nation-state. This argument seems applicable to South Asians in Canada and Britain where political coalitions based on racial identities such as black are similar. Furthermore, this study does not suggest that transnationality is the singular characteristic of Asian migration.

28. See the work of Danielle Bouchard (2001) on the deployments of metaphors of space, location, and mobility in transnational feminist theories and politics. Of course, other critics have rightly pointed out the difficulties of a politics of location that assumes static location and singular coherent subjects. For example, bell hooks (1990) indicates that the current framework of politics of location does not and cannot account for multiple locations and subjectivity. In addition, Richa Nagar (2002) has critiqued the deployment of politics of location by feminist social scientists, particularly by ethnographers. She suggests that reflexivity, positionality, and identity politics have led to an unproductive impasse in feminist scholarship. She suggests that feminists should seek to produce theories and practices that describe how knowledge can be produced not to reinforce privilege but rather to lead to material politics of social change.

29. Anne McClintock (1995), Partha Chatterjee (1993), and Nira Yuval-Davis (1997), for example, are exceptions as they articulate the centrality of gender (with race, sexuality, and class) to understandings of colonialism, nationalism, and postcoloniality.

30. Cathy Cohen (1997) similarly proposes in "Punks, Bulldaggers, and Welfare Queens: The Radical Potential of Queer Politics?" that the potential of queer politics is to illuminate the political possibilities of coalitions based on critiques of normatives.

Chapter 2: Between Hollywood and Bollywood

1. See José Esteban Muñoz's (1999) *Disidentifications.*
2. See Bakhtin's (1981) *The Dialogic Imagination.*
3. The British Film Institute focused on Asian diasporic films as part of their ImagineAsia program. Blending South Asian and South Asian diasporic films, they also sought to distinguish these by attempting to define diasporic films. "Should we insist on a Director of South Asian origin, or funding, or simply a film with distinctive characteristics, imagery and/or content? We were not in the end able to agree but we have generally followed the rule that films in this part of the list should be made by a South Asian director or writer (non resident at the time of making) and have South Asian or Diasporic content" (http://imagineasia.bfi.org.uk/).
4. This analysis of the means and mode of production in relation to the meaning of the text also can be understood as the political economy of film.
5. Scholarship on Asian-American cinema has been extremely limited; in addition to a number of collections and anthologies, the exceptions include the work of Gina Marchetti (1993), Peter Feng (2002a and 2002b), Jun Xing (1998), and Russell Leong (1991).
6. As a first-generation migrant from Taiwan to the United States, Wang has made several well-known films, including *The Joy Luck Club* (1993), *Dim Sum* (1985), and *Eat a Bowl of Tea* (1989).
7. The first film made by an Indian was *The Wrestlers* (Bhatavdekar) in 1899. Dhundiraj Govind Phalke made the first Indian feature film *Raja Harishchandra* in 1913. According to Vijay Mishra (2002), as early as the thirties, the Indian Picture Show Company was formed to export films to Fiji.
8. According to Raymond Williams (1977), structures of feeling are emerging personal and social experiences that are in process and have not been institutionalized or incorporated fully into social formations.
9. For Deleuze and Guattari (1990, 601) a minor literature (or in this case a minor cinema) is characterized by its deterritorialization of language, the connection of the individual to a political immediacy, and the collective assemblage of enunciation. Minor (versus minority) cinema uses the major language but positions itself in terms of its minor practices. Laura Marks (2000, 21) argues that for intercultural cinema, "a politics of identity is limited, since the identities it presents are almost always shifting and emerging. Intercultural cinema appeals to the limits of naming and the limits of understanding, and this is where it is most transformative."

10. Although I disagree with the overuse of these terms, I find them particularly helpful in delineating films that are interstitially located in relation to dominant cinemas—those of Hollywood and Bollywood in particular. More important, the films discussed here are dominant feature-length narrative films, as opposed to documentaries and shorts. Feature-length films generally have an entirely different network of circulation than the latter and are more likely to be distributed through more established transnational commercial networks. Within this group, I include here a variety of films that can be further distinguished by several characteristics including their modes of production, target audience, or themes.

11. As Perminder Dhillon-Kashyap (1988) has noted, there have been earlier Asian films and filmmakers in Britain. She cites *Light of Asia*, a British-German production with an all Asian cast that was directed by Heman Surayi and Franz Osten in 1924 as the earliest example. In addition, she mentions Waris Hussain and Jamil Dehlavi (p. 121).

12. Australia is absent in this discussion mostly as it has a more recent history of migration. I suspect that Australia may become a site of diasporic filmmaking if the nation-state constructs a hospitable political economy. However, considering recent global economic conditions, this is currently unlikely.

13. *Sam & Me* is Deepa Mehta's first feature film. Her earlier work includes documentaries such as *Travelling Light: The Photojournalism of Dilip Mehta* (1988) and *Martha, Ruth, and Eddie* (1988).

14. See Sanjay Sury (2002), "'The Warrior' Loses Oscar Nomination."

15. The film, however, presents the South Asian–American lesbian protagonist as solitary and isolated in relations to other queer desis. The film features no South Asian–American gay/lesbian/bisexual/transgender communities, making invisible the sizeable and visible organizations in many U.S. urban areas.

16. This is not to say that other areas of inquiry such as Asian-American and postcolonial have not informed South Asian diasporic studies but rather that black British cultural studies has been primary.

17. See *Distinction: A Theoretical Critique of the Judgement of Taste* (Bourdieu 1984).

18. Gilroy (1993a), one of the proponents of the term, uses it inconsistently in his scholarship. The "*black*" in the Black Atlantic, for example, does not signify Asian by any account but refers specifically to the African diaspora and the slave trade.

19. See Mercer (1994) for an extended discussion on the development of Channel Four and its television programming during the eighties.

20. Farrukh Dhondy was highly influential in television and other media during this time, assisting not only Kureishi but also Gurinder Chadha and Meera Syal.

21. Kureishi's depictions of blacks have been questioned by several scholars, including bell hooks. Some suggest that Kureishi creates a hierarchy of literate and successful Asians in relation to illiterate and impoverished blacks; hooks (1990), in particular, notes the absence of black women in Kureishi's films, wondering how their absence is always overshadowed by the presence of white feminist women characters.

22. In the United States, Marlon Riggs (1991), bell hooks (1992), Lisa Lowe (1998a), and Peter Feng (2002a) make similar critiques regarding the desire and demand to counter "negative" representations with "positive" ones. Instead, they argue for the necessity of recognizing the negotiated positions of cultural representations within power relations.

23. This dependent relationship has a long history. During the post–World War II period, Britain began to constrain the entrance of Hollywood films to protect its economy. Passing restrictive tariffs and trade laws that limited the total number of Hollywood films in British theaters, the British film industry sought to equalize the exchange by demanding that British films be exported to the United States, where they often played in art-house cinemas. Moreover, it was not only Britain that the U.S. film industry relied on—it was also the British colonies. As Barbara Wilinsky (2001, 74) notes, the "British Empire, accounting for as much as 75 percent of the U.S. companies' foreign box office, was an important market for the film industry and one the U.S. industry wanted to protect and foster."

24. Higson also challenges the idea that British cinema was previously coherent and has only recently become heterogeneous in its emphasis on difference and hybridity. He suggests that this narrative constructs British cinema in unifying narrative with a homogenous past.

25. There are moments in which the father's deployment of tradition as a method of patriarchal control is contextualized within specific historical, geopolitical, and socioeconomic

discourses. For example, the film locates the father's desire to have his youngest son circumscribed at a late age in relation to the father's displacement from the Pakistani community for his exogamous marriage and in relation to his increasing patriotism toward Pakistan during the Indo-Pakistani war. His mobilization of tradition can then be seen as a strategy of resistance and an attempt at authenticity and belonging that employs patriarchal power within the family. The film does not excuse the domestic and child abuse that occurs as a result.

Chapter 3: When Indians Play Cowboys

1. See Bill Mullen (2003) for a recent discussion of the novel in relation to DuBois's internationalist politics.
2. The novel prefigures more recent scholarship in American studies that strives to continually link transnational racial formations, colonialism, and imperialism in the study of American histories and cultures. See Amy Kaplan's (1993) "Left Alone with America" and Ann Laura Stoler's (2001) "Tense and Tender Ties" as two excellent examples.
3. "First generation" refers to those persons who they themselves have migrated, and "second generation" refers to those who are born and raised in diaspora. This encoding of diasporic affiliation along generational lines may mask political differences. As Lisa Lowe (1998a, 63) argues in *Immigrant Acts*, "generation" often functions as an explanatory mechanism for mediating and suppressing political differences within ethnic communities:

    > Interpreting Asian American culture exclusively in terms of the master narratives of generational conflict and filial relation essentializes Asian American culture, obscuring the particularities and incommensurabilities of class, gender, and national diversities among Asians. The reduction of the cultural politics of racialized ethnic groups, like Asian Americans, to generational struggles displaces social differences into a privatized familial opposition. Such reductions contribute to the aestheticizing commodification of Asian American *cultural* differences, while denying the immigrant histories of material exclusion and differentiation.

4. Mira Nair's films engage several diasporic themes, namely, exilic displacement, national (dis)identification, interethnic racism, fragmentation of the nuclear family, and reformation of an alternative family in her films. Frequently, the films begin with a portrayal interrogating the failure of the postcolonial nation-state to form successfully a pluralist society. Most of the films begin with these fissures and failures in postcolonial narratives of nation that lead to diasporic displacement. With the failure of the nation-state, Nair replaces diasporic and national belonging with the possibility of reconstructed home through the formation of alternative families. Even when these homes sometimes fail or are unrootable, home is not sought in the return to the homeland.
5. This is of course a reference to Benedict Anderson's (1991) *Imagined Communities*. The fraternity of the nation is reflected in the masculine homosociality in the relationship between Okelo and Jay as well.
6. In his autobiographical account of Uganda, which provides some of the historical basis of the film, Mahmood Mamdani (1983), African scholar and husband of Mira Nair, recounts soldiers robbing and raping Asians leaving Uganda.
7. My use of *performative* here is in line with Judith Butler's (1999) theorizing of performativity.
8. Though trade between East Africa and South Asia had been ongoing for approximately a thousand years prior to British colonialism, South Asians migrated to East Africa first as indentured servants to build the railroad for the British and then later as an administrative and trading class as subordinate supplements moved from one outpost of the British colonial system to another. Although most workers repatriated after the completion of the railroad, some stayed and were joined by those who were encouraged to build a middle-class population to facilitate and mediate between the white colonial government and the indigenous black Africans.
9. Though less than 2 percent of the Ugandan population, Asians were not a homogenous group and were subdivided by factors such as regional and linguistic identities (e.g., Gujarati and Punjabi), caste differences (e.g., Patels and Darji), and religious identities (e.g., Hindu and Muslim). These differences were significant as some of the working poor Asians socialized,

lived, and intermarried with black Africans and thus also were isolated from their upper- and middle-class Asians counterparts.

10. In the formation of the postcolonial nation-state, all Asians were not equally eligible for citizenship. Factors such as birth land of parent and present citizenship status allowed most, but not all, Asians to be eligible for citizenship, and many had two years to choose either Ugandan or British affiliation after independence. However, as economic and political policies fluctuated toward Africanization (African national control) rather than Ugandanization (Ugandan citizen control) of the government and economy, many Asians were wary of choosing Ugandan citizenship, often fearful of economic redistribution of financial assets as well as their own personal safety. In the end, noncitizen and citizen Asians were expelled from Uganda.

11. Anti-Asian sentiments are framed in the film as merely a response to antiblack racism; moreover, both are presented as illogical in that people of color pitted against each other is unnatural.

12. The racialization of South Asians in the United States has meant negotiating the black and white binary construction of race, often abetting color discrimination within South Asian communities and fostering antiblack racism. Toni Morrison (1992) summarizes it as an identity consolidated in language. She suggests that one of the first words many immigrants learn to say to establish their not-blackness, for example their whiteness, is *nigger*. South Asians seem savvy about the effects of antiblack racism and employ it to their benefit in the film.

13. Although some Asian men and African women married in Uganda, racist and patriarchal concubinage was more frequent. Asians often disapproved of interracial and intercaste couplings and excluded them from the community in the urban areas (Bharati 1972, 160–63). Although the question of intermarriage here is referred to in reference to African female–Asian male and African male–Asian female relationships, it is the latter that was most contested and controversial.

14. Asian-American studies scholars, including Vijay Prashad (2000), Kamala Visweswaran (1997), and Aihwa Ong (1996, 1998, and 1999), address the complex mappings of race and class that outline Asian-American identity in a post-1965 (Immigration Act) and post–civil rights era. The shifting racial and class positions respond to and are maneuvered by specific historical demands of nationalism and citizenship. This "continual flux" has a specific U.S. history. In *A Passage from India,* Joan Jensen (1988, 255) reports that almost 70 percent of early Punjabi immigrants (who were often viewed as "Hindoo" despite that most were Sikh or Muslim) were granted American citizenship between 1908 and 1922 in eighteen states through court cases citing that *white* was synonymous with *Caucasian* and *Aryan.* Several of these court cases were won by arguing for the inclusion of Hindus in the Caucasian race based on anthropological biological scientific discourse. In 1922–23, courts concluded that whiteness (necessary for American citizenship as of 1790) was defined as understood by the "common man." Jensen reports that the U.S. Supreme Court dismissed anthropological race theory's explanation that Indians were Aryans, therefore Caucasians, and therefore white (pp. 256–58). The U.S. Supreme Court ruled on the Bhagat Singh Thind case that *white* was not synonymous with *Caucasian* but rather with the "common" understanding of *whiteness.* Nevertheless, the cases illustrate that some Indian-Americans sought to challenge the racist immigration policies of the United States, not by challenging exclusion policies and identifying with other Asian-American groups but by seeking privilege through racial identification as white. Since then, Indians have lobbied to be considered "Asians" rather than "other" or "white" in the census. In 1974, the Association of Indians in America requested the reclassification of Indians as Asians. Yen Le Espiritu (1992, 124–25) reports that this shift in racial classification was motivated by Indian Americans' possible economic gain through race-based incentive programs, such as affirmative action and set-aside programs. In 1982, following Chinese- and Japanese-Americans' lead, Indian-Americans petitioned to be designated as a socially disadvantaged group. Ironically, at congressional hearings for the reclassification of Indians to Asians on the 1980 census form, Indians cited the case of Thind (Espiritu 1992, 125).

15. See *Racial Castration,* David Eng (2001) for a fuller discussion.

16. This is Sau-ling Wong's (1995) phrase.

17. Okelo forms the third side of the triangle between Kinnu and Jay who both seem to love him deeply, each dealing with his loss differently. In this manner, the film opens up the possibility of interracial desire not only between Kinnu and Okelo but also between Okelo and Jay.

18. What I mean by a noncritical multiculturalism is the theory and practice of inclusionary or additive cultural pluralism positioned against dominant racial narratives and structures of the nation-state in North America and Europe. Multiculturalism often becomes an additive formula celebrating the histories, contributions, and literatures of minorities, in addition to those of the dominant group. It is significant to note that although the goals of multiculturalism are the restructuring of society and the redistribution of power, capitalist forces have frequently been able to manage diversity and multiplicity to their advantage by incorporating, commodifying, and marketing cultural diversity (in its most benign cultural forms—food, music, clothing, and cinema). In this way, multiculturalism has been a historical strategy of cultural pluralism that is symptomatic of the national cultural logics of transnational capitalism.

19. The experience of racism, marginalization, and displacement in migration is complicated frequently by the privilege of class mobility. Therefore, one must be particularly attentive to the function of the diasporic intellectual in institutions in which she (diasporic intellectual) is asked to represent the Third World or as part of the multicultural project. Seen as a repository of authenticity, her race locates her as a native informant or site of knowledge production about the homeland. The feminist diasporic intellectual in the United States is therefore positioned in relation to and asked to represent women of the South (the noncosmopolitan, the indigenous, the subaltern) and women of color or minority women. Diasporic intellectuals often have unrecognized privilege. As bell hooks (1990, 93–94) writes,

    > While it is true that many Third World nationals who live in Britain and the United States develop through theoretical and concrete experience knowledge of how they are diminished by white western racism, that does not always lead them to interrogate the way in which they enter a racialized hierarchy where in the eyes of whites they automatically have greater status and privilege than individuals of African descent.

    See Gayatri Spivak (1991 and 1999), Rey Chow (1993), R. Radhakrishnan (1996), and Timothy Brennan (1989 and 1997) among others for further discussion of the postcolonial and diasporic intellectual.

20. Elsewhere, I argue that the employment of food tropes in South Asian–American cultural productions can especially lend itself to the complicated consumption of multicultural difference.

21. I do not want to create a moral hierarchy between real nomads and metaphorical ones; my point is that each use of the term must be made historically specific so that it is possible to distinguish between them.

22. I thank Danielle Bouchard for pointing out, on one hand, that the notion of civilization requires the progression of a long and linear history and, on the other hand, that U.S. exceptionalism narrates America as the most developed civilization as a result of its severing itself from history to actualize the progressive future of American civilization.

23. Prototypically American, motels also have become the entrepreneurial investments of many Gujarati migrants. Homogeneous and "undescriptively" similar motels across the country have become imprinted with the culture and economics of petty bourgeois Indian-Americans. Motels, as homes away from homes, or dwellings in the midst of travel, stand symbolically at the center of the Indian-American community in the film. See Nabokov's (1958) *Lolita* and Baudrillard's (1988) *America* for extended pronouncements on motels as American.

24. William Least Heat-Moon is a white writer who identifies as Native American and has published several texts on wandering U.S. highways and roads. Sherman Alexie (a Spokane/Coeurs d'Alene Indian) expresses a very similar comment and a different politic in his *The Lone Ranger and Tonto Fistfight in Heaven:* "We were the only real cowboys there despite the fact that we're Indians" (1993, 29).

25. Rosi Braidotti also tries to delineate this fine line: "Speaking as a whitened antiracist post-structuralist European female feminist, I favour figurations of nomadic subjectivity to act as a permanent deconstruction of Euro-centric phallo-logocentrism. Nomadic consciousness is the enemy within in this logic." This call intersects with and is situated in a dialogic exchange with other forms of specifically located rootlessness or diasporas. It lays the foundation for an alliance with them. "Difference, Diversity, and Nomadic Subjectivity" (Website). (2000)

Chapter 4: Reel a State

1. The British group Cornershop is an interesting phenomenon. In contrast to groups such as Asian Dub Foundation and Fun da ment al, they propound less radical but more widely heard politics in their music. For further discussion of these and other British Asian music see the anthology *Dis-Orienting Rhythms* (Sharma, Hutnyk, and Sharma 1996).

2. Though the film was made more than a decade earlier, for many viewers the opening explosion of the film evokes associations with the events of 9/11. Amy Kaminsky has noted the opening also evokes the beginning of *The Satanic Verses* as the characters fall from a plane through the sky.

3. The explosion of Air India flight 182 referenced by the opening sequence of the film illuminates Canadian racism. The Canadian nation-state's response to the explosion attests to the lack of significant changes in reformulating the national imaginary. After the crash, then Canadian Prime Minister Brian Mulroney called Indian Prime Minister Rajiv Gandhi to give his condolences on India's loss. This message of goodwill masks the fact that almost all the passengers on the flight were Canadian citizens and permanent residents of South Asian descent. Thus, the Canadian nation-state, because of its racist configuration of national belonging, detached itself from the incident and responsibility for the lives of these Canadians. Hence, Canadian agencies were quite ineffectual around the issue of the explosion, because Canada saw it is as India's tragedy rather than its own. The film strikes against this ideology in asserting its claim to political power, caricaturing the state response through its depiction of Canadian multiculturalism. Although the film does not depict this particular exchange, many viewers would be aware of this context.

4. Some scholars have argued that camp is dead in the wake of AIDS's devastation on glbt communities. On the other side, scholar Caryl Flinn (1999, 434) argues that camp is not only adequate but also well suited for the task of interrogating the body and death: "Our look into camp's preoccupation with death and decay should lead us not only into a better understanding of camp as a critical endeavor, queer practice, and cultural phenomenon more generally, but also into questions about larger assaults on the female body underway in contemporary political and cultural arenas."

5. Although there is little in the way of racial or gender passing in *Masala,* as is common in discussions of camp, there are frequent exaggerations and excessive representations based on racial, gendered, and classed stereotypes.

6. This debate about the possibility of disidentification is taken up by Slavoj Žižek (1991) and Judith Butler (1993); the latter argues for the space of social transformation from the position of disidentification, while the former evaluates the paralysis of the subject it suggests.

7. Of course, Frantz Fanon (1967) employed psychoanalysis in an understanding of race and colonialism in his *Black Skin, White Masks* much earlier. His analysis of a young white child's scopophilic utterance of "Look, a Negro" similarly configures a colonial gaze as central to racial and gendered processes of identification.

8. Scholars such as Purnima Mankekar (1999b), Patricia Jeffrey and Veena Das (1998), and Amrita Basu (1995) have written on these serials within the context of the postcolonial Indian nation-state, especially focusing on issues of communalism, class, and gender.

9. *Ramayana* is the story of King Dashrath of Ayodhya and his three wives who have produced four sons (Ram, Lakshman, Bharat, and Shatrughan). One of the wives desiring to have her younger son be king forces Dashrath to vow to send Ram into exile for fourteen years upon his adulthood. Ram departs in exile with his wife Sita and his brother Lakshman. In the forest, Sita is kidnapped by Ravana the lord of Lanka. Ram and Lakshman wage a war against Ravana, defeating him and rescuing Sita and returning from exile. As I discuss in another chapter, pregnant Sita is later banished by Ram into the forest to prove his honor. She undergoes and passes a test of purity after raising her twin sons, but she refuses to return with Ram from her exile and is swallowed up by the earth instead.

10. Although there are many characters in *Mahabharat,* the epic focuses on the five Pandava brothers and their wife Draupadi fighting against their one hundred Kaurava cousins. In one of the subplots, one of the brothers loses himself, his brothers, and Draupadi in a game of dice. Draupadi challenges his loss and the passivity of all the onlookers as she questions the propriety of his actions. The winners attempt to disrobe Draupadi by pulling on her sari; she prays to Lord Krishna, beseeching him to save her. As Draupadi's sari is removed, one after another takes its place, thus preventing her disrobing. The epic continues with the Pandavas being

exiled into the forest and then returning to battle against the Kauravas. When one brother questions the morality of killing his own family and war, the Lord Krishna counsels him on dharma and what is right. Ultimately, the Pandavas win the battle and the kingdom, having avenged the many wrongs they have suffered, including the attempted disrobing of Draupadi.

11. In addition, the London film festival organizers, particularly one white viewer, repeatedly refused to screen it, deeming it racist and offensive to Asians. British Asians protested this misinformed "protection" as racist.

12. In the more public traditions of Hindu worship, the priest is also part of the process of darsan. As M. Madhava Prasad (2000) describes, the priest's power lies in the mediation between the divinity and deity, bringing the former to the attention of the latter. This relationship between Shanti and Krishna is unmediated. Krishna appears to Shanti in her everyday acts of religious practice located within the domestic sphere of the home. This interaction sharply contrasts this mode of devotion and faith with the practices of the priest who is featured in the film. As a representative of the power of religious institutions, the priest appears only in contexts in which diasporic affluent patriarchy negotiates with the tokenist multicultural state through the politics of representation, in contexts, in which there is profit.

13. Embedded in my own memories of childhood is a moment of standing and getting darsan while transfixed on Krishna's idol, fully believing that the "real" Krishna would appear if I gazed long and closely enough.

14. Of particular interest is that Singh has the ability to negotiate for the sari trade of Khalistan as a diasporic Sikh located in Toronto.

15. South Asian, particularly Sikh, diasporic involvement in homeland nation-state politics has a long history. In the case of Canada, most of the first South Asian migrants were Punjabi (primarily Sikhs) who settled in British Columbia, working in the timber, railroad, and agricultural industries during the early part of the century. Punjabi soldiers serving in the British army first traveled through Canada on the way to the coronation of Edward VII in 1902; immigration of Punjabi began soon after. Once in Canada, they constituted a relationship with the homeland through remittance, infrequent visits, and when possible sponsorship of relatives and friends. Many participated in the Ghadar Party for the liberation of India. However, immigration laws and citizenship policies limited their numbers and acceptance into Canadian national culture. In 1907, the Vancouver Sikhs formed an organization to safeguard their political and economic interests, since earlier that year Sikhs were denied Vancouver (and therefore federal) voting rights. As British subjects, these Punjabi migrants were said to be equal members of the British empire, supposedly on par with Canadians and Australians. Hence, the British empire placed a few restrictions on the discriminatory treatment of South Asians in Canada, because it was wary of inciting resentment and rebellion against the British government in India. The Canadian government, not wanting to antagonize the British government, tried to control the immigration of South Asians (or Hindoos, the ethnonational/racial term of the time) through a variety of tactics, including a targeted policy stipulating that only those migrants arriving on a direct passage or "continuous journey" from their place of origin would be allowed to enter Canada. Thus, the Canadian state limited migration without resorting to explicit statements of its racial ideologies by framing the ban in terms of transportation rather than nationality or race. This regulation basically affected only South Asians and Japanese (who arrived through Hawaii). For South Asians, there was no direct route to Canada without stopping in Hong Kong or Singapore, and often the migrants arriving were already "twice removed," having lived in Southeast Asia or other locations in the diaspora prior to arrival in Canada. Many Sikhs felt betrayed by the lack of British support given to them as overseas subjects who had served the empire. Even prior to the formation and evolution of anticolonial organizing, the ban on immigration to Canada, through the "continuous journey" act, generated anti-British nationalist activity in Vancouver. One of the first English-language monthlies arguing for Indian nationalism was printed in 1908 in Vancouver by Taraknath Das and sent to India. Though the paper was suppressed in India, it is one connection between the dissatisfaction in the South Asian diaspora and British empire and activism in homeland politics. See also Norman Buchignani, Doreen M. Indra, and Ram Srivastava's (1985) *Continuous Journey: A Social History of South Asians in Canada*.

16. The increased racialization of Sikh and Muslim men in the United States, Canada, and Europe after 9/11 is also, of course, evoked for contemporary viewers. Recent racial formations consistently construct South Asian and Arab men as terrorists.

17. I would like to thank Mary Heather Smith for this contribution.

18. As I discuss Sikh discourses of diaspora and homeland, especially as recent phenomena, nowhere do I mean to imply that Sikhs have not been oppressed by the Indian nation-state. My discussion here is not about the validity and political necessity of Khalistan as a homeland for Sikhs but rather an exploration of how homelands are constituted in relation to diasporas. I understand that my suggestion that the separatist homeland is a recent construction of the Sikh diaspora undermines narratives that claim long and extended histories. This is the common and almost only acceptable claim that groups can make to constitute themselves as a people affiliated with a territory.

19. Scott MacKenzie's (1999) reading of *Masala* suggests that "in relation to cultural production, in many ways, Canada is already postnational and multicultural in nature and therefore offers us insight into what shape a multicultural, postnational cinema might take." Though touted as national Canadian cinema, *Masala* locates itself in opposition to an assimilationist national paradigm and addresses the racism in the narration of the Canadian nation. Therefore, I read it as critical of multiculturalism as it carefully portrays many forms of Canadian racism, from the social in the form of the teenager who murders the protagonist Krishna in a hate crime to the political in the form of the minister of multiculturalism. The state minister is happy to court wealthy support from the Indian community and attend public religious spectacles, but when an Asian postal worker and stamp collector Harry Tikkoo acquires a beaver stamp valued at $5 million dollars, he is visited by another minister, the minister of citizenship and culture, and is told to hand over the artifact of Canadian heritage. Thus the film interrogates exclusionary racist formulations of the nation, as well as the often tokenist state policy of multiculturalism that ineffectively reimagines the nation. Although *Masala* is skeptical about the oppositional potential of political change through Canadian multiculturalism, it nevertheless recognizes that effective resistance involves negotiation with the nation-state.

20. Sikh nationalism is heightened by the political climate not only in India but also in the diaspora. At the beginning of the twentieth century, the Ghadar party provided arms, financial support, and ideological efforts for Indian Independence. Writing about the Ghadar Party, Harjot Oberoi (1994), Arthur Helweg (1989), and Harish Puri (1983) suggest that the movement was inspired as much by Sikh disappointment with the British's indifference to and inaction in regard to U.S. and Canadian mistreatment of South Asians in North America, as it was by the idea of Indian nationalism. Part of the argument of the Ghadar Party for Indian independence was that if Indians controlled their own state, they would have more bargaining power with North American nations on behalf of the immigrants (Dusenbery 1995, 31). Importantly, this diasporic movement was committed not only to transnational politics of South Asia and North America but also to other anticolonial struggles, extrapolating a transnational perspective to decry British imperialism in China, for example (Leonard 1994, 83).

Chapter 5: Homesickness and Motion Sickness

1. I am not suggesting that only men experience or are prone to nostalgia. However, I do argue that nostalgia is a gendered phenomenon.

2. Anne McClintock (1995) comments that in the time of the nation, and here the deterritorialized nation as well, men often represent the future, whereas women are associated with the past. In this case, Baldev is associated with both, as he remembers the past and conjures up the future, while the women seem to be the link to both (either the dancing maidens of the Punjabi village or the means of reconciliation with India).

3. I thank Danielle Bouchard for the precision of her insight here.

4. Bodies and their politics are present in, but not central to, all of these films: in the form of Krishna who lies bleeding at the end of *Masala*, in the form of Rifat who also is abused in *Wild West*, and in the form of sexual relations in *Mississippi Masala*.

5. Scholars contend that illness is a locus of contestation in the defining and controlling of moral and social power. It is imperative to note that I am not suggesting that migration equals illness and I am not operating with the assumption that people are autochthonous with a place and movement from that place makes one "ill" emotionally, psychologically, physically, or otherwise. What I am arguing is that the sicknesses discussed here are produced by oppressions and result from the ways in which migration operates with and is embedded in relations of power.

6. Psychoanalytical understandings of the *unheimlich* or uncanny (Freud 1953) and the unhomely (Bhabha 1994) resonate with my discussions here. Describing an estranged sense of

relocation in the world, the (un)canny provides an understanding of nostalgia in relation to the experiences associated with cultural consumption. I return to this topic later.

7. Many scholars have commented on the social construction of illness in Western philosophy that can be traced through the shifting discourses on disease. In these cases, illnesses, diseases, and disabilities physically mark the dark and deformed self that transgresses social or moral normativities.

8. With this complicated reading of women's agency and location, one should not read the film as only rehashing the formulaic liberal feminist narrative, despite its more normative or standard structure. The film uses a narrative structure that interweaves multiple stories into a web of stories and employs cinematic strategies (such as musical numbers and dream sequences) to disrupt the social realist mode of representation that characterizes dominant liberal (feminist) discourses while it asserts some recuperation of the heteronormative romance.

9. In feminist scholarship, the mother-daughter relationship is privileged as the site of negotiating gender, ethnic, and racial identity and constructions of home (see the work of Leslie Bow (2001), and Carole Boyce Davies (1994), for further discussion). However, in *Bhaji on the Beach,* it is not the mother-daughter relationship, but the relationships between multiple generations of South Asian British women through which identities, home, and communities are (re)worked and no mother-daughter relationships are featured in the film.

10. British state and postcolonial (migrant) discourses mark women as subjects through their relationship with men, for example, through the maintenance of their virginities and reproductive capacities. British state practices of testing migrant women's virginity before approving entrance into the nation-state has been discussed by Avtar Brah (1996) and Pratibha Parmar (1997). (Similar policing of women's virginity occurs at the hands of migrant patriarchies as well.) This is just one example of the state's production and regulation of minority citizens.

11. Ann Stoler (1995) suggests that Foucault does not adequately account for how biopower functioned as a central site of power in colonialism. More recently, Michael Hardt and Antonio Negri (2000) elucidate the production of social beings through the biopower of postmodern neocolonial and late capitalist globalization processes.

12. The public-private dichotomy has been the subject of much feminist theorizing, as in the work of Catharine MacKinnon (1997), who sees the patriarchal family home as equated with the private and the liberal state and its laws with the public. Although not heavily prominent in the film, Ginder's divorce nevertheless illuminates the role and power of law and the state in the "private" sphere of the family. The law often takes contradictory positions regarding the ways it demarcates the rights of immigrant communities to define private cultural practices; see the work of Leti Volpp (2000) for an elucidation of the law's logic. As Aida Hurtado (1989, 850) has commented, "Women of Color have not had the benefit of the economic conditions that underlie the private/public distinction." Alternatively, one can suggest that it is the state reflecting racialized, gendered, and classed interests that defines the realm of the private, and especially the normative bourgeois family. Hence, the state actively produces the space of the private family.

13. For example, in Bernice Johnson Reagon's (1983) insightful article on feminist politics, she argues that women must come out of their homes to build coalitions. Her description of home as a womb suggests that home is associated with safety, comfort, nurture, and the maternal. Similarly, Gillian Rose (1993, 62) suggests that the romanticization of home is related to not only the gendered but also the maternal, construction of place.

14. Coined before the term *nostalgia, heimweh* is a compound of "weh" meaning a cry of pain or of surprise rooted in anger or sadness and "heim" meaning home.

15. See the scholarship of Janice Doane and Devon Hodges (1987), as well as Barbara Creed (1987) for other perspectives on the gendering of nostalgia.

16. Nostalgia has been a significant trope in narratives of nationalism that hearken back to the days when the nation was whole and stable, unhampered by alienation, difference, and change. Progressive critics therefore have critiqued nostalgia, which generally configures a regressive and conservative politics. Kimberly K. Smith (2000) suggests that we may need to rethink nostalgia as signifying alienation from modernity, industrialization, and disciplining. Rather than dismissing all nostalgia as regressive, she suggests that it "figures prominently in struggles over the creation of collective memory precisely because it is a key concept in the political conflict over modernity—an important weapon in the debate over whose memories count and what kinds of desires and harms are politically relevant" (p. 507).

17. Jameson continues, "Faced with these ultimate objects—our social, historical, and existential present, and the past as "referent"—the incompatibility of a postmodernist "nostalgia" art language with genuine historicity becomes dramatically apparent" (pp. 18–19). Anne Friedberg (1991) among others has critiqued Jameson for dismissing all films not about the present as nostalgic for their distance from their historical referent. Kimberly K. Smith (2000, p. 522) responds,

> Nostalgia is a real phenomenon, no doubt, but it may stem from legitimate complaints about modern society; progressives may find it more useful to figure out what those complaints are and take them seriously than to dismiss the unhappiness as irrelevant to a *rational* politics. More troubling, however, is the worry that the theory of nostalgia will delegitimate political movements that are consistent with many progressive goals, such as social ecology and modern ecological agrarianism.

18. Scholars have critiqued Jameson for nostalgizing a modernist past, prior to late capitalism. In this manner, Jameson resembles Marxist theorist Georg Lukacs, who presents the novel as a form representing the fragmentation and alienation from home and community that occurred with capitalism and modernity.
19. See the work of Linda Hutcheon (1997) and David Lowenthal (1985) for example.
20. Rosemary George (1996) argues that if colonial and postcolonial migrant fiction is a sign of homesickness, the converse is also true that homesickness is also a fiction.
21. "Culture" often becomes an explanation and justification for domestic violence. Often, in the case of Asian immigrant communities, the idea of pure cultural difference is used to explain how violence is acceptable in Asian "cultures." In validating this line of reasoning, the law and nation-state employ Orientalist and racist logic to essentialize Asian migrant cultural practices by equating heteropatriarchal cultural nationalism and Asian culture. See the work of Leti Volpp (2000) and Pragna Patel (1997) for discussions of how culture and honor become defenses in the United States and Britain.
22. Domestic violence could be theorized as a form of torture that is state-supported and patriarchal.
23. Spivak's (1997, 1998, 1999) assertion is that subalternity marks the condition of silence (of not being heard), a space that is occupied in her formulations by the nonelite—women, tribals, and peasants.
24. Domestic violence has been the necessary site of much activism in the brown Atlantic. It also has been the site of cultural and academic investigation (see the work of Chitra Divakaruni (1997), Margaret Abraham (2000), and Ananya Chatterjee (2001), for example).
25. This expulsion is spatially rendered within the film as Ginder is forced to flee the space of the domestic house to live in a shelter while Ranjit the abuser remains ensconced in the community and family home.
26. That stigmatization is associated with the divorced or battered woman and not the divorced man is made abundantly clear in the film.
27. The satisfaction of the audience in seeing this moment of what can be called revenge is extremely cathartic within the framework of the film, in part, because the viewer can be interpolated into the position of Asha or Ranjit's younger brother, both of which fulfill the fantasy of revenge and justice. Here, the film substitutes rescue by the community for rescue by romance.
28. Here, I am expanding on the work of John Austin (1986) in theorizing the speech-act, specifically in the performativity of speech that dismantles the binary formulation of speech and action as oppositional.
29. Clearly, there are many levels of "public" within the film.
30. In her article on Asian British feminist activism, primarily by the organization Southhall Black Sisters, Pragna Patel (1997) discusses how the group in the eighties began protesting in front of the houses of men accused of brutalizing and murdering women. Patel discusses how visibility and direct action were strong components for social change and transformation within the community.
31. Conservative and fundamentalist forces also have participated increasingly in aiding abusive men. As Patel (1997) describes, in the early nineties in Britain, a "bounty hunter" began to offer his services of locating and returning young women to the Asian families that they had left. Patel comments that the racist state and the dominant media treated him as if he was a mediator and identified his services as "'salvaging' Asian marriages from the crisis in

modernity" (p. 265). Although women protested this zealot and other conservative men who sought to speak out as representatives of the community, the state following a multicultural logic often supported the efforts of these men over the interests of women to avoid being called racist (p. 268).

Chapter 6: Homo on the Range

1. Sita, as I discuss later, is a mythological Hindu figure who is upheld as a paragon of female virtues, especially in Hindu nationalist discourses.

2. However, in 1942 while still under British rule, Ismat Chugtai (1992) was brought up under indecency charges for her Urdu short story "Lihaaf" (The Quilt). In the story a young girl observes her "auntie" in bed with her maid under a heaving quilt. The case was dismissed by the court, because it was deemed that only those who had knowledge of perversity would understand the story.

3. Kishwar (1998) reads it as anti-Hindu and anti-Indian, that is, as Western. Mehta is painted as a sellout who portrays women and India inaccurately along the yardstick of realism. Kishwar further argues that the sex in the film is boring. Borrowing the same scale of measurement, Parameswaran (1999) in addition to suggesting that Mehta should not have targeted Hinduism, applauds its realist setting but is dismayed by its song and dance numbers. She finds it to be political and posits that she is seduced into analysis by the events in India, despite her first reaction to not "intellectualize or analyze" it. She, like Kishwar, blames Mehta's migrant or diasporic sensibilities for the failure of the film. Both authors also make analogies between "cultural decimation" by colonialism and at the hands of diasporic middle class (secular) intellectual (especially those "holier than thou who decry such events as religious riots and nuclear development in India") (p. 105). This in particular is of interest because it suggests that the diasporic position of supporting the homeland is not to critique Hindutva nationalism. Kishwar also argues quite lengthily that India has no history of persecuting homosexuals and suggests that Mehta paints India as homophobic to garner Western accolades (pp. 5–7). Although Kishwar correctly asserts that homosocial relations between women are prevalent in middle-class urban India, she easily conflates homosocial and homosexual, which are not identical (p. 11). The women's movement position occupied by Kishwar invokes Hindu symbols as a way to counter the Eurocentrism of feminism. Kishwar's work continues to invoke tradition as "points of strength" that can be used creatively. She attempts to wrest control from and employ "tradition" against communal forces. This raises questions of the instrumentality of religion (and tradition) in the postcolonial nation for secular politics and women's movements. As Rajan (1999, 282) writes,

> In a "modernizing" post-colonial nation, the authority of majoritarian religious discourse and practice can only be countered . . . by a clear-cut and visible secular alternative. And to privilege religion as the sole available idiom of the social would be to surrender the hard-won gains of democratic and secular struggles in post-Independence India.

4. *Karva chauth* is a Hindu holiday in which wives fast all day for the health and happiness of their husbands. The fast is broken after sundown when the women are blessed by their husbands and fed food and water.

5. Prasad (2000, 78) suggests that

> in a social formation characterized by an uneven combination of modes of production only formally subordinated to capital, where political power is shared by a coalition of bourgeoisie, rural rich, and the bureaucratic elite, the explanatory scheme in question functions as a disavowal of modernity, an assurance of the permanence of the state of formal subsumption.

6. This is of course a reference to Aihwa Ong's (1999) *Flexible Citizenship;* it is the subtitle to the book.

7. Some critics have read *Fire* as asserting the denial of women's sexuality by patriarchal traditions as the root cause of women's oppression. Indian feminist scholars such as Mary E. John and Tejaswini Niranjana (1999, 581) suggest that

Fire ends up arguing that the successful assertion of sexual choice is not only a necessary but also a sufficient condition—indeed, the sole criterion—for the emancipation of women. Thus the patriarchal ideology of "control" is first reduced to pure denial—as though such control did not involve the production and amplification of sexuality—and is later simply inverted to produce the film's own vision of women's liberation as free sexual choice.

This reading also is offered by Mehta in her own privileged explanation of the film as a reformulation of Catherine MacKinnon's (1997) aphorism that "sexuality is to feminism what work is to Marxism." This collapsing, I argue later, allows Mehta to employ sexuality as a metaphor for gender. Instead, following the work of queer scholars, I suggest that the film links but does not collapse gender and sexuality, seeing sexuality as articulated through gender and class identities in the film. *Fire* aggressively challenges the supposed absence of sexuality in India and the irrelevance of sexuality to Indian feminism, as it asserts the significance of sexuality not just to feminist politics but also to postcolonial understandings of gender, family, and nation.

8. The character of Julie as a Chinese Indian lends a complication to the discourse of nation and modernity. She is configured as marginalized within India because of her race and ethnicity. At the same time, her aspirations to go to Hong Kong suggest an association with the transnational capitalism of cosmopolitan "overseas Chinese."

9. More complicated is the actual viewing of the film *Fire* by different audiences. Some articles report that the film was viewed as pornography by men who came to see the same-sex scenes between Radha and Sita. Often this audience was not characterized as middle class, and therefore, the viewing also crossed class boundaries. The transgression of this cross-class viewing is epitomized in the film by Mundu as he gazes at the women.

10. In his essay on the film *The Wedding Banquet,* Mark Chiang (1998) locates the film's celebration of homosexual identities within an analysis of the global system and postmodernity in opposition to the nation-state and modernity. He writes that in the film,

> the tension between an apparently antihomophobic or homophilic resolution and an antipatriarchal or feminist one is the tension between sexuality and gender as two divergent challenges to the authority of the nation-state. This discontinuity cannot be parsed as one in which sexuality is inherently more or less efficacious a subversion than is gender; rather, we need to attend to who is being recuperated, the first-born son or the working-class woman. (p. 384)

In the case of *Fire,* in which the same-sex relationship is between women, links are drawn between the middle-class women and the working-class man.

11. Compulsory heterosexuality has a long history in U.S. feminist debates. Adrienne Rich (1980) argues that compulsory heterosexuality is a universal condition of the hegemony of marriage. As Blackwood and Wieringa (1999, 55) comment,

> Heterosexual marriage may be the norm in all societies, and often constitutes the only avenue to adulthood, but sexuality does not equal marriage nor does marriage deny women's creation of or participation in other sexual practices, heterosexual or otherwise. It was not *marriage* or *heterosexuality* that oppressed women or constrained their sexuality. The oppression of women's sexuality was located in particular systems in which masculinity and masculine desire were constructed as more valuable and powerful, while women's sexuality was seen as limited or necessarily confined. The corollary to the concept of compulsory heterosexuality was the idea that lesbianism, where it existed, constituted a form of resistance to heterosexuality, the "breaking of a taboo."

In this regard, the association of compulsory heterosexuality with marriage is interrogated in the film. However, my focus is not compulsory heterosexuality but rather heteronormativity.

12. Sita and Savitri are touted as ideal wives by dominant discourses, because they are seen as women who capitulate to patriarchal interests willingly. They are upheld as dutiful (i.e., compliant) and selfless (i.e., sacrificing) at some level. See also Rajan (2002).

13. For example, alternative narratives were discussed at the Columbia University's Sita Symposium. See Ananya Chatterjee (1997) and Nabaneeta Dev Sen (1998) for antihegemonic narratives of Sita.

14. Gopinath's (1997) argument foregrounds the possibilities of South Asian diasporic queer claimings of home in texts such as *Fire*. More relevant to the point I am making here is that Gopinath argues for a queer South Asian sensibility in the cross-dressing scenes of *Fire* that evokes the trope of, but significantly differs from, the politics of cross-dressing and performance in U.S. queer studies.

15. Diasporas participate in the maintenance of patriarchal discourses and practices as well, as I discussed in the previous chapter.

16. I posit that anticommunal and secular are not identical politics, but that discussion is unfortunately beyond the scope of this current discussion.

17. Following the same logic of neocolonialist reviewers, Mahila Samiti (a women's Shiv Sena organization) leader Meena Kambli concluded that the "majority of women in our society don't even know about lesbianism. Why expose them to it?" (cited in Swami 1999, 42–43). Following a similar logic, she also evokes the assertion of pure cultural difference, though claiming a cultural and moral standpoint.

18. The film was actually banned in Singapore and Kenya by pressure from South Asian diasporic residents there. Unfortunately, a discussion of the complexities of those political and social power negotiations cannot be included here.

19. Mehta seems aware of the inability of Western critics to locate the film outside of these hegemonic frameworks. Speaking about the language of the film, she says that she

> thought about translating *Fire* into Hindi, but more for the Western audience rather than the Indian one. Western audiences find a "foreign" film easier to imbibe, easier to accept in its cultural context, if it is in its indigenous language. A foreign film can only be a foreign film if it is in foreign language. And if it isn't, then somehow it is judged (albeit subconsciously), as a Western film disguised as a foreign one. All very complex but true to a larger extent. Well, how to explain to people in the West that most middle-class Indians speak Hinglish? Eventually, I decided to go for the authenticity of spirit of *Fire* rather than people's expectations of what a foreign film constitutes. (Zeitgeist Films Web site, January 14 2003, http://www.zeitgeistfilms.com).

20. Women-only showings or gender segregated shows were made available to allow viewers to watch the film without fear of harassment. The content of the film was thought likely to provoke lewd and sexually explicit responses by working-class and lower class men.

21. It is necessary to distinguish between feminist and fundamentalist critiques of beauty pageants and Western imperialism partially because the right wing movement has successfully seized and implemented the rhetoric and discourses of feminisms in India. Basu (1995) argues they have done just that in framing Hindu women as victims in communalist Hindu nationalist discourse. The flattening out of these differences (between critiques of imperialism and women's victimization) should be of significant concern for feminists and may indicate the necessity of developing and shifting the ways in which we theorize and frame feminist issues as the Hindutva movement appropriates feminist rhetoric.

22. Meaning literally test by fire, the sign refers to the purity test endured by the *Ramayana*'s Sita and the film's Radha.

23. Kumar had recently accepted the Nishane-e-Pakistan award from Pakistan for his contribution to cinema.

24. In regard to Asian-American literature, Maxine Hong Kingston (1989) underwent a similar ordeal as her texts, especially *The Woman Warrior*, were challenged by masculine cultural nationalist scholars as being "inauthentic"and "fake." See King-Kok Cheung (2000) and Laura Hyun Yi Kang (2002) for an excellent discussion of the debates.

25. See Roland Barthes's (1996) "Death of the Author" and Michel Foucault's (1975) "What Is an Author?"

26. Often cosmopolitan or diasporic gays and lesbians are invested in tracing sexuality to a particular precolonial representation or simply adopt an American paradigm as a modular paradigm for all nonheterosexualities.

> The forces of global change means that homosexuality is increasingly interrogated. This also means that some people will benefit from imposing a Western analytic model to explain sexuality; often they will be Third Worlders with a personal or professional investment in modernity. Traditionalists will respond either by denial

(often because of Western-derived moralities) or by seeking to build a nationalist version of homosexuality, with romantic claims to a precolonial heritage which is seen as differentiating them from Western homosexuals. (Altman 1996, 90)

27. Kishwar (1998, 11) writes that the film is lesbian and should not have been made such:

> By crudely pushing the Radha-Sita relationship into the lesbian mould, Ms. Mehta has done a big disservice to the cause of women. . . . I suspect that the net result of this political tract of a film, determined to create programmed individuals, will be to make many women in India far more self-conscious than earlier in their relationships with other women.

But this self-consciousness may result from the greater visibility of lesbian and queer sexualities in the public sphere. Sangini, a hotline in New Delhi, reported an increase in calls after the film (personal communication August 1999).

28. The Indian law on sexuality, like the one on censorship, was enacted during colonial rule from the British Code.

Chapter 7: Sex in the Global City

1. See the work of Linda Basch, Nina Glick Schiller, and Cristina Szanton Blanc (1994) and Yossi Shain (1994), for example.

2. My next project closely analyzes the ways in which dominant Indian cinemas articulate and hail diasporic subjects. Specifically, it examines the cinema of the past decade to mark the changing role of diaspora, noting simultaneously the changing discourses of the state on deterritorialized nationals.

3. Soon after India's nuclear tests, the Indian government used newspaper advertisements to thank not only Indian scientists but also NRIs for their contribution in forwarding India's nuclear capabilities. Recently at the national conference on the Indian diaspora, Prime Minister Vajpayee (2003) again thanked NRIs for standing by India when isolation was used as a threat.

4. However, diasporas may not always respond appropriately by living up to their roles as nostalgic and sentimental benefactors, raising the ire and disappointment of the homeland. Homelands also may resent their economic dependence on diasporic support.

5. In 1996, the city officially changed its name in English from Bombay to Mumbai. Forwarded by Shiv Sena as part of their Hindutva agenda, Mumbai emphasizes Marathi over English. I use both Bombay and Mumbai, the latter primarily because it is frequently used in Gujarati.

6. Dwyer (2000) too refers to Barthes's idea of ex-nomination by which the dominant bourgeoisie unname their privilege and render their processes of normalization invisible.

7. My use of "class" here is not economically, politically, and socially precise and therefore qualified. The histories of the South Asian middle classes have been examined best by those affiliated with subaltern studies. In my more general discussion, I seek not to delineate an exact subgroup of the capital-owning bourgeoisie in economic terms but rather in cultural terms, and therefore I discuss the middle classes as incoherent categories, inclusive of a wide range of income and capital. Thus, what I emphasize are the competing claims to the nation and national culture posed through the rhetoric of modern and tradition.

8. This insight is based on Saskia Sassen's (2001) work on globalization and multicultural cities.

9. The filmmakers distinguish their films from popular and art cinema rather than national cinema. My position argues against this kind of classification distinguishing between highbrow and lowbrow culture and instead emphasizes the ways in which the emerging classes and audiences facilitate and consume new cinematic production. Hence, I refer to parallel and popular cinema as national cinemas in public culture.

10. Of course, Gustad's comment should not suggest homogeneous viewing and interpretative practices for audiences of Bollywood or other Indian cinemas. Moreover, Bollywood cinema is hardly monolithic in its presentation of a coherent construction of diaspora. Nevertheless, it seems quite appropriate and possible to characterize dominant Bollywood cinema with shared characteristics in its presentation of the relationship between diaspora and South Asia.

11. His short films *Corner Store Blues* (1994) and *Lost and Found* (1995) take place in the world cities of New York and Mumbai, respectively. The former film features a young South Asian migrant in New York who is hired by his uncle to run a corner shop in Queens and then

is fired for pursuing his dreams of playing the blues. His hybrid Indian and African-American music uses the blues to voice the failure of the American dream. Similarly, *Lost and Found* focuses on hopes and dreams in the dilemma of a Mumbai shoeshine boy who finds a rich man's wallet. Gustad also has written the novel *Of No Fixed Address* (1998) based on travels from Bali and Paris to Sydney and New York. The novel, like the films, centers around similar themes including a search for self-identity through travel, the relationship between diaspora and the homeland, and the meaning of home. The novel seems to emphasize not the object of searching but the process of searching as the cosmopolitan male character travels from Europe to Southeast Asia, from Australia and India to the United States. Therefore, in *Of No Fixed Address*, displacement and movement are more important than place. The self and identity are in flux, and the subject is made and remade through the journey. Gustad's latest film *Boom!* features, among other stars, Bachchan and focuses on the underworld.

12. Though of course there has been a recent resurgence in Western attention to South Asian and South Asian diasporic literature. Arundhati Roy's (1997) recent Booker Prize and Jhumpa Lahiri's (1999) Pulitzer Prize are examples of the ways in which certain South Asian and South Asian diasporic literature are received and consumed in the West.

13. Dhondy is known for his television and performance productions in England. He is also the author of *Bombay Duck* (1990) a novel that, like *Split Wide Open*, is concerned in part with the exploitation of subaltern street children in India.

14. While I employ the Western term, by no means do I imply that pedophilia is an ahistorical and universal sexual deviancy. I find the term appropriate as the sexual desire here is also seen as transgressive in its crossing of age and power boundaries. Moreover, the English term seems appropriate as the film does employ English as its medium.

15. *Bombay Boys* and *Hyderabad Blues* illustrate the folly of attempting to define diasporic versus Indian films. In this case, both films are made by directors who lived abroad, are financed with support from diasporic communities, and feature plot lines about the displacement experienced by NRI male protagonists upon travel or return to India. Both films also are part of the Filmi Fundas as I discuss later. Nonetheless, distinctions are made between the two. I want to suggest that these films indicate the blurring between the diasporic and the transnational as present in the new middle class.

16. The men are presented in relation to the Indian nation rather than the state initially as they hold passports from the United States, England, and Australia. In contrast to the Indian state's Person of Indian Origin Card scheme aimed at claiming Indian-identified foreign citizens, the film emphasizes their Western citizenship and lack of affiliation to the Indian nation.

17. Rahul Bose, who stars in several of these films, recently wrote, directed, and starred in his own film *Everybody Says I'm Fine!* due for release in 2002–2003; he comments that this new cinema is categorically different from diasporic cinema in that it is about contemporary India by Indians, but a new generation that has absorbed MTV and other media.

18. I am indebted to Danielle Bouchard for this insight.

19. Krishna's character functions less as a vehicle for critiquing diasporic return than it does as a send-up of Bollywood itself.

20. This critique also extends comically to those in diaspora who return to the homeland in imagination alone, garnering awards and praise for their literary productions with nary a visit. A surrealist vignette in Gustad's (1998) *Of No Fixed Address* depicts Rustomji, a character from a Booker Prize–winning Parsee Canadian's pen, coming alive and traveling from Mumbai to Toronto to respond to these literary representations. His mission is to confront the writer Cawas Byramji (based on Rohinton Mistry) about receiving Western accolades and writing about a home that he has not visited in more than twenty years. Here, the embodied homeland literally opposes the authority of the diasporic author. However, challenging simple arguments about essentialism, authenticity, or identity, Byramji justifies his work through being Parsi:

> What proved most difficult was this notion of "home" that he toyed with in the first collection. There, it was clear that home was somewhere between two continents, one foot in each, buried over the Atlantic. . . . But the Parsees are the only ones left on this good earth who haven't a land to call their own. (p. 194)

Gustad emphasizes displacement (as suggested by the title) as separate moments of violence— the first in which Byramji is seriously injured in a hate crime and the second when sixty-year-old Rustomji docks him a blow—indicate that neither home is safe nor accepting.

21. The Hindi word *firengi* is translated in the subtitles as "whites"; I gloss the word here as foreigner. *Goras* (whites or pale ones) and *firengi* were used to refer to the British during colonialism and retain these racial and political references today.

22. I use the term *gay* because Pesi himself identifies in term of his sexual practices. Gay and lesbian identities are not foreign to India. However, not all same-sex practices can be described by either these terms or homosexuality. Same-sex practices in India are neither a product of Westernization and colonialism nor pure indigenous epistemes but rather practices produced by complex transnational and local processes.

23. This is not an essentialist argument suggesting that men cannot and should not make feminist films about women but rather it is to highlight the ways these themes are handled differently by the various filmmakers.

Chapter 8: Conclusion

1. I am most influenced here by the work of Spivak here (1999).
2. Nair is the first Indian and first woman to win the Golden Lion.
3. See Patricia Uberoi (2001) and Vijay Mishra (2002), respectively.
4. See Gayatri Gopinath (1997) for a discussion of how the sangeet opens up queer possibilities.
5. I thank Danielle Bouchard for clarifying this insight.
6. The film also features a romanticized and idealized portrayal of the courtship and marriage of Dubey with the family's servant Alice. In contrast to Aditi and Hemant's wedding, Alice and Dubey's wedding involves a simple garland-exchanging ceremony. The austerity of their wedding, however, does not raise questions regarding the extravagant consumption and display associated with the larger wedding.
7. As Rajeswari Sunder Rajan (1993, 72) points out, "The taking of embattled positions around a raped woman's cause often marks an identity crisis for a group.... Her function in an economy of sexual propriety and property ... becomes an emotional war-cry and the prelude to the virtual disappearance of the concerns of the woman herself."
8. See Saskia Sassen's (1998) *Globalization and Its Discontents*, for example. Sassen, like other feminist scholars, points out that for migrant women there may sometimes be an increased access to the public sphere through their access to and incorporation into the labor market. This exposure fosters agency and increased surveillance in relation to their locations in ethnic communities as well as in dominant public spheres, including vis-à-vis the state.

Bibliography

Abraham, Margaret. *Speaking the Unspeakable: Marital Violence among South Asian Immigrants in the United States.* New Brunswick, NJ: Rutgers UP, 2000.

Ahmad, Aijaz. *In Theory: Classes, Nation, Literatures.* London: Verso, 1995.

Akomfrah, John. *Handsworth Songs.* Black Audio Film Collective, 1986.

Alexander, M. Jacqui. "Not (Any)body Can Be a Citizen: The Politics of Law, Sexuality and Post-coloniality in Trinidad and Tobago and the Bahamas." *Feminist Review 48* (Autumn 1994): 5–23.

Alexander, Karen. "Black British Cinema in the 90s: Going Going Gone." *British Cinema of the 90s.* Ed. Robert Murphy. London: British Film Institute, 2000. 109–14.

Alexie, Sherman. *The Lone Ranger and Tonto Fistfight in Heaven.* New York: Atlantic Monthly, 1993.

Altman, Dennis. "Rupture or Continuity: The Internationalization of Gay Identities." *Social Text* 14.3 (1996): 77–94.

Amin, Samir. *Unequal Development.* New York: Monthly Review, 1976.

Anderson, Benedict. *Imagined Communities: Reflections on the Origin and Spread of Nationalism.* New York: Verso, 1991.

Ansari, Rehan. "Indian Lesbian Film OK'd by Censors." *Inter Press Service News Agency* 24 Nov. 1998. Retrieved 7 Oct. 1999, from http://194.183.22.100/ips/eng.nsf/vwWebMainView/36A62AB5BF888F6F80256A0700552BD8/?OpenDocument.

Anzaldúa, Gloria. *Borderlands/ La Frontera. The New Mestiza.* San Francisco: Spinsters/Aunt Lute, 1987.

Appadurai, Arjun. "Disjuncture and Difference in the Global Culture Economy." *Public Culture* 2.2 (1990): 1–24.

———. "The Heart of Whiteness." *Callaloo* 16.4 (1993a): 796–807.

———. *Modernity at Large: Cultural Dimensions of Globalization.* Minneapolis: U of Minnesota P, 1996.

———. "Patriotism and Its Futures." *Public Culture* 5 (1993b): 411–29.

Appadurai, Arjun, and Carol Breckenridge. "On Moving Targets." *Public Culture* 2.1 (Fall 1989a): i–iv.

———. "Why Public Culture." *Public Culture* 2.1 (1989b): 5–9.

Attenborough, Richard, dir. *Gandhi.* Columbia, 1982.

Attwood, David, dir. *Wild West.* Writ. Harwant Bains. Samuel Goldwyn, 1993.

Austin, J. L. "How to Do Things with Words." *Critical Theory Since 1965.* Ed. Hazard Adams and Leroy Searle. Tallahassee: UP of Florida, 1986.

Axel, Brian Keith. *The Nation's Tortured Body: Violence, Representation, and the Formation of a Sikh "Diaspora."* Durham, NC: Duke UP, 2001.

Bahri, Deepika and Mary Vasudeva. "Transnationality and Multiculturalist Ideology: Interview with Gayatri Chakravorty Spivak." *Between the Lines: South Asians and Postcoloniality.* Ed. Deepika Bahri and Mary Vasudeva. Philadelphia: Temple UP, 1996, 64–89.

Bakare-Yusuf, Bibi. "The Economy of Violence: Black Bodies and the Unspeakable Terror." *Feminist Theory and the Body: A Reader.* Ed. Janet Price and Margrit Shildrick. Edinburgh UP, 1999, 311–23.

Bakhtin, Mikhail. *The Dialogic Imagination.* Ed. Michael Holquist. Trans. Caryl Emerson and Michael Holquist. Austin: U of Texas P, 1981.

———. *Speech Genres and Other Late Essays.* Trans. Vern W. McGee. Ed. Caryl Emerson and Michael Holquist. Austin: U of Texas P, 1986.

Barjatya, Sooraj. *Hum Aapke Hain Koun.* 1994.

Barthes, Roland. "Death of the Author, 1968." *Modern Literary Theory: A Reader.* Ed. Philip Rice and Particia Waugh. 2nd ed. London: Arnold, 1996, 118–22.

Bartlett, Neil. "Forgery." *Camp: Queer Aesthetics and the Performing Subject.* Ed. Fabio Cleto. Ann Arbor: U of Michigan P, 1999, 179–84.

Basch, Linda, Nina Glick Schiller, and Cristina Szanton Blanc. *Nations Unbound: Transnational Projects, Postcolonial Predicaments, and Deterritorialized Nation-States.* Langhorne, PA: Gordon and Breach, 1994.

Basu, Amrita. "Feminism Inverted: The Gendered Imagery and Real Women of Hindu Nationalism." *Women and Right-Wing Movements: Indian Experiences.* Ed. Tanika Sarkar and Urvashi Butalia. London: Zed, 1995, 158–80.

Baudrillard, Jean. *America.* Trans. Chris Turner. New York: Verso, 1988.

Bearak, Barry. "A Lesbian Idyll, and the Movie Theaters Surrender." *New York Times* 24 Dec. 1998: A4.

Benegal, Dev, dir. *English August.* 20th Century Fox, 1994.

———, dir. *Split Wide Open.* Tropic Films, 1999.

Berlant, Lauren. *The Queen of America Goes to Washington City: Essays on Sex and Citizenship.* Durham, NC: Duke UP, 1997.

Bhabha, Homi. *The Location of Culture.* New York: Routledge, 1994.

Bhansali, Sanjay Leela. *Devdas.* 2002.

———. *Hum Dil De Chuke Sanam.* Video Sound, 1998.

Bharati, Agehananda. *The Asians in East Africa: Jayhind and Uhuru.* Chicago: Nelson-Hall, 1972.

Bhatavdekar, Harishchandra Sakharam. *The Wrestlers.* 1899.

Bhattacharjee, Anannya. "The Habit of Ex-Nomination: Nation, Woman, and the Indian Immigrant Bourgeoisie." *Public Culture* 5.1 (1992): 19–44.

Bhattacharyya, Gargi, and John Gabriel. "Gurinder Chadha and the *Apna* Generation." *Third Text* 27 (Summer 1994): 55–63.

Blackwood, Evelyn, and Saskia E. Wieringa, eds. Introduction. *Female Desires: Same-Sex Relations and Transgender Practices Across Cultures.* New York: Columbia UP, 1999.

Bobo, Jacqueline. *Black Women as Cultural Readers.* New York: Columbia UP, 1995.

Bose, Rahul, dir. *Everybody Says I'm Fine!* 2001. India.

———. "New Cinema and the Urban." Bollywood and Beyond Conference. Michigan State University and University of Michigan, Lansing, Michigan, 2–3 Dec. 2001.

Bouchard, Danielle. "Traveling Theory and the Feminist Subject: The Politics of Reading and Writing Selves in Contemporary US Feminisms." Unpublished paper, 2001.

Bourdieu, Pierre. *Distinction: A Theoretical Critique of the Judgement of Taste.* Trans. Richard Nice. Cambridge: Harvard UP, 1984.

Bow, Leslie. *Betrayal and Other Acts of Subversion: Feminism, Sexual Politics, Asian American Women's Literature.* Princeton, NJ: Princeton UP, 2001.

Boyle, Danny. *Trainspotting.* Miramax, 1996.

Brah, Avtar. *Cartographies of Diaspora: Contesting Identities.* London: Routledge, 1996.

Braidotti, Rosi. "Difference, Diversity, and Nomadic Subjectivity." *Magda Michielsens Home Page.* Retrieved 10 October 2000, from http://women.ped.kun.nl/cbt/rosilecture.html.

———. *Nomadic Subjects: Embodiment and Sexual Difference in Contemporary Feminist Theory.* New York: Columbia UP, 1994.

Brandzel, Amy. "Towards a Critical Queer Intersectionality: A Methodology for Feminist Studies." Unpublished paper, 2002.

Brennan, Tim. *At Home in the World: Cosmopolitanism Now.* Cambridge, MA: Harvard UP, 1997.

———. "The National Longing for Form." *Nation and Narration*. Homi Bhabha ed. New York: Routledge, 1990, 44–70.

———. "Cosmopolitans and Celebrities." *Race and Class* 31.1 (1989): 1–19.

Brenner, Neil. "Global, Fragmented, Hierarchical: Henri Lefebvre's Geographies of Globalization." *Public Culture* 10.1 (1997): 135–67.

Buchignani, Norman, Doreen M. Indra, and Ram Srivastava. *Continuous Journey: A Social History of South Asians in Canada*. Toronto: McClelland and Stewart, 1985.

Butler, Judith. *Bodies That Matter: On the Discursive Limits of "Sex."* New York: Routledge, 1993.

———. "Gender Is Burning: Questions of Appropriation and Subversion." *Feminist Film Theory: A Reader*. Ed. Sue Thornham. New York: New York UP, 1999, 336–49.

Campaign for Lesbian Rights. *Silence! The Emergency Is On: Lesbian Emergence*. New Delhi: Campaign for Lesbian Rights, 1999.

Canby, Vincent. "Indian Immigrants in a Black and White Milieu." *New York Times* 19 Feb. 1992: 5.

Cattaneo, Peter. *The Full Monty*. Fox Film, 1997.

Chadha, Gurinder, dir. *Acting Our Age*. Third World Newsreel, 1992.

———, dir. *Bend It Like Beckham*. 20th Century Fox, 2002.

———, dir. *Bhaji on the Beach*. Writ. Meera Syal. First Look, 1993.

———, dir. *I'm British But...*. NAATA, 1990.

———, dir. *A Nice Arrangement*. NAATA, 1991.

———, dir. *What's Cooking?* Trimark, 2000.

Chakrabarty, Dipesh. "Postcoloniality and the Artifice of History: Who Speaks for 'Indian' Pasts?" *Contemporary Postcolonial Theory: A Reader*. Ed. Padmini Mongia. London: Arnold, 1997, 223–47.

Chatterjee, Ananya. "Notes from Dancing Sita: Laments, Fury, and a Plea for Peace." *Proceedings of the Sita Symposium, 1997*. New York: Columbia UP. Forthcoming.

———, dir. *A Wife's Letter*. University of Minnesota, Minneapolis. 13–16 Sept. 2001.

Chatterjee, Partha. *The Nation and Its Fragments: Colonial and Postcolonial Histories*. Princeton, NJ: Princeton UP, 1993.

———. *Nationalist Thought and the Colonial World: A Derivative Discourse?* 1986. Minneapolis: U of Minnesota P, 2001.

Cheung, King-Kok. "Re-Viewing Asian American Literary Studies." *An Interethnic Companion to Asian American Literature*. Ed. King-Kok Cheung. Cambridge, UK: Cambridge UP, 1997, 1–25.

———. "The Woman Warrior versus the Chinaman Pacific: Must a Chinese American Critic Choose?" *Asian American Studies: A Reader*. Ed. Jean Yu-Wen Shen Wu and Min Song. New Brunswick, NJ: Rutgers UP, 2000, 307–23.

Chiang, Mark. "Coming Out into the Global System: Postmodern Patriarchies and Transnational Sexualities in *The Wedding Banquet*." *Q&A: Queer in Asian America*. Ed. David L. Eng and Alice Y. Hom. Philadelphia: Temple UP, 1998, 375–95.

Chopra, Aditya. *Dilwale Dulhaniya Le Jayenge*. Eros, 1995.

———. *Mohabbatein*. Yash Raj, 2000.

Chopra, B. R. *Mahabharat*. Doordarshan Television, India. 1988.

Chopra, Yash. *Dil to Pagal Hai*. Yash Raj Films, 1997.

Chow, Rey. "A Souvenir of Love." *At Full Speed: Hong Kong Cinema in a Borderless World*. Ed. Esther C. M. Yau. Minneapolis: U of Minnesota P, 2001.

———. *Writing Diaspora: Tactics of Intervention in Contemporary Cultural Studies*. Bloomington: Indiana UP, 1993.

Chua, Laurence. "Double Feature." *Black Film Bulletin* 2.3 (1994): 18–19.

Chugtai, Ismat. *The Quilt and Other Stories*. Trans. Tahiri Naqvi and Syeda Hameed. New Delhi: Kali for Women, 1992.

Clifford, James. "Diasporas." *Cultural Anthropology* 9.3 (1994): 302–38.

Cohen, Cathy. "Punks, Bulldaggers, and Welfare Queens: The Radical Potential of Queer Politics?" *Gay and Lesbian Quarterly (GLQ)* 3 (1997): 437–85.

Cohen, Robin. *Global Diasporas: An Introduction*. Seattle: U of Washington P, 1997.

Combahee River Collective. "The Combahee River Collective Statement." *Home Girls: A Black Feminist Anthology*. Ed. Barbara Smith. Latham, NY: Kitchen Table, 1983.

Cornershop. "Brimful of Asha." Perf. Talvinder Singh.

Creed, Barbara. "From Here to Modernity: Feminism and Postmodernism." *Screen* 28.2 (1987): 47–67.

Crenshaw, Kimberlé. "Demarginalizing the Intersection of Race and Sex: A Black Feminist Critique of Antidiscrimination Doctrine, Feminist Theory and Antiracist Politics." *The Black Feminist Reader*. Ed Joy James and T. Denean Sharpley-Whiting. Malden, MA: Blackwell, 2000, 208–38.

Cruz, Jon. "From Farce to Tragedy: Reflections on the Reification of Race at Century's End." *Mapping Multiculturalism*. Ed. Avery Gordon and Christopher Newfield. Minneapolis: U of Minnesota P, 1996, 19–39.

Das, Veena. *Critical Events: An Anthropological Perspective on Contemporary India*. Delhi: Oxford UP, 1995.

Dattani, Mahesh, dir. *Mango Soufflé: A Metrosexual Love Story*. 2002.

Davies, Carole Boyce. *Black Women, Writing, and Identity: Migrations of the Subject*. London: Routledge, 1994.

Davis, Angela. *Women, Race, and Class*. New York: Random House, 1981.

Dehlavi, Jamal, dir. *Towers of Silence*. 1975.

de Lauretis, Teresa. *Technologies of Gender: Essays on Theory, Film, and Fiction*. Bloomington: U Indiana P, 1989.

Deleuze, Gilles, and Felix Guattari. *Anti-Oedipus: Capitalism and Schizophrenia*. Trans. Robert Hurley, Mark Seem, and Helen R. Lane. Minneapolis: U of Minnesota P, 1986.

———. *A Thousand Plateaus: Capitalism and Schizophrenia*. Trans. Brian Massumi. Minneapolis: U of Minnesota P, 1987.

———. "What Is a Minor Literature?" *Out There: Marginalization and Contemporary Cultures*. Ed. Russell Ferguson et al. Cambridge, MA: MIT P, 1990, 59–69.

Dhillon-Kashyap, Perminder. "Locating the Asian Experience." *Screen* 29.4 (1988): 120–26.

Dhondy, Farrukh. *Bombay Duck*. London: Cape, 1990.

Divakaruni, Chitra Banerjee. *The Mistress of Spices*. New York: Anchor Books, 1997.

Doane, Janice, and Devon Hodges. *Nostalgia and Sexual Difference: The Resistance to Contemporary Feminism*. London: Methuen, 1987.

DuBois, W. E. B. *Dark Princess: A Romance*. Introduction Claudia Tate. Jackson: U of Mississippi P, [1928] 1995.

Duggan, Lisa. "Queering the State." *Social Text* 39 (Summer 1994): 1–14.

Dusenbery, Verne A. "Introduction: A Century of Sikhs Beyond Punjab." *The Sikh Diaspora: Migration and the Experience Beyond Punjab*. Ed. N. Gerald Barrier and Verne A. Dusenbery. Columbia, MO: South Asia, 1989, 1–28.

———. "A Sikh Diaspora?: Contested Identities and Constructed Realities." *Nation and Migration: The Politics of Space in the South Asian Diaspora*. Ed. Peter van der Veer. Philadelphia: U of Pennsylvania P, 1995, 17–42.

Dwyer, Rachel. *All You Want Is Money, All You Need Is Love: Sex and Romance in Modern India*. New York: Cassell, 2000.

"Elite Film Personalities Move Supreme Court to Save *Fire*." *Times of India* [New Delhi] 8 Dec. 1998: 1.

Eng, David. "Out Here and Over There: Queerness and Diaspora in Asian American Studies." *Social Text* 15.3–4 (1997): 31–52.

———. *Racial Castration: Managing Masculinity in Asian America*. Durham, NC: Duke UP, 2001.

Enloe, Cynthia. *Bananas, Beaches, and Bases: Making Feminist Sense of International Politics*. Berkeley: U of California P, 1990.

Espiritu, Yen Le. *Asian American Panethnicity: Bridging Institutions and Identities*. Philadelphia: Temple UP, 1992.

Evans, Lissa, and Nick Wood. *The Kumars at No. 42*. BBC. 2001.

Fanon, Frantz. *Black Skin, White Masks*. New York: Grove, 1967.

Feng, Peter X. *Identities in Motion: Asian American Film and Video*. Durham, NC: Duke UP, 2002.

———, ed. *Screening Asian Americans*. New Brunswick, NJ: Rutgers UP, 2002.

"*Fire*: Reaction in India." *Zeitgeist Films*. Retrieved 11 Nov. 2000, from http://www.zeitgeistfilm.com/current/fire/fireindianreaction.html.

Flinn, Caryl. "The Deaths of Camp." *Camp: Queer Aesthetics and the Performing Subject*. Ed. Fabio Cleto. Ann Arbor: U of Michigan P, 1999, 433–57.

Foster, Gwendolyn Audrey. *Women Filmmakers of the African and Asian Diaspora: Decolonizing the Gaze, Locating Subjectivity*. Carbondale and Edwardsville: Southern Illinois UP, 1997.

Foucault, Michel. *The History of Sexuality*. Trans. Robert Hurley. New York: Vintage, 1986.

———. "What Is an Author?" *Partisan Review* 42 (1975): 603–14.

Frears, Stephen, dir. *My Beautiful Laundrette*. Writ. Hanif Kureishi. Orion Classics, 1986.

————, dir. *Sammy and Rosie Get Laid*. Writ. Hanif Kureishi. Cinecom, 1988.

Freud, Sigmund. "The Uncanny." *The Standard Edition of the Complete Psychological Works of Sigmund Freud*. James Strachey ed. and trans. vol XVII. London: Hogarth, 1953, 219–252.

Friedberg, Anne. "Les Flaneurs du Mal(l): Cinema and the Postmodern Condition." *PMLA* 106.3 (1991): 419–31.

Fusco, Coco. "The Other Is In: Black British Film in the U.S." *Institute of Contemporary Arts (ICA) Documents: Black Film, British Cinema*. London: ICA, 1988, 37–39.

Ganetra, Nisha, dir. *Chutney Popcorn*. Seneca Falls, 2000.

George, Rosemary Marangoly. *The Politics of Home: Postcolonial Relocations and Twentieth-Century Fiction*. Cambridge, UK: Cambridge UP, 1996.

Gerstel, Judy. "*Masala* Filmmaker Reaches for Universal Themes, Such as Longing For Home." *Detroit News* 1 Mar. 1992: 6G.

Ghai, Subhash. *Taal*. Melody International, 1998.

————. *Yaadein*. 2001.

Gillespie, Marie. "Sacred Serials, Devotional Viewing, and Domestic Worship: A Case-Study in the Interpretation of Two TV Versions of the *Mahabharata* in a Hindu Family in West London." *To Be Continued ... Soap Operas Around the World*. Ed. Robert C. Allen. New York: Routledge, 1995, 354–80.

Gilroy, Paul. *Against Race: Imagining Political Culture Beyond the Color Line*. Cambridge, MA: Harvard UP, 2000.

————. *The Black Atlantic: Modernity and Double Consciousness*. Cambridge, MA: Harvard UP, 1993a.

————. Lecture. Department of American Studies. University of Minnesota, Minneapolis. Spring 1996.

————. "Nothing but Sweat inside My Hand: Diaspora Aesthetics and Black Arts in Britain." *ICA Documents: Black Film, British Cinema*. London: ICA, 1988, 44–46.

————. *Small Acts: Thoughts on the Politics of Black Cultures*. London: Serpent's Tail, 1993b.

————. *There Ain't No Black in the Union Jack: The Cultural Politics of Race and Nation*. New York: Routledge, 1987.

Givanni, June. Editorial. *Black Film Bulletin* 2.3 (1994): 2.

Gopinath, Gayatri. "Nostalgia, Desire, Diaspora: South Asian Sexualities in Motion." *Positions: East Asia Cultures Critique* 5.2 (1997): 467–89.

————. "On *Fire*." *Screening Asian Americans*. Ed. Peter Feng. New Brunswick, NJ: Rutgers UP, 2002, 293–98.

Gowariker, Ashutosh, dir. *Lagaan: Once Upon Time in India*. Sony, 2002.

Grewal, Inderpal, and Caren Kaplan. "Introduction: Transnational Feminist Practices and Questions of Postmodernity." *Scattered Hegemonies: Postmodernity and Transnational Feminist Practices*. Ed. Inderpal Grewal and Caren Kaplan. Minneapolis: U of Minnesota P, 1994, 1–33.

Grosz, Elizabeth. *Volatile Bodies: Toward a Corporeal Feminism*. Bloomington: Indiana UP, 1994.

Guha, Ranajit. Introduction. *A Subaltern Studies Reader: 1986–1995*. Ed. Ranajit Guha. Minneapolis: U of Minnesota P, 1997.

Gupta, Akhil, and James Ferguson. "Beyond 'Culture': Space, Identity, and the Politics of Difference." *Cultural Anthropology* 7.1 (1992): 6–23.

Gupta, Aruna Mallya. "Film Festivals Ignite: Deepa Mehta's Film *Fire* Wins Awards in Toronto, Chicago." *India Currents* 30 Nov. 1996: D-8.

Gustad, Kaizad, dir. *Bombay Boys*. Kismet Talkies, 1998.

————, dir. *Cornerstore Blues*. Third World Newsreel, 1994.

————, dir. *Lost and Found*. 1995.

————. *Of No Fixed Address*. New Delhi: Harper Collins, 1998.

————, et al. "Filmi Fundas Manifesto." *2000 Goat Island Film Festival Website*. Retrieved 10 Apr. 2001, from http://bzine.bsee.com.au/entertainment/reviews/goatsisland2000.html#2.

————Of Censors, Critics, Copyright and Copycats (and Assorted Other Fundamentalists)." 14 Feb. 1999. Retrieved 14 Jan. 2001, from http://www.the-week.com/99feb14/enter.htm.

————. Interview with Caroline Smith. Retrieved 16 Jan. 2001, from http://www.e.bell.ca/filmfest/98/exclusive/content/inter/gustad.htm.

Hall, Stuart. "Black and White in Television." *Remote Control: Dilemmas of Black Intervention in British Film and Television*. Ed. June Givanni. London: British Film Institute, 1995, 13–27.

————. "Cultural Identity and Diaspora." *Colonial Discourse and Post-Colonial Theory: A Reader*. Ed. Patrick Williams and Laura Chrisman. New York: Harvester Wheatsheaf, 1993, 392–403.

———. "Encoding/Decoding." *Culture, Media, Language.* Ed. Stuart Hall, Dorothy Hobson, Andrew Lowe, and Paul Willis. London: Unwin Hyman, 1980, 128–38.

———. "New Ethnicities." *ICA Documents: Black Film, British Cinema.* London: ICA, 1988, 27–31.

———. "When was the 'Post-Colonial'? Thinking the Limit." *The Post-Colonial Question: Common Skies and Divided Horizons.* Iain Chambers and Lidia Curtis eds. New York: Routledge, 1996, 242–60.

Halperin, David. *One Hundred Years of Homosexuality and Other Essays on Greek Love.* New York: Routledge, 1990.

Hamamoto, Darrell. *Monitored Peril: Asian Americans and the Politics of TV Representation.* Minneapolis: U of Minnesota P, 1994.

Hamamoto, Darrell, and Sandra Liu, eds. *Countervisions: Asian American Film Criticism.* Philadelphia: Temple UP, 2000.

Hanawa, Yukio. "Introduction." *Positions* 4.3 (1996): v–xi.

Hanchard, Michael. "Identity, Meaning, and the African-American" *Social Text* 24 (1990): 31–42.

Hannerz, Ulf. *Transnational Connections: Culture, People, Places.* New York: Routledge, 1996.

Hardt, Michael, and Antonio Negri. *Empire.* Cambridge, MA: Harvard UP, 2000.

Harvey, David. *The Condition of Postmodernity: An Enquiry into the Origins of Cultural Change.* Cambridge, Mass.: Blackwell, 1989.

Helweg, Arthur. "Sikh Politics in India: The Emigrant Factor." *The Sikh Diaspora: Migration and the Experience Beyond Punjab.* Ed. N. Gerald Barrier and Verne Dusenbery. Columbia, MO: South Asia, 1989, 305–36.

Higson, Andrew. "The Concept of National Cinema." *Screen* 30.4 (1989): 36–46.

———. "The Instability of the National." *British Cinema: Past and Present.* Ed. Justine Ashby and Andrew Higson. London: Routledge, 2000, 35–47.

Hill, John. "The Issue of National Cinema and British Film Production." *New Questions of British Cinema.* Ed. Duncan Petrie. London: British Film Institute, 1992, 10–21.

Hoe, Hunt, dir. *Seducing Maarya.* Foreign Ghost, 1999.

hooks, bell. *Black Looks: Race and Representation.* Boston: South End, 1992.

———. *Yearning: Race, Gender, and Cultural Politics.* Boston: South End, 1990.

Hull, Gloria T., Patricia Bell Scott, and Barbara Smith. *All the Women Are White, All the Blacks Are Men, But Some of Us Are Brave: Black Women's Studies.* Old Westbury, NY: Feminist Press, 1982.

Hurtado, Aida. "Relating Privilege: Seduction and Rejection in the Subordination of White Women and Women of Color." *Signs: A Journal of Women in Culture and Society* 14 (1989): 833–55.

Hussein, Waris, dir. *Sixth Happiness.* Dreamfactory, 1997.

Hutcheon, Linda. "The Indian Diaspora: Influence on International Relations." *Modern Diasporas in International Politics.* Gabriel Sheffer ed. New York: St. Martin's 1986, 103–129.

———. "Irony, Nostalgia, and the Postmodern." *University of Toronto English Library Criticism and Theory Resources* 1997. Retrieved 22 Jan. 2003, from http://www.library.utoronto.ca/utel/criticism/hutchinp.html.

Ingraham, Chrys. *White Weddings: Romancing Heterosexuality in Popular Culture.* New York: Routledge, 1999.

"Is the Smoke Around the 'Fire' Just Smoke?" *Asian Age* [New Delhi] 15 Dec. 1998: 19.

Ivory, James, dir. *Howards End.* Sony, 1992.

———, dir. *A Room with a View.* Cinecom International, 1986.

Jain, Madhu, and Sheela A. Raval. "Ire Over Fire." *India Today* [New Delhi] 21 Dec. 1998: 78+.

Jamal, Ahmed, dir. *Majdhar.* 1984.

Jameson, Fredric. *Postmodernism, or, The Cultural Logic of Late Capitalism.* Durham, NC: Duke UP, 1991.

———. *Signatures of the Visible.* New York: Routledge, 1990.

Jayawardena, Kumari, and Malathi De Alwis, eds. *Embodied Violence: Communalizing Women's Sexuality in South Asia.* Atlantic Highlands, NJ: Zed, 1996.

Jeffrey, Patricia, and Veena Das, eds. *Appropriating Gender: Women's Activism and Politicized Religion in South Asia.* New York: Routledge, 1998.

Jensen, Joan. *Passage from India: Asian Indian Immigrants in North America.* New Haven, CT: Yale UP, 1988.

Johar, Karan. *Kuch Kuch Hota Hai.* Yash Raj, 1998.

———. "Globalization, Sexuality, and the Visual Field." *A Question of Silence: The Sexual Economies of Modern India.* Ed. Mary E. John and Janaki Nair. New Delhi: Kali for Women, 1998, 368–96.

John, Mary E., and Janaki Nair, eds. *A Question of Silence: Sexual Economies in Modern India.* New Delhi: Kali for Women, 1998.

John, Mary E., and Tejaswini Niranjana. "Mirror Politics: Fire, Hindutva and Indian Culture." *Economic and Political Weekly* 6–13 Mar. 1999: 581–84.

Jordan, June. *Affirmative Acts: Political Essays.* New York: Anchor, 1998.

Jordan, Neil. *The Crying Game.* Miramax, 1992.

Julien, Isaac. "Burning Rubber's Perfume." *Remote Control: Dilemmas of Black Intervention in British Film and Television.* Ed. June Givanni. London: British Film Institute, 1995, 55–59.

———, dir. *Young Soul Rebels.* Prestige, 1991.

Julien, Isaac, and Maureen Blackwood. *Passion of Remembrance.* Third World Newsreel, 1986.

Kang, Laura Hyun Yi. "Si(gh)ting Asian/American Women as Transnational Labor." *Positions: East Asian Cultures Critique* 5.2 (1997): 403–38.

Kapadia, Asif, dir. *The Warrior.* FilmFour, 2001. UK.

Kaplan, Amy. "Left Alone with America: The Absence of Empire in the Study of American Culture." *The Cultures of United States Imperialism.* Ed. Amy Kaplan and Donald E. Pease. Durham, NC: Duke UP, 1993, 3–21.

Kaplan, Caren. *Questions of Travel: Postmodern Discourses of Displacement.* Durham, NC: Duke UP, 1996.

Kaplan, E. Ann. *Looking for the Other: Feminism, Film, and the Imperial Gaze.* New York: Routledge, 1997.

Kapur, Shekhar. *Elizabeth.* PolyGram, 1998.

Katz, Cindi. "On the Grounds of Globalization: A Topography for Feminist Political Engagement." *Signs: A Journal of Women in Culture and Society* 26.4 (2001): 1213–34.

Katz, Jonathan Ned. "Homosexual and Heterosexual: Questioning the Terms." *A Queer World: The Center for Lesbian and Gay Studies Reader.* Ed. Martin Duberman. New York: New York UP, 1997, 177–80.

Kay, Jeremy. "'Filmi Fundas': The Other Face of Indian Cinema." Retrieved 15 Jan. 2001, from http://www.6degrees.co.uk/en/2/200008ftfilmi.html.

Kim, Elaine H. "Defining Asian American Realities Through Literature." *Cultural Critique* 6 (1987): 87–111.

Kingston, Maxine Hong. *The Woman Warrior.* New York: Vintage, 1989.

Kishwar, Madhu. "Naïve Outpourings of a Self-Hating Indian: Deepa Mehta's Fire." *Manushi* 109 (1998): 3–14.

Krishna, Srinivas, dir. *Lulu.* Alliance, 1996.

———, dir. *Masala.* Strand Releasing, 1991.

———, dir. *Waiting for the Mahatma.* Writ. Srinivas Krishna and Paromita Vohra. 1998.

Kukunoor, Nagesh, dir. *Bollywood Calling.* Eros Entertainment, 2001.

———, dir. *Hyderabad Blues: A Homecoming.* UTV, 1998.

———, dir. *Rockford.* 2000.

Kumar, Manoj. *Paurab aur Paschim* [*East or West*]. 1970.

Kureishi, Hanif. *My Beautiful Laundrette and the Rainbow Sign.* London: Faber and Faber, 1986.

———. *The Black Album.* London: Faber and Faber, 1995.

———. "England, Bloody England." *ICA Documents: Black Film, British Cinema.* London: ICA, 1988, 24–25.

———, dir. *London Kills Me.* Fine Line, 1991.

Lahiri, Jhumpa. *Intepreter of Maladies: Stories.* Boston: Houghton Mifflin, 1999.

Lak, Daniel. "Lesbian Film Sets India on Fire." *BBC News* [London] 13 Nov. 1998. Retrieved 15 Nov. 1998, from http://news.bbc.co.uk/hi/english/world/south_asia/newsid_213000/213417.stm.

Lean, David. *A Passage to India.* Columbia, 1984.

Least Heat-Moon, William. *Blue Highways: A Journey into America.* Boston: Little Brown, 1999.

Lee, Ang. *Crouching Tiger, Hidden Dragon* [*Wo Hu Cang Long*]. Sony Pictures Classics, 2000.

Lee, Robert G. *Orientals: Asian Americans in Popular Culture.* Philadelphia: Temple UP, 1999.

Leonard, Karen. *Making Ethnic Choices: California's Punjabi Mexican Americans.* Philadelphia: U of Temple P, 1994.

Leong, Russell, ed. *Moving the Image: Independent Asian Pacific American Media Arts.* Los Angeles: UCLA Asian American Studies Center, 1991.

Loach, Ken. *Up the Junction.* BBC, 1965.

Lorde, Audre. *Sister Outsider: Essays and Speeches.* Trumansburg, NY: Crossing Press, 1984.

Lowe, Lisa. "Epistemological Shifts: National Ontology and the New Asian Immigrant." *Orientations: Mapping Studies in the Asian Diaspora*. Ed. Kandice Chuh and Karen Shimikawa. Durham, NC: Duke UP, 2001, 267–76.

———. "Heterogeneity, Hybridity, Multiplicity: Marking Asian American Difference." *Diaspora* 1.1 (1991): 24–44.

———. *Immigrant Acts: On Asian American Cultural Politics*. Durham, NC: Duke UP, 1998a.

———. "The Power of Culture." *Journal of Asian American Studies* 1.1 (1998b): 5–31.

Lowe, Lisa, and David Lloyd. Introduction. *The Politics of Culture in the Shadow of Capital*. Ed. David Lloyd, Lisa Lowe, and Frederic Jameson. Durham, NC: Duke UP, 1997.

Lowenthal, David. *The Past Is a Foreign Country*. Cambridge, UK: Cambridge UP, 1985.

Luhrmann, Baz. *Moulin Rouge!* 20th Century Fox, 2001.

Lutgendorf, Philip. "Ramayan: The Video." *The Drama Review* 34.2 (1990): 127–76.

MacCabe, Colin. "Black Film in '80s Britain." *Black Film, British Cinema (ICA Documents 7)*. Ed. Kobena Mercer. London: ICA, 1988, 31–32.

MacKenzie, Scott. "National Identity, Canadian Cinema, and Multiculturalism." *Canadian Aesthetics* 4 (Summer 1999). Retrieved 21 Oct. 2001, from http://www.uqtr.uquebec.ca/AE/vol_4/scott.htm.

MacKinnon, Catharine A. "Sexuality." *The Second Wave: A Reader in Feminist Theory*. Ed. Linda Nicholson. New York: Routledge, 1997, 158–80.

Malhotra-Singh, Angelina. "Sappho's Choice." *Trikone* (April 1999): 10.

Malkani, K. R. "Liberalism: Can We Handle It?" *The Sunday Times of India* [New Delhi] 22 Nov. 1998: 15.

Malkki, Liisa. "National Geographic: The Rooting of Peoples and the Territorialization of National Identity among Scholars and Refugees." *Cultural Anthropology* 7.1 (1992): 24–44.

Mamdani, Mahmood. *Imperialism and Fascism in Uganda*. New York: Heinemann, 1983.

Mani, Lata. *Contentious Traditions: The Debate on Sati in Colonial India*. Berkeley: U of California P, 1998.

Mankekar, Purnima. "Brides Who Travel: Gender, Transnationalism, and Nationalism in Hindi Film." *Positions: East Asia Cultures Critique* 7.3 (1999a): 731–61.

———. *Screening Culture, Viewing Politics: An Ethnography of Television, Womanhood, and Nation in Postcolonial India*. Durham, NC: Duke UP, 1999b.

Marchetti, Gina. *Romance and the Yellow Peril: Race, Sex, and Discursive Strategies in Hollywood Fiction*. Berkeley: U of California P, 1993.

Marks, Laura. *The Skin of the Film: Intercultural Cinema, Embodiment, and the Senses*. Durham, NC: Duke UP, 2000.

Mattelart, Armand. *Mapping World Communication: War, Progress, Culture*. Trans. Susan Emanuel and James Cohen. Minneapolis: U of Minnesota P, 1994.

Mayer, Daisy von Scherler. *The Guru*. MCA/Universal, 2002.

McCann, William H. "Nostalgia—A Review of the Literature." *Psychological Bulletin* 38 (1941): 165–82.

McClintock, Anne. *Imperial Leather: Race, Gender, and Sexuality in the Colonial Contest*. New York: Routledge, 1995.

Mehta, Anurag, dir. *American Chai*. Magic Lamp and Wildcard, 2001.

Mehta, Deepa, dir. "Benares, January 1910." *The Young Indiana Jones Chronicles*. ABC. 1992.

———, dir. *Bollywood/Hollywood*. Mongrel Media, 2002.

———, dir. *Camilla*. Malofilm, 1994.

———, dir. *Earth/1947*. G², 1998.

———, dir. *Fire*. Zeitgeist, 1997.

———. Interview with Ingrid Randoja. *Now On* 5–11 Sept. 1996. Retrieved 18 Sept. 1996, from http://www.nowtoronto.com/issues/16/01/Ent/cover.html.

———, dir. *Sam & Me*. 1991.

——— [Deepa Mehta Saltzman], dir. *Travelling Light: The Photojournalism of Dilip Mehta*. 1988.

———, dir. *Water*. In production.

Mehta, Deepa [Deepa Mehta Saltzman], and Norma Bailey, dirs. *Martha, Ruth, and Eddie*. 1988. Canada. 92 min.

Mehta, Deepa, and Michael Schultz, dirs. *Young Indiana Jones: Travels with Father*. 1996.

Menon, Asha, and Revathi, dirs. *Mitr, My Friend*. Telephoto Entertainments, 2001.

Mercer, Kobena. "Ethnicity and Internationality: New British Art and Diaspora-Based Blackness." *Third Text* 49 (Winter 1999–2000): 51–62.

————. *Welcome to the Jungle: New Positions in Black Cultural Studies.* New York: Routledge, 1994.

Merchant, Ismail. *The Mystic Masseur.* ThinkFilm, 2002.

Metz, Christian. "The Imaginary Signifier." Trans. Ben Brewster. *Screen* (Summer 1975): 14–76.

Mishra, Vijay. *Bollywood Cinema: Temples of Desire.* New York: Routledge, 2002.

Mohanram, Radhika. *Black Body: Women, Colonialism, and Space.* Minneapolis: Minnesota UP, 1999.

Mohanty, Chandra. "Cartographies of Struggle: Third World Women and the Politics of Feminism." *Third World Women and the Politics of Feminism.* Ed. Chandra Talpade Mohanty, Ann Russo, and Lourdes Torres. Bloomington: Indiana UP, 1991, 1–47.

————. "Defining Genealogies: Feminist Reflections on Being South Asian in North America." *Our Feet Walk the Sky.* Ed. Women of South Asian Descent Collective. San Francisco: Aunt Lute, 1993, 351–58.

Morrison, Toni. *Playing in the Dark: Whiteness and the Literary Imagination.* Cambridge, MA: Harvard UP, 1992.

Mohyeddin, Zia, dir. *Here Today, Here Tomorrow.*

Mullen, Bill. "DuBois, *Dark Princess,* and the Afro-Asian International." *Positions* 11.1 (2003): 217–39.

Mulvey, Laura. "Afterthoughts on 'Visual Pleasure and Narrative Cinema,' Inspired by *Duel in the Sun.*" *Framework* 15:17 (1981): 29–38.

————. "Visual Pleasure and Narrative Cinema." *Screen* 16.1 (1975): 6–18.

Muñoz, José Esteban. *Disidentifications: Queers of Color and the Performance of Politics.* Minneapolis: U of Minnesota P, 1999.

Nabokov, Vladimir. *Lolita.* New York: Putnam, 1958.

Naficy, Hamid. *An Accented Cinema: Exilic and Diasporic Filmmaking.* Princeton, NJ: Princeton UP, 2001.

————. "Between Rocks and Hard Places: The Interstitial Mode of Production in Exilic Cinema." *Home, Exile, Homeland: Film, Media, and the Politics of Place.* Ed. Hamid Naficy. New York: Routledge, 1999, 125–47.

Nagar, Richa. "Footloose Researchers, 'Traveling' Theories, and the Politics of Transnational Feminist Praxis." *Gender, Place, and Culture* 9.2 (2002): 179–87.

Nair, Mira. CD liner notes for the soundtrack of *Mississippi Masala.* Burbank, CA: JRS Records, 1992.

————, dir. *Hysterical Blindness.* HBO, 2002.

————, dir. "India." *11'09"01—September 11.* Bac Films, 2002.

————, dir. *Kama Sutra: A Tale of Love.* Trimark, 1996.

————, dir. *Mississippi Masala.* Samuel Goldwyn, 1991.

————, dir. *Monsoon Wedding.* USA Films, 2002.

————, dir. *My Own Country.* Showtime Networks, 1998.

————, dir. *The Perez Family.* Samuel Goldwyn, 1995.

————, dir. *Salaam Bombay!* Cinecom, 1988.

————, dir. *Vanity Fair.* Gramercy Pictures, 2003. UK/US.

Namaste. Dir. Viral Lakhia. 2002.

Newell, Mike. *Four Weddings and a Funeral.* PolyGram, 1994.

Newton, Esther. *Mother Camp: Female Impersonators in America.* Chicago: U of Chicago P, 1972.

Oberoi, Harjot. *The Construction of Religious Boundaries: Culture, Identity, and Diversity in the Sikh Tradition.* New York: Oxford UP, 1994.

O'Donnell, Damien. *East Is East.* Writ. Ayub Khan-Din. Miramax, 1999.

Okihiro, Gary Y. "African and Asian American Studies: A Comparative Analysis and Commentary." *Asian Americans: Comparitive and Global Perspectives.* Ed. Shirley Hune et al. Pullman: Washington State UP, 1991, 17–28.

Olalquiaga, Celeste. *Megalopolis: Contemporary Cultural Sensibilities.* Minneapolis: U of Minnesota P, 1992.

Omi, Michael, and Howard Winant. *Racial Formation in the United States: From the 1960s to the 1990s.* 2nd ed. New York: Routledge, 1994.

Ong, Aihwa. "Cultural Citizenship as Subject-Making: Immigrants Negotiate Racial and Cultural Boundaries in the United States." *Cultural Anthropology* 37 (1996): 737–62.

————. "Flexible Citizenship among Chinese Cosmopolitans." *Cosmopolitics: Thinking and Feeling Beyond the Nation.* Ed. Bruce Robbins and Pheng Cheah. Minneapolis: U of Minnesota P, 1998, 134–62.

————. *Flexible Citizenship: The Cultural Logics of Transnationality.* Durham, NC: Duke UP, 1999.

O'Shea, Marg. "India Songs." *Filmnews* BFI (April 1995): 8.

Ové, Horace, dir. *Playing Away.* Artmattan, 1986.

The Oxford English Dictionary. 2nd ed. 1989.

Palumbo-Liu, David. *Asian/America: Historical Crossings of a Racial Frontier.* Stanford, CA: Stanford UP, 1999.

Pandya, Piyush Dinker. *American Desi.* Blue Rock, 2001.

Parameswaran, Uma. "Disjunction of Sensibility?" *The Toronto Review* (Spring 1999): 99–106.

Parker, Andrew, ed. *Nationalisms and Sexualities.* New York: Routledge, 1992.

Parmar, Pratibha. "Other Kinds of Dreams." *Black British Feminism: A Reader.* Ed. Heidi Safia Mirza. London: Routledge, 1997, 67–79.

Patel, Krutin, dir. *ABCD.* Phaedra, 1999.

Patel, Pragna. "Third Wave Feminism and Black Women's Activism." *Black British Feminism: A Reader.* Ed. Heidi Safia Mirza. London: Routledge, 1997, 255–68.

Patton, Cindy. "Foreward." *Replacing Citizenship: AIDS Activism and Radical Democracy.* Michael P. Brown. New York: Guilford Press, 1997, ix–xx.

Patton, Cindy, and Benigno Sanchez-Eppler, eds. *Queer Diasporas.* Durham, NC: Duke UP, 2000.

Patwardhan, Anand, dir. *Pitra, Putra aur Dharamyuddha* [*Father, Son, and Holy War*]. First Run/Icarus, 1994.

Peters, John Durham. "Exile, Nomadism, and Diaspora: The Stakes of Mobility in the Western Canon." *Home, Exile, Homeland: Film, Media, and the Politics of Place.* Ed. Hamid Naficy. New York: Routledge, 1999, 17–41.

Phalke, Dhundiraj Govind, dir. *Raja Harishchandra.* 1913.

Pinney, Christopher. "Introduction." *Pleasure and the Nation: The History, Politics, and Consumption of Public Culture in India.* Ed. Rachel Dwyer and Christopher Pinney. New York: Oxford UP, 2001.

Povinelli, Elizabeth, and George Chauncey, eds. *Thinking Sexuality Transnationally.* Spec. issue of *GLQ: A Journal of Lesbian and Gay Studies* 5.4 (1999).

Prakash, Gyan. "Postcolonial Criticism and Indian Historiography." *Social Text* 31/32 (1992) 8–19.

Prasad, M. Madhava. *Ideology of the Hindi Film: A Historical Construction.* Oxford, UK: Oxford UP: 2000.

Prasad, Udayan, dir. *Brothers in Trouble.* First Run, 1996.

———, dir. *My Son the Fanatic.* Writ. Hanif Kureishi. Miramax, 1997.

Prashad, Vijay. *The Karma of Brown Folk.* Minneapolis: U of Minnesota P, 2000.

Puri, Harish K. *Ghadar Movement: Ideology, Organisation & Strategy.* Amritsar, India: Guru Nanak Dev UP, 1983.

Radhakrishnan, R. *Diasporic Mediations: Between Home and Location.* Minneapolis: U of Minnesota P, 1996.

Raghunatha, T. N. "BJP Soft Towards Pakistan, Says Thackeray." *Pioneer* [New Delhi] 17 Dec. 1998: 15.

Rajan, Gita. "Pliant and Compliant: Colonial Indian Art and Postcolonial Cinema." *Women: A Cultural Review* 13.1 (2002): 48–69.

Rajan, Rajeswari Sunder. *Real and Imagined Women: Gender, Culture, and Postcolonialism.* New York: Routledge, 1993.

———. "The Story of Draupadi's Disrobing: Meaning for Our Times." *Signposts: Gender Issues in Post-Independence India.* Ed. Rajeswari Sunder Rajan. New Delhi: Kali for Women, 1999.

Ramchandani, R. R. *Uganda Asians: The End of an Enterprise.* Bombay: United Asia, 1974.

"Range." *The American Heritage Dictionary.* Ed. William Morris. 2nd college ed. Boston: Houghton Mifflin, 1982.

Ratnam, Mani. *Bombay.* Amitabh Bachchan Corporation, 1995.

Reagon, Bernice Johnson. "Coalition Politics: Turning the Century." *Home Girls: A Black Feminist Anthology.* Ed. Barbara Smith. New York: Kitchen Table, 1983, 356–69.

Rich, Adrienne. "Compulsory Heterosexuality and Lesbian Existence." *Signs: Journal of Women in Culture and Society* 5.4 (1980): 631–60.

———. "Notes Toward a Politics of Location." *Blood, Bread, and Poetry: Selected Prose 1979–1985.* New York: W. W. Norton, 1986, 210–31.

Richardson, Tony, dir. *A Taste of Honey.* Continental, 1962.

Riggs, Marlon, dir. *Color Adjustment.* California Newsreel, 1991.

Ritchie, Guy. *Lock, Stock, and Two Smoking Barrels*. Universal, 1998.

Robertson, Pamela. "What Makes the Feminist Camp?" *Camp: Queer Aesthetics and the Performing Subject*. Ed. Fabio Cleto. Ann Arbor: U of Michigan P, 1999, 266–82.

Rose, Gillian. *Feminism and Geography: The Limits of Geographical Knowledge*. Minneapolis: U of Minnesota P, 1993.

———. "Women and Everyday Spaces." *Feminist Theory and the Body: A Reader*. Ed. Janet Price and Margrit Shildrick. Edinburgh, Scotland, Edinburgh UP, 1999, 358–70.

Roy, Arundhati. *The God of Small Things*. New York: Random House, 1997.

Rushdie, Salman. *Imaginary Homelands*. London: Granta, 1991.

———. *The Satanic Verses*. New York: Viking, 1989.

Safran, William. "Diasporas in Modern Societies: Myths of Homeland and Return." *Diaspora* 1.1 (1991): 83–99.

Sagar, Ramanand. *Ramayan*. Doordarshan Television, India. 1987.

Said, Edward. *Orientalism*. New York: Vintage, 1979.

San Juan Jr., E. *From Exile to Diaspora: Versions of the Filipino Experience in the United States*. Boulder, CO: Westview, 1998.

Sangari, Kumkum, and Sudesh Vaid, eds. *Recasting Women: Essays in Colonial History*. New Delhi: Kali for Women, 1989.

Sangini. Personal Communication. 20 August 1999.

Sassen, Saskia. *Globalization and Its Discontents: Essays on the New Mobility of People and Money*. New York: New Press, 1998.

———. "Globalization or Denationalization?" *Review of International Political Economy* 10.1 (2003): 1–22.

———. *The Global City: New York, London, Tokyo*. 2nd edition. Princeton, New Jersey: Princeton UP, 2001.

Scarry, Elaine. *The Body in Pain: The Making and Unmaking of the World*. New York: Oxford UP, 1985.

Seizer, Suzan. "Paradoxes of Visibility in the Field: Rites of Queer Passage." *Public Culture* 8.1 (1995): 73–100.

Selvadurai, Shyam. *Funny Boy*. San Diego, CA: Harcourt Brace, 1994.

Sen, Nabaneeta Dev. "When Women Retell the Ramayan." *Manushi* 108 (1998): 18–27.

Sengupta, Ramananda. "Persons of Indian Origin in Some Countries to Get Dual Citizenship." *India Abroad* 17 Jan., 2003: A1+.

Shah, Nayan. "Sexuality, Identity and the Uses of History." *A Lotus of Another Color*. Ed. Rakesh Ratti. Boston: Allyson, 1993, 113–32.

Shain, Yossi. "Marketing the Democratic Creed Abroad: US Diasporic Politics in the Era of Multiculturalism." *Diaspora* 3.1 (1994): 85–111.

Shankar, Lavinia, and Rajini Srikanth, eds. *A Part, Yet Apart: South Asians in Asian America*. Philadelphia: Temple UP, 1998.

Sharma, Sanjay, John Hutnyk, and Ashwani Sharma, eds. *Dis-Orienting Rhythms: The Politics of New Asian Dance Music*. Atlantic Highlands, NJ: Zed, 1996.

Sharpe, Jenny. "Is the United States Postcolonial? Transnationalism, Immigration, and Race." *Diaspora* 4.2 (1995): 181–99.

Shohat, Ella. "Notes on the 'Post-Colonial.'" *Social Text* 31/32 (1992): 99–113.

Shohat, Ella, and Robert Stam. *Unthinking Eurocentrism: Multiculturalism and the Media*. New York: Routledge, 1994.

Shukla, Vijay. *Godmother*. Perf. Shabana Azmi. Yash Raj, 1999.

Shyamalan, M. Night, dir. *Praying with Anger*. Cinevista, 1992.

———, dir. and writ. *Signs*. Buena Vista, 2002.

———, dir. and writ. *The Sixth Sense*. Buena Vista, 1999.

———, dir. and writ. *Wide Awake*. Miramax, 1998.

Sidhwa, Bapsi. *Cracking India*. Minneapolis, MN: Milkweed, 1991.

Silverman, Kaja. *Male Subjectivity at the Margins*. New York: Routledge, 1992.

Smith, Kimberly K. "Mere Nostalgia: Notes on a Progressive Paratheory." *Rhetoric & Public Affairs* 3.4 (2000): 505–27.

Smith, Peter. *A Private Enterprise*. Writ. Dilip Hiro. BFI, 1975. UK.

Snead, James A. "Black Independent Film." *ICA Documents: Black Film, British Cinema*. London: ICA, 1988, 47–50.

Sobchack, Vivian. "Lounge Time: Post-War Crises and the Chronotope of Film Noir." *Refiguring American Film Genres: History and Theory.* Ed. Nick Browne. Berkeley: U of California P, 1997, 129–70.

Sontag, Susan. "Notes on 'Camp.'" *Against Interpretation.* 2nd ed. New York: Anchor, 1986, 275–92.

Spivak, Gayatri. "Can the Subaltern Speak?" *Marxism and the Interpretation of Culture.* Ed. Cary Nelson and Lawrence Grossberg. Urbana: U of Illinois P, 1988a, 271–313.

———. *A Critique of Postcolonial Reason: Towards a History of The Vanishing Present.* Cambridge, MA: Harvard UP, 1999.

———. "Diasporas Old and New: Women in the Transnational World." *Class Issues: Pedagogy, Cultural Studies, and the Public Sphere.* Ed. Amitava Kumar. New York: New York UP, 1997.

———. *Outside in the Teaching Machine.* New York: Routledge, 1993.

———. *The Post-Colonial Critic: Interview, Strategies, Dialogues.* Ed. Sarah Harasym. New York: Routledge, 1991.

———. "Subaltern Studies: Deconstructing Historiography." *In Other Worlds: Essays in Cultural Politics.* New York: Routledge, 1988b, 197–221.

———. "Teaching for the Times." *Decolonizing of Imagination: Culture, Knowledge, and Power.* Ed. Jon Nederveen Pieterse and Vhikhu Parekh. London: Zed, 1995.

Srilata, K. "The Story of the 'Up-Market' Reader: *Femina's* 'New Woman' and the Normative Feminist Subject." *Gender, Media, and the Rhetorics of Liberalization.* Spec. issue of *The Journal of Arts and Ideas* 22–3 (April 1999): 61–72.

Stoler, Ann Laura. *Race and the Education of Desire: Foucault's* History of Sexuality *and the Colonial Order of Things.* Durham, NC: Duke UP, 1995.

———. "Tense and Tender Ties." *Journal of American History* (Winter 2001): 842–64.

Straayer, Chris. *Deviant Eyes, Deviant Bodies: Sexual Re-Orientations in Film and Video.* New York: Columbia UP, 1996.

Sukthankar, Ashwini, ed. *Facing the Mirror: Lesbian Writing from India.* New Delhi: Penguin, 1999.

Suleri, Sara. *Meatless Days.* Chicago: U of Chicago P, 1989.

———. "Woman Skin Deep: Feminism and the Postcolonial Condition." *Critical Inquiry* 18 (1992): 756–69.

Surayi, Heman, and Franz Osten. *Light of Asia.* 1924.

Sury, Sanjay. "'The Warrior' Loses Oscar Nomination." *News India-Times Online* 13 Dec. 2002. Retrieved 13 Dec. 2002, from http://www.newsindia-times.com/2002/12/13/cinema-37-top.html.

Swami, Praveen. "A New Round." *Frontline* [Mumbai] 1 January 1999: 42–43.

Syal, Meera. *Anita and Me.* London: HarperCollins, 1996.

———. *Life Isn't All Ha Ha Hee Hee.* New York: New Press, 2000.

Tandon, Yash. "A Political Survey." *Portrait of a Minority: Asians in East Africa.* Ed. Dharam Ghai and Yash Ghai. Dar es Salaam: Oxford UP, 1970, 68–97.

Tatla, Darshan Singh. *The Sikh Diaspora: The Search for Statehood.* Seattle: U of Washington P, 1999.

Thapar, Vishal. "Fire Scripts Tryst with 'Social Terrorism.'" *Hindustan Times on the Web* 6 Dec. 1998. Retrieved 5 April 1999, from http://www2.hindustantimes.com/nonfram/061298/detFR007.htm.

Thomas, Gerald. *Carry On.* 30 films. 1958–1992.

Tölölyan, Khachig. "Rethinking *Diaspora*(s): Stateless Power in the Transnational Moment." *Diaspora* 5.1 (1996): 3–36.

Trinh T. Minh-ha. "Commitment from the Mirror-Writing Box." *Making Face, Making Soul.* Ed. Gloria Anzaldua. San Francisco: Aunt Lute, 1990, 245–55.

———. *Woman, Native, Other: Writing Postcoloniality and Feminism.* Bloomington: Indiana UP, 1989.

Troche, Rose. *Go Fish.* Hallmark Home and Samuel Goldwyn, 1994.

Turner, Frederick Jackson. *The Frontier in American History.* New York: Henry Holt, 1920.

Uberoi, Patricia. "Imagining the Family: An Ethnography of Viewing *Hum Aapke Hain Koun.*" *Pleasure and Nation: The History, Politics, and Consumption of Popular Culture in India.* Ed. Rachel Dwyer and Christopher Pinney. New York: Oxford UP, 2001, 309–29.

Vajpayee, Atal Bihari. "Welcome Home." *India Abroad* 17 Jan. 2003: A17+.

Van Gelder, Lawrence. "Both Epic and Feminist, From India." *New York Times* 2 Oct. 1996: C16.

Vijayakar, R. M. "New Film Review: *Bombay Boys* Author." *India West* 29 Jan. 1999: C17.

Visweswaran, Kamala. "Diaspora by Design: Flexible Citizenship and South Asians in US Racial Formations." *Diaspora* 6.1 (1997): 5–29.

Volpp, Leti. "(Mis)Identifying Culture: Asian Women and the 'Cultural Defense.'" *Asian American Studies: A Reader*. Ed. Jean Yu-Wen Shen Wu and Min Song. New Jersey: Rutgers UP, 2000, 390–422.

Wallace, Michele. "Race, Gender, and Psychoanalysis in Forties Films: *Lost Boundaries, Home of the Brave*, and *The Quiet One*." *Black American Cinema*. Ed. Manthia Diawara. New York: Routledge, 1993, 257–71.

Wallerstein, Immanuel. *The Capitalist World-Economy*. London: New Left, 1980.

Wambu, Onyekachi, and Kevin Arnold. *A Fuller Picture: The Commercial Impact of Six British Films with Black Themes in the 1990s*. London: British Film Institute, 1999.

Wang, Wayne, dir. *Dim Sum: A Little Bit of Heart*. Orion Classics, 1985.

———, dir. *Eat a Bowl of Tea*. Columbia, 1989.

———, dir. *The Joy Luck Club*. Buena Vista, 1993.

Warner, Michael, ed. "Introduction." *Fear of a Queer Planet: Queer Politics and Social Theory*. Minneapolis: U of Minnesota P, 1993.

Webber, Andrew Lloyd. *Bombay Dreams*. Comp. A. R. Rahman. Dir. Steven Pimlott. Prod. Andrew Lloyd Webber and Shekhar Kapur. Apollo Victoria Theater, London. 2002.

Wei, William. *The Asian American Movement*. Philadelphia: Temple UP, 1993.

Weiner, Myron. "Labor Migrations as Incipient Diasporas." *Modern Diasporas in International Politics*. Ed. Gabriel Sheffer. New York: St. Martin's, 1986, 47–74.

Westwood, Sallie. "Gendering Diaspora: Space, Politics, and South Asian Masculinities in Britain." *Nation and Migration: The Politics of Space in the South Asian Diaspora*. Ed. Peter van der Veer. Philadelphia: U of Pennsylvania P, 1995, 192–221.

Wilinsky, Barbara. *Sure Seaters: The Emergence of Art House Cinema*. Minneapolis: U of Minneapolis P, 2001.

Wilkinson, Kathleen. "Filmmaker Deepa Mehta is on Fire." *Lesbian News* 23.2 (1997): 38+.

Williams, Raymond. "Structures of Feeling." *Marxism and Literature*. London: Oxford UP, 1977, 128–35.

Wong, Sau-ling C. "Denationalization Reconsidered: Asian American Cultural Criticism at a Theoretical Crossroads." *Amerasia Journal* 21.1–2 (1995): 1–27.

———. *Reading Asian American Literature: From Necessity to Extravagance*. Princeton, NJ: Princeton UP, 1993.

Wong, Shelley Sunn. *Notes from a Damaged Life: Asian American Literature and the Discourse of Wholeness*. Ph. D. dissertation. Berkeley: U of California P, 1993.

Wood, Nick. *Goodness Gracious Me*. BBC2. 1998–2000.

Xing, Jun. *Asian America Through the Lens: History, Representations, and Identities*. Walnut Creek, CA: Altamira, 1998.

Yudice, George. "We Are *Not* the World." *Social Text* 31/32 (1992): 202–16.

Yuval-Davis, Nira. *Gender and Nation*. Thousand Oaks, CA: Sage, 1977.

Žižek, Slavoj. *The Sublime Object of Ideology*. New York: Verso, 1991.

Zwigoff, Terry. *Ghost World*. MGM and United Artists, 2001.

Filmography

Alain, Jannu, dir. Shutter. 2001. US.
———, dir. *Taxi Bhaiya.* 1997. US.
Amin, Rahul, dir. *Flame in My Heart.* 1983. UK.
———, dir. *A Kind of English.* 1986. UK.
———, dir. *Moviewallah.* 1992–3. UK.
———, dir. *Purbo London.* 1978. UK.
———, dir. *Rhythms.* 1994. UK.
Andersen, Erika Surat, dir. *Lifting the Blackout: Images of North Korea.* Cinema Guild, 1989. 54 min.
———, dir. *None of the Above.* 1993. US. 22 min.
———, dir. *Questioning.* 1991. US.
———, dir. *Turbans.* NAATA, 1999. US. 30 min.
Anderson, Vashti, dir. *Looking at Ourselves.* 1997. 56 min.
———, dir. *Zara Mirage.* 2002. US. 12 min.
Attwood, David, dir. *Wild West.* Writ. Harwant Bains. Samuel Goldwyn, 1993. UK. 85 min.
Aubier, Pascal, dir. *Com'mon.* Writ. Madhurika Sona Jain. Perf. Sarita Choudhury.
Hima, B., dir. *Coming Out, Coming Home: Asian Pacific Islander Queer Families' Stories.* 1996. 30 min.
———, dir. *Straight for the Money: Interviews with Queer Sex Workers.* 1994. US. 59 min.
———, dir. *Vicious.*
Hima, B., and Eliza O. Barrios. *Lick.* 1995. US.
Bald, Vivek Renjen, dir. *Mutiny: Asians Storm British Music.* 2003.
———, dir. *Taxi-Vala/Autobiography.* 1994. US. 48 min.
Bali, Kavita, dir. *Aunti.* 1993. 4 min.
———, dir. *Birth of a Butterfly.* 1993/2002. US. 4.5 min.
———, dir. *Distant Souls.* 1993/2002. US. 5.5 min.
———, dir. *Image Kaleidoscope.* 1993. 4 min.
———, dir. *Namaste Papaji.* 1997. US. 15 min.
———, dir. *To Serve One's Country.* 1992/2002. US. 3 min.
———, dir. *Urban Peacock.* 1994. 8 min.
Basu, Raj, dir. *Aaghat* [*Anguish*]. 1997. US.
———, dir. *Wings of Hope.* 2001. US.
Benegal, Dev, dir. *English, August.* 20th Century Fox, 1994. India. 118 min.
———, dir. *Shabana.* Tropic Films, 2002. India. 30 min.
———, dir. *Split Wide Open.* Tropic Films, 1999. India. 100 min.
Bhagat, Darshan, dir. *Karma Local.* Karma LLC, 1999. US. 84 min.

Bhasin, Neeraj, dir. *My Friend Su.* 2001. India. 55 min.
————, dir. *Touch the Sky.*
Bhattacharya, Uday, dir. *Circle of Gold.* 1988. UK. 52 min.
Bose, Rahul, dir. *Everybody Says I'm Fine!* 2001. India.
Brown, Barry Alexander, dir. *Lonely in America.* Arista Classics, 1992. US. 94 min.
Cabreros-Sud, Veena, dir. *10 in America.* US.
————, dir. *Mummers.*
————, dir. *One Night.* 2000. US.
————, dir. *Rain.* 1997. US. 4 min.
————, dir. *Sisters N Brothers.* 1994. 4 min.
————, dir. *Stretchmark.* 1996. US. 9 min.
Chaddha, Anmol, Naomi Iwasaki, Sonya Mehta, Muang Saechao, and Sheng Wang, dirs. *Yellow Apparel: When the Coolie Becomes Cool.* 2000. US. 30 min.
Chadha, Gurinder, dir. *Acting Our Age.* NAATA, 1993. UK. 30 min.
————, dir. *Bend It Like Beckham.* Twentieth Century Fox, 2002. Germany/UK/US. 112 min.
————, dir. *Bhaji on the Beach.* Writ. Meera Syal. First Look, 1993. UK. 100 min.
————, dir. *I'm British But…* NAATA, 1990. UK. 30 min.
————, dir. *A Nice Arrangement.* NAATA, 1991. UK. 11 min.
————, dir. *Rich Deceiver.* BBC, 1995. UK. 110 min.
————, dir. *What Do You Call an Indian Woman Who's Funny?* Third World Newsreel, 1994. UK. 18 min.
————, dir. *What's Cooking?* Trimark, 2000. UK/US. 109 min.
Chatterjee, Sanjeev, dir. *Bittersweet.* Cinema Guild, 1994. US. 39 min.
————, dir. *Pure Chutney.* Writ. Amitava Kumar. 1998. US. 42 min.
————, dir. *The Shadow of History.* 1996.
Chatterjee, Sanjeev, and Amitava Kumar, dirs. *Travel Advisory.* 1997. 9 min.
Cheang, Shu Lea, dir. *Fresh Kill.* Writ. Jessica Hagedorn. Strand Releasing, 1994. US. 80 min.
Chopra, Tanuj, dir. *Big Brother.*
————, dir. *Uljhan.* 1999. US.
Chowdhry, Maya, dir. *Monsoon.* 1992. Canada.
————, dir. *Running Gay.* Facets Multimedia, 1991. US. 20 min.
Chuhan, Kuljit, dir. *Raag, Glitter and Chips.* UK.
Coelho, Shebana, dir. *Desi: South Asians in New York.* NAATA, 2000. US. 58 min.
Coelho, Shebana, and Shashwati Talukdar, dirs. *Ghosts.*
Cooney, Sean, dir. *24-Seven.* US. 8 min.
Cran, William, dir. *Chachaji, My Poor Relation: A Memoir by Ved Mehta.* Writ. Ved Mehta. Icarus Films, 1978. 58 min.
Crossland, Harvey, dir. *The Burning Season.* Primedia, 1993. Canada. 104 min.
Crusz, Robert, dir. *The Census.*
————, dir. *Inbetween.* Third World Newsreel, 1992. UK. 42 min.
Dargan, Amanda, and Susan Slyomovics, dirs. *The Painted Bride.* Queens Council on the Arts, 1991. 25 min.
Das, Sarba, dir. *Mausi.* 2000. US. 10 min.
Dasilva, Jason, dir. *Lest We Forget.* In production.
————, dir. *Olivia's Puzzle.* 2001. Canada. 12 min.
Dehlavi, Jamil, dir. *The Blood of Hussain.* Cinegate, 1980. Pakistan/UK. 112 min.
————, dir. *Born of Fire.* Vidmark, 1983. UK.
————, dir. *Immaculate Conception.* Pakistan/UK. Barcino Barcino, 1992. 120 min.
————, dir. *Jinnah.* Dehlavi Films, 1998. Pakistan/UK. 110 min.
————, dir. *Towers of Silence.* National Film Development, 1995. Pakistan.
Dewshi, Alnoor, dir. *Anton and Minty.* 1995.
————, dir. *Bekky ykkeb.* 2001. UK. 3 min.
————, dir. *Do You Love Me?* 2001. UK. 3 min.
————, dir. *Jomeo and Ruliet.* 2000. UK.
————, dir. *Latifah and Himli's Nomadic Uncle.* 1992.
————, dir. *Shush.* 2002. UK. 1 min, 11 sec.
Fernando, Rohan, dir. *Cecil's Journey.* 2002. Canada. 54 min.
————, dir. *Fade to Black.* 2001. Canada. 84 min.
————, dir. *La Cucaracha.* 1996. 10 min.

Fernando, Sonali, dir. *The Body of a Poet: A Tribute to Audre Lorde.* Women Make Movies, 1995. US. 29 min.
———, dir. *India Calling.* Channel 4, 2002. UK. 50 min.
———, dir. *Kala Pani —Across the Black Water.* 1997.
———, dir. *Shakti.* 1993. UK.
Frears, Stephen, dir. *My Beautiful Laundrette.* Writ. Hanif Kureishi. Orion Classics, 1986. UK. 94 min.
———, dir. *Sammy and Rosie Get Laid.* Writ. Hanif Kureishi. Cinecom, 1988. UK. 97 min.
Fried, Elise, dir. *Do You Take This Man? Pakistani Arranged Marriages in LA.* 1990. 22 min.
Friedman, Daniel, and Sharon Grimberg, dirs. *Miss India Georgia.* 1997. US. 57 min.
Ganatra, Nisha, dir. *Chutney Popcorn.* Seneca Falls, 2000. US. 92 min.
———, dir. *Drown Soda.* 1997. US.
———, dir. *Fast Food High.* CCI, 2003. Canada/US. 92 min.
———, dir. *Junky Punky Girlz.* 1996. US. 12 min.
Ganti, Tejaswini, dir. *Gimme Somethin' to Dance To!: What Is Bhangra?* 1995. US. 18 min.
Gardela, Isabela, dir. *Tomandote? Two for Tea.* Spain. 93 min.
George, Renuka, dir. *Little Indias.*
Gerber, Tony, dir. *Side Streets.* Cargo/nuMedien, 1998. US. 130 min.
Grace, Terrance, dir. *Mr. Ahmed.* Third World Newsreel, 1994. 52 min.
Graverson, Rebecca, dir. *Illusions of an Other Place.* 2000. 18 min.
Gulati, Sonali, dir. *Barefeet.* 2000. 5 min.
———, dir. *Sum Total.* 1999. US. 4 min.
Gulati, Sonali, Byron Karabatsos, and Antonio Paez, dirs. *Where Is There Room?* 2002. US. 8 min.
Gundu, Bob. *The Transfer.* 2002. Canada.
Gunnarsson, Sturla, dir. *Such a Long Journey.* Optimum Releasing, 1998. Canada/UK. 113 min.
Gupta-Smith, Vismita, dir. *For Straights Only.* 2001. 22 min.
Gustad, Kaizad, dir. *Bombay Boys.* Kismet Talkies, 1998. India. 105 min.
———, dir. *Boom.* Quest Films, 2003. India.
———, dir. *Corner Store Blues.* Third World Newsreel, 1994. 48 min.
———, dir. *Lost & Found.* Third World Newsreel, 1995. India. 28 min.
Hakim, Khaled, dir. *When I Was Just a Little Girl.*
Hart, Jayasri Majumdar, dir. *Power and Fear.* 1990.
———, dir. *Roots in the Sand.* NAATA, 1998. US. 57 min.
———, dir. *Sisters of Selma.* In production.
Hidier, Tanuja Desai, dir. *The Test.*
Hidier, Tanuja Desai, and Nisha Ganatra, dirs. *The Assimilation Alphabet.*
Hoe, Hunt, dir. *Seducing Maarya.* Foreign Ghost, 1999. Canada/India. 107 min.
Hüseyin, Metin, dir. *Anita and Me.* Writ. and Perf. Meera Syal. Icon, 2002. UK. 92 min.
———, dir. *It Was an Accident.* Pathé, 2000. UK. 96 min.
Hussein, Waris, dir. *The Sixth Happiness.* Dreamfactory, 1997. UK. 97 min.
Jafri, Shiraz, dir. *The Adventures of the FOB Factor.* 1997. US. 5 min.
———, dir. *The Arrangement.* Awaaz, 2003. US. 100 min.
———, dir. *Indian Buffet.* 1997. US. 4 min.
———, dir. *Jungli Fever.* 1998. US. 20 min.
Jagessar, Rohit, dir. *Guiana.* RBC Films, 2000. US. 112 min.
Jain, Madhurika Sona, dir. *Afreen.*
———, dir and writ. *Vasarma's Lovers.* Hypnotic, 2000. US. 12 min.
Jayamanne, Laleen, dir. *A Song of Ceylon.* 1986. Australia. 51 min.
Jaysekera, Kingsley, dir. *Bombay Bazaar.* UK.
Jhaveri, Siraj, dir. *Ma/Baap.* 1994. 30 min.
Kabir, Yasmine, dir. *Duhshomoy [A Mother's Lament].* 1999. Bangladesh. 26 min.
———, dir. *My Migrant Soul.* 2001. Bangladesh.
Kaderali, Amyn, dir. *Little Man.* 1997. US. 12 min.
———, dir. *Take the A Train.* 2002. US. 16 min.
Kakati, Buboo, dir. *A Letter Home.* Frameline, 1998. US. 6 min.
———, dir. *Off Duty.*
———, dir. *A Question of Virtue.* US. 2000. 10 min.
Kalal, David Dasharath, dir. *Five Minutes to Cloud Boundary.* 2001. US. 8 min.
———, dir. *Love Song for Persis K.* 1996. US. 9 min.
———, dir. *WoW.* 2001. US. 9 min.

Kalal, David Dasharath, and Gita Reddy, dirs. *Hindustan.* 1995. US. 4 min.

Kapadia, Asif, dir. *The Sheep Thief.* 1997.

———, dir. *The Warrior.* FilmFour, 2001. UK.

Kapoor, Sarah, Kristi Vuorinen, and Christina Lamey, dirs. *Don't Pass Me By.* 1999. 40 min.

Kashyap, Keshini, and Dharini Rasiah, dirs. *A Crack in the Mannequin.*

Kaul, Amitav, dir. *Ustra.* 1998. US. 7 min.

Kaul, Pooja, dir. *Winter Trail.* 2001. UK. 11 min.

Kazimi, Ali, dir. *Narmada: A Valley Rises.* Peripheral Visions Film and Video, 1994. Canada.

———, dir. *Passage from India.* 1998. 22 min.

———, dir. *Shooting Indians: A Journey with Jeffrey Thomas.* 1997. Canada. 56 min.

———, dir. *Some Kind of Arrangement.* National Film Board of Canada, 1997. Canada. 44 min.

Keerthisena, Buddhi, dir. *Mille Soya* [*Boungiorno Italia*]. Cinema Buddhi, 2002. Italy/Sri Lanka.

Khalid, Lubna, and Tania Cuevas-Martinez, dirs. *Haters.* 2001. US. 30 min.

Khan, Keith, dir. *Aiya's Apple, Aisha's Eye.* Britain.

Khan, Yusuf Ali, dir. *Skin Deep.* 2001. UK. 8 min.

Khanna, Nathalie, dir. *Gay Bombay.* 1994. UK. 30 min.

Khurana, Swati, and Leith Murgai, dirs. *Desi Dub.* 1997. US. 25 min.

———, dir. *Jalpari.* 1996. US. 25 min.

Kohli, Hardeep Singh, dir. *The Drop.* 2000. UK. 7 min.

Korya, Dilesh, dir. *Bhangra Heads.* 2000. UK. 24 min.

———, dir. *Once Upon a Time in Southhall.* UK.

———, dir. *Sari.* UK.

Krishna, Lalita, dir. *It's About Time.* Canada.

———, dir. *Ryan's Well.* 2001. Canada. 50 min.

———, dir. *What Held It All: The Making of Cosmos.* 1999. Canada/India. 50 min.

Krishna, Srinivas, dir. *Forever.* 1999. US. 15 min.

———, dir. *Lulu.* Alliance, 1996. Canada. 96 min.

———, dir. *Masala.* Strand Releasing, 1991. Canada. 105 min.

———, dir. *Tell Me What You Saw.* 1994. Canada. 7 min.

———, dir. *Waiting for the Mahatma.* Writ. Srinivas Krishna and Paromita Vohra. 1998.

Krishnan, Indu, dir. *Knowing Her Place: A Documentary.* 1990. 40 min.

Kukunoor, Nagesh, dir. *Bollywood Calling.* Eros Entertainment, 2001.

———, dir. *Hyderabad Blues.* UTV, 1998. India.

———, dir. *Rockford.* 2000.

———, dir. *Teen Deewarein.* 2002. India.

Kureishi, Hanif, dir. and writ. *London Kills Me.* Fine Line, 1991. UK. 107 min.

Lakhia, Viral, dir. *Namaste.* 2002.

Luthra, Avie, dir. *Baby.* FilmFour, 2002. UK. 12 min.

———, dir. *Cross My Heart.* 2003. UK.

———, dir. *A Family Business.* 1993. UK. 10 min.

———, dir. *Fast-tricity.* UK.

———, dir. *Hot and Cold.* UK.

———, dir. *Love from Above.* 1995. UK. 10 min.

———, dir. *Melons in Winter.* UK.

———, dir. *Quack.* UK.

———, dir. *Shopkeeping.* 1998. UK/US. 14 min.

Maan, Shakila Taranum, dir. *A Quiet Desperation.* 2001. UK. 90 min.

———, dir. *Restless Sky.* UK.

———, dir. *A Thousand Borrowed Eyes.* UK.

Majid, Hajira, dir. *Ifti.* 1998. US. 20 min.

Malladi, Aparna, dir. *Mitsein.*

———, dir. *Nupur.* 2001. US. 10 min.

Manuel, Peter, dir. *Tan-Singing of Trinidad and Guyana: Indo-Caribbean "Local-Classical Music."* 2000. 50 min.

Marfatia, Heeraz, dir. *Birju.* 2001. India/US. 14 min.

Marjara, Eisha, dir. *24 Hrs.* 1990.

———, dir. *Desperately Seeking Helen.* 1998. Canada. 80 min.

———, dir. *The Incredible Shrinking Woman.* 1994.

Mayer, Daisy von Scherler, dir. *The Guru.* Prod. Shekhar Kapur. MCA/Universal, 2002. UK. 94 min.

Mehta, Anurag, dir. *American Chai.* Magic Lamp and Wildcard, 2001. US. 92 min.

Mehta, Deepa [Deepa Mehta Saltzman], dir. *At 99: A Portrait of Louise Tandy March*. 1975. Canada. 24 min.

———, dir. *Bollywood/Hollywood*. Mongrel Media, 2002. Canada. 103 min.

———, dir. *Camilla*. Malofilm, 1994. Canada. 95 min.

———, dir. *Earth/1947*. G^2, 1998. Canada/India. 110 min.

———, dir. *Fire*. Zeitgeist, 1997. Canada/India. 104 min.

———, dir. *The Republic of Love*. Seville Pictures, 2003. Canada.

———, dir. *Sam & Me*. Writ. Ranjit Chowdhry. 1991. Canada. 94 min.

——— [Deepa Mehta Saltzman], dir. *Travelling Light: The Photojournalism of Dilip Mehta*. 1988.

———, dir. *Water*. In production. Canada/India.

Mehta, Deepa [Deepa Mehta Saltzman], and Norma Bailey, dirs. *Martha, Ruth, and Eddie*. 1988. Canada. 92 min.

Menon, Asha [Revathy], dir. *Mitr—My Friend*. 2001. India. 99 min.

Merchant, Ismail, dir. *Cotton Mary*. Universal International, 1999. France/UK/US. 124 min.

———, dir. *The Courtesans of Bombay*. Channel 4, 1983. UK. 73 min.

———, dir. *In Custody*. Sony Pictures Classics, 1993. India/UK. 126 min.

———, dir. *The Mystic Masseur*. ThinkFilm, 2002. India/Trinidad and Tobago. 117 min.

Mehta, Richie, dir. *Anamika*. 2002. Canada. 5 min.

———, dir. *One Night in My Dreams*. 2002.

Michell, Roger, dir. *The Buddha of Suburbia*. Writ. Hanif Kureishi. BBC, 1993. UK. 222 min.

Mohabeer, Michelle, dir. *Child-Play*. Third World Newsreel, 1997. Canada/Tobago. 15 min.

———, dir. *Coconut/Cane and Cutlass*. Women Make Movies, 1994. Canada/Guyana. 30 min.

———, dir. *Exposure*. From *Five Feminist Minutes*. National Film Board of Canada, 1990. Canada. 8 min.

———, dir. *Manufacturing Gender*. In production.

———, dir. *Parkdale Portraits*.

———, dir. *Two/Doh*. Canadian Filmmakers' Distribution Centre, 1996. 5 min.

———, dir. *Under the Knife*. In production.

Mootoo, Shani, dir. *u.m.* Video Out, 1996. Canada. 30 min.

———, dir. *English Lessons*. Video Out, 1991. Canada. 3 min.

———, dir. *Her Sweetness Lingers*. Video Out, 1994. Canada. 12 min.

———, dir. *Lest I Burn*. Video Out, 1991. Canada. 4 min.

———, dir. *View*. Video Out, 2000. Canada.

———, dir. *Wild Woman in the Woods*. Video Out, 1993. Canada. 12 min.

Mootoo, Shani, and Kathy High, dirs. *Gûerita and Prietita*. Video Out, 1995. Canada/US. 20 min.

Mootoo, Shani, and Wendy Oberlander, dirs. *A Puddle and a Compass*. Filmmakers' Cooperative, 1992.

Moyeddin, Zia, dir. *Here Today, Here Tomorrow*.

Mudan, Balvinder D. [Balvinder Dhenjan], dir. *Desi Remix: Chicago Style*. Third World Newsreel, 1996. UK/US. 46 min.

——— [Balvinder Dhenjan], dir. *The Pyre*. Third World Newsreel, 1996. 4 min.

———, dir. *Square-Shaped Fingernails*. 1999. UK. 18 min.

——— [Balvinder Dhenjan], dir. *What Are Our Women Like in America?* Third World Newsreel, 1994. US. 12 min.

Mukherji, Kevin, dir. *American Storytellers*. Clearwater Pictures, 2000. US. 90 min.

———, dir. *Car Fever*. 1981. US. 30 min.

———, dir. *Death and Taxis*. 2000. US. 90 min.

———, dir. *Michael Kapoor*. 1981. US. 30 min.

———, dir. *Note One of Them's You*. 1983.

Mundhra, Jag, dir. *Monsoon*. New Films International, 1998. US.

Nair, Mira, dir. *Children of a Desired Sex*. 1987.

———, dir. *Hysterical Blindness*. HBO, 2002. US. 96 min.

———, dir. "India." *11'09"01—September 11*. Bac Films, 2002. France/UK.

———, dir. *India Cabaret*. 1985.

———, dir. *Jama Masjid Street Journal*. 1979.

———, dir. *Kama Sutra: A Tale of Love*. Trimark, 1997. India. 117 min.

———, dir. *The Laughing Club of India*. 1999. India/US. 28 min.

———, dir. *Mississippi Masala*. SCS Films, 1992. US. 118 min.

———, dir. *Monsoon Wedding*. USA Films, 2002. France/India/Italy/US. 114 min.

———, dir. *My Own Country*. Showtime Networks, 1998. US. 95 min.

——, dir. *The Perez Family.* Samuel Goldwyn, 1995. US. 115 min.
——, dir. *Salaam Bombay!* Cinecom, 1988. India. 114 min.
——, dir. *So Far from India.* 1982. US. 52 min.
——, dir. *Vanity Fair.* Gramercy Pictures, 2003. UK/US.
Nanji, Meena, dir. *It Is a Crime.* 1996. 5.5 min.
——, dir. *Voices of the Morning.* NAATA, 1992. 15 min.
——, dir. *Women and War.*
Nawaz, Zarqa, dir. *BBQ Muslims.* NAATA, 1996. Canada. 5 min.
——, dir. *Death Threat.* NAATA, 1998. Canada. 19 min.
Nousheen, Farah. *Nazrah, A Muslim Woman's Perspective.* In production.
Nurudin, Azian, dir. *Bitter Strength: Sadistic Response Version.* 1993. US. 3 min.
——, dir. *A Gun Is Useless in a Dead Girl's Hands.* 2000. US. 3 min.
——, dir. *Malaysian Series 1–6.* Frameline, 1986/1987. US. 15 min.
——, dir. *Nancy's Nightmare.* Frameline, 1988. US. 7 min.
——, dir. *Self-Immolation as an Anachronism.* 1988. US. 4 min.
——, dir. *What Do Pop Art, Pop Music, Pornography, and Politics Have to Do With Real Life?* Frameline, 1990. US. 20 min.
——, dir. *Wicked Radiance.* Frameline, 1992. US. 5 min.
O'Donnell, Damien. *East Is East.* Writ. Ayub Khan-Din. Miramax, 1999. UK. 96 min.
Ové, Horace, dir. *The Art of the Needle.* 1966. UK.
——, dir. *Baldwin's Nigger.* 1968.
——, dir. *Orchid House.* 1991. UK.
——, dir. *Playing Away.* ArtMattan, 1986. UK/US.
——, dir. *Pressure.* 1976. UK. 120 min.
——, dir. *Reggae.* Impact, 1971. US.
Pahuja, Nisha, dir. *Bollywood Bound.* 2002. Canada. 85 min.
Pandya, Piyush Dinker, dir. *American Desi.* Blue Rock, 2001. US. 100 min.
Parasher, Prajna Paramita, dir. *I Left My Eyes Behind in Video Frames.* 1989. 16 min.
——, dir. *Yeh hi hai Heiroglyphics of Commodity.* 1998. India/US. 45 min.
Parasher, Prajna Paramita, and Deb Ellis, dirs. *Unbidden Voices.* Women Make Movies, 1989. US. 32 min.
Parmar, Pratibha, dir. *Bhangra Jig.* Women Make Movies, 1990. UK. 4 min.
——, dir. *Brimful of Asia.* Channel 4, 1998. UK. 24 min.
——, dir. *The Colour of Britain.* CrossCurrent Media, 1994. UK. 58 min.
——, dir. *Double the Trouble, Twice the Fun.* Women Make Movies, 1992. UK. 24 min.
——, dir. *Emergence.* Women Make Movies, 1986. UK. 18 min.
——, dir. *Flesh and Paper.* Women Make Movies, 1990. 26 min.
——, dir. *Jodie: An Icon.* Women Make Movies, 1996. UK. 25 min.
——, dir. *Khush.* Women Make Movies, 1991. UK. 26 min.
——, dir. *Memory Pictures.* Frameline, 1989. UK. 24 min.
——, dir. *Memsahib Rita.* BBC, 1994. UK. 20 min.
——, dir. *A Place of Rage.* Women Make Movies, 1991. US. 52 min.
——, dir. *The Righteous Babes.* Women Make Movies, 1998. UK. 50 min.
——, dir. *Sari Red.* Women Make Movies, 1988. UK. 11 min.
——, dir. *Sita Gita.* 2000. UK. 24 min.
——, dir. *Warrior Marks.* Women Make Movies, 1993. UK. 54 min.
——, dir. *Wavelengths.* Women Make Movies, 1997. UK. 15 min.
Parson, Matthew, dir. *Tom, Dick, and Haresh.* 1997. India/UK. 14 min.
Patel, A. K., dir. *Out of State.* 2001. US. 4 min.
Patel, Krutin, dir. *ABCD.* Phaedra, 1999. US. 105 min.
Patel, Nilesh, dir. *A Love Supreme.* 2001. UK. 9 min.
Patel Rajesh, dir. *I Write What I Like.* UK.
Patnam, Premika, dir. *Burning Bridges.* 10 min.
Patwardhan, Anand, and Jim Monro, dirs. *A Time to Rise.* 1981. Canada.
Poore, Grace, dir. *The Children We Sacrifice.* Women Make Movies, 2000. 61 min.
——, dir. *Voices Heard, Sisters Unseen.* Women Make Movies, 1995. 75 min.
Prasad, Udayan, dir. *Brothers in Trouble.* First Run, 1996. UK. 102 min.
——, dir. *My Son the Fanatic.* Writ. Hanif Kureishi. Feature Film, 1997. Britain. 87 min.
Randera, Safiya, dir. *Health Status Survey.* 2000. Canada. 12 min.

————, dir. *Jangri*. 1998. Canada. 7 min.

Rao, Jay, dir. *Raju's Blind Date*. 2001. Canada.

Rasool, Kay, dir. *ANGAN*.

————, dir. *Hot Curry*.

————, dir. *My Journey, My Islam*. Women Make Movies, 1999. Australia. 56 min.

————, dir. *Temple on the Hill*. Australia.

Rathod, David, dir. *West Is West*. 1987. US. 50 min.

Ray, Sandeep Bhusan, dir. *Leaving Bakul Bagan*. 1993. US. 43 min.

Reddy, Prerana, dir. *(Un)Suitable Girls*. 2000. US. 28 min.

Rohan, Meena, dir. *Skin Deep*. Writ. Paromita Vohra. 2000.

Rony, Fatimah Tobing, dir. *On Cannibalism*. Women Make Movies, 1994. 6 min.

————, dir. *Concrete River*. 1996.

————, dir. *Demon Lover*. 1998.

————, dir. *Everything in Between*. Frameline, 2000. 26 min.

Saigal, Sunil, dir. *Lipstick Dreams*. 2001. 46 min.

Saluja, Harish, dir. *The Journey*. 1997. US. 96 min.

Samarthya, Ambika, dir. *After*. 2001. US. 8 min.

————, dir. *Theen*. US. 16 min.

Saraf, Sujit, dir. *Asphyxiating Uma*. US.

————, dir. *Bugaboo*. 1999. US. 82 min.

Saran, Nishit, dir. *A Perfect Day*. 2001. India. 80 min.

————, dir. *Project Flower*.

————, dir. *Summer in My Veins*. 1999. India/US. 41 min.

Sarin, Ritu, dir. *Shadow Circus: The CIA in Tibet*. 1998. Britain. 49 min.

————, dir. *The Trials of Telo Rinpoche*. Britain/India/Kalmykia. 1994. 49 min.

Sarin, Ritu, and Tenzing Sonam, dirs. *The New Puritans: The Sikhs of Yuba City*. NAATA, 1985. 27 min.

————, dirs. *The Reincarnation of Khensur Rinpoche*. Zeitgeist, 1991. India/UK. 62 min.

Sawhney, Punam, dir. *The Goddess Method*. 2000. Canada. 6 min.

Saxena, Devashish, dir. *The Chase*. 2000.

————, dir. *Karma*. 2000. 92 min.

————, dir. *Wedded Bliss?* 2002.

Saxena, Gita [Gitanjali], dir. *The Avocado Vegetarian Turtle*. Canadian Filmmakers' Distribution Center, 1988. 3 min.

————, dir. *Bolo! Bolo!* Crosscurrent Media/NAATA/V-Tape, 1991. Canada. 30 min.

————, dir. *New View, New Eyes*. V-Tape/Women Make Movies, 1993. Canada/India. 50 min.

————, dir. *No Such Number*. 1996. 20 min.

————, dir. *Only Enough to Ignite*.

————, dir. *Second Generation Once Removed*. V-Tape, 1990. Canada. 19 min.

————, dir. *Wallflower*. Canadian Filmmakers' Distribution Center, 1989. Canada. 5 min.

Saxena, Gita, and Shauna Beharry, dirs. *Chocolate Is an Indian Word*. 1996. 22 min.

Saywell, Shelley, dir. *Legacy of Terror: The Bombing of Air-India*. 1999. Canada. 60 min.

Sen, Mitra, dir. *Just a Little Red Dot*. 1996. Canada. 35 min.

Sen, Nandana, dir. *Arranged Marriage*. 1996. US. 14 min.

Sen, Somnath, dir. *Leela*. 2002. India/US. 97 min.

Seth, Gaurav, dir. *Darkness*. 1990. 5 min.

————, dir. *The Essence*. 1993. 20 min.

————, dir. *An Example to the World*. 1994. 20 min.

————, dir. *Five Minutes To. . . .* 1991. 10 min.

————, dir. *Guilty or Not*. 2001. Canada. 43 min.

————, dir. *Iskusstvo Umirat* [*The Art of Dying*]. 1995. Russia. 60 min.

————, dir. *Journey of Self-Discovery*. 1998. 10 min.

————, dir. *A Passage to Ottawa*. 2001. Canada. 90 min.

————, dir. *Prabhupada: A Lifetime in Preparation*. 1996. India. 50 min.

————, dir. *Sweetheart*. 1992. 20 min.

————, dir. *The Walk*. 1989. 10 min.

Shah, Byron, dir. *The Mischievous Ravi*. 1998. US. 13 min.

Shetty, Anula, dir. *Being Native/Alien*. 1999. 9 min.

————, dir. *Border Crossing*. 2001.

————, dir. *Cosmic Egg.*
————, dir. *Paddana, Song of the Ancestors.* 1999. US/India. 40 min.
————, dir. *Tele/Kinetics.* 1999. US. 20 min.
Shoaib, Samia, dir. *Camilla.* 1995. 12 min.
Shroff, Beheroze, and Caroline Babayan, dir. *A Life after Death.* 1997. 50 min.
————, dir. *Sweet Jail: The Sikhs of Yuba City.* 1985.
Shyamalan, M. Knight., dir. *Praying with Anger.* Cinevista, 1992. US. 107 min.
Siddartha, Chandra, dir. *The Inscrutable Americans.* Tricolor Communications, 2000.
Sikand, Nandini, dir. *Amazonia.* Women Make Movies, 2001. US. 8 min.
————, dir. *The Bhangra Wrap.* NAATA, 1994. 20 min.
————, dir. *Don't Fence Me In.* Women Make Movies, 1998. 55 min.
Singh, Cyrus Sundar, dir. *Film Club.* 2001. Canada.
————, dir. *Walla.* 5 min.
Singh, Digvijay, dir. *Maya.* Narai, 2001. India. 105 min.
Singh, Nidhi, dir. *Khush Refugees.* NAATA, 1991. US. 32 min.
Sivakumaran, Nick, dir. *Diwali.* 2001. US. 16 min.
Syed, Alia, dir. *Fatima's Letter.* 1994.
————, dir. *Spoken Diary.* 2001.
Syed, Tanya, dir. *Chameleon.* 1990. UK. 4 min.
————, dir. *Delilah.* 1995. UK. 9 min.
————, dir. *Salamander.* 1994. UK.
Taghioff, Michelle, dir. *Home.* 1992. US. 37 min.
————, dir. *The Visitor.* 1997. US. 18 min.
Talati, Jigar, dir. *Fly.* 1999. Canada. 20 min.
————, dir. *The Market Square.*
————, dir. *The Stand Up.*
Talukdar, Shashwati, dir. *Any Number You Want.*
————, dir. *Live Spaces.* 1990. 17 min.
————, dir. *My Feet Remember Movement.*
————, dir. *My Life as a Poster.* NAATA, 1996. 7.5 min.
————, dir. *Ravings of a Geometry Lover.*
————, dir. *Retro/Action.*
————, dir. *Rumination and Advice from Dr. Abbey Polk.*
————, dir. *Snake-Byte.* 1997. US. 10 min.
————, dir. *Unable to (Re)member Roop Kanwar.* 1997. 16 min.
Tan, Yen, dir. *Happy Birthday.* 2002. US. 93 min.
Thakur, Shanti, dir. *Circles.* 1997. 58 min.
————, dir. *Crossing Borders.* 1992. 25 min.
————, dir. *Domino.* 1994. 45 min.
————, dir. *Kairos.* 2002.
————, dir. *Seven Hours to Burn.* Women Make Movies, 2000. Canada/US. 9 min.
————, dir. *two forms.* 1998. 4 min.
Ting, Emily, dir. *What's Love Got to Do With It?* 2002. US. 30 min.
Trepanier, Tania, dir. *Dance Can Do All That.* 2002. 20 min.
————, dir. *Seahorses.* 2002. 12 min.
————, dir. *Sugar and Spice.* 1997. Canada. 10 min.
Vachani, Nilita, dir. *Eyes of Stone.* 1989.
————, dir. *Sabzi Mandi Ke Heere* [*Diamonds in a Vegetable Garden*]. 1993. Greece.
————, dir. *When Mother Comes Home for Christmas.* 1995. Germany/Greece/India. 109 min.
Vellani, Shafeeq, dir. *The Changing of the Light.* 1999. UK.
————, dir. *Circling the City.* UK. 25 min.
————, dir. *Darwish.* 1994. UK. 12 min.
————, dir. *New Blood.* 20 min.
————, dir. *See Red.* 1998. UK. 15 min.
Venkatachallam, Usha, dir. *Smoke/Smokescreen.* US/India. 18 min.
Vohra, Paromita, dir. *Annapurna, Goddess of Food.*
————, dir. *A Short Film about Time.* 1999. 11 min.
————, dir. *Unlimited Girls.* 2002. 94 min.

Index